Shakespea
the Actor and th
Purposes of Pla

Meredith Anne Skura

The University of Chicago Press

Chicago and London

Meredith Anne Skura is professor of English at Rice University. She is the author of *The Literary Use of the Psychoanalytic Process* (1981) and has contributed frequently to *Daedalus, New Literary History,* and other journals.

The University of Chicago Press, Chicago 60637
The University of Chicago Press, Ltd., London
© 1993 by The University of Chicago
All rights reserved. Published 1993
Printed in the United States of America
02 01 00 99 98 97 96 95 94 93   1 2 3 4 5

ISBN: 0-226-76179-7 (cloth)
       0-226-76180-0 (paper)

Library of Congress Cataloging-in-Publication Data

Skura, Meredith Anne, 1944–
    Shakespeare the actor and the purposes of playing / Meredith Anne
  Skura.
      p.   cm.
    Includes bibliographical references and index.
    1. Shakespeare, William, 1564-1616—Knowledge—Performing arts.
  2. Shakespeare, William, 1564, 1616—Characters—Actors. 3. Theater—
  England—History—16th century. 4. Theater—England—History—17th
  century. 5. Actors—Great Britain—Biography. 6. Acting in
  literature. 7. Actors in literature. I. Title.
  PR3034.S58 1993
  822.3′3—dc20
                                                    93-17317
                                                    CIP

⊗The paper used in this publication meets the minimum requirements of the American National Standard for Information Sciences—Permanence of Paper for Printed Library Materials, ANSI Z39.48-1984.

For Marty, Rebecca, and Vivian

Contents

Preface and Acknowledgments

*T*his book attempts to reconstruct something of the mental climate in which Shakespeare's plays were written, particularly those aspects affecting and affected by his experience as an actor. Shakespeare's texts were produced specifically for public consumption in circumstances limited by economic and political constraint and, thus, were shaped in many ways by the culture in which he worked. But my assumption throughout this study is that texts are overdetermined, that they respond to internal as well as to external pressures, neither of which can be reduced to a function of the other. The stories told by Shakespeare's plays, and the strategies employed, answer not only cultural but also individual needs, some of which are not consciously acknowledged and may be left over from early, even infantile, stages of development as shaped by the world Shakespeare was born into. The work of psychoanalytic and feminist critics, particularly Janet Adelman, C. L. Barber, Coppélia Kahn, Carol Neely, and Richard Wheeler, provides a continuing, though not always explicit, foundation for my approach to Shakespeare here. But, on the whole, this book addresses directly neither the public field of discourse outside the theater nor, except in part of chapter 3, the intimate particulars of Shakespeare's early experience or unconscious fantasies. It attempts to locate a middle ground between large social forces and private fantasies, that is, to describe the way outer and inner reality interact to produce the personal, but not private, view of the world in Shakespeare's plays.

Drama, or rather the theater, is the most obvious intersection of public and private, and this was even more true in sixteenth- and seventeenth-century England. The dichotomy between public and private of course meant something different for Shakespeare than for us. But whether we locate him in an age newly aware of its power to deconstruct a stable medieval social self and to fashion new ones, in an age when the humanist illusion of a unified interior self had not yet been produced, or in a period progressing slowly toward individualism, what matters for the present study is that the wooden O of his theater was important in defining his position. If one of the defining characteristics of early modern England was a movement toward enclosure and privatization of space, theater, which projected intimate passion onto a public stage for communal attention, was an enclosed space that was at once public *and* private. Whatever "persons" were taken to be, theater and the actors personating them put them in question by framing their production on stage. Role-playing, the theater's stock-in-trade, created artificial persons that offer clues to understanding early modern subjectivity, much as our study of artificial intelligence suggests models for understanding our own.

Although focused on Shakespeare, then, the book draws on and, I hope, contributes to various discussions of the Elizabethan-Jacobean stage. I note three sorts of inquiry that have been particularly important to my thinking though neither in practice nor in theory is it possible to separate them cleanly. The first is concerned with the metaphysical or ontological implications of the "world as stage" metaphor: life as dream, man as role-playing animal. While not directly relevant to the study of a practicing actor, it is nonetheless important because Elizabethan actors were both the source of and affected by the period's historically determined notion of the theatricality of the self and by what Francis Fergusson has called their "idea of a theater." The ancient topos of the *theatrum mundi* took concrete form in Renaissance drama, shaping the architecture of the stage, the language of the plays (where "act" and "play" take on double meaning and characters often see their experience as tragedy or pageant), the scripted action (often with literal or implied inner plays), and perhaps the actors' own justification for their calling. The issue at stake in these comparisons between world and stage is the illusion of human power—the Player King's speech in *Hamlet*'s inner play, for example, addresses his position as player scripted into a play as much as his position as King in that play's narrative:

> I do believe you think what now you speak,
> But what we do determine oft we break. . . .
> Our wills and fates do so contrary run
> That our devices still are overthrown:
> Our thoughts are ours, their ends none of our own.
>
> (*Ham.* 3.2.181–82, 206–8)

But all discussions of the *theatrum mundi* in Renaissance drama are complicated by the uncertain boundary between world and stage, and most bear witness to the real power of theatrical illusion.

A more direct influence on the present study is Anne Righter's *Shakespeare and the Idea of the Play,* which begins at the other end of the same topos, with the stage rather than the world, and studies its implications for Shakespeare's attitude toward plays. Metadramatic studies like those of Lionel Abel, Sigurd Burckhardt, James Calderwood, and Alvin Kernan, who are interested in the way in which the plays are about their own creation, are similarly important. Though metadramatic awareness can extend to any aspect of the stage, text, or production, the primary emphasis in these critics is on the experience of the playwright (or, if on the actor, on his relation to the playwright rather than to his audience), with not only explicit inner plays, but all the action, seen as analogy for the playwright's experience. Burckhardt and Calderwood see the kings and heroes in the history plays, for example, as playwrights trying to order their material and reshape reality.

The metaphysical critic moves from the *theatrum mundi* metaphor to the world and the metadramatic critic to the theater, but both regard the play as mirror, whether of reality or of artistic process. A third sort of criticism, which has also contributed to the present study, has shifted attention from mimesis to performance and from author to actor and audience. In Shakespeare studies, this criticism emerged first from studies of Elizabethan theater as a social process shaped by popular ritual (S. L. Bethell, C. L. Barber, Robert Weimann, Michael Bristol) and has been influenced by more general twentieth-century theories about the theatrical event (Ortega y Gasset, Bertolt Brecht, Antonin Artaud, Jerzy Grotowski). "Performance criticism," as it has come to be called, sees the text as a blueprint for production with which we can come as close as possible, so far, to an understanding of the historically specific experience of acting on an Elizabethan stage. Some performance critics emphasize the script as a set of directions for mimesis, for the actor creating a stage illusion, and shift attention from the words to the text's silences, implied gestures for players, blocking patterns, stage imagery, and visual spectacle (Bernard Beckerman, John Russell Brown, Alan Dessen, Anne Slater). Others emphasize the script as a set of directions for performance, as a means for the actor to make contact with his audience (Weimann, Michael Goldman, David Wiles). The latter studies once focused on the audience's engagement in or detachment from the illusion created by the play (Maynard Mack) but recently have concentrated on other interactions between actor and audience and the possibility (or felt impossibility) of mutual acknowledgement between character and audience (Stanley Cavell, a theorist of performance if not a performance critic per se). I have drawn heavily on the work of all of these performance critics, especially as they have attempted to answer questions about the specific theatrical conditions Shakespeare took for granted. What distinguishes the present work from previous psychoanalytic or biographical studies, in fact, is that it "analyzes" Shakespeare's texts in the context of performance conditions and the Elizabethan actor's subculture. I have tried, in other words, to combine Caroline Spurgeon's attention to patterns in the text and a psychoanalyst's attention to motivated language, with Michael Goldman's attention to the actor's experience of playing to an audience and the theater historians' reconstruction of the specifically Elizabethan actor's experience.

I have looked for varied effects of playing: not only in Shakespeare's way of representing players, but in his way of representing all the world as a one-time player might have seen it.

More specific debts are easier to locate though more difficult to describe or to acknowledge adequately. Chapter 2 benefited from the generous and careful commentary of G. K. Hunter and S. P. Cerasano; Alan Grob and Marianne Novy read and commented at length on an early draft of the entire manuscript; David Bevington and Richard Wheeler read a later draft and responded with wonderfully detailed comments to which I have returned many times in reshaping the material; Anne Few read and discussed at least two versions of the entire manuscript, each time teaching me something new. Finally, the book would not have been possible without the advice and support of my husband and colleague, Martin Wiener, who read and talked about too many versions to count, and who has been patient when too often I have been distracted writing them. Though none of the chapters has been previously published, I have had the opportunity to present portions of them to various audiences, from whose responses I have happily profited. Some of the material on *Love's Labour's Lost* and *Henry VI* (parts of chapters 4 and 9) was presented in lectures at the MLA, the Shakespeare Association of America, the City University of New York, and Boston University; the material on *Julius Caesar* was presented at the Philadelphia Psychoanalytic Institute, the Freud Symposium, and the International Conference on Elizabethan Theatre, Waterloo, Ontario; and portions of chapters 1 and 2 were presented at the MLA. I am grateful for the institutional support I have had while working. Rice University provided sabbatical and leave time without which I could not have done the research for this book, and the National Endowment for the Humanities provided a year during which the bulk of it was written. My thanks also to Antje Thole, who worked heroically on the details of the final copy, and to Terry Munisteri, who negotiated the difficult passage from typescript to computer.

Sources for Texts Quoted

The following editions have been used for sixteenth- and seventeenth-century texts cited. Unless otherwise noted, dates for all plays are taken from Yoshiko Kawachi, *Calendar of English Renaissance Drama 1558–1642* (New York and London: Garland Publishing, 1986). Nondramatic texts are indicated by an asterisk. Bibliographic details for twentieth-century texts are given at first citation in the endnotes.

* *The Actors Remonstrance or Complaint for the Silencing of their profession and banishment from their severall "Play-Houses."* In Hazlitt, *English Drama and Stage,* 259–65.

Arden of Faversham, ed. Martin White. The New Mermaids. London: Ernest Benn; New York: W. W. Norton, 1982.

Barry, Lording. *Ram-Alley; or, Merry Tricks.* In Hazlitt, *Old English Plays,* 10:271–380.

* Beard, Thomas. *The Theatre of Gods Judgements.* London: Adam Fflip, 1612.

Beaumont, Francis. *The Knight of the Burning Pestle,* ed. John Doebler. Regents Renaissance Drama Series. Lincoln: University of Nebraska Press, 1967.

Chapman, George. Regents Renaissance Drama Series. Lincoln: University of Nebraska Press. *Bussy D'Ambois,* ed. Robert J. Lordi, 1964; *The Gentleman Usher,* ed. John Hazel Smith, 1970.

Chapman, George, Ben Jonson, and John Marston. *East-Ward Hoe.* In *The Plays of John Marston,* ed. H. Harvey Wood, 3:83–171. Edinburgh and London: Oliver and Boyd, 1939.

* Chettle, Henry. *Kind-Hartes Dreame.* In *Henry Chettle, "Kind-Hartes Dreame" (1592); William Kemp, "Nine Daies Wonder" (1600),* ed. G. B. Hamson, 3–65. Bodley Head Quartos 4. London: John Lane, 1923.

Cooke, John. *Green's Tu Quoque, or The City Gallant.* In Hazlitt, *Old English Plays,* 11:173–289.

* Davies, John. *Microcosmos.* In *The Complete Works of John Davies of Hereford,* ed. Alexander B. Grosart, 1:48–88. Edinburgh University Press, 1878.

* Dekker, Thomas. *The Non-Dramatic Works of Thomas Dekker,* ed. Alexander B. Grosart. London: Hazell, Watson, and Viney, 1885. *The Belman of London,* 3:61–170; *The Guls Horn-Booke,* 2:193–266; *The Ravens Almanacke,* 4:167–266; *The Wonderfull Yeare,* 1:71–148; *Worke for Armourers, or The Peace is Broken,* 4:85–166.

*Erasmus, Desiderius. *The Praise of Folly,* trans. Clarence H. Miller. New Haven and London: Yale University Press, 1979.

*Earle, J. *Micro-Cosmography, or A Piece of the World Discovered in Essayes and Characters,* ed. Gwendolen Murphy. Waltham St. Lawrence: Golden Cockerel Press, 1928.

The Famous Victories of Henry the Fifth Containing the Honourable Battle of Agincourt. In *The Oldcastle Controversy: "Sir John Oldcastle," Part 1, and "The Famous Victories of Henry V,"* ed. Peter Corbin and Douglas Sedge, 145–99. Manchester: Manchester University Press, 1991.

Fletcher, John. *The Faithful Shepherdess.* In *The Works of Francis Beaumont and John Fletcher,* ed. Arnold Glover and A. R. Waller, 2:372–445; see also 518–27. Cambridge: Cambridge University Press, 1906.

Fletcher, John, and Francis Beaumont. *The Maid's Tragedy,* ed. Howard B. Norland. Regents Renaissance Drama Series. Lincoln: University of Nebraska Press, 1968.

*G[ainsford?], T. *The Rich Cabinet Furnished with Varietie of Descriptions.* In Hazlitt, *English Drama and Stage,* 228–30.

*Golding, Arthur. *Shakespeare's Ovid Being Arthur Golding's Translation of the "Metamorphoses,"* ed. W. H. D. Rouse. Carbondale: Southern Illinois University Press, 1961.

*Greene, Robert. *The Life and Complete Works in Prose and Verse of Robert Greene,* ed. Alexander B. Grosart. The Huth Library. London: Hazell, Watson, and Viney, 1881–83. *A Disputation between a Hee Conny-Catcher and a Shee Conny-Catcher,* 10:193–278; *Greens Groatsworth of Wit,* 12:98–160.

——— *The Scottish History of James the Fourth,* ed. Norman Sanders. The Revels Plays. London: Methuen, 1970.

*Harsnett, Samuel. *A Declaration of Egregious Popish Impostures* . . . . London: James Roberts, 1603.

Hazlitt, W. Carew, ed. *The English Drama and Stage under the Tudor and Stuart Princes 1543–1664.* London: Wittingham and Wilkins; Chiswick Press (The Roxburghe Library), 1869.

——— *A Select Collection of Old English Plays.* 4th ed. London: Reeves and Turner, 1874.

*Heywood, Thomas. *An Apology for Actors.* In *"An Apology for Actors" (1612) by Thomas Heywood and "A Refutation of the Apology for Actors" (1615) by I. G.,* ed. Richard H. Perkinson. New York: Scholars Facsimiles and Reprints, 1941.

Jonson, Ben. *The Complete Plays of Ben Jonson.* Ed. G. A. Wilkes. Oxford: Clarendon Press, 1982. *Bartholomew Fair,* 4:1–122; *Cynthia's Revels,* 2:vii–117; *Poetaster,* 2:119–228; *Sejanus,* 2:229–348; *Volpone, or The Fox,* 3:vii–120.

King Edward III, rev. and ed. Karl Warnke and Ludwig Proescholdt. Pseudo-Shakespearean Plays 3. Halle: Max Niemeyer, 1886.

A Knack to Know a Knave. In Hazlitt, *Old English Plays*, 6:503–91.

Kyd, Thomas. *The Spanish Tragedy*. In *The Works of Thomas Kyd*, ed. Frederick Boas, 1–99. Oxford: Clarendon Press, 1901.

*Lyly, John. *The Complete Works of John Lyly*, ed. R. Warwick Bond. 1902; reprint, Oxford: Clarendon Press, 1973. *Euphues*, 1:83–375; *Endimion*, 3:6–80.

*M., R. *Micrologia: Characters, or Essayes of Persons, Trades and Places*. London: T.C., 1629.

Marlowe, Christopher. *The Complete Works of Christopher Marlowe*. 2d ed., ed. Fredson Bowers. Cambridge: Cambridge University Press, 1981. *Dr. Faustus*, 2:121–271; *Edward II*, 2:1–119; *Tamburlaine*, 1:71–252.

Marston, John. *The Plays of John Marston*. 3 vols, ed. H. Harvey Wood. Edinburgh and London: Oliver and Boyd, 1939.

Massinger, Philip. *The Roman Actor*, ed. William Lee Sandidge. Princeton: Princeton University Press, 1929.

May, Thomas. *The Heir*. In Hazlitt, *Old English Plays*, 11:513–84.

Middleton, Thomas. *A Mad World, My Masters*, ed. Standish Henning. Regents Renaissance Drama Series. Lincoln: University of Nebraska Press, 1965.

Middleton, Thomas, and Thomas Dekker. *The Roaring Girl*, ed. Andor Gomme. The New Mermaids. London: Ernest Benn; New York: W. W. Norton, 1976.

Munday, Anthony. *John a Kent and John a Cumber*, ed. Muriel St. Clare Byrne. Malone Society Reprints. Oxford: Oxford University Press, 1923.

*——— *A Second and Third Blast of Retrait from plaies and Theaters*. In Hazlitt, *English Drama and Stage*, 97–156.

Munday, Anthony, et al. *Sir Thomas More*, ed. Vittorio Gabrieli and Giorgio Melchiori. The Revels Plays. Manchester and New York: Manchester University Press, 1990.

Nashe, Thomas. *The Works of Thomas Nashe*, ed. Ronald B. McKerrow. Oxford: Basil Blackwell, 1966. *Pierce Pennilesse His Supplication to the Divell*, 1:137–245; *Summer's Last Will and Testament*, 13:227–95.

Norton, Thomas, and Thomas Sackville. *Gorboduc, or Ferrex and Pollux*, ed. Irby B. Cauthen. Regents Renaissance Drama Series. Lincoln: University of Nebraska Press, 1970.

The Pilgrimage to Parnassus, The Return from Parnassus, The Second Part of the Return from Parnassus. In *The Three Parnassus Plays (1598–1601)*, ed. J. B. Leishman. London: Ivor Nicholson and Watson, 1949.

*Platter, Thomas. *Thomas Platter's Travels in England 1599*, trans. Clare Williams. London: Jonathan Cape, 1937.

*Rankins, William. *A Mirrour of Monsters,* ed. Arthur Freeman. New York and London: Garland, 1973.

S., W. *The Lamentable Tragedy of Locrine.* In *The Shakespeare Apocrypha,* ed. C. F. Tucker Brooke, 37–65. Oxford: Clarendon Press, 1908.

Shakespeare, William. The Arden Shakespeare. London: Methuen, except where noted. *As You Like It,* ed. Agnes Lathan, 1975; *The Comedy of Errors,* ed. R. A. Foakes, 1962; *Coriolanus,* ed. Philip Brockbank, 1976; *Hamlet,* ed. Harold Jenkins, 1982; *Henry IV, Part One,* ed. A. R. Humphreys, New York: Random House, 1960; *Henry IV, Part Two,* ed. A. R. Humphreys, New York: Random House, 1966; *Henry V,* ed. John H. Walter, 1954; *Henry VI, Part One,* ed. Andrew S. Cairncross, 1962; *Henry VI, Part Two,* ed. Andrew S. Cairncross, 1957; *Henry VI, Part Three,* ed. Andrew S. Cairncross, 1964; *Henry VIII,* ed. R. A. Foakes, 1957; *Julius Caesar,* ed. T. S. Dorsch, 1955; *King John,* ed. E. A. J. Honigman, 1954; *King Lear,* ed. Kenneth Muir, 1952; *Love's Labour's Lost,* ed. Richard David, 1951; *Macbeth,* ed. Kenneth Muir, 1951; *Measure for Measure,* ed. J. W. Lever, 1965; *The Merchant of Venice,* ed. John Russell Brown, 1955; *The Merry Wives of Windsor,* ed. H. J. Oliver, 1971; *A Midsummer Night's Dream,* ed. Harold F. Brooks, 1979; *Much Ado About Nothing,* ed. A. R. Humphreys, 1981; *Othello,* ed. M. R. Ridley, 1958; *Richard II,* ed. Peter Ure, 1956; *Richard III,* ed. Antony Hammond, 1981; *The Taming of the Shrew,* ed. Brian Morris, 1981; *The Tempest,* ed. Frank Kermode, 1954; *Timon of Athens,* ed. H. J. Oliver, 1959; *Titus Andronicus,* ed. J. C. Maxwell, 1953; *Troilus and Cressida,* ed. Kenneth Palmer, 1982; *Twelfth Night,* ed. J. M. Lothian and T. W. Craik, 1975; *Two Gentlemen of Verona,* ed. Clifford Leech, 1969.

——— *Shakespeare's Sonnets,* ed. Stephen Booth. New Haven and London: Yale University Press, 1977.

* *Tarlton's Jests, and News Out of Purgatory,* ed. James Orchard Halliwell. London: Shakespeare Society, 1844.

Tomkis, Thomas. *Lingua.* In Hazlitt, *Old English Plays,* 9:331–463.

The True Chronicle Historie of King Leir and his three daughters. In *Narrative and Dramatic Sources of Shakespeare,* ed. Geoffrey Bullough, 7:331–402. London: Routledge and Kegan Paul; New York: Columbia University Press, 1973.

*Vaughan, William. *The Spirit of Detraction, Conjured and Convicted in Seven Circles.* London: W. Stansby for George Norton, 1611.

Webster, John. *The Duchess of Malfi,* ed. Elizabeth M. Brennan. The New Mermaids. New York: Hill and Wang, 1966.

W[ilson], R[obert]. *The Three Ladies of London.* In Hazlitt, *Old English Plays,* 6: 245–370.

Wily Beguiled. In Hazlitt, *Old English Plays,* 9:219–330.

Introduction

*T*he British actor Simon Callow tells about preparing for a marathon one-man performance in which he was to read all of Shakespeare's sonnets. Trying to feel his way into the poems, Callow found himself identifying more and more deeply with the poet as lover because he himself was then in love with a fair young man. This helped, but the real turning point came when Callow discovered, as he says, that "I knew [Shakespeare]; and I knew what he was, in the root of his being—he was an actor."[1] What in the sonnets' love story made Callow think of actors? And what might it have meant to Shakespeare, born four hundred years before Callow, to be an actor?

As we know, sixteenth-century writers like Thomas More saw themselves as actors caught in a script played out on the *theatrum mundi,* while others like Marlowe saw themselves as protean actors free to take what form they wished.[2] An interest in the theatricality of everyday life has led twentieth-century commentators to assume that all Elizabethans were actors in some sense, fashioning selves and being fashioned in the process.[3] But humanist allusions to the *theatrum mundi* originated without reference to a professional theater, and recent studies of self-fashioning and social construction similarly make use of theatrical discourse without literal reference to the stage. These studies are no more dependent on the theater itself than are narratives about the *Narrenschiff* dependent on navigation or those about the "dance of death" on choreography. By contrast, Shakespeare's involvement with the stage was concrete. No matter how many Elizabethans may have figuratively "acted," Shakespeare was one of the very few who wound up a common player on the public stage, "playing" in ways very different from the courtier's self-fashioning behind the scenes. With hindsight we think of Shakespeare as a man destined to become a playwright, and easily dismiss his early stint as a player as one of the incidental costs of his ultimate career as chief writer for Lord Chamberlain's Men. But his contemporaries knew him first as an actor, "excellent in the quality he professes," as Chettle said in 1592.

Shakespeare chose to be an actor despite the fact that in the late 1580s, when he probably came to London, playing was a high-risk business and by no means the obvious career for the son of a former Stratford bailiff with a family of four to support. Even after he established himself as a playwright, Shakespeare chose to remain a player—unlike Anthony Munday

1

or Ben Jonson, who also began as actors but left the quality behind when they made their reputation as writers. There is no record of Shakespeare's appearance on stage after 1603, but many records bear witness to his continuing reputation as a player; the 1623 Folio lists him first among the "Principall Actors in all these Playes," and he was remembered as an actor long after. In 1640 he was still being eulogized as "that famous Writer and Actor," and anecdotes about the roles he took were still circulating in the eighteenth century.[4] Shakespeare's choice indicates a unique perspective both on stage playing and on the playing that was part of everyday life; it is a perspective that Callow detected in the sonnets but which we have not for the most part attempted to recover.

Recent studies of the place of the Renaissance stage and its social and ideological function have posed their questions from the point of view of the observer and his—and more recently her—interests. From Jonas Barish's study of a timeless "antitheatrical prejudice"[5] to studies of drama's specifically Jacobean containment of subversion, theater's effect on its audience has been our primary interest. We have yet to use our understanding of the theater's position to get at the experience and interests of the actors themselves and to ask what their daily life was like on such a stage at such a time.[6] The prevailing emphasis on audience is appropriate to our largest concerns. After all, to analyze a performance from the point of view of the actor, Stephen Booth says, is like describing a meal from the point of view of the entrée (a metaphor about which we will have more to say later).[7] But no account of theater can be complete without reference to the exchange between actor and audience which provides its occasion—and therefore no account can ignore the actor's point of view. Michael Goldman has argued that the modern actor's effort to create a character becomes part of the meaning of any play, and that his charismatic presence is at the heart of the audience's experience in the theater.[8] Certainly as we become increasingly aware of the intersubjective nature of experience we need to look more closely at what the actor feels as it impinges on the spectator, as well as looking at whatever prejudices the spectator brings to the theater.

Theater historians have been justly cautious in attempting to reconstruct even the factual outlines of players' lives, and their caution should guide any inquiry. Elizabethan actors have not left the copious records typical of their opponents like the prolific William Prynne, who saw plays as Satan's work. But, like other minorities made to serve symbolic functions in the discourse of the majority, players left indirect traces on that discourse, and some left texts of their own, most significantly the plays written by men who had been on the stage themselves: Richard Tarlton, Robert Wilson, Anthony Munday, Ben Jonson, Thomas Heywood, Nathan Field, Robert Armin, Samuel and William Rowley, Richard Brome, and, of course, William Shakespeare. These texts are by no means a transparent source of information about playing, but they do allow us to glimpse some patterns of thematic and metadramatic concern. Many actor-playwrights, for example, show interest in intricate plots, male cross-dressing, and ostentatious *offstage* roleplaying, at times complicated or multiplied—Munday's John a Kent dresses up as his opponent John a Cumber, who has disguised himself as John a Kent; Neville, in Field's *Woman is a Weathercock* (1609), appears in two disguises while Scudamore attends a masque disguised as Neville; and Armin designed *Two Maids of More-Clack* (1607–8 [1608]) so that he could play two contrasting roles; Jonson and Shakespeare place characters not only in situations of role-playing but also in discomforting moments of exposure and audience-consciousness.[9] Concerns like these emerge most directly in the portrayal of literal players and plays, but they also manifest themselves in every aspect of text and performance—in a play's other thematic and metadramatic concerns, in its language, its patterns of movement on stage, and its dramatic strategies. Shakespeare's plays are by no means "about" acting at every moment discussed here. But as Goldman says, everything Shakespeare wrote "reflects his dramatic bent . . . because it shows us a response to life for which drama was finally necessary."[10] Similarly the actor's "response to life" affects not only his moments on stage, but also the way he positions himself in relation to the Other, to authority, to time, to desire, and to death.

What follows is not only a reading of the plays but also a reading of the man who wrote them—the man who also wrote the sonnets, and who tells us something about himself even before we read the work by having chosen to be an actor. This book addresses the question of what it might have meant to be an actor in the sixteenth and early seventeenth centuries and moves on to the question of how Shakespeare's acting might have shaped his texts and the performances they imply. There is a danger of circularity in using the plays to define an actor's perspective and then finding it in them; to add an external point of reference, the discussion begins in chapter 1 by surveying modern perspectives on acting. Onstage, acting is not only a matter of playing roles but also of obsession with display and exposure, with power and humiliation. Both as mimesis and as performance, acting today is an intense and ambivalent experience, focused unrelentingly on the actor's body. More than those in other professions, the actor puts himself on the line for every performance, displaying his body for public approval; he is engaged in an intimate exchange with the audience which, in the words of one actor, "both appalls and uplifts." Actors are narcissists who delight in the audience's approval; as the song says, "Nowhere could you get that happy feeling,/ When you are stealing that extra bow."[11] But behind such satisfactions may lie the insecurity of narcissism in its clinical sense, a mirror-hungry personality that needs applause to shore up a fragile sense of self. The emotional stakes evoke the all-or-nothing intensities of childhood, and can give an audience the power of the maternal gaze to validate or destroy. This emotional intensity is relived in the actor's volatile relation to the director during rehearsal and, again, when he stands alone before a crowd which can make him its idol—or its victim. In performance the theatrical confrontation takes on the excitement of the hunt, recalling not only the ambivalent intimacy of the love hunt, but also the plenitude of mob emotion.

Even if we think we understand the modern actor, however, we might well ask what he has in common with his Elizabethan predecessors. T. J. King traces "a great chain of acting" unbroken from Shakespeare, through Christopher Beeston and twelve other links, to Laurence Olivier,[12] but what sort of continuity can such a chain guarantee? Chapter 2 argues that there are other, more important continuities. Like the modern actor's the Elizabethan player's "profession has in it a kind of contradiction," said J. Earle in 1628, "for none is more dislik'd, and yet none more applauded."[13] Despite obvious differences, the more we learn about Elizabethan culture and playing conditions—about the audience, the social construction of the actor, the social and economic pressures affecting theater companies, and the day-to-day details of rehearsal and performance—the more it seems that their stage, even more than ours, would foster the ambivalence and regressive concerns typical of modern actors and that it would make the player even more vulnerable to the fantasies modern actors report regarding the fickle mob. The popular image of the Elizabethan player—seen over and over as a "proud beggar"—embodied a paradox intriguingly similar to the one we describe today as the insecurity of narcissism. Chapter 2 ends with a discussion of two Elizabethan roles which had their proud beggary scripted for them: the Clown, who alternately hectored and wheedled the audience throughout the play, and the Epilogue, who kneeled for applause at the end. A conventional role of course tells us nothing about what the actor felt playing it. But the prominence of the begging stance suggests how important it was to the idea of theater in Shakespeare's time, and contemporary testimony reveals how closely it reflects what actors feel today. Chapter 3 suggests that one way to understand what it meant to Shakespeare to be a player is to look more closely at Richard III, the seminal figure, himself both an actor and a perfect actor's medium, who takes over the last of the early history plays. Most commentators, including some within the play itself, have identified Richard as a player in Elizabethan terms. Richard's strange power over the court—and over us—can, however, also be seen to derive from an ambivalence toward himself and toward his audiences much like the one modern actors describe. The chapter ends by suggesting that although Richard is an unlikely self-portrait, it is revealing to read Shakespeare's own life and his presentation of Richard in "dynamic and speculative relation to one another,"[14] with an eye for the repetitions and distortions that pervade a text and its sources. The most compelling connection between Shakespeare and the charismatic player he created lies not so much in specific biographical details as in the pervasive duality of Richard's histrionic flair: he is electrically attractive when he is "on"—and yet he is a cripple, all too aware that "no creature loves me" (R3 5.3.201). This is precisely the contradiction that animates the sonnets, where Shakespeare comes closest, though by no means all the way, to speaking in his own voice.

The second part of the book considers Shakespeare's presentation of acting in the rest of the canon. Just as Shakespeare's life can be illuminated by reading it against that of the players he invented and the real ones who played them, his fictive players can be illuminated when read against what we know about his life, about actors, and about Elizabethan theater. The more marginal nature and function of Shakespeare's later players can be as revealing as Richard's stranglehold on his play. Some of the most important Shakespearean themes, rhetorical patterns, and dramatic strategies emerge first in the players' scenes, then disperse and mature into the extended body of the later plays. The sequence is revealing in what it shows both about Shakespeare's continuing concerns and about the way each play responds to the particular conditions of its own performance. Chapters 4 and 5 examine a series of "great house" plays, all of which are about, and some of which may have been written for, private performance for a "great man" who has something of the status the modern actor accords his director. The series includes all Shakespeare's literal players (in *Love's Labour's Lost, The Taming of the Shrew, A Midsummer Night's Dream,* and *Hamlet*) as well as some notably histrionic hangers-on, like Falstaff (in *Henry IV* and *The Merry Wives of Windsor*), whose profession entails, at least in part, playing with and for a great man and singing for his supper. All Shakespeare's players—unlike actual Elizabethan players—are itinerants or local amateurs, as if Shakespeare had taken seriously the antitheatricalists' slur about the actor as proud beggar going from one man's house to another, dependent on aristocratic hospitality. They endure their own version of modern actors' fantasies about showing off for a parent, as well as their own version of heckling—or worse—from the mob. In some of the plays, the players are comically attacked as well as laughed at, and the disguised Falstaff in *The Merry Wives of Windsor* is finally "pinched" and "dis-horned" like a deer at bay (*Wiv.* 4.4.60–64). The myth of Actaeon, which structures Falstaff's reversal from hunter to hunted, lies behind the experience of other actors in the canon as well. Allusions to the hunt continue to turn up in the later plays, where Shakespeare's attention turns from the beggarly player to the lord who finances and directs the play. Some of the figures considered at the end of chapter 5 are not literally players or directors, nor, I believe, are they intended as figures for actors. They are, however, caught in moments and exchanges of the sort which actors experience onstage and which fascinated the actor Shakespeare. Thus the chapter ends with a discussion of *King Lear,* not a story about acting, but a retelling of the great house story first presented as Sly's adventure after being thrown out by the Hostess. It is of all the plays the most focused on the actor's "instrument," his body, and on his hunger for recognition, and it addresses most powerfully the experience of spectatorship and response.

Chapter 6 discusses the ways in which playing was theorized and suggests a link between Actaeon's—or Falstaff's—fateful reversal and the prevailing Renaissance theory of theater as mirror or reflecting glass. Hamlet's formulaic advice to the players sounds simple: the purpose of playing is to hold the mirror up to nature. But theatrical optics are more complex, and the variety of relations possible in the dynamics of spectatorship suggest that drama has more purposes than Hamlet prescribes. In particular it mediates the mutual hostility between player and audience, hostility which animates Hamlet himself when he plays the fool and when he uses a play to catch the king. The chapter goes on to consider other discussions of the mutuality of the actor-audience relationship—by Ulysses in *Troilus and Cressida* and by Julia in *Two Gentlemen of Verona*—each of which, appropriately enough, is used tendentiously to affect its own audience.

Chapter 7 suggests that the actor's ambivalent relation to the audience, thematized and theorized within the plays, also underlies Shakespeare's best-known image cluster, the "dog, licking, candy, melting group called up by the thought of false friends or flatterers."[15] This cluster proves to be only half of a larger cluster in which the fawning spaniel turns into a cur or circle of curs surrounding a helpless victim and attacking or "pinching" him; it merges with the imagery of the hunt. The two-faced dog is often called up during those reversals and identifications between hunter and hunted which Shakespeare associated with the fate of a player, surrounded by a flattering audience who might at any moment turn on him. Flattery was so important to Shakespeare that he explored its vicissitudes in a series of "flattery plays," which in their own way turn out to be as much about theater as the great house plays. Like Shakespeare's players, the men at the center of *Richard II, Julius Caesar, Coriolanus,* and *Timon of Athens,* each enjoy a dream of greatness maintained by the flattering ministrations of unreliable followers, both the intimate friends who begin by serving them and the public which begins by cheering them. But intimates and public both betray them, calling up scenes like those in a modern actor's fantasies about showing off for a doting but dangerous mother or performing for an adoring but fickle mob. Each man then fears that he will have to turn and flatter his flatterers. Only two are explicitly called actors, but each experiences an actor's agonies of presentation before a crowd as fickle as any theater audience. And each is subject to the dizzying reversals of dominance that hold actor and audience together in the theatrical exchange.

Shakespeare's repeated vision of reversals—of display, entrapment, and attack—is bound up with his view of playing. Chapter 8 suggests that in associating the performer with the victim of a violent mob, Shakespeare was not eccentric, although his vision was more emphatic than others'. Shakespeare could have seen at least two types of popular entertainment in which the performer was a victim and the performance could be deadly. The first was bearbaiting, and the second was the cycle of mystery plays culminating in the baiting and crucifixion of Christ. At some level the bear's suffering had special significance for Shakespeare; the language of the bear ring appears at climactic moments in Shakespeare's early tragic sequences in the histories and the comedies and again at similar points in *Twelfth Night* and the great tragedies. And, as the histrionic Richard II realized, Christ's story lends itself even more tantalizingly to an actor's fantasies. The actor, Grotowski said, is isolated up there in front of us not for us but instead of us. Christ's passion in the cycles of mystery plays gives new meaning to "the actor's passion," as one recent study of acting is called. Shakespeare's plays are marked by an interest in the self-sacrificing man of sorrows, like Antonio in *The Merchant of Venice,* and in the theatricality of the "good death" in an age when such rites of passage were public occasions. The sacrificial stance, important as it may be on occasion in the plays, emerges most consistently, however, in the dedications to his poems and in the sonnets. Chapter 8 argues that the self-presentation in these texts is closely related to the presentation of the actor's experience elsewhere in the canon. It ends by considering the brief—and notorious—passages in the sonnets where many readers have heard Shakespeare refer explicitly, and derogatively, to his profession as an actor. It suggests how intricately connected these passages are to the other presentations of acting in the canon, not only in their explicit reference to the stage, but in the language used and the way in which the stage shifts unstably between figure to ground, peripheral yet central to the sonnets' concerns.

Much of this argument elaborates on the ways in which the player is not only someone who plays roles but someone exquisitely aware of his audience and his relation to them—an awareness that recreates both the intimacies of the earliest relationships and the impersonality of public display.

The Afterword is less a conclusion than a gathering and rearrangement of Shakespeare's several variations on the physical locus in which the actor's exchange with the audience took place, "the wooden O," the charmed circle in which an audience enshrines or entraps the player. Together the examples suggest one final way in which the phenomenology of playing helped shape the plays.

Chapter One

"Being an Actor": An "Up and Down, In and Out Life"

The bow at the end of her famous concert act was Dietrich distilled. She would stand there, arms outstretched, her body ramrod straight, and then bend over in a graceful arc, so deep her nose would virtually touch the floor. It was the ultimate expression of humility and arrogance, at the same time.

New York Times, 15 May 1992

*T*he way to begin understanding what it is to be an actor is to listen to actors themselves. What follows is an impression drawn from a selective sampling of letters, autobiographies and biographies, read in the context of remarks by other theater people, by theorists of the theater, and by psychologists.[1] No one can generalize about being an actor in such a way as to describe—let alone begin to explain—*the* actor's experience for every actor, or even for any one actor at every moment. There are, however, patterns linking these rather different discourses to create a useful body of commonly accepted material about twentieth-century actors.

One fundamental assumption shared by actors, theater people, theoreticians, and psychologists is that there are two aspects to acting, although these are not always separated. The first is mimesis or role-playing; the second is performance, establishing a "real" relation to an audience.[2] Richard Burton told about amusing some friends one day by "doing" John Gielgud, then noticing that his listeners had frozen and were staring behind him. There was Gielgud himself who, having secured everyone's attention, pronounced cordially, "Generally veddy good mimes do not make veddy good actors," and walked away.[3] Whatever his motives for this comment, Gielgud demonstrated with it the highly charged transaction between actor and audience which no actor, however good a mime, can afford to ignore. Theater always involves both mimesis and performance, though at different times various theaters have veered toward one or the other of these poles. The naturalistic theater on the proscenium stage stressed mimesis and eliminated any interplay between actor and audience which might interfere with the illusion. In this century, however, the balance has on the whole shifted toward performance, although powerful spokesmen have drawn theater in each direction: Konstantin Stanislavski's inner-directed theories of acting toward mimesis, Bertolt Brecht's political theater and Antonin Artaud's theater of cruelty toward audience-directed performance. In our own self-conscious era, theorists have fixed their gaze on the apparatus of theater and the participatory theater "event."

It's not that mimesis is not important to actors; it is vital. Debates about mimetic technique not only monopolize technical manuals but constitute probably the largest proportion of acting theory. How does one get outside the self to create another character? How to effect the change? Should one follow the American method, the intuition-and-frenzy school, or the cooler, more technical British approach? Does one cultivate a warm heart, a cool head—or both? Psychologically, mimesis is at least as important to actors as it is to theoreticians. It is "by means of a series of identifications that the personality is constituted and specified" in the first place,[4] and acting allows the performer a rare second chance to reorganize those identifications to his greater satisfaction. He can be someone else—someone he would never dare to be offstage. "The actor's freedom" allows him to escape the rigidities of everyday life—whether they be the limits imposed by propriety, by profession, or by gender roles.[5] It depends on a fluidity of identity which may affect the actor's life offstage as well as on; the long-standing association between actors and homosexuality or bisexuality, for example, makes psychological sense insofar as a flexible identity in general entails flexibility in gender identity, gender style, and sexual orientation. But primarily the actor's aptitude for identification defines his being onstage. Many actors have described the need—the drive—simply to act. Sometimes it is described as a need to express or let out something inside, other selves or "phantoms," that wells up from memory and fantasy.[6] Some describe an uncontrollable need to imitate someone outside the self, to pick up the accent of someone across the room, or to walk like whoever happens to be beside them. But a "need" or "drive" it is. Again and again actors say that they are "only really alive when they're on stage,"[7] that they are depressed and anxious between roles.[8]

Not only is the actor most alive when playing, but by playing he can effect a "Zulu magic" as Callow calls it. The actor is a "hungan," a human being possessed momentarily by a spirit from another world above, below, or inside himself, or a "shaman" who sends his own spirit to that world.[9] He can even create new life. For Stanislavski, to create a role is to give birth to a character (according to Michael Redgrave, "the period of gestation for a great part is the same as that for a child: nine months"). John C. Gustin's subjects saw "creating a new character" as a "rebirth" for themselves.[10] This magic the actor shares with the playwright. Ionesco, for example, has described the thrill of bringing characters to life:

> To incarnate phantasms, to give them life, is a prodigious, irreplaceable adventure . . . [I] was overcome when, during the rehearsals of my first play I suddenly saw characters move on the stage who had come out of myself. I was frightened. By what right had I been able to do this? Was this allowed? . . . It was almost diabolical.[11]

The difference is that the actor makes this diabolical magic with his own body.

It is not always a matter of a new life; the magic extends to a power to bestow immortality or even to raise the dead. In their interviews with some forty actors Seymour and Rhoda Fisher found subject after subject who saw what they were doing on stage as a way to give new life to that which is lifeless, to "feel you are part of re-creation."[12] The actor is a ghost, uncanny in his ambiguous duality,[13] one of the "living dead" who both is and is not who he seems to be.[14] The feeling is particularly strong if either the play or its content dates from the past. Harley Granville-Barker argues that when new actors "revive" an old play they do in a real sense give it new life.[15] Revivals entail not so much new invention but the power of perpetuating what has been, and they satisfy the commonly expressed desire "to bring back the past," to feel "oneself as part of an historical continuity," as if what is being warded off is the passage of time and the separation from others who have gone before. As one actor said, "I've always been interested in what went on back there and trying to keep it for what goes on ahead." Ultimately, all these feelings are related to "a concern about mastering decline, decay, and death."[16] Among the many superstitions in this most superstitious of all professions—as Tallulah Bankhead said, "You name it, honey, I believe in it"—is that tin trunks are unlucky "because they resemble coffins, and anything which even remotely resembles or reminds you of death is to be avoided."[17] Two curiously similar reports of childhood memories provide tangential but suggestive evidence of such a need. Actors in separate studies by different authors recalled a mother who found a dead chicken or mouse, put it in the oven, and revived it—as if the actor's self-image is built partly in identification with the mother's life-giving and life-sustaining role.[18] Fisher and Fisher conclude that the actor's attempt to rise "above his own individual existence is of fundamental importance in understanding his endless and difficult experimentation with different identities."[19] Acting is an escape.

Nonetheless, despite this emphasis on the creation or the revival of other selves, acting is never really an escape from the self. An actor, whatever his role and whatever his method for getting into a role, is always announcing himself *as an actor* and asking the audience to respond to *him*. Olivier didn't become a character, Peter Hall commented, he performed it.[20] "Don't be funny," Redfield was advised when preparing to play Guildenstern: "Be interesting. The lines are funny. You are interesting." On some stages the actor overshadows the character, as in the days when Mercutio, having died off-stage, would return to the thunderous cheers of the audience, while the play stopped dead.[21] But even in less self-indulgent periods the actor remains, waiting for the cheers. Audience and actor are linked by "invisible strings," as Olivier called them, crackling with the electricity of a secret affair conducted in public. The involvement generated by this exchange—as much as the power of mimesis—creates the magic of theater for the audience as well as for the actor. This is no less true for the postmodern actor who resists becoming a transparent medium for a character, trying to substitute another exchange for the one Olivier counted on.[22] This interaction charges live theater—which doesn't need to be as self-conscious about the process as "living theater" was—with an energy no film can have. In film there is only the fiction and its mechanical medium, but something "real" happens in the theatrical space when the fiction is staged.

The locus of that reality is the actor's body. No matter how successful an actor is in transforming himself into another character, his body, a residue of resistant mass, is still the same body. "Put bluntly," says Bert O. States, "in theater there is always a possibility that an act of sexual congress between two so-called [fictional characters] will produce a real pregnancy."[23] Even in David Hwang's M. Butterfly where the beautiful heroine M. Butterfly turns out to be a man, the audience is ready to distinguish between "her" two sets of fictional genitalia, one more fictional than the other, and the real one exposed when the actor undresses at the end. What this means is that the actor, as many are fond of saying, is his own instrument. Stanislavski's exercises, designed to give an actor access to his emotions, begin with physical movement. Performance in this sense means exposure of the most intimate—and most primitive—aspect of self to the scrutiny of others; the ego, as Freud says, is first a body ego. Acting is the provocative business of displaying one's body on stage for public approval. It is "emotional nudity," says Redfield, as stark as physical nakedness.[24] The actor is "'up there' under lights in a performance rite which at once appalls and uplifts him, which he both longs for and dreads." "It's like walking on stage naked—naked and looking awful!" "You're naked. You're stripped down. You're put out there to fall flat on your face or triumph." "The actors are all alone with a thousand strangers." No wonder Stuart W. Little and Arthur Cantor call their chapter on stage fright "The Naked Actor," and Stephen Aaron calls one of his "A Thousand Strangers."[25]

As Callow puts it, "When it boils down to it, you . . . your face, your body, and your personality, is what you sell," and when you don't get the part, "it's you nobody wants."[26] There is something illegitimate about even legitimate theater, and many actors class themselves with other forms of entertainment altogether. "A music hall entertainer," said Granville-Barker. "A juggler, a street-singer, a prize-fighter," said Redfield.[27] He is a hustler, a flatterer, a seducer—a prostitute, said Grotowski; a whore, said Brecht.

For actors performing, then, there really is always something at stake—actors, Artaud said, are "like victims burnt at the stake, signaling through the flames."[28] The salvation of society is what Artaud thought was at stake, but for each actor it is his own salvation as well. The material stakes are high enough; good performances get you jobs and bad ones can lose them. But it's not just a matter of a job. The actor "puts himself on the line for every performance." He "comes alive" on stage not just because he is taking on a role but because the audience has a life-and-death power to validate or destroy him. "A child seeking to please his parents . . . a lover wooing his mistress, a soldier going to battle," Little and Cantor call the actor, claiming that actors will do almost anything for the favor of these strangers.[29] Why would anyone go through all this? "Actors are narcissists," Redfield explains: "Otherwise they would not be actors."[30] Even discounting offstage gossip that supports such a stereotype, it is clear that performance on stage generates immense narcissistic rewards. Applause, momentarily at least, calms an actor's megalomaniacal greed for approval and attention, his most childish "look at me!" As the song says, "Nowhere could you get that happy feeling,/When you are stealing that extra bow." The massed audience becomes for a moment an actor's only and most significant Other. Sybil Thorndike describes

> that curious sensation we have when entering the stage, as of one's other half-being waiting to be transformed. An expectant force is there, not just separate men and women but an entity, a personality in the larger common soul of the mob. This mob-soul is a force that is continually baffling us, it is always an unknown quantity. On our first entrance before a word has left our mouths, we are conscious of this large thing confronting us. Sometimes one knows it is a thing to be fought and struggled with in order to move it and use it, and on these occasions the performance is a big effort, as every sensitive actor will tell you. At other times one is conscious of a something that is feeding one with life.[31]

An actor will endure daily poverty, anxiety, and grueling work, all for one more chance at the "performance rite which both appalls and uplifts him, which he both longs for and dreads." The twin delusions of love and power fed by the audience's attention are irresistible. The actor may risk going "naked in front of a thousand strangers," but the rewards are worth it. "To have a thousand people waiting on your every move . . . and it's you they're watching! You're ruling the roost." "When you feel you have them, when you know you've got them, what a wonderful feeling!" "The actor's high," says Terry Kaiser, is "the ability to control the audience. It is power; and it is beyond power."[32]

As in any intimacy, of course, where there is love there is also hate. The actor works by "seduction and intimidation," Otto Fenichel concluded in one of the earliest psychoanalytic studies of acting, freed to indulge in such otherwise antisocial behavior by the unreality of the theatrical context.[33] The actor is not only a lover but a soldier going to battle, or both at once: "the audience is the dragon to be slain, the woman to be raped," said Burgess Meredith, sliding all too easily between the alternative descriptions.[34] Or as one actor in analysis put it, "I want to fuck the audience right up the ass."[35] The actor will do anything *for* these strangers—and anything *to* them—to get what he wants. Goldman sees the play's fiction taking its life from the actor's thrust into a role and his aggressive "thrust outward to make connection in performance, to create and control a response." Actor and audience, he says, are the hunter and the hunted.[36] Nor is it always certain who is who; hostility gives way to fear of retaliation, and the actor's own hostility is felt as coming from the audience. Richard Burton's strength, Redfield claims, derived from his "warlike energy" and "his love of blood sublimated only by his fear of being killed."[37] Every good actor must have a gladiator instinct. In another manifestation of the hostility of the encounter, Olivier used to stand behind the curtain before opening nights calling voicelessly to the critics, "You bastards!"[38] Wiles identified a more "calculated hostility" in the Brechtian actor working to create an alienation effect, but hostility nonetheless.[39] Theater jargon, which predates both Brecht and Olivier and is still in use, also bears witness to hostility in triumphant announcements phrased as war cries—We killed them! We mowed 'em down tonight! We laid them in the aisles! We brought down the house! The actor's goal is a "hit" or, better, a "smash hit."[40] The aims of the revisionist "theater of cruelty" and of Peter Handke's *Offending the Audience* grow out of an aspect of theater which has always been present in the actor's experience.

Despite everything, for some actors the delight in display is unalloyed. It hardly takes a psychoanalyst, however, to suggest that the insecurity of narcissism in its clinical sense may lie behind such satisfaction or that the obsessive need to perform can be the symptom of a "mirror-hungry personality" who needs audience confirmation to shore up a fragile sense of self.[41] The need for applause is a need to heal a nakedness beyond nakedness—"a basic fault," the universal "castration" Jacques Lacan describes, the "narcissistic wound," as Heinz Kohut calls it—that rends a remembered or imagined early wholeness.[42] While most of us find some way to compromise, displace, or deny the pain of longing which early losses leave, actors seem to be driven to assuage the nostalgia for unalloyed love and power through performance—and to be therefore always vulnerable to renewed loss, new wounds. "Acting," it has been said, "is to want, to want, and to want again."[43]

Anecdotal evidence of actors' insecurity abounds. "Actors feel like bad people," say Fisher and Fisher, describing the sense of moral inferiority expressed in Rorschach test results.[44] A sense of physical inadequacy often accompanies or overshadows the moral insecurity. Dustin Hoffman, "who subscribes to Bette Davis's theory that no one who likes himself goes into acting," says if he had been tall and handsome he would have been a doctor.[45] Maureen Stapleton says of actors, "we are . . . the deformed children of the world,"[46] and Simon Callow picked *two* hunchbacks as role models. I had been "overwhelmed at an early age by two acting performances," Callow says: "Olivier's Richard [III] and Laughton's Hunchback [of Notre Dame], and . . . was liable at any moment to become possessed by one or the other."[47] So fascinated with Charles Laughton that he wrote a biography of him, Callow implies that Laughton's self-hatred—exposed and yet quieted by identifying with the Hunchback—is more typical than not among actors.

At times, even applause is not good enough to still the self-doubt; the actor must be wildly famous and "loved by the world."[48] "Any actor I don't recognize doesn't even exist," says Redfield, implying that the same is true if someone doesn't recognize him.[49] "The insecurity is endless," say Little and Cantor.[50] Sir Henry Irving always walked to the theater on first nights in order to absorb the "open, unashamed adoration of all he met on his royal progress—paper sellers, flower girls, shopkeepers, ordinary pedestrians"—to mitigate the "nightmare of insecurity and inadequacy which haunted him." The insecurity, we may assume, was related to his image of the hostile audience in the theater—an image he helped perpetuate by always providing free tickets to his long-estranged wife, who sat there "gazing at him with cold, implacable hatred, willing him to fail."[51] Little and Cantor quote a director's advice to "always tell an actor he was marvelous. Lie in your teeth." They add their own recommendation: "Opening nights call for bravura flattery. There is no such thing as too much adulation. Nothing is really enough after a smashingly successful opening, not even a full-dress parade through Times Square with . . . cheering crowds, and the victorious star throwing kisses in triumph."[52]

If even a merely modestly sized cheering crowd is not enough, a hostile audience can destroy an actor. They expose him as the loser he always was; they see through to the wound which had driven him to play roles for them in the first place. And if the audience applauds this time, the actor's fate, as Tyrone Guthrie says, is to be "writ in water."[53] Acting is truly a self-consuming artifact. No matter how good you are, you're only as good as your last performance. Disappointment is almost inevitable, because even a successful performer implicitly depends on external sources for the self-esteem that can never really give happiness unless it comes from inside. Applause barely suffices to cover the wound temporarily, not to heal it. At the moment of success the actor may feel omnipotent, an adored monarch surrounded by admiring subjects who will love and obey him even if he performs badly or not at all. But the reality is that he must capture the audience's love and attention over and over again; his greatest terror is that they will have no response but will be oblivious to his existence.

Obviously narcissism and insecurity aren't enough to make a great actor. If they were, universities alone would generate enough theater to put Broadway out of business. As Stanislavski says, the actor must surpass his narcissism. He must resist the temptation to play up to the audience—which is often a temptation to play down to them, going for the easy laughs or the bravura soliloquies. Every actor true to his art must sometimes be a "kamikaze pilot," Stephen Booth says; Colly Cibber made a similar complaint in other terms two hundred years before.[54] Nonetheless, the conflict between transcendent art and dependence on the audience's response never disappears. An actor can ward off dependence in various ways: by inflating himself or devaluing the audience as a ragtag crowd who don't know anything, by denying any pleasure in their response and scorning the pliant suckers for being so easily manipulated, by withdrawing and pretending indifference, or if worse comes to worst by identifying with the audience's superiority ("Look at all those important critics come here just to watch me!"). The temptation to play to the audience remains and generates a hostility as intense as the attraction. The actor hates himself for wanting so much to please them, and hates them for "making" him do it. His resentment adds to the already charged adversarial relationship.

Although the actor's talent cannot be explained by narcissism, narcissism is always there. In other words, at the heart of what makes an actor is something passionate, irrational, and conflicted, the sort of thing most of us repress but which the actor depends on to make a living. It's no wonder then that actors suffer from the irrational tyranny of stage fright or that first-night paralysis can conceal potential violence. As the editors of the theatrical dictionary *The Language of Show Biz* describe it, the phenomenon of stage fright "in another connotation is known as buck fever and may render a skilled marksman on a hunting party unable to pull a trigger"[55]—an occupational hazard of Goldman's "hunters." The more skilled the actor the worse the panic, and it never goes away. Stage fright strikes at the moment of confrontation, when the actor steps onstage and realizes that his grandiose fantasies are finally to be tested. After intimate preparation in the studio, the first onstage rehearsal, even without an audience, is "like emergence from the womb."[56] The first performance for a hall full of strangers is correspondingly worse.

Not that actors are the only ones who face stage fright. It is common among other performers, though many of them have a conductor or at least a familiar musical instrument with them, while the actor is alone. Stage fright is common even among nonperformers who suffer from shyness, but the professional performer, suffering as much or more than anyone else, chooses an occupation which brings this plague on him regularly. Olivier's stage fright was so bad that at times he had to beg his fellow actors not to leave him alone on stage even for soliloquies. Asked, "Do you like acting?" Stewart Granger replied, "Would you like being scared every night?"[57] Clearly at some level he did like it or he would not be there, but that didn't keep him from being afraid. When the stakes are high, so is the anxiety, and the stakes must be high if the actor is to be any good. "I wouldn't give a nickel for an actor who isn't scared," said one producer. "You have to have it or you go on flat as a pancake."[58] What scares the actor is the same fear that generates the electricity of live performance—walking the razor edge between success and failure each time the curtain goes up.

Actors across the board agree about what happens in stage fright. The precursors, which are different for different actors—sleeplessness for one, stomachaches for another—are replaced by an almost animal fear, ranging from mild to paralyzing. Donald Kaplan, describing the cases he has watched, identifies two aspects to the attack. The first is "blocking": the actor is paralyzed by naked vulnerability, his lines and movements are all forgotten, unavailable, and he simply cannot function. This usually does not last more than a few moments, although it can feel considerably longer. The second is "depersonalization," in which even if the actor performs, *he* isn't performing; he stands beside himself, watching himself like a stranger. His body feels like an alien mechanism which he doesn't know how to control, suddenly awkward as he tries to remember how to coordinate the limbs, distribute the weight of the torso, make sounds. Both reactions, irrational as they may seem, effect the only kind of fight-or-flight reaction available to an actor, short of running out of the theater or shooting into the audience. The first, painful as it may be, postpones the moment of confrontation; the second removes the actor from the confrontation as his body obediently goes through with it.[59]

* * *

The origins of stage fright are more obscure than its characteristics. Nonetheless they are equally relevant to an understanding of performance. Stage fright, rather than being an accidental irritant that can be cured, is only the most visible manifestation of the largely unconscious processes that drive all actors and fuel their connection with the audience. It is frightening to "go out in front of all those people" not because of present danger, but because doing so calls up the thrills and terrors of two other highly charged encounters: the child's isolation before his mother, as either cherished darling or appendage, defenseless against abuse, and the adult's isolation before a crowd, as either idol or victim. The evocation of each releases powerful emotional responses usually kept in check by the structure of social relationships. Onstage they are released, first, by the actor's need to draw on his own emotional depths in order to create a character and, second, by the presence of the massed audience that performance requires. These confrontations are the subtext for performance, whatever the play is ostensibly about.

It is a commonplace among directors that actors are like children, but this means more than being spoiled. Actors are in touch with the emotions, attitudes, and fluidity of childhood. They have access to a way of being from a time when being was not yet so rigidly molded by intellectual and social structures that modify impulse and contradict fantasy. When actors talked to him about stage fright, therapist-director Aaron realized, "we were in the realm of dreams and fantasies"—a realm that originates in childhood.[60] Nearly every aspect of an actor's life encourages regression: being a member of a familylike community, being able to take on new identities, rehearsing under the benevolent protection of a director, and enjoying daily both the narcissistic pleasure of exhibiting himself and the challenge of begging, flattering, and commanding an audience to validate his sense of self. But acting, because it provides a way of reworking primitive concerns, also leaves the actor open to devastating repetitions of them. Access to childhood is a major source of the volatility of the actor's life onstage and off.

In particular, just as the actor's exhibitionism draws on the ecstatic and grandiose narcissism of a child, he is liable to reexperience, with a child's intensity, narcissistic wounds from a time when the ego was even more fragile and the audience more powerful. An actor's fear of failure calls up the spectrum of loss every child experiences once he notices the discrepancy between his grandiose fantasies about himself and his real powerlessness in the adult world. As Jacques Lacan has said—and perhaps he is the prophet for our era, even if not its best psychologist—subjectivity is a wound. Self-consciousness begins with the sense of loss.

This developmental history is relived every night on stage, starting with presubjective glimmerings, from before the self was perceived as separate from its sustaining context. Narcissistic fulfillment then is based on physical sensation, the oceanic bliss of maternal nurturance and holding—milk to drink, a cradling embrace, and a reassuring gaze. It is focused on the "snout" or perioral region, the forward tip of the self at birth, the interface where the infant's "primal cavity" meets the external world to take in supplies via sight, taste, smell, and touch.[61] Failure of self-esteem at this stage—the infant's narcissistic wound—is an endless, gaping wound of need, an annihilating terror of deprivation and helplessness. Any brief delay or disappointment is, to his immature nervous system, total, a terror of falling, of being detached from the supporting mother, of starving and drying out (thirst and hunger not yet being separated), or even of suffocating. Its remnants in adult stage fright—or in everyday shyness—can be similarly all-encompassing. The actor is overcome by general paralysis, but the symptoms often affect the snout region in particular—feelings of being trapped and suffocated, shortness of breath, dryness of mouth, blushing, or, figuratively, "losing face."[62] These are usually allayed by comforting hand-mouth gestures, replacements for the mother's missing oral ministrations—smoking, drinking, nervously touching the mouth and face—natural mechanisms, we might note, forbidden to the actor.

That the actors' onstage experience involves this oral level is suggested by the image of the prompter, for example, "feeding" one lines.[63] In actress Nancy Parker's description, "If you are an empty vessel, the words you speak fill you up."[64] Perhaps most vivid, when an actor forgets his lines, he "dries up" or simply "dries." Actors frequently include accounts of terrifying episodes of "drying" in their memoirs. One amateur actor said the only other experience he'd had like it was watching someone put a gun to his daughter's head during a robbery. The actor looks not only to his role but also to the audience to fill his emptiness, to feed and sustain him with the attention and applause that he "strive[s] for like the oxygen supply itself."[65] The exchange is so primitive, however, that boundaries between self and other disappear, and actors can feel as if the voracious need were coming from the audience instead. Callow recalls one performance, in a poverty-stricken Irish neighborhood, where he felt "a hunger from the audience, a feeling they were getting something they had done without for too long," and another where the audience's "appetite for the play was insatiable."[66] They had come to dine at the "culinary theater" of which Brecht so disapproved—and which Stephen Booth implied when he spoke of the actor as entrée.

An actor can enjoy the arrangement so long as he receives enough response to feel successful, whole, and generous. Then he believes that he has them eating out of his hand, that he is "spreading the jam on thick," as Redfield said of Burton's Hamlet.[67] But if he is frightened he looks into what Stanislavski called the "black hole beyond the proscenium arch" and is struck with terror.[68] Even the gaping auditorium itself can leer mockingly at the cast, like Mae West beckoning to a group of Boy Scouts, "Come on you teentsie weentsies, fill me up. Acres and acres of me, and I'm all yours."[69] The gleaming semicircle of balconies becomes a set of jaws waiting to devour him, a "primal cavity" as hungry and empty as his own.[70] Even when the performance goes well, actors "give a lump of themselves to each moment of stage life," as if "throwing out lumps of bleeding flesh as offering to the audience."[71] For actors, these primitive feeding experiences are, not surprisingly, often registered visually as "looking" or "being looked at," both of which are part of a child's experience at the breast as it takes in its mother's gaze along with her milk; the "infant's omniverous eye," as it has been called, is almost as central as his mouth. The infant's gaze and ocular identifications are the precursors of exhibitionist drives that emerge later and are as ambivalent as the purely oral exchanges that precede them.[72]

Narcissistic triumphs and wounds from later dyadic or mirror stages of development are less total but can be equally devastating when reactivated in performance. Mirror-stage narcissism derives from the child's newly developed sense of himself as a physically separate entity. It is based on pride in his body and its parts and functions, over which he has recently gained such exhilarating control—learning to stand up, to walk away from his mother, and to monitor his own boundaries. An infant's self-esteem depended on taking in supplies, wherever they came from; now the child's esteem depends on putting out and showing off for someone specific out there. The child who has just learned how to walk is at the pinnacle of narcissistic delight but needs to have his prowess confirmed by his mother, to know that he is the apple of her eye.[73] From this stage comes the childish exhibitionism which everyone attributes to actors, the delighted and un-self-conscious call to "look at me!" Some of this is necessary for rapport with audiences; too much can lead to what Jack Lemmon has called "a bad case of the cutes," when an actor believes that he is "not only amusing but adorable."[74]

The narcissistic wound at this stage derives from humiliation at the body's failure before an audience. Delighted exhibitionism then becomes involuntary exposure; the object of admiration becomes a target for derision. The more grandiose the original self-image, the worse the humiliation; the opposite of fame is shame.[75] The process is not unique to the stage. It draws on experiences which are almost inevitable in the difficult process of learning to define and control our physical apparatus. Indeed, as Edmund Wilson suggests in his study of the Philoctetes myth, superior artistic strength is often figured as inseparable from a debilitating wound; the warrior with the invincible bow suffers a putrid wound in his leg (Oedipus's name means both "I know" and "wounded ankle").[76] Or, we might say, claims to superiority are inseparable from wounds. Although it is found elsewhere, susceptibility to this kind of symbolic wound is rampant among actors and kept alive by the conditions of performance. Bruno Bettelheim's study *Symbolic Wounds* describes a group of disturbed teenagers who formed a club with an initiation ritual involving the periodic wounding and letting of blood from "a secret part of their bodies." Bettelheim traces the wounding to envy of women and menstruation, but, whatever else may have influenced their ritual, Bettelheim observes in passing that what brought the youngsters together in the first place was their desire to become actors and to participate in the glamorous nightlife of entertainers. We might guess that the theatrical ambition and the punishment were related.[77]

Certainly adult actors perceive their stage fright as linked to overextended ambition. Olivier traced his adult paralysis back to a performance as a choirboy at school, when he tried to show off by performing without his music and promptly forgot every note. Callow likens stage fright to a fear of being caught out pretending, and tells how Don Henderson "touched a nerve" in rehearsal by whispering in his ear, "They rumbled you yet?"[78] "Shame and anxiety," Fenichel says, "arise from the dread of being exposed as a sham, of having expropriated something, of adorning oneself with borrowed plumes."[79] A good percentage of the colorful theater superstitions work to ward off the gods' wrath, as if actors were aware of their own hubris and were trying to evade inevitable punishment. One must never wish an actor good luck.

Part of the shame when failure does occur derives from the fear, acquired relatively late in life, of having one's fantasy exposed, from suddenly seeing the difference between a grandiose self-image and a flawed performance—and seeing how unacceptable such self-inflation is to ordinary standards. But although "shame" implies this sort of intellectual discomfort, it is rooted in bodily shame (and manifested in physical signs like blushing), just as exhibitionism is based on bodily display. Any performance can evoke memories of physical childhood performances. The two are connected in Nicholas Craig's parodic memoirs, when he invents—one presumes it is invention—a history of childhood stage appearances during which his costume fell down and "inadvertently 'revealed all'" or "afforded the audience a full view of my masculinity."[80] It is a joke, of course, but one which appears in the first chapter as if a natural part of the mythology. Many of the cant words for failure in the theater evoke the toddler's navigational disasters. While a good play "takes off," a bad play is a "flop," prompting actors to moan, "We just lay there, flat as a pancake." Failure brings everything that the precurtain well-wisher is warding off when he calls "Break a leg!" When one actor makes another lose control, he "corpses" him, turns him into a mere body no longer able to perform wonders.

There is also the—again primitive—fear of losing control of what is inside the body. Part of a child's narcissism at this stage is his newly developing ability to control both what goes into and what comes out of his body, to guard his own boundaries. Traces of the early concern remain, and the emotional discharge in acting, if not applauded, can seem as awkward and socially unacceptable—as "dirty" and "messy"—as a physical discharge. Freud's well-known anecdote about urinating in front of his parents, though on a very private "stage," illustrates the dynamics. The young Freud was using the chamber pot in his parents' bedroom, not without pride in his prowess, when his father, observing the breach in manners, said, "This boy will come to nothing." The boy's purely physical shame became inseparable from his later, more intellectual ambitions.[81] Rex Harrison begins his autobiography by explaining that an actor needs a "special charge of inner energy" without which, "everything, the whole performance, will be wasted. It will—as we actors say—all go down your shirt front, and into the stage." Redfield's free associations were similarly loose when he described his fear that a production of *Hamlet* in which he was to play Rosencrantz was not going to work. He feared his *Hamlet* would turn out like a play in which George Washington appeared onstage atop an actual white horse, who promptly emptied his bowels before the audience.[82] (In France, we might note here, well-wishers send performers on stage with a cry of "Merde!" as their way of warding off the worst.)

Narcissism at a still higher, or "triadic," level of development entails the oedipal competitions signaling entry into what Freud called "civilization" and Lacan "the Symbolic." Self-esteem for a child at this stage depends not only on showing off for the mother but also on showing up potential rivals and winning her away from them. Actors are notorious for their jealousies and rivalries and are said to compete bitterly for the attention of their beloved audience. It's not that vicious competition is unique to the theater, only that it is particularly overt there. Being an actor "has the savage appeal of the cockpit," it is a "ghastly" profession, "a cutthroat business," no matter how civilized it may be in other ways.[83] Even the magisterial Olivier, on hearing that another had been chosen in his place to guide the National Theater, said he felt as if his "mother's milk was being taken from me and fed to some marauder's brat." And perhaps drawing on a different aspect of alimentary fantasy, John Bryan's ritual for avoiding stage fright is to go to "the lavatory, sit on the seat, and silently recite the names of actors he admires."[84]

Performance itself, then, fosters the dreams and fantasies from childhood which generate stage fright. But in addition the actor's history often leaves him more under the influence of childhood than other people are. Generalizations are inadequate, but the lives of well-known actors do seem to follow a pattern of pain and loss, as countless best-selling stage and screen

"autobiographies" testify.[85] Crisis or chronic stress prevents satisfactory so-
lution of childhood conflicts and precludes "normal" development within
the usual social channels. Actors are the creative children whose external
lives happened to offer the stage as an option for fantasy satisfactions—
Olivier's, for example, raised as he was in a family of players descended
from Ellen Terry—or whose internal economy led them from the beginning
to elaborate fictional identifications as escapes from unbearable reality, as
painters-to-be choose visual escapes and writers verbal ones. Several of the
Fishers' subjects recalled the seductive effects of their first school play or
church Nativity play, and many actors remember choosing—or feeling chosen for—their calling quite early. Olivier imitated his minister father at the
altar; Sir Michael Redgrave felt that the theater was the most magical place
in any town.[86]

More specific it is difficult to be; Fisher and Fisher do, however, find one
biographical consistency in the actors they studied that implies the continuing influence of childhood. Their typical subject remembered—or still
felt—his mother's importance in his life, for better or for worse, and remarked on the absence—literal or emotional—of his father.[87] This finding
is borne out by a casual sampling of autobiographies and anecdotal collections. Olivier's mother, described in his autobiography as "my heaven, my
hope, my entire world, my own worshipped mummy," died when he was
twelve, leaving him at the mercy of an indifferent father.[88] From the time
Laurence was born, the senior Olivier, having already sired the only two
children he wanted, considered the boy a nuisance and treated him as such.
As one commentator suggests, Laurence's habitual lying as a child seems to
have grown out of "some desperate search for the role or personality that
would at last appease the parental god."[89] The search might help explain
his habitual acting as well. Simon Callow's father disappeared into Africa
soon after the boy was born. At home young Simon became "a monstrous
show-off and infant transvestite, mostly with and for my flamboyant grandmother" (who had "run away to go on stage before the First World War").
Callow also "regaled astounded twelve-year-olds with my jelly dance
and . . . won first prize in a fancy dress competition as a can-can dancer";
it is perhaps not unrelated that, after having been snubbed by the senior
box officer in his first theater job as box-office boy, Callow "felt that I'd
made a major break-through the day he greeted me with, 'What do you
want, cunt?' "[90]

There are other variations on the pattern. Dustin Hoffman's father gave
him neither approval nor attention, but his mother, we are told, was his
inspiration in shaping *Tootsie*'s Dorothy Michaels, a dubious honor.[91] Josh
Logan, in his autobiography, shrugs off his father as a mystery about whom
people stopped talking when Josh entered the room. Josh lived with his

mother and her family and went to kindergarten next door at Mansfield Female College, running home at recess to get his mother to sew up costumes for the daily plays the class put on.[92] Robin Williams's father was physically present but so distant and imposing that Robin nicknamed him "Lord Viceroy of India." His mother, an amateur comic who kept whoopee cushions at home and "did not blanch at the prospect of pulling halved rubber bands out of her nostrils on national television," had more in common with him. The father threatened to move out somewhere, anywhere where there was no rubber, but Robin was impressed for life by this unusual incarnation of the phallic mother. "You don't forget that for a while," he says. "Like, well, that's your *mom,* man, with the rubber bugger."[93]

An acting career seems an understandable consequence of growing up without a resident male authority or role model and being "something of a mother's boy" (as Rex Harrison described himself), especially if the female authority encourages dressing up, emotion and fantasy, or "women's" activities that a father might look down on—as did Callow's grandmother, Logan's mother, and, in another way, Charles Bronson's mother, who was so poor she made him wear his sister's dress to school.[94] Even if a mother doesn't particularly sanction dressing up, identifying closely with her can give a boy a sense of himself as alternate male and female selves. Philip Weissman, in fact, argues that all acting begins when an infant responds to his doting mother's "billing and cooing" by joining her and playing along. Most boys begin to resist this intimacy and move toward their father's world quite early, but future actors may not. Girls, who are freer to continue such maternal identifications, "engage in play action and play acting more universally and with more spontaneous freedom than [do boys]."[95] A man who becomes an actor is thus "develop[ing] aspects of himself which originate in his identification with his mother"—a woman—and in doing so is following a path of development more like the girl's than the boy's. This dual openness to identification with women may "help to explain why male actors have been effective in playing female roles in so many societies" and why actors have so often been seen as feminine.[96]

Even if she does nothing else, then, a mother helps train an actor in childhood by encouraging his female identification. Many mothers, if actors' reminiscences are accurate, implicate their sons even more deeply into role-playing and its rewards and into identification with the mothers' lives, behavior, and values. Many actors report having had scripts laid out for them in childhood by a mother whose orders gained significance in the absence of a father. Like Olivier, they learned early on that their own selves would not do, that others had to be manufactured; small wonder that they began to feel more at home acting than not. Logan opens his autobiography with this account of his introduction to theatrical life:

> When I was two, my mother fed me beauty instead of cod liver oil. Beauty
> cured everything. "Just think of flowers, lacy leaves, horses' manes, or being
> happy—and you will be." Being *un*happy was forbidden. Should I fall on the
> floor, bump my head and burst out crying, she became diversionary. "Think
> how poor Mister Floor feels! Apologize to Mr. Floor." Blubbering with self-pity
> I would bend down to the planks and say, "Ex-cuse me, M-M-Mister Floor."

Logan's mother had taken him and his sister to see D. W. Griffith's *Judith of
Bethulia* because she was a Sunday school teacher and "thought it might
decorate our minds." But when Judith produced her sword and held it over
Holofernes' neck, "Mother pushed our faces behind the seats in front, saying, "Duck yo' heads and think o' fields of yellah daisies!"[97]

The popular image of the "stage mother" is grounded in reality; mothers
in actors' accounts tend to exert a powerful influence over their children's
lives, if not actually "directing" them. Some of these mothers are driven by
thwarted theatrical ambitions of their own; others, like Logan's mother,
simply have strong beliefs which they are willing to impose. Others have
made it clear that their child must take the place of a dead spouse or sibling—a task which can lead either to psychosis or to facile, but despised,
acting ability. Whatever her preoccupation, a narcissistic mother caught up
in her own needs helps train an actor, not—as one might expect—by totally ignoring the child and failing to mirror his efforts, but rather by doing
so only when he conforms to her demands and expectations. He is encouraged to achieve or excel—even to be independent—but only on her
terms.[98] The mothers of stars who cowrote the ambiguously titled *Star
Mothers* introduce their book with a defense of the much-maligned "strong
mother," but in doing so they inadvertently testify to precisely the sort of
maternal involvement which shakes identity and creates actors. "At the core
of [stardom]," they write:

> mother looms large—probably larger than life. . . . An opinionated, purposeful
> mother who is strong, and yes, perhaps even domineering, who has an agenda
> for her children's lives but also sees them as people in their own right . . . is
> healthy. . . . The children may grow up bearing this burden that they "have to
> do it to please mother," but while they are pleasing mother they often, without
> admitting it, tend to like it. And also become *very* famous.[99]

In other words, what a mother wants is not only best for her, but also best
for her child, no matter what the child thinks. Holt, Cher's mother, bla-
tantly merges herself with her famous daughter in the opening anecdote of
her book. She tells about going to see Cher at the Hollywood Bowl with
her father, Cher's grandfather, and manages to turn the anecdote into an
image of herself on stage when she digresses to tell how her father pointed

to Cher and said, "'That's you up there! That's you up there made over!' (Daddy had brought me to Los Angeles from Oklahoma City when I was ten. Because of my singing, everyone there told him I could be a star.)"[100] To her mother, Cher is not only her mother's unique creation ("a child without a real father," Holt calls her) but a stand-in for the mother herself.

No wonder many actors, accustomed to maternal dominance and never having had a "real" father, are dependent on their directors. If a judgmental audience can arouse regressive feelings and fantasies about powerful parents during performance, the director's authoritative presence has at least as much power, in that it conforms more closely to the parental model. Aaron argues that much of the contemporary actor's stage fright derives from the terror of being suddenly separated from the director who has supported him like a mother and coached him like a father through weeks of rehearsal. Whatever his role in stage fright, however, the figure of the director—often jokingly referred to as "father," "father-confessor," or even, in one production of *Cat on a Hot Tin Roof,* "Big Daddy"—is entwined with the actor's fantasies about and reactions to his role and his performance of it, and the director's presence encourages childhood analogies.[101] An actor, like a dependent child, first wants to get the part from the director, then wants help from him, and then praise. Particularly in the early stages of preparing a play, while actors are still trying to intuit their way into a role and play with it, the director is reassuringly always there as an auxiliary observing ego, in charge of the regressive process and making it safe. Gradually the director imposes his paternal law on their behavior, arousing the discontent of a child being introduced to civilization. Then (as they feared he would) he withdraws, leaving them on their own.

Finally, whatever childhood legacy an actor brings to performance is enhanced by the presence of an audience—with its own fantasies, both individual and collective—which provides the other half of the theatrical exchange. For if theater calls up ambivalence and the irrational in an actor, it does the same for the audience. We respond intensely to both the character performed and the actor's performance. "When Richard Burton plays Hamlet, the audience not only becomes Hamlet, it also becomes Richard Burton playing Hamlet."[102] We identify with Burton the supernatural shape-shifter and with Burton the defiant exhibitionist up there with all eyes on him. But as we admire his power to transform himself, we also recoil from what it produces—an uncanny hybrid, one of us but not one of us, a deceptive creature we "hold in contempt [but] secretly envy."[103] Theater's power to attract is immense, but Barish has traced an accompanying "antitheatrical prejudice" which has tainted reactions to performers throughout history. Audiences recoil from what Barish calls theater's ontological subversiveness[104] in creating alternate realities that threaten their own—that both defy natural law ("But there *is* no moon tonight!") and undermine trust in social mores and in each other ("He looks as if he really loves her, but offstage he's married to someone else!"). As with the actor's ambivalence—he is both lover and soldier—the audience's response draws both on an intellectual stance and on passionate identifications and aversions, as the spectators project their own best or worst impulses onto the lightning rod of the actor's body.

And once there is more than one spectator, the audience becomes something else—a crowd, even a mob or a pack, as Thorndike described it—its responses magnified and multiplied. Not every collection of people necessarily becomes a crowd, but the actor provides a focus which creates a unified response in the theater—the more so, paradoxically, because of each individual spectator's ambivalence toward him. Cole argues that the theater creates optimal conditions for uniform crowd response, and cites several studies in social psychology which find that behavior is most contagious when people have two opposing impulses both directed at a central figure.[105] When the actor embodies our projected "ego ideal," as Freud described it in *Group Psychology and the Analysis of the Ego,* he becomes more than human and the crowd adores him. He is a kind of god, a totem, or at least a seer or divine spokesman. Edith Oliver in that most secular of media, *The New Yorker,* describes the actor, half seriously, as a priest: "An actor practices a calling that sets him apart from the rest of us, formally estranging him in order that, in the fashion of priests and judges, he can serve as our chosen surrogate."[106] Such comments, somewhat overwrought for today's critical calculus, point to the ritual aspects of theater—that is, not so much to a genealogy of the theater as to an analogy between theater and those formal ceremonies which hold a community together by compelling not only attention but assent. This is another source of the "magic" of theater, which Genet tried to exploit and Brecht to suppress.[107] Peter Brook celebrates ritual or "Holy Theatre" and Artaud calls for, we might say, an unholy (but equally sacred) "theater of cruelty," but both evoke the power of mass emotion. Actors work to unite an audience and generate communal response. Olivier, according to Richard Burton, was driven to dazzle the audience and turn them into "a thunderstruck mob. . . . More than anything else, I think, he wants to homogenize them into one entity, one mass impulse . . . mass hysteria."[108]

But crowds are notoriously unstable. The actor who has rehearsed to fantasies of "a full-dress parade through Times Square with . . . cheering crowds, and the victorious star throwing kisses in triumph"[109] is always aware of the alternate scenario in which the triumphal procession he leads becomes a vicious pack chasing down its prey. The rock star adored by screaming fans one moment can be trampled and attacked by them in the next, as they move from an ecstasy of attraction to an ecstasy of repulsion. The actor is still isolated above the mass of spectators, but now as the sacrificial victim instead of the priest. Once aroused, the fury of a "baiting crowd," as Elias Canetti calls it in his eccentric but insightful *Crowds and Power,* is fueled by hatred for all they have suddenly made their victim symbolize. Such crowds, Canetti argues, originate ultimately in the hunting pack—itself based on the hungry animal pack—which ran down a living object in order to kill and incorporate it. The mob sights its prey and attacks it in unison—a shower of spears, arrows, or stones marking the "culmination of rapacious looks directed at him" in pursuit and ambush. Of course, the human pack is restrained, in part because even as they attack they identify with the prey: "Man does not lie in ambush and turn persecutor with impunity. Anything of this kind which he actively undertakes, he experiences passively in himself, in exactly the same form."[110] We cannot help running with the hare when we hunt with the hounds. In a theater the crowd is also subdued by a variety of other, more important, constraints—the marked separation of the stage from the seats; formalized expectations about entrance, display, applause, and closure; and, above all, decorum. The crowd is "stagnant," in Canetti's term. But the potential for violence remains, and although theater audiences are not very likely actually to kill, psychological violence is not uncommon. When Redfield said acting was "like going out into the bull ring," he explained that "the danger to the body is slight but the danger to the ego is mortal."[111] The very gaze which the audience collectively focuses on an actor recalls the pack's unified rapacious looks, and the tomatoes or boos they throw are as cutting as spears.

The actor's power derives from an intense ambivalence which makes him vulnerable to the terrors of live performance—both to his own stage fright and to the audience. The audience's experience depends on equally powerful ambivalences about itself and about the actor who calls up the ambivalences and for a moment embodies them. Theater depends on the exchanges and mutual identifications that result. These draw on emotions first generated by "performances" for the mother, whose responses shaped the actor, as well as on the emotions of the crowd, which now reshapes him into either god or victim, totem or taboo. When Brook condemns the twentieth century's "deadly theatre"[112] he refers to a detached leisure-time activity in which both content and responses are predictable and safely limited: boring theater, for both actor and spectator. What actors talk about when they describe their most intense moments on stage is, by contrast, a theater that can *in fact* become deadly for them and for the audience—or can feel as if it had.

Chapter Two

Elizabethan Players: Proud Beggars "Now Up and Now Down"

. . . your fine, elegant rascal, that can rise
And stoop (almost together) like an arrow;
Shoot through the air, as nimbly as a star . . .
And change a visor swifter than a thought!
This is the creature had the art born with him.

Mosca in Jonson's *Volpone*

*I*n many ways actors in today's theater would hardly recognize its noisier, more popular, and, it would seem, emotionally less intense Elizabethan counterpart.[1] Nonetheless in our era of the global village and electronic bulletin boards, theater (unlike cinema) has retained the intimacy villages once had. In an era mistrustful of "presence," drama maintains a convincing illusion of immediacy, resistant to postmodern technology and fragmentation. Although it too has begun to change, in basic ways today's actor resembles his earlier counterpart. The theater still thrives on its double ambivalence: the onstage tension between actor and character on the one hand, the love and hate between stage and gallery on the other. Playing, now as in Shakespeare's time, isolates the actor before a crowd of watchers as mimesis transforms him into another being; but no matter how complex, alienated, or self-conscious the relation between actor and role, there is always an actor as well as a character, both engaging the audience in the performance and alienating them from it. Theater is still a matter of emotional projections that can generate intense feelings. Indeed, with more radical changes in the circumstances of contemporary theater, we might more accurately say that theater had disappeared than that it had been changed.[2]

Nor is the resemblance limited to these minimal continuities. The more we learn about Elizabethan culture and playing conditions—about the audience, the social construction of the actor, the political, economic, and cultural pressures affecting the theater companies, and the day-to-day details of rehearsal and performance—the more it seems that their stage, even more than ours, would foster the ambivalence and regressive concerns typical of modern actors, and would make the player even more vulnerable to the fickle mob of modern actors' fantasies. The previous chapter began with actors' accounts of their experience in performance and moved toward the audience's experience; lacking such direct evidence from sixteenth- and seventeenth-century players, this chapter begins with accounts provided by their audiences, about whom we know more.[3] The first section attempts to sort fact from fantasy in the reports about the player's offstage life that constitute a large part of our evidence. The following section turns more directly to the player's experience onstage, and to the ways in which mimesis and, especially, performance were part of that experience, just as they are for today's actors. The chapter ends with a discussion of the Clown, who alternately heckled and begged from the audience, and the Epilogue, who came forward at the end of a play to ask the audience for applause. Each of these actors had scripted for him a relation to the audience remarkably like the one modern actors describe; in the case of clowns like Robert Wilson who wrote their own scripts, the roles are particularly suggestive.

The Player Offstage: Fact and Fantasy

Some facts are clear without having to depend even on audience testimony. The Elizabethan player, like modern actors, was an anomaly. The English have always had both a tremendous appetite for drama and at the same time a suspicion of anyone living what they called a "minstrel's life,"[4] anyone who professed drama as a vocation and thus fell outside the usual social categories. From the beginning, players suffered the paradoxical response described by modern actors. On the one hand, they brought welcome diversion and caused a stir which overstimulated moderns find hard to imagine.[5] Though at times they were turned away or paid not to play, in the overwhelming majority of cases players were welcomed, just as fictional players are when portrayed on stage.[6] Hamlet is not only delighted to receive the players from the capital but can greet them all personally, noting that the boy is "nearer to heaven than when I saw you last by the altitude of a chopine" (*Ham.* 2.2.422–23). Even the haughty lord in *Taming of the Shrew* welcomes the troupe heartily and recognizes specific players when the traveling company arrives at his house.

> This fellow I remember
> Since once he play'd a farmer's eldest son. . . .
> I have forgot your name; but, sure, that part
> Was aptly fitted and naturally perform'd.
>
> (*Shr.* Ind.1.81–85)

Demand—and reward—for players was great enough that provincial visits multiplied even in the 1590s, when Admiral's and Chamberlain's companies were establishing themselves in London.

But on the other hand, the strolling players were a potential threat to the authorities. To the crown and to the local officials the traveling players were little better than the groups of "masterless men," rogues and vagabonds, or even than the "sturdy" but lawless beggars who roamed the countryside. The latter have lost much of their import for twentieth-century students of drama, though the new visibility of the homeless in our cities may change that. But Elizabethans were terrified of beggars, who not only epitomized the fears of a society dependent on already slipping hierarchies, but also posed a real physical threat when banded together.[7] Considering the association of players with these other vagabonds, it was an achievement for them to have survived at all. They did so in two ways: by strengthening their ties to the aristocrats in great houses and at court and, progressively, by establishing themselves on public stages just beyond the reach of London authorities. Neither tactic, however, allowed the player to escape the stigma which was placed on the earliest vagabonds, and which—more to the point—is much like that placed on contemporary actors. The player's life was hedged with conditions which could have been taken from a modern actor's fantasy. Then as now social construction of the player was a curious amalgam of partial truths left over from his peripatetic past, hard-nosed response to the day-to-day realities of his commercial enterprise, and irrational fantasies or prejudices that had less to do with contemporary realities than with the provocative confrontation between player and spectator that still defines theater.

At first the great house was "the alpha and omega of Elizabethan playing."[8] Noble households could be counted on to employ players for part of the year, while for the rest the patron's livery exempted players from the statutes against vagabonds and encouraged their acceptance when they traveled. As the most important patrons drew their troupes into the circle of court politics, competing with one another to entertain the queen, the players learned the codes of aristocratic taste, and in the process of making themselves good enough to appear before a queen, a pastime was elevated to a "quality."[9] Patronage helped determine which troupes survived, what role they took in London politics, and to some degree how and what they played.[10] As public theaters multiplied, however, the players' relation to their nominal lords became less important. But the relation remained vital in fantasy long after it declined in fact.[11] The great house dominated the representation of players, particularly in Shakespeare's plays, even as it disappeared from their lives. The typical play-within-a-play was a private performance for some great man, though not the troupe's patron. The great house was important in part because its hierarchical structure provided a ready figure for the ambiguous, even contradictory relation between actor and audience which occurs at any performance, public or private. In the great house the players would be included as childlike dependents of a

noble patron—a situation where the contradictory hopes and fears characteristic of modern actors could actually come true. On the one hand, as
Bradbrook suggests, the players' livery and their presence in aristocratic
households allowed them to masquerade as "members of the gentlemanly
profession of serving men."[12] Shakespeare was not the only player who
thought even more grandly and applied for a coat of arms.[13] On the other
hand, a player's "service" could include duties besides playing, as if he, like
any other servant, were as valuable swelling a procession as in exercising
his quality.[14] When the Lord Chamberlain's Men played before an elite audience of student gallants at Gray's Inn in 1595 they were described as "a
sort of base and common fellows," though they probably included among
them, as Bradbrook dryly comments, both Shakespeare and Burbage.[15]
Even the courtesy required by noblesse oblige in a private house could be
demeaning. Notice that the Lord in Shakespeare's *Shrew,* enthusiastic as he
is about the player's performance, has forgotten his name, a Coriolanus-like
condescension. Others did not even care about the performance, only about
the gift of service it implied. So Shakespeare's Theseus implies when Hippolyta complains that the rude mechanicals are mangling their play:

> The kinder we, to give them thanks for nothing.
> Our sport shall be to take what they mistake:
> And what poor duty cannot do, noble respect
> Takes it in might, not merit . . .
> . . . in the modesty of fearful duty
> I read as much as from the rattling tongue
> Of saucy and audacious eloquence.
> Love, therefore, and tongue-tied simplicity
> In least speak most, to my capacity.
>
> (*MND* 5.1.89–105)

Theseus most appreciates players when they are "tongue-tied," so overcome
with "love" and "fearful duty" that they forget their lines; then all the credit
goes to him and not to them.[16] Munday's Sir Thomas More is equally paternal though less patronizing to the players he welcomes: "if art fail," he says,
half expecting it to do so, "we'll inch it out with love" (*More* 3.2.132).
Performances often mattered even less to other audiences.[17] The earliest
interludes were written to accommodate a break for eating between the
acts, and all were liable to interruptions (as in *Love's Labour's Lost, Sir
Thomas More,* and *Travels of Three English Brothers,* where only two lines
of prologue are spoken before the interruption) and rude remarks from the
spectators (*Love's Labour's Lost; A Midsummer Night's Dream; Hamlet;* Marston's *Histriomastix;* and Middleton's *Mayor of Queenborough*). The show—
or "sport"—was always subordinated to the social occasion which framed

it; the players were hired help. The very means of displaying his skill to the great thus also demeaned the player, a paradox on which John Davies drew in what he took to be appropriate praise for Shakespeare: "Hadst thou not plaid some Kingly parts in sport, / Thou hadst bin a companion for a King."[18] Even for ordinary spectators the player's livery could not rescue him from the accusation of beggary which was part of the standard anti-theatrical rhetoric. Players might pretend to be supported by their nominal masters, but in reality, Stephen Gosson said in 1579, these parasites still lived "by merry begging, maintained by alms, and privily encroach upon every man's purse."[19] In the following year Munday attacked the noblemen themselves for sending out their own players to live on "alms of other men, passing from country to country, from one Gentleman's house to another, offering their service, which is a kind of beggary."[20] And Brome's *Jovial Crew, or, The Merry Beggars* was still exploiting the analogy in 1641, when it showed a group of beggars putting on a play at a country house.

A similar paradox dogged the "common" player, who was both extremely popular and continually under attack as permanent London theaters multiplied. By 1595 the new industry was drawing some 15,000 spectators a week and was increasingly integrated into the life of the city.[21] Plays and performances helped shape, more profoundly than either players or audience could know, the culture that produced them. Serving some of the functions once performed by then-vanishing popular and religious rituals, theater did more than simply gather people. From its vantage point outside the workaday world—a permanent holiday on the south bank—the saturnalian pattern of comedy, as well as the sacrificial pattern of tragedy, also drew on ritual's power to convene a crowd and to channel its energies into socially sanctioned forms.[22] Though modern commentators disagree on whether this resulted in clarification or carnivalization, that is, whether it served as a recuperative safety valve or produced genuine subversion, all agree on the importance of theater's deep and not always recognized ties to social life. On a more mundane level, theater was "the only major medium for social communication, the only existing form of journalism and only occasion that existed for the gathering of large numbers of people other than for sermons and executions" and state occasions.[23] As it is today, theater was a natural medium for social debate. Plays not only attacked general abuses like usury, but also particular individuals. Cutting Dick, a notorious cutpurse, was the hero of a lost play,[24] and the heroine of Middleton's *Roaring Girl,* Marion Frith, or Moll Cutpurse, came dressed as a man and sat on stage to see herself represented.[25] The players, as Hamlet said, will "tell all," and better a bad name after you are dead than their ill report while you live (*Ham.* 3.2.138). Even ordinary citizens might find themselves looking at duplicates of themselves on stage, in toto or, as in Dekker's *Guls Horn-*

Booke (1609), represented by some telling trait like a feather or a red beard.[26]

Individual players became as vital a part of London life as the theater. Few Elizabethans are mentioned so often in the surviving records as the clown Richard Tarlton, and Edward Alleyn and Richard Burbage were still recalled years after their deaths. In defenses of the stage, the achievements of specific players were cited to justify the whole theatrical endeavor.[27] These men were stars as we know them today, and appreciative audiences were as aware of the player as of the character. Hamlet seems less impressed by Pyrrhus than by the First Player who "does" him so naturally,[28] and when Nashe celebrated the return of the old war hero Talbot to "triumphe againe on the Stage," he does not forget to mention the "Tragedian that represents [Talbot's] person" before "ten thousand spectators at least."[29] Heywood also distinguishes between character and actor when he boasts about "the drunkards so naturally imitated in our playes, to the applause of the Actor, content of the auditory, and reproving of the vice."[30] Audiences scorned the drunkard but admired the actor.

Some audiences of course failed to distinguish between the actor and the character he played, and were interested in his offstage as well as onstage life.[31] Ferdinand in Webster's *Duchess of Malfi* (1612–14 [1614]), for example, observes that "a good actor many times is curs'd / For playing a villain's part" (*Malfi* 4.2.283–84). More telling, every actor took something of his charisma with him offstage. Thomas Platter mentions among London's attractions a tavern "visited by players almost daily"—much as Hollywood guides identify hangouts where tourists might glimpse current stars.[32] Ben Jonson helped satisfy his audience's curiosity specifically about the sexual life of the players by including gossip about the offstage transvestite activities of the boy-actor Richard Robinson.[33] Later, especially with the opening of the private theaters, gallants took to socializing with the stagers. It became the fashion for ladies to invite players for dinner and to fall in love with them. As the courtesan says in Middleton's *Mad World*, "I could find in my heart to fall in love with that player now, and send for him to a supper. I know some i'th' town that have done as much" (5.2.33–35).[34] Apparently it was more than some, and it cut across all classes. Barry implicates the middle class in *Ram Alley, or, Merry Tricks* (1607–8 [1608]):

> What do you say to a citizen's daughter
> Who was never in love
> With a player, that never learnt to dance . . .
> Might not she in time prove an honest wife?

> (5.1.369)[35]

Earle points both lower and higher: "The waiting women Spectators are over-eares in love with [the player], and ladies send for him to act in their

Chambers."[36] (Compare, in chapter 1, Henry Irving basking in the adoration of nineteenth-century flower sellers.) Jonson seems especially struck by the ladies' admiration for players; not even puppets are exempt: Leatherhead, puppet master at Bartholomew Fair, introduces his male lead this way: "This is he, that acts young Leander, sir. He is extremely beloved of the womankind" (*Bartholomew Fair* 5.3.73–74).[37] By 1623 an empress's love for a player could become the turning point of tragic action in Philip Massinger's *Roman Actor*. Custom did not stale the player's offstage charisma, which lasted until the theaters closed—and disappeared only when they did. Or so the anonymous author implies in *The Actors Remonstrance or Complaint for the silencing of their profession and banishment from their severall Play-Houses* (1643). Now that the actors are out of work, he says, they are deserted by everyone, even "their verie Mistresses, those Buxsome and Bountifull Lasses that usually were enamoured on the persons of the younger sort of Actors, for the good cloaths they wore upon the stage, beleeving them really to be the persons they did only represent."[38] So long as they performed, the players were accorded all the power theater had over its spectators.

However, the player's visibility in the theatrical enterprise also meant that he bore the brunt of the city's ambivalence about theater. "His profession has in it a kind of contradiction," as Earle was still saying in 1628, "for none is more dislik'd, and yet none more applauded."[39] Despite the audiences hurrying to pay their pennies, the players had many enemies— apparently even among theater people—and for better or worse, it is on these whom we must depend for much of the rest of our information.[40] Even before the permanent theaters were built, humanists had been suspicious and moral critics galled to see the ungodly players not only getting away with such transgression but being applauded for it.[41] As the theaters multiplied, so did the criticism. The attack was carried out by some half-dozen writers at the most, and largely under the banner of religion, but it accorded with the attitude of city fathers in their official edicts, and it seemed to draw on a reservoir of prejudice in the population at large. The series of antitheatrical sermons and pamphlets, which punctuated the period from the late 1570s to the early 1590s, enjoyed a brief renewal at the end of the century, and finally exploded in William Prynne's encyclopedia of complaints just before the theaters closed. Gathering momentum, the critics' complaints about "fleshly and filthy" content expanded into complaints about unruly crowds and playing on Sundays when people should be at church—that is, to playing under certain conditions, whatever the content—and finally, in extreme cases, to playing at all under any circumstance, even for educational purposes at the universities.

These writers assumed that theater had extraordinary power to shape anyone who came near it, and they objected to the terrible effect it had on the masses;[42] but their main focus was on the player.[43] If we take the critics at their word, the players were a colorful lot. Playing was idolatry; simply by daring to represent reality, players reversed the hierarchy of creativity in which man is subordinate to god.[44] In addition, the players dedicated themselves to ungodly idleness; they were dishonest, diseased, and improvident usurers.[45] But above all they dealt in the flesh; they were procurers and willing cuckolds, and, always, they were as obscene as the scandalous characters they represented.[46] The king may have had two bodies but the player most emphatically had only one. As Munday argued:

> As for those stagers themselves, are they not commonlie such kind of men in their conversation, as they are in profession? Are they not as variable in hart, as they are in their partes? Are they not as good practisers of Bawderie, as in-actors? . . . If (it be his nature) to be a bawdie plaier, and he delight in such filthie & cursed actions, shal we not thinke him in his life to be more disordered, and to abhor virtue?[47]

The actor, Munday says, necessarily resembles the bawdy characters he plays. No matter that the player also plays virtuous characters; that doesn't mean that he is virtuous, but only proves that he is "as variable in hart, as [he is] in [his] partes."

In particular the custom of employing the cross-dressed boy actor to play women proved that he was sexually "variable." The player provoked every "mate" in the audiences to "sort his mate," go home and "play the *Sodomite* or worse," as the audience's passion was projected onto the actors, who were assumed to keep "queans and Ganimedes" and to be sodomites themselves.[48] Tom Stoppard's twentieth-century version of the boy player available for various offstage positions and entertainments may or may not accurately represent what went on between the Chamberlain's player-queen and his fellows (or his audience), but it is certainly what some of that audience thought went on. J. Cocke's satire on the "common" player includes the observation that "If [the player] marries, hee mistakes the Woman for the Boy in Womans attire, by not respecting a difference in the mischiefe: But so long as he lives unmarried, hee mistakes the Boy, or a Whore for the Woman."[49] So unassailable was the assumption of the player's wantonness that it was used to refute the standard arguments that plays provided moral instruction. "If any goodnes were to be learned at Playes it is likely that the Players them selves which committ every sillable to memory should profitte most," Gosson says with mock open-mindedness, "but the daily experience of their behaviour sheweth, that they reap no profit by the discipline them selves."[50]

Today's reader will detect ulterior motives behind the antitheatricalists' moral outrage and will sort through the accusations with care before accepting such an image of players.[51] Religious authorities, who resented not only the players' "sinfulness" but also the competition for Sunday audiences, and civic authorities, who feared both seditious content and unruly crowds that gathered to see it, could both profit by exaggerating those dangers. Nor, as Henry Chettle complained at the time, could one trust the testimony of merchants, who resented the players' competition for Londoners' spending money, and the fact that they "played" while others had to work. In 1603 Henry Crosse's purely moral objection to the players' bringing kings, "Prophets and Patriarkes" on stage to be "derided, hist, and laught at," was immediately followed by a more pragmatic objection to these nouveaux riches impostors or "buckorome gentlemen," who "growe rich" and "purchase lands by adulterous Playes."[52]

Finally, an irrational antitheatrical prejudice as Jonas Barish describes it, or at least an ambivalence, joined the religious, economic, and political biases to further distort the surviving descriptions of players. Given that even today actors believe it can be fatal to say the name *Macbeth*, it is not surprising that Elizabethan antitheatricalists viewed plays as if they were called up from witches' cauldrons and believed that Burbage as Dr. Faustus could call up a real devil, that divine wrath made the Bear Garden collapse, and that the blasphemous actor who played Christ in a mystery play was suddenly struck ill.[53] But even if spectators did not take the play as literal truth subverting reality, they distrusted the fiction *as* fiction and the player for perpetrating it so flagrantly. The "dread of the stage," associated with the Puritans if not with religion per se, was in part a quite secular dread of anything that roused such strong feelings and fantasies.[54] The Puritan "catalogue of horrors," Barish notes, focuses on

> anything that gives pleasure and is patently designed as recreation—and even more obsessively on sexuality and effeminacy, as though to underscore the author's aversion to anything—dancing, love-making, hair-curling, elegant attire—that might suggest . . . sexuality, this being equated with femininity, with weakness, with the yielding to feeling, and consequently with the destruction of all assured props and boundaries.[55]

The complaints are so extreme that, at least to a modern ear, they sound unmistakably defensive. The questions put to the "rascal beadle" by King Lear in madness might as easily be put to the Puritan critics of the stage:

> Why dost thou lash that whore? Strip thine own back;
> Thou hotly lusts to use her in that kind
> For which thou whipp'st her.
>
> (*Lr.* 4.6.159–61)

The Elizabethan player, even more than our actors, was marked as the Other whose strangeness fascinates and repels, the charismatic transgressor who all too easily becomes a screen for the projection of the audience's disowned impulses.[56]

The testimony of unreliable antitheatricalists was supplemented by testimony from similarly unreliable playwrights. Society's ambivalence toward theater was thoroughly internalized within the playhouse community, as playwrights redirected the familiar antitheatricalist claims onto the quality. If society considered theater in general "parasitical," a "caterpillar" preying on the otherwise industrious commonwealth, then writers called the players parasitical, growing wealthy by reciting lines that someone else had written. The player can do nothing on his own, according to the playwrights; he is a "puppet," an "antick," an "ape." The London Corporation objected to presenting the queen with plays that had been "commonly played in open stages before all the basest assemblies," but Ben Jonson, like Greene and Nashe before him, took the full force of his loathing for the common stage out on the "common players."[57] The enmity may have helped fuel the "war of the theaters" at the end of the century, when, as Rosencrantz says, "the poet and the player went to cuffs" (Ham. 2.2.353). Chambers speculates that the revival of boy companies in the first place may have been the playwrights' way of fighting the adult players, though here, as in the war itself, many other factors were involved.[58]

Unlike the Puritans, playwrights didn't bother with religious or moral rationalizations for their disapproval and were quite overt about their envy of the players' financial success. Complaints like the Scholar's in *Second Part of The Return from Parnassus* (1601) were common:

> . . . ist not strange this mimick apes should prize
> Unhappy Schollers at a hireling rate?
> Vile world, that lifts them up to hye degree,
> And treads us downe in groveling misery.
> *England* affords these glorious vagabonds,
> That carried earst their fardels on their backes,
> Coursers to ride on through the gazing streetes,
> Sooping it in their glaring Satten sutes,
> And Pages to attend their maisterships:
> With mouthing words that better wits have framed,
> They purchase lands, and now Esquiers are namde.
>
> (5.1.6–16)

The Scholar's bias is made explicit when he complains that the vile world lifts *them* up but treads *us* down. In Jonson's typically more vituperative expression of envy, the antagonism between players and "men of worship" is obvious from the beginning. Here is Captain Tucca in *The Poetaster* (1602) calling Histrio the Player:

Do you hear? You, player, rogue, stalker, come back here: no respect to men of
worship, you slave? What, you are proud, you rascal, are you proud? Ha? You
grow rich, do you? And purchase, you twopenny tear-mouth? (3.4.107–11)

But the problem with such attacks is that they contradict what we know
from other sources. Even though there may have been, by the end of the
century when Jonson was writing, some factual basis for envying players'
wealth, the antagonism had begun at least as early as 1580 (if we count
Munday's pamphlets, which accuse the players of offering "their games for
lucre sake"), before playing became really profitable.[59] Certainly in the late
eighties and early nineties, when Marlowe attacked the "jigging veins of
rhyming mother wits" (*Tamburlaine* Pro.1), Nashe made occasional swipes
at players, and Greene attacked Shakespeare as an "upstart crowe," the
player still lived a precarious life at the edge of poverty. In fact the *Parnassus* "mimick" in his "Satten sute" (1601) sounds suspiciously similar to
Greene's player in *Groatsworth of Wit* (1592), as if the characterization
were as much a convention as a portrayal of real actors. Greene's is already—most implausibly at that time—as rich and gentrified as the one in
Parnassus:

> A Player, quoth *Roberto,* I tooke you rather for a gentleman of great living; for
> if by outward habit men shuld be censured, I tell you, you would be taken for a
> substantiall man. So am I where I dwell (quoth the player) reputed able at my
> proper cost, to build a Windmill. What though the worlde once went harde
> with mee, when I was faine to carrie my playing Fardle a footbacke . . . it is
> otherwise now; for my very share in playing apparrell will not be solde for two
> hundred pounds. (*Parnassus,* 131)

Greene not only takes a shareholder to be a representative player—hardly
the case—but also overestimates the value of a share, as Stubbes similarly
exaggerated the player's sexual extravagance.[60]
   Like the Puritans alert to evidence of debauchery, the playwrights seem
all too ready to think of the players as rich. The *Parnassus* complaint, for
example, makes it sound as if the players always lived like nobility:

> *England* affords these glorious vagabonds, . . .
> Coursers to ride on through the gazing streetes,
> Sooping in their glaring Satten sutes,
> And Pages to attend their maisterships.
>
> (5.1.10–14)

But it is unlikely that the Scholar saw many players gadding about this way
in the streets. Onstage actors wore clothing that would have been the mark
of wealth, status or arrogance on anyone else. But off duty, no player could

present himself so magnificently, nor ever make use of the satin suits: their contracts forbade them to take the costumes out of communal storage in the theater.[61] Only a very few players could afford "coursers to ride on through the gazing streetes"; this complaint must refer to the players' usual parade entry into a town or through the city *as players* with the company animal.[62]

The attackers themselves regularly undermine the claim that players were rich by simultaneously accusing the player of poverty. They simply recast the old complaint about vagabonds into commercial terms: "Howsoever hee pretends to have a royall Master or Mistresse," J. Cocke wrote scornfully in 1615, "his wages and dependance prove him to be the servant of the people."[63] In fact disgust about the city player's wealth never did counteract the old image of the strolling player as less than a servant—as a beggar, always ready to humiliate himself in public to earn a penny, and "groveling on the stage"[64]—little better than the *Parnassus* Scholar trodden down to "grovelling misery." If the player grows rich, as Jonson's Tucca jeers, he is at the same time only a "twopenny tear-mouth" (*Poetaster* 3.4.110–11). Not long before Greene was envying the shareholder worth two hundred pounds, pamphleteers were referring to stagers who "for one poor penny" play "ignominious fools for an hour or two together,"[65] and to players who were "Asses for travelling all daie for a pennie."[66]

To a large degree these attacks tell us more about the attackers than about the players. Something seems to be going on in the stubbornly contradictory image of the wealthy penny-grubbing player, as if writers felt that the player was getting away with something he had no right to, whether it was money, sexual license, or social climbing. Or, perhaps more than any particular transgression, it was a matter of what we would now call "attitude." The one accusation that appears again and again in the attacks on players is that they are "proud." Henry Crosse, for example has only scorn for the parvenu "buckorome gentlemen," players "puft up in such pride and selfe-love, as they envie their equalles, and scorne theyr inferiours,"[67] and Nashe complains about the insolence of the "vainglorious Tragedians" (1589).[68] Like Crosse's, many of these attacks are directed simply at the player's social climbing. Gosson accuses the player not only of "prating on the stage" but of doing the same when he "comes abrode":

> [the players] jet under gentlemens noses in sutes of silke, exercising themselves ᵗoo prating on the stage, and common scoffing when they come abrode, where they looke askance over the shoulder at every man, of whom the Sunday before they begged an almes.[69]

But other attacks on the proud actor are directed not so much at social pretense as at professional pride, to which playwrights felt he had as little right as to his money or genteel status. The players in *Histriomastix* (Marston's version, 1599), which may date originally from just this period, refuse to pay their would-be playwright, Chrisoganus, the only decent character in the play, the customary ten pounds; they are too proud.[70] Such pride is a matter of more than social ambition, as John Davies implies when he takes it on himself to scourge "men most base that are ambitious," i.e., the players:

> Good *God!* That ever *pride* should stoop so low,
> That is by nature so exceeding hie:
> Base *pride,* didst thou thy selfe, or others know,
> Wouldst thou in *harts* of Apish *Actors* lie,
> That for a *Cue* wil sel their *Qualitie?*
> Yet they through thy perswasion (being strong),
> Doe weene they merit *immortality,*
> Only because (forsooth) they use their *Tongue,*
> To speak as they are taught, or right, or *wronge.*[71]

Actors are so proud of their achievements on stage that they think they deserve immortality—when in fact all they've done is to ape the playwright's words. Here it's not the actor's status or money that is envied (though Davies scorns his willingness to sell his quality or talent), but his self-satisfaction, his admiration of his own talent. The lean and hungry Greene complained that the players "waxe proud" and "too full of self-liking and self love," suggesting perhaps a dislike fanned by envy not only of the player's supposed wealth but also of his undeserved fame, his glitter as well as his gold.[72] The *Parnassus* Scholar envies the certainty that "gazing streetes" of people would admire the player and envy his (unlikely) ownership of his own courser and page, but Henry Chettle attacks a "contempt" which has nothing to do with either money or clothing and could refer as much to the player's general air of self-satisfied superiority as to his social pretensions. Chettle seems to suggest that the player's contempt is fueled by his being at the center of everyone's attention: "Divers of them [players] *beeing publike in everie ones eye,* and talkt of in every vulgar mans mouth, see not how they are seene into, especially for their contempt, which makes them among most men most contemptible" (italics added).[73] The player thinks that because he has made himself flashy enough to be "in everie ones eye" no one will see through him to diagnose the contempt for others that is part of his own self-glorification.

* * *

Nonetheless, even though Gosson and the others are unreliable witnesses, the consistency with which they describe the player's attitude suggests that they may have been responding to something in the player as well as to their own prejudice. What was the reality behind this image of the proud beggar of a player? How was playing different from being a goldsmith's apprentice, as Robert Armin had been, or a brewer, as Anthony Jeffes became later?[74] Because people then were identified so closely with their callings—and were shaped so extensively by them—the question is even more pertinent for Shakespeare's biography than for Olivier's. We have of course no first-person testimony—no autobiographies like Callow's—and unfortunately the players' lives, as William Ingram says, "have for the most part passed into unrecorded oblivion."[75] Little evidence remains to answer the questions we would like to ask about what it felt like to be a member of a troupe or to worry about censorship, the plague, court preferences, and popular taste. But there are hints in the meager record, and some players have left texts of their own which suggest certain habits of mind, recurring themes, and internal consistencies or contradictions. There can be no proof about what actors felt, but the circumstantial evidence suggests enough resemblances between Elizabethan and contemporary actors' lives to justify some analogies.

The differences between the two periods are of course more obvious, and we should begin with those. In some ways Elizabethan players actually led more settled lives than today's actors who must live precariously from job to job. All acting then was repertory acting, and many players lived with their families in the neighborhood of the theater, where parish registers record the usual procession of events—marriages, births, illegitimate births, and deaths. When players petitioned the Privy Council in the early 1580s for the right to play in the city, they did so in the name of their family responsibilities. Players' wives occasionally worked as gatherers (money takers) in the theaters,[76] and, judging from a well-known letter sent by Ned Alleyn's apprentice to Mrs. Alleyn when the players were on tour, in that household at least there was a warm family circle including both boy and servants.

For many players playing was no doubt a job to which they had been led simply because they belonged to an acting family (as was Burbage), because they were orphaned and turned over to the children of the revels, or for other mundane reasons.[77] As their opponents said, playing was a commercial venture, both in the long term and, as players would be reminded daily, in the short, when the take was counted and distributed after each performance. Like other professionals, players banded together to form hierarchically organized guildlike structures ("brotherhoods" as Cocke mockingly calls them), in which the sharers, or partners who had invested money to create the organization, were sharply divided from the hirelings. When soldiers bully the players and steal their rich costumes in *Histrio-*

mastix, they wittily excuse their behavior by explaining, "now we are the Sharers / And you the hired men." Sharers, who made the theatrical decisions about plays and (probably) casting, often included outstanding players like Alleyn and Burbage. The fictional Sir Thomas More and Hamlet, both known more for their love of playing than for their love of gold, joke about earning a share in a cry of players by acting. But sharers were not always the best players; their economic rather than histrionic credentials granted them what respect they had among theater's opponents. Even Gosson distinguished between sharers and their "hang-byes"; more than twenty years later, when Middleton's ridiculous upstart Sir Bounteous in *Mad World* hears that the actor before him is the greatest sharer and "may live of himself" (5.1.40)—that he does not need to earn his living playing— he immediately changes his tone from patronage to respect. By contrast, the hired men—and "Iohannes fac totum[s]" who performed "mechanical labor," as Greene said—took secondary roles, or worked as stagehands.[78] Finally there were the boy-actors, who had been apprenticed (or bought) to serve senior players (Henslowe acquired one for eight pounds in 1597); both Nathan Field and Richard Brome, players who later took to writing, are called "servants" (probably apprentices) of Ben Jonson.[79] It was all very orderly and well organized.

But nonetheless, despite the unmodern regularities imposed by both feudal hierarchy and bourgeois commercialism, there were many similarities to the unsettled lives of today's actors. Though (as the critics insisted) for a very few playing could be "one of the lightning careers of a speculative and chaotic age,"[80] for many it was neither rising nor even secure. Dekker may have joked that even the "worst player's Boy" could hope someday to be a sharer himself, but the majority never realized such hopes.[81] Even the better players, like William Bird, could end a long and successful career in poverty. "Theater entrepreneurship was perilous,"[82] and the sharers themselves were not always secure.[83] Many companies failed to survive city opposition, plague, the vagaries of public approval, and the increasing restrictions on patrons. The Lord Chamberlain's Men themselves were put to fear when their patron died in 1596. Thomas Nashe wrote to his friend that the players "are piteously persecuted by the Lord Mayor and the Aldermen; and however in their old Lord's time they thought their estate settled, it is now so uncertain they cannot build upon it."[84] Ten years later when Sir Bounteous in Middleton's *Mad World* is told "there are certain players come to town," he replies:

By the mass, they are welcome; they'll grace my entertainment well. But for *certain* players, there thou liest, boy; they were never more uncertain in their lives. Now up and now down, they know not when to play, where to play, nor

what to play; nor when to play for fearful fools, where to play for Puritan fools,
nor what to play for critical fools. (5.1.27–33)

Sir Bounteous described the player's up-and-down life three hundred and
fifty years before Joshua Logan adapted the phrase to title his autobiography,
and though the knight's emphasis was more on the external troubles caused
by foolish audiences, the similarity between the two accounts is telling.

Concluding his account of the hired men in his *The Profession of Player,*
Bentley cites the record of John King, aged forty-eight, who "for the space
of these 30 years past and upwards . . . hath been a hired servant to the
company of sharers of the players of the Red Bull." King was promised
wages "certain by the week," but also told by the sharers that "if at any time
it should happen the getting of the said company to be but small and to
decrease then he should not have his whole wages." Bentley concludes: "As
so often one comes back to the constant precariousness of the theater. That
men like John King stayed with such a hazardous occupation for thirty
years seems as irrational in 1623 as similar conduct by modern players
seems today."[85]

It is impossible to generalize about the private, as opposed to financial,
irregularities which Puritans claimed to find among these people, who
seem on the whole to have been family men. The St. Giles, Cripplegate,
parish register for 10 February 1587 records the baptism of a child named
"Comedia, base-borne daughter of Alice Bowker," her theatrical name chosen presumably because, "as she [Bowker] saith the father's name is
W[illiam] J[ohnson]; one of the Queene's players."[86] Thirty years later
the same register records the birth of "base-borne" "Edward," named
(proudly?) after his father "Edward Shakespeare, the player," a nephew of
William Shakespeare.[87] But in this, players seem no different from their
fellow citizens. As for assumptions about the actors and their boys, the
most we can say is that the speculation is not surprising in an era when
boys (unlike men) offstage were commonly known as objects of desire;
most reported cases of "sodomy" during the period involved adult—often
married—men and their young male servants, or schoolmasters and their
boys, situations exactly like that of the boy actors and their masters. As
many have argued, given the universality of the convention cross-dressing
must have been taken for granted on most occasions, but the homoerotic
potential of such moments must also have been readily available for exploi-
tation.[88] Whether the boys were ravishing or not, their plays were known
for sexually suggestive style and lines, and gossip flourished about their
relation to their masters. When the Citizen's Wife in *The Knight of the Burning Pestle* sees her apprentice Rafe in a play, she sees only the "pretty child"

beneath the role.[89] But Middleton saw "a nest of boys able to ravish a man." Gabriel Harvey was perhaps alluding to the relations between the masters of the early boys' companies and their helpless charges when he describes Lyly's position in the troupe as "Vicemaster of Poules."[90] In the adult companies, where there were fewer boys, things may have been different. But Jonson, Marston, and Chapman, though writing for the boy players, all describe adult performances with boy actors where the homoerotic attachments are clear and the suggestion is that the boys served as the actor's ingles.[91] And one of the seedy actors in *Histriomastix* keeps, or is kept by, an *adult* "ingle" who interrupts a rehearsal at one point bandying suggestive compliments on his sword (4.1).[92]

We will almost certainly never know whether the accusations of sexual impropriety are true or, if they are, what meaning they would have had. But even if they were all false, the important fact is that players were so widely taken to be promiscuous that they would have had to live in the shadow of social stigma. The player's offstage life differed in enough other ways from most other professions to match the popular image of him as a transgressor and, whether or not any given player actually transgressed, he had to live with that image. Players would not all have been the target of such frenzied homophobia as Prynne's, but they would always have been vulnerable to a satirist like J. Cocke, who used his claim that the player mistook "the Boy, or a Whore for the Woman" as final proof of the player's baseness. The social stigma of this embryonic "new estate" extended beyond the Puritans and politicians to ordinary citizens whom the players would encounter in daily transactions that affected their lives.[93] It has for example left its trace in at least a few court records where "litigants tried to score easy points by appealing to common prejudice." In 1577 when Richard Hickes "went to law against the stage player Jerome Savage, [he] described Savage in a suit as 'a verrie lewd fellowe' because 'his Chieffe staie of lyvinge is by playinge of interlude.'"[94] Anyone becoming a player would know that his choice entailed precisely the kind of stigmatization which makes parents uneasy when their children go on the stage today. Even Tarlton, who dared to tease the queen, who could ask Sidney to be godfather to his son and then ask Walsingham to take over, was kept in his place as a fool; and, more to the point, he died "without any real property."[95] Similarly, although he was beloved by the thousands who came to see him on stage, when he refused to step out of the way of "a spruce young gallant . . . in white sattin" on the street, "the gallant, scorning that *a player* should take the wall . . . drew his rapier" (italics added). Even an ordinary spectator in the gallery took offense when Tarlton made horns at him—not because of the horns but "because a player did it."[96] As "Tarlton" said, in a 1598 epigram dedicated to him, "I was extold for that which all despise."[97]

The Player Onstage: Mimesis and Performance

The player John King's social status, then, would have made his daily life not only financially hazardous, as Bentley observed, but also socially diffi- cult. Bentley's conclusion seems even more inescapable: staying with such an "occupation for thirty years seems as irrational in 1623 as similar con- duct by modern players seems today."[98] It would be impossible to deter- mine whether or not the "character of the player," as described in several collections of "characters,"[99] was "irrational," and it would be anachronistic to describe the player's "character" in the sense which that word has for us, though a few tantalizing shreds of evidence do support the cliché of tem- peramentality. The fines and stern warnings found in players' contracts, and mentioned, for example, in *Histriomastix,* suggest that many players were not dependable in this matter. Burbage had a reputation for temper, and Chambers went so far as to speculate that there is "a certain instability of temperament, which the life of the theatre, with its ups and downs of for- tune, its unreal sentiments and its artificially stimulated emotions, is well calculated to encourage."[100] Less melodramatically, we might speculate that some found the financial gamble worth the risk, or may even have found the irregularity of a player's life congenial.

But there is another way to look for traces of the player's "character." Instead of trying to document players' "irrational" attitudes toward the off- stage details of their lives—wages and job stability, to say nothing of sexu- ality—we might look more closely at the onstage experience of a player, both in rehearsal and in performance. There is even less evidence about the day-to-day experience of players onstage—what it felt like to go on a thrust stage and be applauded or booed by several thousand people close at hand—than there is about their offstage lives. We have no revealing quotes from Elizabethan autobiographies. But circumstantial evidence suggests that playing in Shakespeare's time entailed—and therefore could reward— the same exercise of mimetic power in role-playing and the same perfor- mance skills it does today. Such evidence might help explain the motivation for playing which Bentley could not find in the financial record.

Playing then as now was a matter of pride. My informal impression is that no other trade was assumed to be so available for general judg- ment—understandably, since none was so public. However money-minded a player may have been, this was not a hack job. There were even special displays in which audiences wagered on competing actors.[101] In ordinary performances, individual actors were singled out, praised for their skill (at times in the text of the play itself), or criticized for the lack of it, and it was assumed that they would improve with experience and "study." As the Epilogue to Chapman's *Bussy D'Ambois* put it:

> The best deserving actors of the time
> Had their ascents, and by degrees did climb
> To their full height, a place to study due.[102]

There is little evidence about what study (as opposed to experience) might have entailed for Chapman's boy player. But, although the official position of "director" was not established until this century, there are indications that someone did "instruct" or "guide" the players in sixteenth- and seventeenth-century productions, just as actor-managers did in the nineteenth century. Erasmus includes a "guide" or "manager" in *The Praise of Folly,* his allegory of the *theatrum mundi;*[103] and both real amateurs and boy actors were assumed to need guidance. When the aristocrats organize a performance in Shakespeare's *Love's Labour's Lost* for example, they feel it necessary to coach their would-be player, Moth, even though he already "well by heart hath conn'd his embassage." Boyet reports that "Action and accent did they teach him there; / 'Thus must thou speak, and thus thy body bear'" (*LLL* 5.2.99–100). Prospero makes sure that Ariel has "performed to the point" in the tempest scene (*Tem.* 1.2.194) he directed and later praises Ariel and the rest of the "rabble" for following his direction perfectly:

> Of my instruction hast thou nothing bated
> In what thou hadst to say: so, with good life
> And observation strange, my meaner ministers
> Their several kinds have done.
>
> (*Tem.* 3.3.85–88)

Some evidence suggests that, as one German visitor wrote in 1613, the same condition prevailed among adult professionals: "even the eminent actors have to allow themselves to be taught their places by the dramatists."[104] In other words, there seems to have been then, as there is today, a parental figure about whom fantasies might collect during the actors' daily work on their roles. The apprentices and recruits from the boys' companies would have been accustomed to direction, and, as Heywood says in his defense of the theater, in the case of any actor, "imperfections may be by instructions helped."[105] Someone, whether dramatist or actor-manager, must have given the instructions.

Certainly nearly every one of the extant plays of the period which portray playing do so in a way that suggests that someone was assigned just such a function.[106] Although these inner plays usually represent amateur rather than professional productions—the sort of pageants which in actuality almost always had a "presenter"—playwrights may also have drawn on their professional public stage experience in creating them. Will Summers instructs his actors as well as presenting them in Nashe's *Summer's Last Will and Testament* (1592), privately produced for Whitgift at Croydon, but perhaps drawing on Nashe's experience in writing for the public stage. When John a Cumber organizes "the lads of the parish" for a private performance in Munday's *John a Kent and John a Cumber* he says, "Ile give ye apt enstructions,"[107] and Skelton takes charge of the framed play in Munday's *Death and Downfall of Robert, Earl of Huntingdon* (1598). Even the rude crew in *Histriomastix* seems to designate someone to take charge of their rehearsals. Shakespeare's Armado has charge of the pageant in *Love's Labour's Lost,* in *Hamlet* the professional players defer to the First Player's decisions, and Quince the carpenter is clearly the producer-director in *Midsummer Night's Dream's* inner play.[108]

The psychological significance of the player's relation to a "director" is even more a matter of speculation. It is certain, however, that Shakespeare emphasized the dependent relation between the player and such omnipresent patron-managers as Theseus in *Dream,* the Lord in *Shrew,* Hamlet, Prospero, and if we count him, the Duke in *Measure for Measure,* who literally serves as father confessor in the real-life play he directs. This figure invariably accompanies Shakespeare's inner plays and becomes, as we shall see in chapters 4 and 5, a vital part of his representation of the player's experience. There is no way of knowing how an actual player's relation to such a figure might have corresponded to the modern actor's relation toward his director-father. Nonetheless it is interesting to observe how many of the most well known sixteenth- and seventeenth-century players had lost their fathers early. Success for Edward Alleyn and Nathaniel Field was facilitated by the fact that each orphaned youth adopted a father figure connected with the theater: Henslowe in the case of Alleyn,[109] Jonson in the case of Field. Ben Jonson, who entered the theater as an actor, was himself a posthumous child. The loss of his father, as well as the loss of his children, may have fed the marked concern with father-son relationships in his plays, and may also have had something to do with his leaning toward the stage.[110] Even Rafe, the amateur player in Beaumont's *Knight of the Burning Pestle* (1607), is "a fatherless child" (2.94), taken under the wing of the Citizen's Wife. Such data are of course merely suggestive; many Elizabethans lost parents and did not become actors. But the consistency is nonetheless of interest and suggests that the Elizabethan stage, like our own, might have been more attractive to men who had grown up without close ties to a father who could provide a satisfactory model and career. It is of particular interest in light of Shakespeare's apparent "loss" of his father to financial, social, and perhaps psychological decline.

We are on more certain ground when we move from rehearsal to the two aspects of an actual presentation of the plays, mimesis and performance. Many sixteenth- and seventeenth-century texts testify to the importance of mimesis to Shakespearean actors. As they do now, discussions of acting focused on the player's mimetic ability, and sixteenth-century role-playing required as great a fidelity to "nature" as method acting does today. We don't find the plays realistic, but audiences did then—and complained when they didn't. Even Richard Edwards claims verisimilitude for his stiff-legged *Damon and Pithias* (1564); his Prologue promises that things "doone of yore in longe time past, yet present shalbe here, / Even as it were dooynge now, so lively it shall appeare."[111] Years later, dismissing Edwards and his ilk, Hamlet insisted on his own version of faithfulness to the "modesty of nature" (*Ham.* 3.2.19), but "nature" remained the goal. To play was to do the part "to the life," so that, as Heywood boasted, the audience felt "as if the Personater were the man Personated."[112] Both friendly and unfriendly audiences, as we have seen, could confuse actor and character as if there were no difference.[113] But there is still the question of what "personating" meant to the personator and whether it entailed the same kind of identification with his role that today's actors experience. Shakespeare's actors sawed the air with oratorical flourishes and used conventional gestures to express fear, anger, love or other passions; Falstaff used an onion rather than a sad memory to make his eyes red for performance.[114] Working as they did "from the outside in," as we now say, how could a player lose himself in his role? If nothing else, the dizzying repertory schedule which required him to keep several such roles in mind at once ought, we now feel, to preclude any psychological involvement with the characters he played.

These are important objections, but we should be careful not to over-estimate the differences between "personating" then and now. Shakespeare distinguished between stock gestures (and expressions) which seemed artificial and those which did not; an actor should have been capable of making similar distinctions.[115] The fact that a player used stereotyped gestures does not preclude his identifying with the feelings believed to motivate such external signs of emotion. It may be as anachronistic to assume that stylized acting cannot be sincere as it is to assume that sixteenth-century players felt exactly as ours do about their roles. Assumptions about the effects of repertory playing are also tricky. Obviously, in a month when the company performed a dozen or more different plays, demands on the player would be tremendous. But twentieth-century actors have said that it is easier to identify with a changing sequence of repertory roles than to stay in character for long-run performances day after day. We know that today's actors can memorize several different roles "on different tracks" or "in different compartments" of the mind;[116] Shakespeare's actors, trained from school days to memorize and listen to long passages, might have found it even easier. And an occasional remark, like Richard Flecknoe's that Burbage "never (not so much as in the Tyring-House) assum'd himself again until the Play was done," leaves the possibility open that Shakespeare's actors identified with their roles.[117] Certainly the player's emotional involvement in his role was very much an issue of debate at the time.

From the plays themselves we know that the majority of plays-within-plays in Renaissance drama are performed, not by disinterested professionals, but by offstage amateurs who are very much involved in their roles.[118] For lovelorn women like Rosalind in Shakespeare's *As You Like It,* and for paralyzed rulers who disguise themselves to effect their real wishes, role-playing was almost always a means of self-expression and self-knowledge. Rosalind was not necessarily a figure for the professional player but there are suggestions that professionals could be just as involved as the amateurs were. In the Induction to Marston's *Antonio and Mellida* (1599–1600 [1599]), for example, when the actors are gossiping among themselves before the play begins, one of them, Alberto, questions another's praise of a witty remark: "Umph; why 'tolerably good . . .'? Go, go; you flatter me" (Ind.41–42). The other, Forobosco, defends himself by claiming that he was simply speaking as his character would: "Right; I but dispose my speech to the habit of my part" (Ind.43). In the same Induction, another actor excuses his fellow's bombast in offstage conversation by explaining that "'tis native to his part" (Ind.88), as if he were identifying himself with that part. *Antonio and Mellida* is unusually self-conscious about its status as a play, but is not necessarily a less accurate reflector of playing conditions. Theorists as well as playwrights assumed that insofar as an actor was like an orator, he would have to feel the character's emotions in order to be effective. According to Renaissance understanding of physiology, passion was a physical force moving outward from the heart to the external body and thence to an observer; a merely feigned emotion would be less forceful and would therefore not affect the spectator as powerfully.[119] Thomas Dekker implies that the right author can actually transform an actor into the man he seems. "Give me" that playwright, he says, who

> Can give an Actor, Sorrow, Rage, Ioy, Passion,
> Whilst hee again (by selfe same Agitation)
> Commands the *Hearers,* sometimes drawing out Teares
> Then smiles, and fills them both with *Hopes & Feares.*[120]

Players themselves, understandably, have left no clear testimony about whether or not they could tell the personator from the personated, or to what degree they identified with their roles. Philip Massinger's Roman actor insists that he is unaffected by his roles (*The Roman Actor* [1626] 4.2.44–51), and Shakespeare's Richard III claims—smugly—that players remain aloof. "Come," he demands of Buckingham,

> canst thou quake and change thy colour,
> Murther thy breath in the middle of a word,
> . . . As *if* thou were distraught and mad with terror?
>   (*R3* 3.5.1–4; italics added)

But whatever Richard says, his roles do have a truth of their own for him. He may "play" at wooing Anne, for example, but he enjoys thereby doing precisely what he had said was impossible for him: bewitching the ladies.[121] And by the end of *Richard III* Richard is in reality "distraught and mad with terror" (*R3* 3.5.4)—as if, however much Richard thinks he is in control of his emotions, Shakespeare knows that he is not. It is also interesting that Shakespeare elsewhere uses something like Richard's description of successful acting to indicate its opposite—stage fright destroying an actor's pretense. Richard sees the actor's quaking and mid-word pauses as signs of successful hypocrisy; Theseus in *A Midsummer Night's Dream* sees the same symptoms as signs of real fear:

> . . . I have seen them shiver and look pale,
> Make periods in the midst of sentences,
> Throttle their practis'd accent in their fears,
> And, in conclusion, dumbly have broke off.
>   (*MND* 5.1.95–98)

T. W. Baldwin's theory of "acting lines" written into plays for specific actors presumably playing—and identifying with—themselves over and over, has been discredited, partly because of disagreement about the presence of such lines in the plays themselves, and partly because there is no evidence for them in surviving plots and cast lists.[122] But even though playwrights did not always create roles specially for each actor in a company, there might well have been a less institutionalized interplay between actor and role—as there is for today's actors who do not limit themselves to a particular "line." Munday, said to have been an actor himself, accused the players of choosing "those partes which is most agreeing to their inclination, and that they can best discharge."[123] Munday meant to disparage the people who played such wanton parts. But the actor Thomas Heywood made the same assumption in his praise of players: "Actors should be men pick'd out personable, according to the parts they present."[124] Players could have been "personable" to the characters they personated, even if the roles were not created specifically for them. The ambiguity is precisely what characterizes acting theory today. It suggests that acting then—as it does now—moved between the poles of identification and technical distancing, rather than implying that Shakespearean acting was a wholly different experience from ours.

It is even possible that role-playing was a moving enough experience to convey some of the magical power that actors feel today when they "bring a play to life"—though again, the testimony comes from playwrights rather than actors, and none took such powers literally. Joseph Roach, however, argues that rhetorical "inspiration" was taken almost literally as the experience of being animated by the spirit of another being.[125] The very vocabulary of the theater lent itself to imaging the player as revenant: he was a "shape," a "shadow," a creature from another world. Revenge masques lent themselves to false resurrections: Hieronimo's revelation of his son's body at the end of his inner play, Vindice's use of his fiancée's skull in his, or Hoffman's sideshow of his father's skeleton and Otho's body. The high drama of counterfeit deaths was a popular ingredient in many plays, and there was a market for "real" stage resurrections as well.[126] The best known claim for drama's restorative power is Thomas Nashe's praise of the tragedian who brought "brave Talbot" to life on the stage "after he had lyne two hundred years in his Tombe," to which we shall return in examining Shakespeare's histrionic heroes in the early plays.[127] But the notion of "bringing a play to life" appeared elsewhere as well. Amateur playwright John Jones, for example, complained that the players had refused his request to have "the Promethean fire of action infused into" his play.[128] And Ben Jonson drew on the notion—appropriately enough—in his elegy to the player Edward Alleyn, ending with the claim that "'Tis just, that who did give / So many *Poets* life, by one should live." Flecknoe's *Praises of Richard Burbage* repeats the claim: "'Twas only he gave life unto a play; / Which was but dead, as 'twas by the author writ, / Till he by action animated it."[129]

If Shakespeare's actors, like ours, were praised for and took pleasure in their mimetic skills, they also knew that mimesis was not enough. "Performance," or the relation between actor and the audience, which determines so much of a modern actor's fantasy life, was even more important then and more capable of providing immediate narcissistic gratification whatever the theatrical venue: market square, amphitheater, hall theater, or private performance. This aspect of acting was even more like the acting we know today. Despite the obvious differences between Shakespeare's stage and ours, the experience of putting one's body on display has not changed all that much over the centuries. Our knowledge of details may be limited, but we do know that the Elizabethan player was on display in a world hungry for display. It was an age of "ostentation" and of reciprocal speculation—of the "centripital gaze," as Northrop Frye called it—"which, whether addressed to mistress, friend or deity, seems to have something about it of the court gazing upon its sovereign, the courtroom gazing upon the orator, or the audience gazing upon the actor."[130] Today we speak of a cinematic "gaze," voyeuristic and predatory, rooted in the totalizing privacy of a mother's mirroring gaze. But the attention then focused on the player was more a communal and reciprocal affair. The intense private gaze between the mother and child, rather than being repressed or relegated to equally private encounters, was continually replayed in various social rituals, eroding the boundaries, as Frye suggests, and therefore giving all kinds of public display—and most especially the theater—the intensity of what we call private experience. Shakespeare's actors would have expected to find the stage a site for reinforcing intimate emotion by public display, and for drawing the crowd's attention to their bodies. Webster describes the way in which, "by a full and significant action of body, he [the actor] charmes our attention," and draws ears as well as eyes toward him: "sit in a full Theater, and you will thinke you see so many lines drawne from the circumference of so many eares, whiles the *Actor* is the *Center*."[131] The actor, Henry Chettle said, is "publike in everie ones eye, and talkt of in every vulgar mans mouth"; "no man need be more wary in his doings," Earle agrees, "for the eyes of all men are upon him."[132]

Finally the star system, as we have seen, not only put players on display but made them into charismatic creatures, as idolized by some as they were feared by the Puritans. There are indications that sixteenth-century stars had something of our actors' star mentality as well, narcissism and all. Sir John Davies was certain that, "naught goes on there [onstage] but to be seene"; as Redfield said three centuries later, "actors are narcissists. Otherwise, they would not be actors."[133] Many players, Foakes suggests, apparently preferred "the leading role in a hack company to a subordinate role in a good one."[134] Or, as Dekker commented, there are players, who, "out of ambition to wear the *Best Ierkin* (in a *Strowling Company*) or to Act *Great Parts,* forsake the stately and our more than *Romaine* Cittie Stages, to travel upon yᵉ hard hoofe from village to village for chees & buttermilke."[135] The ambition to be a star rather than part of a well-respected company suggests that narcissistic delight in personal display, as well as social and professional pride, was fueling the player's ambition. Some of the evidence cited to prove that Elizabethan acting was highly stylized may actually be evidence that players were willing to break an otherwise naturalistic illusion in order to steal that extra bow. Thus among J. Cocke's 1615 complaints about the common actor is the fact that "when he doth hold conference on the stage; and should looke directly in his fellows face; hee turnes about his voice into the assembly for applause-sake, like a Trumpeter in the fields, that shifts places to get an echo."[136] The Shakespearean player, hoping, as Webster said he could, to attract a circle of ears as well as eyes, is not only mirror-hungry; he is also echo-hungry in a theater that could provide the kind of approval Drayton (1600) describes: "With Showts and Claps at ev'ry little pawse, / When the proud Round on ev'ry side hath rung."[137]

Invested so heavily in applause, actors were as vulnerable then to audience disapproval as they are now. Frye mentioned only the centripetal gaze focused on occasions of celebration and epiphany, but Elizabethans who elevated their gaze toward kings and priests also lowered it to criminals at executions, to cuckolds in skimmington rites, and to two-headed monsters at fairs. If they remembered watching the baiting of Christ in the annual Passion plays, they now flocked to watch bearbaitings all year round.[138] Even in the amphitheaters they not only admired real gallants above stage, but also saw real pickpockets tied "to a post on our stage, for all people to look at."[139] They were accustomed to venting their opinions in "theaters" far more interactive than ours—an interaction with Shakespeare both included within his narratives and invoked in his own audiences, as we shall see.[140] Players were always dependent on this "monster," as actor Nathan Field called the audience, who "clapped his thousand hands / and drowned the scene with his confused cry."[141] Such investment in one's audience was not part of other professions whatever concerns for the market other trades might have aroused. The actor in Marston's *Antony and Mellida* who fears he is unsuited for his part looks "dusky" [gloomy] because he knows "I shall be hiss'd at, on my life now" (Ind.66). The audience threw tomatoes at Tarlton in the 1580s, and while the missiles may have diminished as time went on, the invectives did not.[142] With stakes like this, Bottom, Shakespeare's portrait of the actor as childishly narcissistic exhibitionist, may have had more specific satiric point than we have realized.[143]

In any case the actor could hardly ignore the audience's reactions. The Elizabethan audience was literally closer to the players than ours; they were competing for the same space onstage in the hall theaters, and at the actors' feet in the amphitheaters if not onstage there as well.[144] Of course some spectators were busy eating or showing themselves, but on the whole, they seem to have been noisily involved with the action.[145] The ranting in the amphitheaters might have kept spectators from the more subtle varieties of identification we associate with playgoing, but not from the mass emotion. Actor Gerard Murphy claims that the reconstructed Swan theater is a much more intimate stage than ours today. "You do not need to shout when you are whispering."[146] Commenting on the implications of the Rose and Globe excavations, Tony Church, who has played at the Swan, observed:

> You have to play to people that are all around you, but also over your head. You have to make certain that your eyes reach into all those spaces. You have to

acknowledge their existence at some point in every sequence. That must have been the case at the Globe. To be surrounded on three sides by a tall wall of very closely spaced, heavy breathing, probably smelly people must have been like playing in the middle of a football club.[147]

Acoustical difficulty may even have tied the player more closely to his audience. Laurence Olivier believed that the advent of the microphone destroyed vaudeville by disturbing the exchange between performer and audience:

> The stand-up act with the microphone clasped in his hand had a weapon of unbeatable calibre, thereby taking from the audience the right to send him cowering off the stage in response to their mercilessly vociferous refusal to have further patience with him. Thus the solo artist had robbed himself of his own gallantry. The admiration that the audience would happily have given to deserving cases would no doubt have been forthcoming, but not with that unsportingly unbeatable weapon clasped in their hands.[148]

Only when the entertainer walked away from the mike, Olivier noted, did the audience come alive as they used to.

If the physical layout of the theaters demanded intimacy between player and audience, so did the acting style. Acting was more formal than ours but that didn't necessarily imply distance; the most formal rituals can be the most moving. Much more so than today, successful acting—even successful *mimesis*—was defined not in terms of the actor's ability to "personate" a character, but in terms of his ability to move the audience to laughter or to tears. The player's passion was "lively" or lifelike only to the degree the audience responded as if it were. The player who "personate[s] Hieronimo," says a character in Thomas May's *Heir,* paints grief

> "in such a lively colour, that for false
> And acted passion he has drawn true tears
> From the spectators."[149]

To those who feared it, in fact, theater assaulted the audience's senses as well as emotions. Jonson tried to counteract this vulgar effect by appealing to the ear rather than the eye, but for others the ear itself was a dangerous organ.[150] The players, Gosson feared, "by the privie entries of the eare, slip downe into the hart, & with gunshotte of affection gaule the minde."[151] Like Burton "spreading the jam on thick" or Callow playing to the "hungry audience" in Ireland, the Elizabethan player appealed to the audience by feeding it. Plays, Philip Stubbes feared in 1583, were "sucked out of the Devills teates to nourish us in ydolatrie, hethenrie, and sinne." And in 1615, I. H. was still complaining about the "loathsome and unheard-of Ribauldry, suckt from the poysonous dugs of Sinnesweld Theaters."[152] A parting insult from one of the boy actors in Chapman's *All Fools* (Queen's Revels, 1604) suggests that the fare offered in that very different theater for a very different audience, twenty-five years later, was equally capable of being seen as food: "We can but bring you meat, and set you stools, / And to our best cheer say, you are all—welcome."[153] No playgoer believed he was eating a play, any more than he believed Talbot had been resurrected in *Henry VI*. But such metaphors are not irrelevant, particularly since players had provided food at times, and when they did not, the audience nonetheless (as the nutshell-littered excavations at the Rose and the Globe confirm) ate.[154]

Players suffered from stage fright, just as ours do. The sheer amount of memorizing necessary to maintain the repertoires made it likely that players would forget their lines. Handfuls of Marlowe are added to Shakespeare in the quartos. Thomas Hughes objected that the actors left out lines from his *Misfortunes of Arthur*, and the Clerk in Middleton's *Mayor of Queenborough* complained that the actors "fribble out" theirs (*Mayor* 5.1.360). Inner plays frequently staged the need for a prompter; the Prologue in *Wily Beguiled*, for example, assumes the players are still hastily learning their lines: "What ho! where are these paltry players? still poring in their papers and never perfect [or, as the modern actor would say, "word perfect"]? For shame, come forth; your audience stays so long, their eyes wax dim with expectation."[155]

The Prologue doesn't mention how his imperfect actors feel, but Jonson's Bartholomew Cokes knows that players can be "flustered" (*Bartholomew Fair* 5.3.104), and Nashe describes a similar nervousness in the players who put on *Summer's Last Will and Testament* (1592) at Croyden for Archbishop Whitgift:

> *Actors,* you Rogues, come away, cleare your throats, blowe your noses, and wype your mouthes ere you enter, that you may take no occasion to spit or cough, when you are *non plus*. And this I barre, over and besides: that none of you stroake your beardes to make action, play with your cod-piece poynts, or stād fumbling on your buttons, when you know not how to bestow your fingers.[156]

Jonson's Amorphus in *Cynthia's Revels* (1600–1) takes it for granted that the "neophyte player" will be "daunted at the first presence" (3.1.3–4), as Shakespeare's amateur Moth is before his royal audience in *Love's Labour's Lost* (*LLL* 5.2.158–73).[157] But it wasn't only the neophyte who was daunted.[158] At any point in a performance or a career, a "player is much out of countenance, if fooles doe not laugh at them, boyes clappe their hands, pesants ope their throates, and the rude raskal rabble cry excellent, excellent."[159] Accusations like these suggest that the player's "pride" entails a psychological investment in display that we now associate with narcissism, as well as implying the external airs inseparable from pride. With so much at stake, the "unperfect actor on the stage," as Shakespeare called him in the sonnets, was always subject to fear that strikes him dumb (Son. 23, 1–2). And to judge by the contexts in which Shakespearean characters refer to forgetting their lines, the experience was associated with emotions as extreme and irrational as those actors describe today. Not only were Elizabethan actors frightened like modern actors; their fear apparently evoked similar fantasies. The sonnet speaker calls himself an unperfect actor only when he finds that he cannot express either his love or his need for his beloved; it is not a situation implying emotional distance. Richard III's failure of nerve as king (R3 4.4.452–55) takes "the form of an actor's forgetting his lines."[160] Richard II is a "tedious" actor (R2 5.2.24–26) when being unkinged, and Coriolanus a "dull actor" (Cor. 5.3.40) when forced to do the thing he feels will annihilate him. Stage fright signaled narcissistic threats of great importance for the player Shakespeare.

Proud Beggar Onstage: Clown and Epilogue

Two typical Elizabethan roles consisted largely, if not entirely, of performance rather than mimesis. In each the player came forward as "himself," and in each he showed an ambivalence toward the audience like the one modern actors describe. The first, the Clown, was the archetypical actor. As theater was to society and the player to the theater, the Clown was to the player: the epitome of everything lawless and base. To insult a player, his enemies called him a clown—an "antic," said Greene; a "fool," said Nashe; a "motley to the view," said Shakespeare. He embodied the "aberrant impulse" or, as Barber called it, the "saturnalian misrule" associated with theater in general—the "carnivalesque" or "grotesque" departure from the normal world.[161] The first stars in England were clowns, and later clowns like Pope, Greene, and Singer were among the most famous Elizabethan and Jacobean players. Clowns were often gifted writers or performers on their own; more than any other single group they seem to have shaped the period's drama. Many became managers of their companies, and eventually clown actors like William Rowley were themselves recognized as official collaborators.[162]

The character he played explained both part of the Clown's appeal and his ability to represent all players. Like the players generally, the Clown was a social outcast, usually a "rustic" (though at times he appeared in citified form as a collier, miller, or other mechanical), and much of the humor arose from his being a hick in the metropolis, as many actors actually were. He was a product of the "hostility to the peasant class which characterizes a great part of the literature of the later Middle Ages and the Renaissance" and of the London tendency "to treat in burlesque fashion whatever came from the country."[163] Like the player, he was above all a physical and passionate creature. His emotional volatility generated many of his routines; even as the other players were learning not to out-Herod Herod, the clown howled, yelled and, in a well-known skit, wept copiously.[164] He made scurvy faces, used props (sticks, shoes, animals) and depended so heavily on nonverbal "business," as Thomas Fuller observed, that anyone else speaking his lines wouldn't be funny. Much of his humor consisted of the slapstick aggression now relegated to cartoon animals. As playwright John Fletcher complained, just because a player can "abuse his fellow," he thinks he's "a first class clown." The most famous of the three surviving anecdotes about Tarlton's routines tells how, having been boxed on the ear, Tarlton passed the blow on to poor John Cobbler—and called him a clown for taking it.[165] A second, the Book-keeper's recollection of Tarlton in *Bartholomew Fair,* tells how he was beaten by his fellow Adams.[166] In the third, from Peacham's 1638 recollection, Tarlton, playing the youngest of three sons, insulted his dying father. The rest of the clown's "trunk-hose humor" depended on scatology and sex, probably in that order. The clown dropped his slops, farted, pissed, and threw up freely, and Slipper in Greene's *James IV* provided a description of his diarrhea attack (2.1.185–90). While Gosson complained that the players were "uncircumcized philistines," Tarlton told the audience about his troubles with his prepuce.[167] At home with death as well as dirt, the Clown could collect shoes from dead soldiers, play with corpses, or pretend to be one himself, always seeming able to rebound into life.

But what mattered more than the Clown's character was the performative dimension of the role—its relation to the audience. The Clown was the player closest to the nonmimetic roots of theater in ritual celebrations, popular pastimes, and folk tradition. He was related to the offstage fool and scapegoat of mummers' plays and morris dances, to the entertainers who helped mountebanks sell the "waters of life," to the devils and goblins of folklore (Tarlton's ghost appeared in a book with Robin Goodfellow), to historical court fools and jesters, and to the rogues and tricksters of popular tales. Like these, the Clown engaged the audience directly, whether to gather the crowds as clowns had done for road shows, to tell them about the action, or to cover for actors who missed their cues. He also played himself. The audiences at a Queen's play didn't come to see "a clown"; they came to see Tarlton. They laughed as soon as they saw Tarlton's well-known face peeping out from behind the door, whatever role he played; and they were always alert to self-references, like the clown Bubble's allusion to

the clown-actor "Greene," when everyone knew he was played by Greene
(*Greene's Tu Quoque* [1609] 11: 240).

It is in the clown's role that we come closest to first-person testimony
from Elizabethan actors and closest to seeing the intimate and ambivalent
relation to the audience which twentieth-century actors like Callow describe. Only one Elizabethan player, the famous clown Robert Wilson, has
described what it felt like to cater to the incorporative aspects of audience
demand, but he corroborates Callow's sense of an actor throwing out lumps
of bleeding flesh to the audience. Wilson's play *Three Ladies of London*
(1581)[168] includes a hungry clown who decides to give up his ill-paying
job, become a beggar, and sing for his food and drink—in this case at least,
to perform is to ask to be fed. Within five lines, however, the relationship
has reversed itself and his audience is trying to eat him:

> But yonder is a fellow that gapes to bite me, or else to eat that which I sing.
> Why, thou art a fool; canst thou not keep thy mouth strait together?
> And when it comes, snap at it, as my father's dog would do at a liver.
> But thou art so greedy,
> That thou thinkest to eat it, before it comes nigh thee.

Apparently what the Clown offered was not "caviare to the general" (*Ham.*
2.2.433) but something rather more edible. After his song, he returns to
the theme of the hungry audience:

> Now, sirrah, hast eaten up my song? and ye have, ye shall eat no more today,
> For everybody may see your belly is grown bigger with eating up our play.
> He has fill'd his belly, but I am never a whit the better,
> Therefore I'll go seek some victuals; and 'member, for eating up my song
>   you shall be my debtor.[169]

The stories about Tarlton, to the degree we can depend on them, repeat
another aspect of the contemporary actor's descriptions of what it feels like
to confront an audience. The anecdotes suggest that Tarlton's famous ex-
temporizings, like those of our own stand-up comics, often depended on a
repetitive streak of mutual abuse.[170] Vaughan recalls that when Tarlton
came on stage to hear "no end of hissing" instead of being greeted with the
"civil attention" he expected, he broke into "this sarcasticall taunt":

> I liv'd not in the Golden Age,
> When Jason wonne the fleece,
> But now I am on Gotam's stage,
> Where fooles do hisse like geese.[171]

If the people threw pippins at Tarlton, he rhymed insults back at them. When someone in the gallery pointed at him, Tarlton pretended to take it as an insult, gave the man the horns, and got so much the best of him in the ensuing exchange that "the poore fellow, plucking his hat over his eyes," left the theater.[172] Other clowns playing to the same audiences would have to be similar enough to satisfy the public's taste for what was after all an extremely conservative and traditional kind of performance.[173]

The Clown's liminal position between the play and the audience has fascinated modern critics, who have emphasized the Clown's alienation as index of wider social tension outside the theater. Italian director Dario Fo, who has made use of the modern clown's comedy for savage political satire, observes that "clowns always speak of the same thing, they speak of hunger: hunger for food, hunger for sex, but also hunger for dignity, hunger for identity, hunger for power. In fact they introduce questions about who commands, who protests."[174] Although scholars do not always agree about whether the Clown's presence tended to work out social conflicts or exacerbate them, they have shown how important the figure can be.[175] But the Clown's relevance to questions of "who commands, who protests" outside the theater was mediated by power transactions inside the theater. More so than the rest of the play, the Clown's act depended on that ambivalent confrontation between isolated player and massed audience which today's actors find both "uplifting and appalling," and the Clown experienced the extremes of ostentation and ignominy familiar to all players. Although he could manipulate the laughter of thousands of spectators, he was always a beggar saying, "Here I am; laugh at me please," leaving himself vulnerable to their hostility. As the Stagekeeper says in the prologue to the *Second Part of Return to·Parnassus,* to "fool it" for the audience entailed obsequious flattery. Coriolanus saw the demand for his public appearance before the crowd as a demand to "fool it" or play the clown for them (*Cor.* 2.3.120). The Clown was the figure who drew the crowds to the theater, in part because he epitomized its quality.

Along with the Clown, the players who spoke most directly and self-consciously to the audience were the Prologue and Epilogue, and they too were beggars. As they called attention to the boundaries between play and reality, each almost always apologized for the play. First, the Prologue came before the noisy preperformance audience to stake a claim for theatrical space and attention, but he sweetened his audacity with flattering acknowledgment of the crowd. Today's reader may see the Prologue's humility—in *Henry V,* for example, he refers to the audience as "gentles, all"—as a sign of mutual respect between players and audience, but Elizabethans saw it for the tendentious formality it was.[176] The Prologue's obsequiousness was mocked in *The Return from Parnassus* (1599–1601), for example, where he has barely begun his speech to the "Gentle—" before the Stage-Keeper breaks in scornfully:

> Howe, *gentle* say youe, cringing parasite?
> That scrapinge legge, that droppinge *curtisie,*
> That fawninge bowe, those sycophants smoothe tearmes,
> Gained our stage muche favoure, did they not? . . .
> Sirra be gone, you play noe prologue here,
> Call noe rude hearer *gentle, debonaire.*
> Wele spende no flatteringe on this carpinge croude.[177]

The crowd is not "gentle" but "rude" ; the Prologue is merely a "cringing," "scrapinge," "fawninge" flatterer—and so, it is implied, are his fellow actors. The great god Proteus himself was known as a flatterer, and the protean players were flatterers both in the sense of "praising excessively" and in the more general sense of "courting and fawning on" (literally "smoothing or flattening" the way) or even of "seducing." Rankins's *Mirrour for Monsters* (1587), a vitriolic attack on players, includes flattery among their chief vices, calling them hypocrites and "Judas[es]," "fawning parasites" :

> . . . these Players . . . pinne Cushions under the elbowes of young wits, to make them snorte in securitie, & present before theyre eyes, as well in life as continuall exercise, such inchaunting Charmes and bewitched wyles, to alienate theyr mindes from vertue, that hard wyll it be for a wit well stayde to abyde the same.[178]

Although the fashion for prologues came and went during the period, many, like Rankins, continued to mistrust all flattering players "as well in life" as onstage, assuming they always had at least one "politician" among them who "works out restraints [on playing], makes best legs at court, and has a suit made of purpose for the company's busines."[179] Abject flattery was taken to be a cover for self-serving greed, if not arrogance. And it was, as we shall see in chapter 7, a topic of great interest to the player Shakespeare.

Epilogues were equally given to extravagant and ambiguous gestures toward the audience at the end of the play. The vainglorious tragedian who had been jetting about on stage in his satin suit suddenly came forward and got down on his knees to beg for applause. "The King's a beggar now the play is done," says the actor who played the King in *All's Well that Ends Well* (*AWW* Epi.1).[180] The submissive posture originated long before with the liveried players who were really servants, and it was still being recalled in 1606 when Middleton's Follywit kneels to his uncle, saying, "This shows like the kneeling after the play; I praying for my Lord Owemuch and his good countess" (*Mad World* 5.2.180–81). But as time went on, the Epilogue's

humility became increasingly outrageous, a tacitly acknowledged extravagance which attributed to the audience impossible powers. They could for
example provide May's heroine in *The Heir* (1620) with a restorative dowry:

> Our heir is fall'n from her inheritance,
> But has obtain'd her love: you may advance
> Her higher yet; and from your pleas'd hands give
> A dowry, that will make her truly live.

> (Epi.1–4)

They could bring Chapman's D'Ambois (*Bussy D'Ambois,* 1604) back to life:

> With many hands you have seen D'Ambois slain,
> Yet by your grace he may revive again.

> (Epi.1–2)

When Prospero appears as Epilogue to *The Tempest* no longer a powerful
magician but a helpless suppliant, he even attributes to the audience the
power of God's grace:

> My ending is despair,
> Unless I be relieved by prayer,
> Which pierces so, that it assaults
> Mercy itself, and frees all faults.
> As you from crimes would pardon'd be,
> Let your indulgence set me free.

> (*Tem.* Epi.17–20)

The Player-Duke-Magician is in "bands" (bonds), "wants" skill, may "fail"
or end in "despair," and, instead of a dukedom or revenge, wants only "to
please." By contrast, the audience is not only "good" and "gentle" but stands
in the position of the deity who receives what sounds like the Lord's
Prayer.[181] The Epilogue "strive[s] to please you every day," as Feste said
(*TN* 5.1.407), but as in the case of the Prologue—and the rest of the players—audiences knew that such conventions were not always to be trusted.

* * *

Elizabethan actors, then—at least enough of them to generate comment—were seen in much the same terms as we see actors today; and despite the obvious differences, there is evidence to suggest that playing on
the Shakespearean stage was similar in many ways to playing today. This
fact alone does not entitle us to assume that the inner springs of action in
both cases are similar; or that the actor Shakespeare felt the same way, saw
himself as a proud beggar, and had the same unconscious fantasies as to-

day's actors, though, as I have suggested, there is some indication that this is true. The best evidence for such assumptions about Shakespeare remains the texts which Shakespeare himself left. The next chapters examine some recurring concerns in these texts and suggest their resemblance to the modern actor's fantasies about childhood and about confrontation with a volatile crowd.

Chapter Three

Richard III: Shakespeare's "False Glass"

And I for comfort have but one false glass,
That grieves me when I see my shame in him.

Duchess of York, Richard III (2.2.53–54)

*S*hakespeare, being an actor himself," suggests Sir Laurence Olivier's biographer, "was a playwright who wrote parts as much as plays."[1] However arguable an assessment of Shakespeare's prevailing habits, this claim seems true enough of *Richard III*, the culmination of the first *Henriad*'s civil wars and Shakespeare's first fully developed tragedy; the play is a showcase for Richard, Duke of Gloucester, as he makes himself into Richard III. The *Henriad*'s vicious warfare is spectacular, but Richard towers over its blood and horrors; he is both ringmaster and star attraction, and his presence, balanced by that of his nemesis, Queen Margaret, organizes the play. Audiences invariably appreciate Richard's power over them; his magnetic personality makes him, as Anne Righter says, more "an example of the power of the actor than . . . a figure of treachery and evil."[2] Or rather of the way the "power of the actor" can be bound up with treachery and evil. It is an ideal acting part; Richard Burbage was known for it in the sixteenth century, and both David Garrick in the nineteenth and Olivier in ours made their reputation playing Richard.[3] In creating his first tragedies Shakespeare thus simultaneously created his first histrionic character. One way of understanding what it might have meant to Shakespeare to be an actor is to look more closely at this charismatic figure who is both himself an actor and a perfect actor's medium. Richard is the first of several figures in the plays who seem vicariously to embody the actor in the playwright Shakespeare, in part by taking on the role of Vice, the morality play actor who was most like a playwright.

Richard III: "False Glass"

As an actor, Richard is a "proud beggar," his magic derived from the familiar sources modern actors describe, and driven by a similar ambivalence about displaying his body. In the *Henriad* he has command of Marlovian rhetoric to encourage his father's ambition:

64

> ... And, father, do but think
> How sweet a thing it is to wear a crown,
> Within whose circuit is Elysium
> And all that poets feign of bliss and joy.
>
> (*3H6* 1.2.28–31)

Richard's own ambition emerges as he sets out to win the crown for himself and makes his famous narcissistic announcement: "I have no brother, I am like no brother . . . I am myself alone" (*3H6* 5.6.80, 83). But if Richard starts out as an arrogant hero like Tamburlaine, he quickly becomes a devious "politician" like Barabas—with all the beggarly fawning that such a posture may entail.[4] Despite his protestations that he "cannot flatter and look fair" (*R3* 1.3.47), that his "tongue could never learn sweet smoothing word" (*R3* 1.2.172), he can, and it does. He boasts that he can "[c]hange shapes with Proteus" (*3H6* 3.2.192) and although his ultimate goal in doing so is the crown, his immediate concern is always to please—and often to seduce—his present audience. The god Proteus himself was a seducer, but Shakespeare seems to have found the image of player as seducer especially congenial, and to have dwelt on the abjection as well as the power of that position. Indeed, he chose to follow Richard's Machiavellian Prologue with a fawning courtship scene; Shakespeare's arch player is *introduced* as a wooer, whose fawning, like the actor's, is allied with erotic vulnerability.

Richard's courtship of Lady Anne certainly exploits the potential for both pride and beggary. Having killed Anne's husband and father-in-law, he boldly approaches her at the funeral, and is soon claiming outright that he is fit for her "bed-chamber" (*R3* 1.2.114).[5] But he finally sways her only through an equally extreme submission. He not only endures her scorn when she calls him "hedgehog" (*R3* 1.2.104) and spits on him; he himself bares his throat and offers her his sword—an abject gesture recalling the female Phaedra's masochistic offer of herself to Hippolytus in Seneca's play.[6] The confusion over his motives is indicative of the proud beggar's conflict. On the one hand Richard says that the courtship of Anne is purely political—he will marry "not all so much for love / As for another secret close intent" (*R3* 1.1.157–58); this is the man who had previously denied any need for love:

> I . . . have neither pity, love, nor fear . . .
> And this word "love," which greybeards call divine,
> Be resident in men like one another,
> And not in me.
>
> (*3H6* 5.6.68, 81–83)

But, as several critics have noted, the marriage to Anne "does not advance the career of Richard in the least" and suggests that he may need Anne's love more than he admits.[7] His glee at her capitulation gives him away:

> Was ever woman in this humor woo'd?
> Was ever woman in this humor won?
> What, I that kill'd her husband and his father:
> To take her in her heart's extremest hate,
> With curses in her mouth, tears in her eyes,
> The bleeding witness of her hatred by . . .
> And yet to win her, all the world to nothing!
> Ha!
>
> (R3 1.2.232–43)[8]

Richard's delight is genuine, however concealed beneath irony. Anne's love is not so much politically as psychologically necessary for Richard—the way it is psychologically necessary for an actor. Anne is the "amorous looking glass" Richard says he "was not made to court" (R3 1.1.15);[9] and once he wins her, she mirrors back a more handsome image of himself:

> And will she yet debase her eyes on me . . .
> On me, that halts and am misshapen thus? . . .
> Upon my life she finds—as I cannot—
> Myself to be a marvelous proper man.
> I'll be at charges for a looking-glass,
> And entertain a score or two of tailors . . .
> Since I am crept in favour with myself,
> I will maintain it with some little cost . . .
> . . . Shine out, fair sun, till I have bought a glass,
> That I may see my shadow as I pass.
>
> (R3 1.2.251–68)

As Barber and Wheeler put it, "The pleasures of love as Richard imagines them are narcissistic—the sort of loving we get in the show-off courting of *Love's Labour's Lost*"—or in any actor's effort to court the audience.[10] Similarly, Richard's attention in love—like an actor's—is focused on his own body, whether he sees it as "misshapen" or as "proper" (R3 1.2.255, 259). More relevant to our concern with the actor's development, Richard not only has an actor's need for an audience's admiration, closely associated with his need to be admired by women, but a history that, according to contemporary psychology, would have made him a mirror-hungry actor from his earliest days. Public man that he is, Richard is the Shakespearean character most fully defined in terms of family and past.[11] The play provides a psychological myth of origin for actors as it positions Richard in relation to his mother's powerful hostility and his father's ultimate weakness.[12] The Duke of York, Richard's father, is a failure, though a colorful one. Claimant to the throne, he is the sole representative of old-fashioned heroism in the second and third parts of *Henry VI,* and he is charismatic enough to have had one version of *Henry VI, Part Two* named after him.[13] Yet he would have withdrawn his claim without Richard's prompting, and when he finally loses the battle, he is humiliated by his enemies and made into a laughable Player King, a mere pretender.[14] He dies helpless in the *Henriad* and is never mentioned in *Richard III*—except once, when Richard tells Anne (suggestively) that York's death was less disturbing to him than is his unrequited love for her (*R3* 1.2.160).

As in the case of modern actors, however, it is Richard's mother who had the most effect on him when she rejected him at birth. "Love foreswore me in my mother's womb," he had announced:

> . . . She did corrupt frail Nature with some bribe,
> To shrink mine arm up like a wither'd shrub;
> To make an envious mountain on my back . . .
> To shape my legs of an unequal size;
> To disproportion me in every part,
> Like to a chaos, or an unlick'd bear-whelp
> That carries no impression like the dam.
> And am I then a man to be beloved?
> O monstrous fault, to harbor such a thought!
> (*3H6* 3.2.155–64)

Richard means that no ladies will love him now, as an adult—that the very idea is "monstrous":

> I'll make my heaven in a lady's lap. . . .
> And 'witch sweet ladies with my words and looks.
> O miserable thought! and more unlikely,
> Than to accomplish twenty golden crowns.
> (*3H6* 3.2.148–51)

But the lady his thoughts return to is his mother, the very first lady in whose "lap" he sought heaven.[15] The play returns to her as well, for she appears—quite unhistorically—to forswear Richard before our eyes and to make her loathing for him clear.[16] Though Richard is arrogant in dealing with the audience outside the fiction, his audiences with his mother reveal his more obsequious side. The first time he sees the Duchess he kneels to ask for her blessing, as he had kneeled when he asked for Anne's love. The Duchess responds with the first half of the traditional formula—asking God to make Richard meek and obedient—but stops

short of "the butt-end of a mother's blessing" and pointedly does not ask
that God make him die a good old man. "I marvel that her grace did leave
it out," Richard notes ironically (R3 2.2.10–11). In their second confrontation, the Duchess joins the old queens Margaret and Elizabeth, forming
a triplet of wailing women, as if Richard, like Macbeth, were himself
"witched" by the Three Sisters: "In the breath of bitter words let's smother
/ My damned son, that thy two sweet sons smother'd" (R3 4.4.133–35).[17]
The women literally block his army's march; and when he asks, "Who
intercepts me in my expedition?" his mother's reply is murderous: "O, she
that might have intercepted thee— / By strangling thee in her accursed
womb" (R3 4.4.136–38).[18] She finishes not just with an incomplete blessing this time, but with a curse:

> Take with thee my most grievous curse,
> Which in the day of battle shall grieve thee more
> Than all the complete armour that thou wear'st.
> My prayers on the adverse party fight.
>
> (R3 4.4.188–90)

The Duchess had begun her complaint by citing Richard's atrocities
against the little princes, but these lead her back to the mirroring atrocities
she wishes she had perpetrated on him when he was an infant prince himself. Richard "smother'd" the two princes, and she now wants to smother
Richard, but also thinks back to the way she could have strangled him in
the womb. In the Duchess's eyes, Richard was guilty before he murdered
anyone, guilty simply for being born—or rather for being born the person
he was and not someone else. She reminds him that his birth was "a griev-
ous burden" that brought her "torment and agony" (R3 4.4.168, 164), and
Margaret recalls that he was born a monster—not so much deformed as
already on the attack (R3 4.4.47–49). Not that he needs reminding:

> I have often heard my mother say
> I came into the world with my legs forward. . . .
> The midwife wonder'd, and the women cried
> "O Jesu bless us, he is born with teeth!"
>
> (3H6 5.6.70–75)

It has not seemed necessary to ask why the Duchess should have rejected
so monstrous a child, but one might still ask what motivates the narrative
which so bemonstered him. Richard's monstrosity, seen sympathetically,
may simply have been maleness misunderstood, and the Duchess's "hell-
hound," in Margaret's terms (R3 4.4.48), simply a male child asserting his
energy in a display of teeth and feet, and defying her fantasies about a baby

girl more like herself.[19] Richard certainly feels that he "carries no impression like the dam" (*3H6* 3.2.162), a failure as much of gender as of species. He counters her description of himself as potent infantile menace with one of himself as a crippled infantile victim, with unequal legs and a withered arm. In recalling his birth, Richard vacillates between two responses to the ambiguously described abnormality. Sometimes he plays his role of "hell-hound" (or "carnal cur"; *R3* 4.4.48, 56) to the hilt. The women say he was born with teeth, so he responds:

> And so I was, which plainly signified
> That I should snarl and bite, and *play the dog.*
> > (*3H6* 5.6.76–77; italics added)

But at other times he sees himself as enfeebled and victimized:

> . . . sent before my time
> Into this breathing world scarce half made up—
> And that so lamely and unfashionable
> That *dogs bark at me,* as I halt by them.
> > (*R3* 1.1.20–23; italics added)

It is the combination rather than either partial account that best describes Richard.

In any case, the Duchess now clearly prefers his more obedient brothers, and she exacerbates the political rivalry among them by her preferential bestowal of love. Elsewhere in *Richard III,* scenes between the playfully sparring boy princes suggest childhood analogies for Richard's fratricidal competition; their mother herself compares the two princes invidiously and "make[s] growing up . . . into a competition."[20] Even Richard's courtship of Anne is a kind of competition with his brother Edward for success in love. Richard's proposal closely imitates Edward's earlier proposal to Lady Jane in *Henry VI, Part Three,*[21] which Richard had spied on, jealous both of Edward's potential heirs—and his sexual potency.[22] With Anne Richard proves that he can attract a widow too.

It may also be that the Duchess cares so little for Richard because she cares so much for the dead, most of whom died at Richard's hands. Richard of course mourns for no one. Indeed he acts as if he can replace the dead as easily as he can give life to a new role, or as easily as he can beget a child. When he approaches Edward's mourning widow Elizabeth, trying to get permission to marry her daughter, she tells him there is no way to win her "Unless thou couldst put on some other shape, / And not be Richard that hath done all this" (*R3* 4.4.286–87). No problem. "If I have kill'd the issue

of your womb," he tells Elizabeth, "To quicken your increase, I will beget /
Mine issue of your blood upon your daughter" (*R3* 4.4.297–98). And when
she protests, he repeats his promise to resurrect the dead through a macabre act of procreation, described as a burial:

> *Elizabeth:* Yet thou didst kill my children.
> *Richard:* But in your daughter's womb I bury them,
>   Where, in that nest of spicery, they will breed
>   Selves of themselves, to your recomforture.

(R3 4.4.422–25)

Elizabeth's dead child, "buried" in her daughter Elizabeth's womb, will rise
phoenixlike from that womb: people are replaceable, Richard implies, just
as they are reshapable.

But the women remain unconvinced. Old Queen Margaret, Richard's
nemesis, insists on mourning those who have been sacrificed to what she
sees as a cruel if poetic justice: "Thou hadst a Richard, till a Richard kill'd
him. . . . / . . . Thy Edward he is dead, that kill'd my Edward; / Thy other
Edward dead, to quit my Edward" (*R3* 4.4.43, 63–64). And Richard's
mother, the Duchess, always appears in mourning for those she has lost.[23]
Shakespeare modeled the Duchess on Seneca's Hecuba, *the* mourning
mother in Renaissance literature.[24] If this mother failed to act as a mirror
for Richard, it may have been in part because she sees Richard only as a
potential mirror for herself or for her dead husband—a role he fails to
fulfill: "I, for comfort, have but one false glass [i.e., Richard], / That grieves
me when I see my shame in him" (*R3* 2.2.53–54). Richard's response to his
mother's latest rejection—as perhaps throughout his life—is to try again.
Just after his mother walks off cursing him, Richard slides over to Elizabeth,
a substitute "mother" ("for I must call you so," he tells her; *R3* 4.4.412), and
tries to woo her daughter.[25] Throughout the action Richard makes detours
like this from the crown to do just what he said he could not do: "'witch
sweet ladies with my words and looks" (*3H6* 3.2.150). The man who refused to accept his role as rejected child presents himself as "too childish-
foolish for this world" (*R3* 1.3.142), harmless as an "infant that is born
tonight" (*R3* 2.1.71), a compliant "child" (*R3* 2.2.153)—paradoxically playing himself after all.[26] And even when aiming at the crown, rather than
seizing it directly he tries to witch the general public—as he had witched
Anne—into choosing him themselves. Desperate for popular support, Richard "play[s] the maid's part" himself (*R3* 3.7.50) when Buckingham rounds
up a crowd of extras to offer Richard the crown so he can pretend to reject
it.[27] Like a modern actor Richard plays to the audience both as the one
beloved woman and as a potentially adoring—though in this case recalci-
trant—crowd.

The man who never had a mother's mirroring love will spend his life recasting his image for an endless sequence of audiences. Richard himself links his rejection and his histrionic drive, leaping from one to the other when he first announces himself in *Henry VI, Part Three*:

> Love forswore me in my mother's womb. . . .
> I'll drown more sailors than the Mermaid shall;
> I'll slay more gazers than the basilisk;
> I'll play the orator as well as Nestor,
> Deceive more slily than Ulysses could,
> And, like a Sinon, take another Troy.
> I can add colours to the chameleon,
> Change shapes with Proteus for advantages,
> And set the murderous Machiavel to school.
>   (*3H6* 3.2.153, 186–93)[28]

It's not only that Richard uses deception for evil ends—the traditional Machiavel's behavior. For Richard, more unusually, the performance serves as revenge on the world that rejected him and refused to look on him with favor ("Out of my sight!" Anne had ordered. "Thou dost infect mine eyes"; *R3* 1.2.153). Now he will return their destructive gaze. His "unavoided eye is murderous" (*R3* 4.1.55), the Duchess warns. Anyone who listens to him (as to the mermaid) or looks at him will die. "I'll slay more gazers than the basilisk," he says, reversing the basilisk's power to kill what it gazes at—killing instead what gazes at him (*3H6* 3.2.186–87).

If this is the origin of Richard's theatrical flair, no wonder it proves dangerous to him as well as to his audience. Any drive that comes with such a history is doomed to turbulence, and Richard's is no exception. Richard's story almost parodies the modern actor's history of narcissistic wounds, subjective crisis, and dependence on the mirroring response of others, all of which make performance an ambiguous achievement. Richard's conflicted ambition—and the cool theatrics he claims it requires—are important, because they reveal much about Shakespeare's other "players," and perhaps also about Shakespeare's own ambivalence toward the stage. Richard's ambition had at first sounded reasonable, unconflicted. He cannot find "heaven in a lady's lap" (*3H6* 3.2.148), he says, so he will make the "golden circuit" (*2H6* 3.1.352) of the crown his "Elysium" (*3H6* 1.2.30):

> T'account this world but hell
> Until my misshap'd trunk that bears this head
> Be round impaled with a glorious crown.
>   (*3H6* 3.2.169–71)

But it is not easy to reach the crown:

> I do but dream on sovereignty;
> Like one that stands upon a promontory
> And spies a far-off shore where he would tread. . . .
> I know not how to get the crown,
> For many lives stand between me and home:
> And I,—like one lost in a thorny wood,
> That rents the thorns and is rent with the thorns,
> Seeking a way and straying from the way,
> Not knowing how to find the open air
> But toiling desperately to find it out—
> Torment myself to catch the English crown.
>
> (3H6 3.2.134–36, 172–79)

Because Richard's desire for the crown is a displacement of his desire for the "Love [that] foreswore [and deformed him] in his Mother's womb," as Janet Adelman argues, the crown (like all such desperate displacements) begins to take on the characteristics of that original goal: "Even as he shifts from the misshaping womb to the image of the crown, the terrifying enclosure of the womb recurs, shaping his attempt to imagine the very political project that should free him from dependence on ladies' laps."[29] As soon as Richard describes his ambition for the golden "circuit" of the crown, it becomes as claustrophobic as the womb, keeping him from the "open air" or smothering him. The crown threatens to smother Richard just as his mother wishes she had strangled him in her womb. In addition, Adelman argues, "through the shifting meaning of 'impaled,' the stakes [pales] that enclose him protectively turn into the thorns that threaten to impale him."[30] In other words, the crown, and the histrionics necessary to win it, are as dangerous as women.

Richard does not mention acting in these lines, but in the lines immediately preceding, Shakespeare reminds us that the character "Richard" is also an actor, physically present on a stage jutting out into the audience. When Richard likens himself to

> one that stands upon a promontory
> And spies a far-off shore where he would tread,
> Wishing his foot were equal with his eye,
> And chides the sea, that sunders him from thence,
> Saying he'll lade it dry to have his way,
>
> (3H6 3.2.135–39)

he uses one of the metaphors used elsewhere in the period's drama to refer to the raised stage itself—as "promontory" thrusting in upon the audience, a ship or an island surrounded by a sea.[31] The solitary actor playing Richard, standing well downstage, suggests Ralph Berry, is the man on the promontory staring out over the sea of spectators' heads at the imaginary crown which they themselves prevent him from reaching.[32] Suggesting the importance of the conceit by dwelling so long on it, Richard seems to threaten not only the king but also the audience/sea which stands between him and the king's crown:

> So do I wish the crown, being so far off;
> And so I chide the means that keeps me from it;
>   [Does he look threateningly out at the audience here?]
> And so I say I'll cut the causes off,
>   [gesture toward the audience?]
> Flattering me with impossibilities.
>
>   (3H6 3.2.140–43)

As we shall see, the men throughout Shakespeare's plays who seek something like the crown's "circuit" of Elysium by striding to the center of the "wooden O," also find that the amphitheater's protective enclosure can both stifle and penetrate.[33]

Richard III: Shakespeare's Glass?

Although Shakespeare created a character whose motives may seem explicable by twentieth-century tactics, we can neither assume that Richard is a self-portrait nor generalize from the play to Shakespeare's own history of narcissistic wounds or his own motives for acting. But it is nonetheless revealing to read Shakespeare's life and the account of Richard's life in "dynamic and speculative relation to one another,"[34] with an eye for repetition and analogy. Such patterns, while unlikely to reveal radically new meaning either for play or biography, can enrich both. To take a relatively trivial example, the one anecdote we have about Shakespeare's childhood suggests that, like Richard, he was not only an actor but also had a natural gift for making comedy out of violence. John Aubrey reports that Shakespeare "when he kill'd a Calfe, he would doe it in a high style, and make a Speech,"[35] and biographers, after some speculation about Shakespeare's apprenticeship to a butcher, now suggest that Aubrey may have been referring to Shakespeare's role in a Christmas mumming play, perhaps accompanied by what Nashe elsewhere calls "some kil-cow conceit."[36] A version of it was still extant earlier in this century, calling for several boys to play the butcher and the calf, and to catch the calf's blood in a bucket. The older version may have been a solo ventriloquist act—like some of the stage clowns' self-debates—between the killer and the calf; there is record of one man's being paid for the whole performance early in the fifteenth century.[37] The anecdote is interesting because it reinforces the impression, given by the plays themselves, that clowning was important to Shakespeare.[38] Whether he himself killed a calf, or whether the anecdote was created with hindsight to explain an adult gift, it reminds us that, although he is best known for his late "wise fools," Shakespeare was already a master of the clown scenes when he began writing.[39] Still more important, from the beginning of his writing career Shakespeare the playwright had a clown's ability to connect with the audience. He was already, in Emrys Jones's words, "a formidably confident technician of the emotions," just as Richard is.[40] And, like Richard, he was keenly aware of the actor's body, whether in pain—the blinding of Gloucester in *Lear*—or simply in motion—Antony being hauled up to the monument in *Antony and Cleopatra*. Just such a "concern for the physical comes into particularly sharp focus" at numerous moments throughout the canon and "becomes fundamental to the play's argument."[41]

The most compelling connection between Shakespeare and Richard lies not so much in any biographical details, but in the duality of Richard's histrionic flair which provides their context. Richard's self-confidence makes him electrically attractive when he is "on"—and yet he is a cripple, all too aware that "love forswore me in my mother's womb" (*3H6* 3.2.153). This is precisely the contradiction that animates Shakespeare's sonnets, with their vacillation between erotic and professional ambition on one hand and, on the other, self-effacement, even self-abasement, before his beloved. Richard's confidence in his creative power is matched by the sonnet poet's boasting that he can make the young man immortal and has won his love. But the unlovable Richard, "deformed," "halt," and "lamely," Wheeler and Barber suggest, also embodies everything the poet feels when his beloved young man rejects him and "my glass shows me myself indeed" (Son. 62, 9)—"lame, poor . . . despised" (Son. 37, 9) and "outcast" (Son. 29, 2).[42] It is in the sonnets that Callow heard the voice of an actor, and there, as we shall see in chapter 8, that the poet's strategies of self-representation repeat his representations of actors throughout the canon. There is a similarly Richardian duality in the wise fools, Shakespeare's later versions of the Vice. Although the detached sophistication of these characters (Touchstone, Feste, Thersites, Lavatch, and *Lear's* Fool) is often said to be actor Robert Armin's contribution to the plays, Armin seems rather to have been limited to creating ordinary clowns (and to have been fascinated by unwise, natural fools) until he collaborated with Shakespeare.[43] Instead, it may have been Armin's Richard-like physique—squat, ugly, doglike—and his gift for projecting multiple identities[44] that inspired Shakespeare to create the series of creatures occupying the same theatrical space that he had first staked out for Richard.[45]

We might even see Richard as Shakespeare's "Hunchback of Notre Dame," the role which actor Charles Laughton made into a form of exorcism for his own self-loathing.[46] Like Richard, Laughton's twentieth-century hunchback is victim of a shameful deformity that could nonetheless be used to win him love. Not that Shakespeare lavished any sentiment on his hunchback. Richard may pretend to be a harmless innocent like Quasimodo, but Shakespeare animated him with the rage that can seethe beneath such a posture. Nonetheless Richard, like Quasimodo, is made to play out a similarly sacrificial trajectory, from hero-monster to scapegoat, in exaggerated emotional color. Laughton's film opens as Quasimodo is lifted up and crowned "king," naively delighted at the "honor" bestowed on him by the cheering crowds; it moves toward the moment when Quasimodo, trying to save the heroine he worships, sees her recoil in loathing and is then publicly whipped for his "attack"—while the same crowd laughs and throws stones at him. Richard opens his play anticipating triumph, and leaves it as humbled as Quasimodo.

Analogies between *Richard III* and the biographical record are even more speculative than those between the play and other texts like the sonnets. We can, however, speculate about the genesis of a text like *Richard III* without trying to reduce its meaning to its origin. And although we can have no proof that Shakespeare's vision of Richard embodied fantasies about himself, we can try to piece together what Natalie Davis calls "conjectural knowledge and possible truth,"[47] here about Shakespeare's inner life, since that is the only kind of knowledge we can have. In any case, certain parallels between play and life are suggestive, particularly when they sketch similar origins for Richard's and Shakespeare's theatricality. Shakespeare's father, like Richard's (and like many a modern actor's), failed to live up to his own expectations. John Shakespeare's career began promisingly, but he ended his life as useless to any ambitions William may have had as York was to Richard's.[48] A solid citizen, owner of several properties before he married Mary Arden, John Shakespeare held increasingly important positions in Stratford and finally, when William Shakespeare was four, was made bailiff, "the highest elective office Stratford had to offer."[49] For several years the Shakespeares enjoyed what must have been a full and prosperous life. Beginning about 1576, however, when Shakespeare was twelve, John Shakespeare stopped attending his accustomed official meetings, withdrew from the public life that provided most of the Shakespeare records until then, and sank into what seems to have been financial decline. He stopped paying taxes, mortgaged valuable property, and did not repay debts.[50] "English villages," Michael MacDonald says, "were bound together by bewilderingly complex networks of credit and debt," which created important status as well as financial relations among the villagers.[51] This made debt, though common, doubly upsetting when it became unpayable. Among the two thousand or so cases seen by Napier, the early seventeenth-century "psychiatrist" whose notebooks MacDonald edited, for example, "debt was by far the greatest single source of anxiety." One patient was so "crossed with debts that it broke his wits and senses," and another grew "mopish and fearful," lamenting "that they will take away his goods and he shall be undone."[52]

Given these realities, Shakespeare's portrayal of the "doom" (*Err.* 1.1.2) awaiting a benign bankrupt like Egeon in *The Comedy of Errors* or Antonio in *The Merchant of Venice* takes on added power. *Errors,* perhaps written in the midst of John's troubles, is particularly suggestive if it draws on Shakespeare's familial experience of debt.[53] It represents the "public humiliation"[54] of and the "fear of processe of debt" in the lives of both father and son, and it recounts the father's pitiful fear that, "perhaps, my son, / Thou sham'st to acknowledge me in misery?" (*Err.* 5.1.321–22). Even if John did not, as Joseph Padel has speculated, sink into an Egeon-like depression, the scattering of Mary's inheritance undermined the family's finances and made a stark contrast with happier days.[55] Gone were the furs and badges of office, the public recognition of John's status, the daily power that financial security brought, and even the daily busy-ness of John Shakespeare's former occupation. In their place was the community's no doubt welcome but probably embarrassing sufferance—John was kept on the rolls for several years though he did not attend meetings and was not taxed the customary amount.

John Shakespeare's decline came just at the time when an adolescent needs a strong father who can withstand the boy's rebellious independence. If today's teenager is "successfully" to resolve the renewed generational conflict which puberty brings, he must revise his childishly idealized images of his father to bring them more in line with reality. Then he can gradually replace the image of an omnipotent hero—whom he must either worship or fight—with the image of a man he can hope to imitate himself.[56] One hesitates to generalize across the centuries, but Natalie Zemon Davis has suggested that boys in sixteenth-century France experienced at least some aspects of what we now call adolescence, and Steven R. Smith finds that London apprentices in the sixteenth and seventeenth century fit Erik Erikson's description of today's adolescents. The apprentices Smith describes seemed engaged in the "role experimentation," "sexual confusion," and search for adult identity typical of modern teenagers.[57] They veered between rebelliousness, as in the case of the notorious George Barnwell "immortalized in a seventeenth-century ballad," and model behavior, like Dick Whittington's, designed to assuage their "anxiety for approval of adults." The process entailed both a struggle against servility to their actual masters and identification with fictional heroes possessed of "the manly virtues displayed on the battlefields of France and of the Holy Land . . . and with the romantic virtues of Johnson's 'nine worthies,' " both of which provided raw material for popular "apprentice literature."[58]

Several decades earlier and in the provinces, Shakespeare's biological maturation might not have been culturally encoded in quite the same way, but it is nonetheless likely to have created many of the pressures the apprentices felt from their masters. John Shakespeare's decline effectively removed him as a powerful guardian just as William was beginning the difficult process of growing out of the need for one. Without a father— whether he has died, disappeared, or is merely "shamefully" weak as in so many of Shakespeare's plays—it is not easy for a young man to assume a stable male identity of his own.[59] The loss of his father can leave him with a need to search for the idealized vision of the father he didn't have, and a need to cling to someone else who is powerful, because he himself feels so weak.[60] The plays often depict a bereft son's search for an ideal father—the "absent father"[61]—or the effort to "restore" him in one way or another.[62] John's failure prevented him from passing on the expected inheritance to his son. Instead the hierarchy was reversed and Shakespeare had to go to court to help John make repeated (and unsuccessful) claims to the family inheritance and to a coat of arms. John Shakespeare's son, like York's son Richard, had to achieve the honor his father failed to win; the arms were finally granted.

If John Shakespeare was weak in some ways, William's mother Mary was more formidable, at least socially; she brought John an honorable name, the gentry status of the Ardens otherwise out of his reach. It was through the female line that John, like York, would claim his coat of arms (2H6 2.2.33–51). As nearly all psychoanalytic and feminist critics agree, the plays reveal pervasive assumptions about women's encompassing and dangerous maternal powers, and, to Shakespeare, Mary may have seemed formidable in other ways as well. John Shakespeare's failure would have brought the Shakespeare family configuration closer to the one modern actors describe, when so many of them tell about weak or absent fathers and about the importance of their mothers during childhood. In the late 1570s, when the advantages John had brought to the marriage were rapidly eroding and threatening to take Mary Arden's inheritance with them, John's public decline might have been paralleled by one within the family if William imagined, or perhaps observed, a strong mother's dissatisfaction with a husband who could no longer provide for her.[63]

Add to this configuration the fact that the Shakespeares lost a child just at this time, when seven-and-a-half-year-old Anne, the fourth of the five living siblings, died in 1579. There is reason to believe that brother-sister relations in the sixteenth century were particularly close,[64] and that the death of a sister would therefore have been difficult for the surviving siblings, just as it is today.[65] The poet who could sympathize with a hunted rabbit and an injured snail could hardly have been unmoved by Anne's death, the first he had experienced in the family.[66] The loss might have been more striking because Anne died only about two weeks before Shakespeare's fifteenth birthday.[67] The celebration of Shakespeare's birthday that first year—and perhaps for years after—would have been overcast by memory of Anne's death. Edgar I. Fripp has suggested that the death of Katherine Hamlet, who drowned at Stratford in 1579, may have left its mark on Ophelia's drowning in Hamlet.[68] If so, not only the accidental similarity of the name but also the coincidence with his sister's death could have been responsible.

It is even more likely that the adult Shakespeares were affected by the loss of Anne. Contrary to Lawrence Stone's caution against assuming anachronistically that sixteenth-century parents grieved for dead children,[69] subsequent studies have argued convincingly that parents were as devastated then by losing a child as they are now.[70] Napier's records provide numerous examples of the "searing grief experienced by bereaved mothers," prompting him to cite the Marquis of Winchester's book of platitudes: "The love of the mother is so strong, though the child be dead and laid in the grave, yet always she hath him quick in her heart."[71] Though there can be no proof, it is likely that John and Mary Shakespeare suffered as we would from the loss of a child—and as Constance does for the loss of Arthur, and as Leontes and Hermione do for the loss of Mamillius. It is even possible that the Shakespeares conceived another child to fill the gap. One year after Anne's death, Mary Shakespeare gave birth to Edmund, in circumstances that would likely have discouraged giving birth at that time unless she had been trying to produce a "replacement child." John had scant means of supporting even the family he had already, and the child seems to have been named after Mary's brother Edmund, to whom the Shakespeares had mortgaged Mary's property—emphasizing their dependence on him.[72] Not only were the Shakespeares deeply in debt, but John was about fifty years old, and, at forty, Mary's childbearing career had been over for some time. After giving birth regularly at intervals of two-and-a-half years or less from 1563 to 1574, she had managed to prevent conception for the previous five years in an age with no contraceptive technology; but within two months of Anne's death she was pregnant again. If Edmund was to some degree conceived and treated as Anne's replacement, his subsequent career makes psychological sense, at least from a twentieth-century point of view. Replacement children, whose parents consciously or unconsciously expect them to undo their sibling's death, suffer because they are torn between the need to express their own desires and their need to win parental approval by being somebody else.[73] In extreme circumstances such children can become psychotic; in less extreme ones they can develop a talent for—though also an ambivalence about—acting. The one thing we do know about Edmund is that he was an actor, apparently taken under the protective wing of his oldest brother in London, but perhaps already inclined that way, having learned how to play roles long before he got to the city.

It isn't only adolescent crises and John Shakespeare's failure that can help illuminate Shakespeare's choice of career. Even earlier, Shakespeare, like many of today's actors, had experienced a series of deprivations which might help explain his turn toward the stage as well as his vulnerability to John's misfortune. Such deprivation did not necessarily entail unique hardship on Shakespeare's part—many of his countrymen were more truly "death's familiars"[74] than he, and were not so privileged economically as he was even after his father's fall. His early travails need only have constituted the inevitable natural shocks that flesh is heir to—and that creative children, Phyllis Greenacre has observed, are far more vulnerable to than others.[75] Shakespeare's uniqueness lay not in his difference from but rather in his unique responsiveness to what Claudius in *Hamlet* dismissed as our "common" fate, the "necessary losses," as one popular book now calls them, or narcissistic wounds which we see as painful prerequisites to maturity. For most people, infantile crises like these seem irrelevant to adult lives and mythologies, but even the earliest crisis can leave lasting effects which are the basis for those mythologies. There is more justification in Shakespeare's case than in most for looking to early experience to illuminate adult creativity, simply because the plays present so much of it. In an age when even diarists tended to pass over childhood, Shakespeare was unusual in giving children such attention.

From the beginning there were losses that might have intervened in Shakespeare's development and predisposed him towards the self-denial which hones an actor's skills. Shakespeare may have been born into a house of mourning, and may even have himself been a replacement child like his brother Edmund.[76] We do know that Shakespeare's position as firstborn was complicated by the fact that a sister—and probably two sisters—had died in infancy before he was born.[77] The first, Joan, born in September 1558, probably died "in 1559 or 1560, when burial entries are sparse in the registers."[78] The second, Margaret, was born in December 1562 and died in April of the following year, only four months old.[79] Shakespeare was conceived two months after Margaret died, and Mary Shakespeare might well have been still mourning for her lost daughters when her son arrived.[80] Stone's strictures about indifference to death are scarcely less applicable for a babe-in-arms than in the case of Anne. Evidence about supposed parental indifference to newborns has seldom distinguished (the less accessible) maternal from paternal responses.[81] Fathers may not become attached to children until later, but many mothers have been both anxious and hopeful for months before a child arrives. Patricia Crawford finds in seventeenth-century female writers "an attempt at empathy with the infant even before its birth," and Alice Thornton referred to the "sweete infant in my wombe."[82] Mothers today, even of stillborn or aborted children, mourn copiously and can suffer for years afterwards.[83] Mothers then seem no different, judging from the number of Napier's patients who suffered the "lacerating effect . . . of infant deaths," as MacDonald describes it. The additional "desperation of the childless," which Napier observed, would also have applied when the children lost, like Mary's, were the first or only ones.[84]

Although John and Mary Shakespeare were no doubt relieved and joyed when their third child, William, survived the dangerous postnatal period and the 1564 plague, which carried off some two hundred Stratfordians, Mary's relation to her new son might nonetheless have been affected by her earlier losses. At best she would have been especially worried about this third infant, and at the worst she might have tried to re-create her lost daughters through William. The eldest-born's blissful paradise would already have been marred by contingency. If Shakespeare was to some degree expected to play out a script written for another child, the role might have been even harder for him than for Edmund. The replacement position is hardest on a gifted child whose identity is unusually flexible. In addition, it is harder when the first child dies in infancy, because then the surviving sibling has to live up to an idealized image of a child who didn't live long enough ever to disappoint parental fantasies.[85]

Richard's mother the Duchess, let us hope, bears little resemblance to Mary Shakespeare. But if Shakespeare was in fact a replacement child conceived after the death of two sisters, and if he remembered his mother in mourning for the three siblings he survived, it is interesting that the Duchess always appears in mourning. Did Shakespeare's mother, like Richard's, find him a "false glass" for his two dead sisters?[86] Did she therefore prefer Shakespeare's more docile younger brother Gilbert who stayed home, made no hasty marriage, and took over his father's role as bourgeois businessman? Certainly critics agree that the sibling rivalry which haunted Richard is important in Shakespeare's plays. "Brother hatred," fratricidal rage and competition, and doubling among adult brothers are vital to the plays.[87] Rivalry is indicated in Shakespeare's frequent allusions to the stories of Cain and Abel, Jacob and Esau, and the prodigal son.[88] Even as young children, siblings like *Richard III*'s two princes act out rivalries, and Richard's own jealousy is directed toward boys and an infant, as well as toward his adult brothers. In *Winter's Tale* "the connection between male jealousy and female childbearing" is clear,[89] and the rivalry between the adult "twins" Leontes and Polixenes for pregnant Hermione is juxtaposed with a scene in which seven-year-old child Mamillius is ousted from his pregnant mother's "lap" by his yet-unborn sibling.[90]

Barber argues that the first of Shakespeare's "natural shocks" came when he was two-and-a-half and his brother Gilbert was born. As first and only son of a young wife with a busy older husband, William would have been reigning monarch of the paradise to which Barber and Wheeler see allusions in the sonnets.[91] The sense of being "mother's undisputed darling," as Freud wrote in connection with Goethe's career (and his own), gives a child "the triumphant feeling, the confidence of success, which not seldom brings actual success with it."[92] Young William might have resembled "my lady's eldest son," as Beatrice describes such a boy in Much Ado About Nothing, "evermore tattling [talking away]" (Ado 2.1.8–9), or any of the beloved and precocious boys who appear on stage: Macduff's son left alone with his mother when Macduff deserts them, the fatherless Prince pursued by Richard III, or Mamillius. But then his brother Gilbert arrived and William was, on an infantile scale, "by a brother's hand / Of life, of crown, of queen at once dispatch'd" (Ham. 1.5.74–75). In less extravagant terms, if William was anything like displaced eldest sons today, the loss of his mother's undivided attention would have constituted a major upheaval at the center of his world even before his father failed him later. In the plays, Shakespeare singles out the third year—roughly the age William was when Gilbert was born—as an abrupt break from the world of maternal nurturance and a time of human and even natural disaster. "Thou wast not / Out three years old" when exiled (Tem. 1.2.40–41), Prospero tells Miranda, at which time she was taken from the care of "four or five women" (Tem. 1.2.47) and set afloat with her outcast father. Juliet was three when her old nurse put wormwood to her dug and weaned the child—the very day an earthquake shook the world (Rom. 1.3.23).[93] It was the age ("two and three years old"; Cym. 3.3.101) when the princes in Cymbeline were kidnapped from their real parents, when the servant Tranio in Shrew was bought from his parents to be brought up by a stranger (Shr. 5.1.74), and when Rosalind began to converse with her magician uncle (AYL 5.2.60–61).[94]

Richard's rage at being born crippled and disowned is justified by the play, and so is his jealousy of Edward's "unlook'd for issue" (3H6 3.2.131). But both might draw on Shakespeare's experience of ordinary family rivalries, particularly in a family where the usual succession of siblings was capped by the appearance of Edmund late in Shakespeare's life; issue even more "unlook'd for" than the rest. The rage roused by a new sibling can be terrifying to a small child who can't easily distinguish between desire and fact and who can't tolerate ambivalence.[95] Afraid that his fury might actually kill his mother or his rival, a child will often deny all jealousy, setting up a lifelong proclivity towards self-denial and identification with the enemy. The "enemy" in this case is a ridiculously helpless infant who nonetheless matters vitally to his mother, a "naked new-born babe" (*Mac.* 1.7.21) striding with mysterious power into his life.[96] Better to enjoy the mother's ministrations vicariously through such a rival than to destroy him and risk her anger. Still better to identify with the mother's life-giving and nurturing capacity, with her cherishing maternal role, and to participate vicariously that way.[97] (Compare the three actors, cited in chapter 1, who remembered watching their mothers bringing a chick or mouse back to life by heating it in the oven.) Such identification would fit with the impression many of his contemporaries had of Shakespeare as a sweet and gentle man,[98] and of what Keats called his "negative capability."[99]

Richard gave up competing for love to make his Machiavellian way to the crown; it has been suggested that the competitiveness missing from the life of gentle Shakespeare went into writing plays, a deflection that worked for him, although it did not seem to work either for Marlowe or Jonson. As playwright, Barber argues, Shakespeare can be a "hidden executioner [in tragedy] or disruptive lord of misrule [in comedy]."[100] He can also fight vicariously—as in the person of Talbot in *Henry VI, Part One* for example—for his own immortality. But competitive aggression also, and perhaps more directly, finds outlet in acting—whatever the role—and in commanding an audience's response. Or, more exactly, the conflict between aggression and self-denial finds expression in the player's vacillation between proud ostentation and humble beggary, between domination and submission. It is a vacillation which not only marks Richard III and the sonnet poet, but as we shall see also characterizes both Shakespeare's other histrionic characters, and those heroic figures who confront amphitheater-like public crowds.[101]

Reading the record in light of the plays in this way suggests that the self-effacement which acting demands, and the identification with women which characterizes many modern actors, may both have begun very early for Shakespeare, starting when he tried to meet the expectations of a mother who had just lost two daughters.[102] Any feminine identification, in particular, would have been strengthened later by identifying with his mother's nurturing role when other babies began to arrive. Then, when his sister Anne died near Shakespeare's fifteenth birthday, her ghost would have joined those of the two sisters who had made way for William in the first place, making it all the easier for him to take up the "feminine" position so valued by his mourning mother. As John Shakespeare suffered his reversals, William would have been practiced in taking up the "woman's part" rather than openly competing with his father—another helpless rival—in his decline. It would have been good preparation for a player-to-be: avoiding a fixed identification with male authority and learning to identify with roles more like his mother's. Such experience might also help explain why Shakespeare's plays not only concern themselves so often with female power, but also contain so many star roles for boy "actresses." In what he read as well as what he wrote, Shakespeare seems to have been drawn to stories about women both weak and strong—the stories of Hecuba and Medea on the one hand, and Ariadne and Dido on the other—whose lives he drew on to create even his male characters. Such transgender sympathies may also contribute to the homoerotic aspects of the plays and the poems; it is, after all, the suffering woman, Helena in *All's Well That Ends Well,* who most resembles the poet of the sonnets in his love for a heartless young man. But finally, the feminine identification contributes much more pervasively to Shakespeare's theatrical empathy in general, not just to the creation of female or feminine roles.

Speculation about the parallel childhoods of Richard and William aside, the biographical record for the adult Shakespeare begins, like Richard's, with an unusual courtship, followed by ambitious claims on the theatrical crown. The most immediate outcome of the early years we have described was to make Shakespeare not an actor but a father. William's marriage to Anne Hathaway, though it may have followed from the romantic accident that biographer Schoenbaum describes, may also have had some less random determinants. Schoenbaum describes the young Shakespeare's careless but not unusual summer courtship of an eligible neighbor to whom he was probably already betrothed. But the striking fact is that, as a result of that seemingly impetuous affair, a brief two years after his middle-aged mother had mourned one child and borne his father another, William had impregnated a woman eight years older and of somewhat higher social class than he, and soon after that he was married—to a woman who, we might add, was still in mourning for her father.[103] There is a hint of Richard's sadomasochistically exaggerated Petrarchan mode of courtship[104] in Shakespeare's own courtship of Anne Hathaway if sonnet 145 was written for Anne. That poem describes the woman's original rejection of the poet, followed by her pity and a change of heart when, "hate from hate away she threw, / And saved my life saying, not you."[105] If Richard's courtship of Anne was unusual, so was Shakespeare's—not, however, as nineteenth-century scholars believed, because of Anne's premature pregnancy, a common phenomenon among betrothed couples.[106] Its oddness lies in her agreeing to it at all.

Marriage then was undertaken neither lightly nor usually so early. It bestowed adult rights and responsibilities on a young man; until they could be sure of meeting those responsibilities, few married. Although there were exceptions, most young people supported themselves and did not move in with their parents.[107] On average men (apart from the aristocracy) married in their mid- or late twenties (brides of course were substantially younger). John Shakespeare himself had carefully waited to acquire status and property before he brought home a wife. Could he look with favor on the hasty marriage of a son who proclaimed his independence by marrying, then brought his bride home to live with his parents in an already overburdened household? Like Antipholus of Syracuse in *The Comedy of Errors,* who crosses the ocean and proposes to a foreign woman—but thereby winds up in the arms of his mother and bankrupt father after all, Shakespeare after his marriage was only more tightly bound into the family network. Was Shakespeare trying to show his father that he too could conceive a child? To show his mother that if she were going to withdraw from him because her daughter died, and then betray him with John, he could find in Anne's lap metal more attractive? Did the liaison help "undo" Anne Shakespeare's death by impregnating an Anne (the child would be called Susanna)? [108] Whatever the motives, Susanna arrived in 1583, followed by twins less than two years later. Then equally suddenly, Shakespeare was gone from Stratford altogether, leaving his family behind (again). Having rushed into fatherhood and marriage in the wake of his family's decline, Shakespeare seemed equally ambivalent about starting a family of his own.

It wasn't long then before Shakespeare became a player after all,[109] and began his career—if tradition is accurate—by playing versions of the fatherly role which he had left behind in Stratford.[110] He moved from what he might see as "acting out" ambivalence in life to being an actor on-stage—whether he joined a company of players as they passed through Stratford; went to serve as tutor in some great house where he participated in amateur theatricals which led to London connections; or, like Hamlet, was in the capital for other reasons but haunted the playhouses enough to memorize the players' lines. Given both the social stigma of playing, and the financial insecurity that made it seem irrational to Bentley for John King to continue playing, it is noteworthy that Shakespeare left family and Stratford for such a risky, if potentially profitable, career. Certainly his continued commuting or bachelor life in London would have been an oddity among the players. Among the no doubt varied factors that contributed to Shakespeare's decision, perhaps there were irrational reasons which made a life on the stage attractive to Shakespeare as well as to John King. The next chapter turns to Shakespeare's representation of playing to examine in more detail what "life on the stage" meant for Shakespeare and in what ways it might have been attractive.

Chapter Four

Player King as Beggar in Great
Men's Houses—I

*J*ust as Shakespeare's life can fall into new patterns when read in the context of players Elizabethan and modern, Shakespeare's fictional players look different when read against what we know about his life, about Elizabethan theater, and about actors today. Perhaps the most striking fact is that Shakespeare created so many players: three plays each include a play-within-a-play (*Love's Labour's Lost, A Midsummer Night's Dream,* and *Hamlet*); one is framed as a play by its extensive Induction (*The Taming of the Shrew*); and at least eight others have masques or other playlike elements (*Titus Andronicus, Henry IV, Part One, The Merry Wives of Windsor, As You Like It, Timon of Athens, The Winter's Tale, The Tempest, Henry VIII*). Renaissance drama was permeated with histrionic self-consciousness, but interest usually focused more on the world as stage than on the stage itself, and surprisingly few of the plays-within-plays (called "inner plays" here) in Shakespeare's time were put on by (even temporarily) professional players.[1] Of these even fewer were performed on the public stage along with Shakespeare's. Tellingly, many of the inner plays that do exist were created by known or suspected players. Anthony Munday created or coauthored four early inner plays (*John a Kent and John a Cumber, Sir Thomas More, The Death of Robert Earl of Huntington* and *The Downfall of Robert Earl of Huntington*) and Ben Jonson and Thomas Heywood two later ones; the clown William Rowley had a hand in creating Kempe's abortive performance in *The Travels of Three English Brothers*; and Richard Brome (a suspected actor) created two inner plays produced after Shakespeare's death. In other words the likes of the professional Player King in *Hamlet,* or even of the amateur Bottom, are hard to find, especially on the public stage; and where we find them, they often signal an actor's bias.[2]

Shakespeare's view of players is suggested not only by their numbers but also by the particular bias of his portraits. Although his own experience lay primarily on the up-to-date public stage in London, Shakespeare's players all conform to the outdated antitheatricalist's image of the player as itinerant, a proud beggar living on alms. In a period when players were moving away from aristocratic patronage to commercial theater, Shakespeare accentuated the displacement and social inferiority implied by the former. His plays include professionals like the troupe in *Shrew* and Hamlet's old friends from Wittenberg (both used "better than they deserve"), as well as amateurs, like the villagers in *Love's Labour's Lost,* the mechanicals in *Dream* (identified as "the rabble" in the stage directions), and, we might include, the "rabble" in *Tempest* who put on Prospero's masque. The professionals in *Shrew* and *Hamlet* betray no bias on Shakespeare's part; they are if anything quite competent (unlike the corresponding players in the analogous *A Shrew* play). The players we remember, however—the ones given substantial roles—are the amateurs, who are all laughably inept.

In fact Shakespeare's players are confined to a series of "great house plays"; neither established in the city (like the players who feel superior to the Citizen and his Wife in *The Knight of the Burning Pestle*), nor traveling independently (like the players in *Histriomastix*), they depend on aristocratic hospitality—and in *Dream* they must even compete for it. Despite Shakespeare's own status as shareholder in the most important London company, his players are all defined by contrast to the greatness embodied in the house, and they are bound by a relation of service, if not subservience, to the resident great lord.[3] It is true that the lord usually welcomes the players graciously, not only rewarding the performance but often taking part by giving instructions, adding some dozen or sixteen lines, or presiding as unofficial master of revels. The players typically hope to win his affection and approval, as well as the much-needed monetary reward. But despite his cordiality, from the great man's point of view the player is mere "sport," or a jester, like that "harlotry player" Falstaff. Many of the players are in fact either the play's literal clowns or closely related types, and they fit the sixteenth-century image of player as foolishly proud despite his baseness.

In addition, the lord is identified not only by birth and wealth, but also by the particularly masculine activities of warfare and the hunt, which was the peacetime equivalent of aristocratic warfare. In America, where hunting was so long a mundane necessity and is now associated with lower social classes, neither the forest nor the hunt has the same mythic or ideological significance it had for Shakespeare.[4] Forests were disappearing in early modern England and practical hunting for food had long since been replaced by a ritualistic procedure which, although a central activity in the lives of the ruling class, was no less symbolic than the occupations of pastoral shepherds and of Robin Hood's merry men. The "forest" was not just any woods but a specially marked aristocratic space; the object of the hunt was a specially marked deer, chosen according to elaborate seasonal and social rules; and the hunt itself was an elaborately artificial ceremony, most artificial in the butchering of the animal (the "unmaking," "undoing," or "breaking") and in the curée, the formal rewarding of the hounds. It involved its own specialized language and was far more important as a social marker than as a source of meat. The resulting activity was an odd combination in which the savagery of the pack was overlayed with exquisite elegance, a mixture of sacrifice and butchery mocked by Tudor humanists and Jacobean satirists alike. The player is defined as foil for this manly warrior or hunter whom he has come to serve. The contrast thus encompasses not only that between King and Beggar or King and Clown, but that between man and woman, man and boy, or even man and beast. This contrast is caricatured by Jonson in Volpone's staff of house entertainers, the dwarf and the hermaphrodite, who may or may not be his children, and the protean Mosca, who is his Venus. Shakespeare has no hermaphrodites, but it is notable that all the males in the canon who dress as women are located in the great house plays. On the face of it this seems perfectly explicable: men *must* dress as women in inner plays. Cross-dressing is natural enough in *Dream,* where Flute takes on Thisbe's role as the object of Bottom/Pyramus's desire simply because he is part of a play—like the Player Queen in *Hamlet.* But cross-dressing moves off the literal stage and into the "real" world of the great house plays. In *Shrew* the page in the frame also puts on woman's clothes to serve as Sly's wife (*Shr.* Ind.103–30);[5] in the Falstaff plays, Falstaff himself plays Mother Pratt in earnest (and may play Hotspur's wife offstage); and in *Wives* Anne Page's would-be suitors each finds himself married to a boy dressed as a fairy. Once players enter, their gender instability as well as their ontological subversiveness can spread quickly.

Although the player's situation improves somewhat in the later plays, perhaps influenced by Shakespeare's own rising status, it is never entirely transformed. The result is an image of playing in general which exaggerates the twentieth-century actor's sense of himself as child before a parent or lone figure before a crowd: Shakespeare narratizes the discrepancy between actor's and audience's power, points up the confrontation between the player's grandiose ambitions and the threat of humiliation, and infantilizes the player. He also situates the theatrical encounter in the charged atmosphere of warfare or the hunt, where at any moment the hunter can become the hunted—surrounded by a pack of critics—though the confrontation is usually limited to an exchange of gazes rather than physical encounters. The following two chapters will examine in roughly chronological order the "great house plays," which include Shakespeare's literal players (in the early cluster of *Shrew, Love's Labour's,* and *Dream* and in *Hamlet*), as well as some of the closely related hangers-on (in the Falstaff plays and *Troilus*) whose roles, at least in part, entail playing for a great man and singing for their suppers. They will also suggest that since most of these plays not only were about, but may have been written for, actual private performances in great houses, they may represent responses to the specific occasions of their own performance. Shakespeare's presentation strategy, already implicated in the plot, is manifested as well in a prologue or epilogue, and in the degree to which the action meets or thwarts audience expectations about genre, tone, and decorum. The two chapters lead to a brief discussion of *King Lear,* which can be seen as the heir of the great house plays although it has no inner play and is not about players. The great house influence on *Lear* suggests that Shakespeare's actor identity could affect far more than the literal players in the plays—not only by elaborating the familiar Renaissance trope of role-playing, but also by returning his attention to the painful and reversible relationship which defines the actor and his audience.

Armado and Costard in the French Academy: Player as Clown

The Taming of the Shrew, framed as theater by its Induction, is almost certainly earlier, but the pageant in *Love's Labour's Lost* is the first Shakespearean inner play proper. Since the players' roles call for comedians in the modern sense, their entry here marks the first confrontation in the canon between King and Clown and establishes Shakespeare's opposition between the player and the aristocratic world of heroes from whom he begs alms.[6] Ferdinand, King of Navarre, is the "great man" in *Love's Labour's Lost* and though he may have "sworn out house-keeping" (*LLL* 2.1.103), he cannot escape from his duty as host, either to the visiting princess or to the players who help him to entertain her. And when the motley players in *Love's Labour's Lost* perform their Pageant of Worthies, they gain access not only to Navarre's academic retreat in his country house, surrounded by its "curious-knotted garden" (*LLL* 1.1.242), but to the entire world of manly aristocratic heroics which it represents. This is a world shaped by the ideology of honor and driven by the heroic thrust toward "fame" as a means of establishing an eternal name, and transcending all that is base and shameful in mortality. It naturally encourages the rituals and "activities that are most integral to the whole idea of aristocracy—leading troops in a patriotic war against the King's enemies."[7] This world had been the first object of Shakespeare's dramatic attention in the "heroical histories" of the first *Henriad,* which opens with the death of Henry V and the funeral proclaiming "death's dishonorable victory" (*1H6* 1.1.20), and is dominated by Talbot's effort to fight on in Henry's name and transcend death through heroic fame.[8] Talbot's project in *Henry VI, Part One* is symbolized by his devotion to the rituals of the Order of the Garter, with its implicit opposition between heroic fame and cowardly shame: "*Honi soit qui mal y pense.*" His failure is signaled by the rituals of the aristocratic hunt when Talbot, who was accustomed to penetrating enemy cities, at last finds himself surrounded by the French and "bounded in a pale" like "a little herd of England's timorous deer, / Maz'd with a yelping kennel of French curs" (*1H6* 4.2.45–47).

Love's Labour's Lost might not seem at first to belong in such company, but it continually alludes to the heroic tradition drawn not only from the English chronicles which furnished the plot of *Henry VI*, but also from the lives of the famous "Worthies"—beginning with Hercules, whose labors supply the title of *Love's Labour's Lost*.[9] Similarly, both in its structure and its major concerns, *Love's Labour's* mirrors Shakespeare's *Henry VI, Part One*. Certainly Navarre's men see themselves as members of the illustrious company of departed heroes like *Henry VI's* St. George and Henry V. *Love's Labour's Lost* is an oddly death-conscious comedy; and, scholars though they are, Navarre and his fellow votaries fancy themselves above all to be chivalric warriors battling against "the huge army of the world's desires" in order to transcend "death's dishonorable victory," as it was called in *Henry VI*, or "the disgrace of death," as it is called here (*LLL* 1.1.3, 10; *1H6* 1.1.20). And just as their serious work drives them to stalk the elusive "fame that all hunt after all their lives," in their leisure they devote themselves to the aristocratic hunt, seen as appropriate entertainment for a royal princess. The play refers insistently to the hunting party which provides the first occasion for the "bookmen" to mingle with the Princess's entourage. There Navarre spurs his horse hard upon the hill and reveals his "mounting mind." Indeed the whole play is cast as a reversible "hunt," and Navarre and his men meet a fate like Talbot's. The love-struck Berowne complains, "The king he is hunting the deer; I am coursing myself: they have pitched a toil [set a snare for the deer]; I am toiling in a pitch" (*LLL* 4.3.1–2).[10] Meanwhile the Princess jokes about the deer she kills and, as she prepares to shoot her bow, likens herself to a "curst wi[fe]" who "subdues a lord" (*LLL* 4.1.36, 40).[11] Navarre and his votaries had entered boldly commanding that "fame, that all *hunt* after in their lives, / Live register'd upon our brazen tombs" (*LLL* 1.1.1–2; italics added). Now the hunters are hunted and the suitor-shooters shot.

Navarre's aristocratic ideals thus run exactly counter to the base, effeminate pastime of playing,[12] and the players here are mere foils showing that Navarre's heroic ambition turns out to be no better than the "Pageant of Worthies," where everyone is "o'er-parted." Military prowess in early modern Europe was indeed spectacle—nowhere more visibly so than in the French wars from which Shakespeare took the names of Navarre and his men (and to which he may already have alluded in *Henry VI, Part One*).[13] Shakespeare was not alone in mustering his grandeur for his stage. Marlowe had made fun of soldiers who march in garish robes like players in *Edward II* (1591–93 [1592]), and one reason for the reluctance of the players in *Histriomastix* (1598–99 [1599]) to go to war is the fear that the soldiers would steal their "playing parrell" and "strout it in the field" (286)—a joke that loses its point unless soldiers were already known for strouting. The

popularity of Braggadocchio suggests that they were.[14] Even when not paro-
died, the soldier was represented as an actor on display for spectators, subject to the actor's extremes of fame and shame.[15]

Shakespeare's glorious soldier, heroic Talbot himself, is introduced on
display, high in a tower where he has been "watched . . . even these three
days" (*1H6* 1.4.16) by the master gunner below. For Talbot, fame and success in war entail a physical display of prowess, so that he can terrify the
French, whose "whole army stood agaz'd on him" (*1H6* 1.1.126). Similarly,
when failure threatens Talbot, it threatens in the form of public shame
when the French witness his inability to live up to his role. Recounting his
captivity in France, what Talbot most deplores is the shame of public
exposure:

> In open market-place produc'd they me
> To be a public spectacle to all:
> Here, said they, is the Terror of the French,
> The scarecrow that affrights our children so.

And Talbot directs his heroic fury not at his captors but at his audience:

> Then broke I from the officers that led me,
> And with my nails digg'd stones out of the ground
> To hurl at the beholders of my shame.
>
> (*1H6* 1.4.38–45)[16]

Later he is almost trapped by the Countess, who locks him within her walls
and laughs at his heroic pretense; and before he finally dies the general of
the encircling French forces announces that "these *eyes,* that *see* thee now
well coloured, / Shall *see* thee wither'd, bloody, pale and dead" (*1H6* 4.2.37–
38; italics added).[17] Appropriately enough, Talbot sees death itself as an
audience, "Thou antic Death, which laugh'st us here to scorn" (*1H6* 4.7.18).

But the comparison which likens a soldier to an actor works the other
way too. Navarre and his men are struggling with precisely the ambition
and its discontents that lead people—including Armado and company—to
the stage. We have heard the twentieth-century actor described as "a soldier
going into battle,"[18] and heard about his "warlike energy" and "gladiator instinct." The sixteenth-century *Hamlet,* the most theatrical of Shakespeare's
plays, pairs the soldier and actor as well, when Hamlet compares himself
first to a player, then to the soldier Fortinbras, and when at the end he is
carried "like a soldier to the stage" (*Ham.* 5.2.401).[19] Not long before *Hamlet,* Shakespeare's most heroic soldier, Henry V, had encouraged his warriors into the breach by telling them to *act* like tigers, while the Chorus of
that play encouraged the audience to strain and work like soldiers.[20]

In *Love's Labour's Lost,* therefore, Navarre's sense of himself as warrior, as well as his search for fame and immortality, provide a model as well as an antitype for theatrical ambition.[21] Navarre's world represents everything drama aspired to in its proudest claims. More than ten years would pass before John Davies would complain that players "weene they merit immortality," and thirty before Massinger's Roman actor could claim outright that he played for "glorie, and to leave our names / To after times."[22] But the grandiose fantasies of twentieth-century actors—that acting can make contact with the past or recreate life—were already inscribed in the praise topoi used by Thomas Nashe and Thomas Heywood in their defenses of Renaissance drama. Drama, for these men, was almost synonymous with a pageant of worthies that both recognized and created heroic immortality. We have already had occasion to cite Nashe's famous testimony to the power of *Henry VI,* which we might see as Shakespeare's own "Pageant of Worthies":

> How it would have joyed brave *Talbot* . . . to think that after he had lyne two hundred yeares in his Tombe, hee should triumphe again on the stage and have his bones newe embalmed with the teares of ten thousand spectators at least . . . who, in the Tragedian that represents his person, imagine they behold him fresh bleeding.[23]

Nashe concludes with a less well-known but even more sweeping claim for all drama: "There is no immortalitie can be given a man on earth Like unto Playes."[24] Heywood's emphasis is on the power the play has over the audience, but he too insists on the way in which theater goes beyond creating mere "shadows" or "forms": "To see a souldier shap'd like a souldier, walke, speake, act like a souldier: to see a *Hector* all besmered in blood, trampling upon the bulkes of Kinges. . . . To see as I have seene, *Hercules,* in his own shape hunting the Boare, knocking downe the Bull . . . Oh, these were sights to make an *Alexander!*"[25] Webster's *Excellent Actor* (1615) makes the same claim: "A man of deepe thought might apprehend, the Ghosts of our ancient *Heroes* walk't again, and take [the player] (at severall times) for many of them."[26] Neither Nashe, Heywood, nor Webster really believe in reincarnation; just as the same complaints turn up again and again in the antitheatricalist tracts, resurrection had clearly become part of the standard defense of drama. Yet there is something in their praise that sounds like Macbeth's awe at the line of eight real kings raised up in the witches' show (*Mac.* 4.1.111, stage direction)—or like the scholars struck with admiration at Faustus's ability to raise Alexander and his paramour from the dead "in their own shapes" (*Dr. Faustus* 4.1[1233]).[27] Faustus's opening complaint in Marlowe's play was that no human doctor could raise the dead; apparently in some minds the players could.[28] If nothing else, the player was the one who brought a play to "life," and the idea of resurrection, as we have seen (chap. 2), inhabited the language of the theater.

Perhaps then, the pageant of dead white male worthies in *Love's Labour's Lost* serves as parodic displacement not only of Navarre's overblown aspirations but also of Shakespeare's own theatrical aspirations in *Henry VI*— just as Pyramus and Thisbe would soon parody his efforts at romance in *Romeo and Juliet.* In any case the pageant certainly serves to expose the proud beggars in *Love's Labour's Lost* who arrange to perform it for the king. Shakespeare devotes an unusually large proportion of lines and even whole scenes to these characters, whom Berowne dismisses as a crew of walking stereotypes from the commedia dell'arte—"the pedant, the braggart, the hedge-priest, the fool, and the boy" (*LLL* 5.2.536)—but who are remarkably well developed as individuals.[29] They include the flamboyant Spaniard Armado, his page Moth, and Costard, retainers who have been invited into the academe to provide "sport" for the bookmen. They are joined by the local villagers, the pedant Holofernes, his parasite, Nathaniel the Curate, and Constable Dull, who help put on the pageant. The players run the gamut from narcissistic would-be stars to less-talented hired (in this case drafted) men, just as Quince's troupe does in the Athens of *A Midsummer Night's Dream* and as London companies did. Preparations for this performance may provide a glimpse of what went on in Elizabethan performances, though we have no way of knowing whether the power struggles among actors here, the preference for typecasting, the threat of stage fright, and the rudeness of the audience are models for, or nonsensical distortion of, professional practice.

In any case the performance gives a glimpse of would-be actors as Shakespeare saw them. Most revealing among these actors is the group's leader, Armado, another version of Shakespeare's proud beggar. Though he is a braggart soldier by stereotype, Armado has a good deal of the braggart player about him. He resembles Robert Greene's equally spruce and arrogant player in *Groatsworth of Wit.* Greene's player boasts to Roberto that he can make "a prettie speech," and reports that he had "terribly thundred" the twelve labors of Hercules on stage, in a role not very different from those in the pageant.[30] Even Holofernes, a vain man himself, sees through Armado's similar bombast:

> his humour is lofty, his discourse peremptory, his tongue filed, his eye ambitious, his gait majestical, and his general behaviour vain, ridiculous, and thrasonical. He is too picked, too spruce, too affected. . . . I abhor such fanatical phantasimes, such insociable and point-devise companions. (*LLL* 5.1.9–13, 17–19)

Armado's sensitivity however distinguishes him from Greene's unworthy charlatan and makes him an important indicator of Shakespeare's attitude toward actors. Armado's pride is not only a matter of social pretense, but an involvement with self and self-image that suggests something like what we now mean by narcissism. He is as concerned with emotional as with sartorial style, and he cannot even fall in love without playing a role. When Jaquenetta steals his heart Armado desperately seeks "some mighty precedent" to shore up his shattered sense of self: "Comfort me, boy," he asks his clever page, "What great men have been in love?" (*LLL* 1.2.60–61). And, like Richard III, if Armado is proud and thrasonical, he nonetheless finds himself in humiliating pursuit of a most unlikely woman. Like Richard with Lady Anne, Armado veers between brazen self-assertion and abject submission, claiming to be the Nemean lion to Jaquenetta's lamb, the King to her Beggar—then vowing at the end to hold the plow three years for her.

Armado is awed both by his female audience—as Navarre and his men are by theirs—and by the king for whom he organizes the Pageant of Worthies. He is a fawning courtier thoroughly concerned with pleasing his audience and, like all Shakespeare's later players, he feels an exaggerated, even childlike, deference for his lord and patron. For him, self-esteem is inseparable from Navarre's approval. When he learns that "the king would have me present the princess, sweet chuck, with some delightful ostentation" (*LLL* 5.1.102–4), he takes it as sign that his theatrical duties have "singled [him out] from the barbarous" (*LLL* 5.1.73). He never suspects that he has been included in the festivities as mere sport, and is assumed to be no better than a "Monarcho," or court fool.[31] If we take his unwitting innuendoes seriously, Armado finds an almost obscene pleasure in serving Navarre and being his "familiar":

> Sir, the king is a noble gentleman, and my familiar, I do assure ye, very good friend. For what is inward between us, let it pass . . . for I must tell thee, it will please his grace, by the world, sometime to lean upon my poor shoulder, and with his royal finger, thus, dally with my excrement, with my mustachio; but, sweet heart, let that pass. . . . some certain special honours it pleaseth his greatness to impart to Armado, a soldier, a man of travel, that hath seen the world: but let that pass. The very all of all is, but, sweet heart, I do implore secrecy, that the king would have me present the princess, sweet chuck, with some delightful ostentation, or show, or pageant, or antic, or firework. (*LLL* 5.1.87–104)

As he prepares a pageant for "The posteriors of this day" (*LLL* 5.1.80–81), Armado, with unconscious camp, elaborates the king's patronage into an indecent fantasy of something "inward" between them as the king's "royal finger" dallies with Armado's excrement.

Before the pageant is over—or rather interrupted, as nearly all Shakespeare's inner plays are—Armado and his fellows experience the extremes of egotism and shame inherent in a player's life. Some of them are truly "shame-proof" (Berowne's wishful claim; *LLL* 5.2.508): Holofernes begins the project ridiculously overconfident about his worthiness to play three Worthies, and nothing that happens during the performance can faze Costard, who walks off barely containing his delighted "I hope I was perfect" (*LLL* 5.2.554), despite the audience's rudeness to him. But when the audience is unrelenting in its seemingly motiveless malignity toward the poor players, others fall apart. Holofernes, like Tomkis's "fresh player" or T. G.'s "bashful" player, is literally put "out of countenance."[32] Nathaniel is so afflicted by the audience's scorn—"A conqueror, and afeard to speak!" (*LLL* 5.2.573–74)—that he forgets his lines and must "run away for shame" (*LLL* 5.2.574). He responds to their rejection just as Boyet predicts the would-be lovers will respond to the ladies' rejections: "Why, that contempt will kill the speaker's heart,/ And quite divorce his memory from his part" (*LLL* 5.2.149–50). The men attack not only the acting but the very shape and odor of the actors' bodies, taking advantage of their physical vulnerability: Nathaniel smells; Holofernes' face is too thin, like a "death's face"; and (spoken sarcastically) Armado's "leg is too big" in the "calf" and the "small" (*LLL* 5.2.562, 607, 631–34). If Armado's devotion to the King evokes the familial fantasies modern actors describe, his experience during the performance itself suggests the modern actor's sense of being held at bay by Canetti's baiting crowd. The players become scapegoats. "Only the savage shame one feels toward an unworthy part of oneself," Thomas Greene notes, "could motivate the gentlemen's . . . (quite uncharacteristic) cruelty."[33] It is a telling analysis of audience psychology.

In the end, Armado, insulted in his effort to present Hector, suffers the worst reversal. Like Navarre claiming to be heir to all eternity, Armado has staged a heroic drama and attempts (à la Nashe and Heywood) to bring dead heroes to life. But instead the pageant turns into an unheeded memento mori, a "death's face in a ring," as Berowne calls Holofernes (*LLL* 5.2.607). When "Alexander" comes on stage to announce that, "when in the world I lived, I was the world's commander" (*LLL* 5.1.557), his words only remind the audience that in the world he does not live any longer. Then too, Armado's play, as much as Navarre's own efforts, is interrupted by the messenger from France announcing the death of the Princess's father. More painful for Armado than the metaphysical failure of his fictional pageant, is the real-life defeat that it accompanies. Costard interrupts "Hector" in midspeech and accuses Armado of getting Jaquenetta pregnant.

"Dost thou infamonize me among potentates?" Armado cries (*LLL* 5.2.670), ready to fight for his honor; and the bookmen crowd around to laugh not at Hector but at Armado. The poor Spaniard endures an almost literal re-alization of the actor's fear of being naked in front of an audience, when Costard challenges him to strip to his shirt and Armado is forced to admit, shamefully, that he has none ("I go woolward for penance"; *LLL* 5.2.701–2). The man who played Hector, and who identified with the King when he quoted the ballad of "The King and the Beggar" to Jaquenetta, is humiliated in front of his King. He is a portrait of the actor as vulnerable narcissist.

* * *

But Shakespeare's satiric thrust in *Love's Labour's Lost* is aimed more at the aristocrats than the actors; even their attack on the players reflects back on themselves. The joke is not so much on the clownish players as on Navarre and his men, whose plans are interrupted when Marcade breaks up the play. Besides, *Love's Labour's Lost* exudes a confidence and delight in itself as theater which contradicts its mockery of the pageant. Its self-assurance emerges not least in the way it teases its offstage aristocratic au-dience, both by inviting their complicity in the play's dense allusiveness and private jokes, then refusing them the expected happy ending, and by suggesting that they are as unsatisfying an audience as Navarre and his fellows.

Sly in the Cotswold Manor: Player as Beggar

At about the same time that Shakespeare was recreating heroic kings in the early history plays and would-be heroes in *Love's Labour's Lost,* he also cre-ated one of Renaissance drama's most memorable beggars, Christopher Sly in *The Taming of the Shrew.* The heroical histories told a story of men striv-ing for a histrionic greatness; *Shrew* tells the story of a beggar who has it thrust upon him. A textual connection between the comedy and the histo-ries is suggested by the fact that *Shrew*'s main plot adapts details from the first *Henriad,* and Sly's plot may be related to the histories more holisti-cally.[34] (Sly actually tells the hostess to "look to the chronicles" if she wants to verify his claim about his origins; *Shr.* Ind. 1.3–4.) Even apart from the history plays, however, the antithesis between king and beggar provides an important context for the performance in *Shrew,* just as the contrast be-tween king and clown does for the pageant in *Love's Labour's Lost.*

The antithesis between king and beggar was rooted in Scripture and legend, and it found frequent expression in a hierarchal world where the opposition between rich and poor, powerful and powerless, was every-where evident. But the theme of the King and the Beggar "seems to have

Tamora and Titus. Drawing of a scene from *Titus Andronicus* (1595?). Manuscript, library of the Marquess of Bath, Longleat House.

exercised a peculiar hold on [Shakespeare's] imagination."[35] The vivid contrast between King and Beggar (in Shakespeare's version, at times, Emperor and Beggar, or Caesar and Beggar) was most often evoked to point the lesson about their common mortality. A king, grand as he is, Hamlet discovers, may go progress through the guts of a beggar. Alexander and even "Imperious Caesar, dead and turn'd to clay, / Might stop a hole to keep the wind away." (*Ham.* 5.1.206–7). "'Tis paltry to be Caesar," says Cleopatra at a similar moment, "the dung"[36] is both "the beggar's nurse and Caesar's" (*Ant.* 5.2.27–28). The scene of "The Beggar and the King" (*R2* 5.3.78), as Bolingbroke calls it in *Richard II,* was a favorite of Shakespeare's.

But the reversal which most preoccupied Shakespeare was different. Unlike his fellow dramatists Shakespeare seems fascinated by the emotional relationship between the king and the beggar, and by the fact that the king and beggar might change places in relationship to one another. The traditional pairing of king and beggar had often led out of the graveyard—via the lesson of *theatrum mundi*—into the playhouse, and for Shakespeare too, the reversal was associated with theater and with the magnificent Player King who must kneel at the end of the play and beg the audience for ap-

Isabel and Angelo. From Nicholas Rowe's edition of *Measure for Measure* (London, 1709). Folger Shakespeare Library.

Volumnia and Coriolanus. From Nicholas Rowe's edition of *Coriolanus* (London, 1709). Folger Shakespeare Library.

plause. The king, who takes his status for granted, may find himself having to beg for it from the very beggar he scorned before—just as Richard II's histrionic meditation about kings and beggars begins when he discovers that he must kneel and beg favors from his former subject:

> Thus play I in one person many people,
> And none contented. Sometimes I am king,
> Then treasons make me wish myself a beggar
> And so I am.
>
> (R2 5.5.31–34)

Even the Protean Richard III's climb to kingship was inseparable from his tendency to play the beggar, and to kneel both to his mother and to Lady Anne.

Further implications of this reversal are suggested by "The Ballad of the King and the Beggar," mentioned some five times in the plays, which Armado cites as precedent when he courts Jaquenetta. Probably obscene, perhaps popular enough to have been made into a play or jig, the ballad tells the story of King Cophetua's love for the beggar maid Penelophon, and thus has inscribed in it not only class but gender hierarchies.[37] (The two descents were already associated on stage; a boy actor, for example, could play both woman and beggar.[38]) Reversal in this case would make the king not only base but feminine, and merely to be in love with a beggar—to beg her favors—implied a reversal. Armado tries to transform his humiliating infatuation with the dairymaid into a Caesarlike victory over her. He writes in the imperative voice, and identifies with the King:

> More fairer than fair, beautiful than beauteous . . . have commiseration on thy heroical vassal! The magnanimous and most illustrate King Cophetua set eye upon the pernicious and indubitate beggar Zenolophon, and he it was that might rightly say, *veni, vidi, vici;* which, to annothanize in the vulgar (O base and obscure vulgar!) *videlicet,* he came, saw, and overcame. . . . Who came? the king: why did he come? . . . to overcome. To whom came he? to the beggar: . . . who overcame he? the beggar. The conclusion is victory: on whose side? the king's. (*LLL* 4.1.63–76)

But he winds up playing the beggar and asking for her commiseration.[39]

Sly is quite literally a beggar. Although he calls himself a tinker, he is identified both by Shakespeare in the speech headings and stage directions, and by the Lord in the text, as "beggar"—and indeed a "tinker" was not much different from a beggar.[40] He is also a player, although he is not included among the literal Players who arrive at the Lord's manor. Those Players are relatively respectable members of their class; and they are greeted graciously, though with some condescension when the Lord not only expresses his preference in dramatic style—"aptly fitted and naturally perform'd"—but also gives them a lesson in manners—"I am doubtful of your modesties" (*Shr.* Ind. 1.85, 92). Shakespeare's impeccable strollers may even have been created as an answer to the boorish and beggarly players in *Histriomastix*.[41] The strollers' professional performance, however, is presented as only part of a larger amateur "play" in which the clownish Christopher Sly, though unwittingly, stars as chief player. It is Sly, not the literal Players, who resembles "Guts" and "Gulch" among Sir Owlet's men in *Histriomastix*—and who resembles the clownish Players in Shakespeare's own *Love's Labour's Lost* and *Midsummer Night's Dream*. His experience parallels that of *Shrew*'s literal Players and presents it in another register; he shows the regressive underside of the patron-player relationship and the emotional stakes in it. Gracious as the Lord is to the Players, he is even more generous to Sly, and Sly's transformation is the dream version of the Player's welcome. Sly's playing, like that of Richard III, seems associated with Shakespeare himself. Sly's Warwickshire induction sets forth a fantasy which will reappear in Bottom's story and Falstaff's before it emerges transformed in Lear's tragedy. Sly is a player only unwittingly but despite—or because of—that fact his story encodes a narrative about the meaning of acting, its origins, its wished-for benefits, and its dangers. The story is a myth of origin for playing, though also of much else. It ridicules the player's social ambition and yet indulges Armado's fantasy of being accepted by the great lord who calls for the play.

Thus, although part of the joke is that Sly is a theatrical innocent who doesn't know a play from a tumbling trick, at heart he is as much a role-player as Armado or Bottom. He may never have seen a play, but his speech is larded with quotations from contemporary blockbusters like *The Spanish Tragedy*. Even more fundamental is his Pistol-ian rhetoric ("Therefore *paucas pallabris,* let the world slide. Sessa!" *Shr.* Ind. 1.5), and the remarkable number of offstage roles he has played, from peddler to bearherd to lord of the manor. Like the clownish players in *Love's Labour's Lost* and *Dream,* Sly is a typical clown in a typical clown's plot. In person he is lawless, sensual, and boorish: a comic butt. He may even have been a clown in the technical sense, played by the troupe's comic.[42] It is true that the outlines of his plot can be traced to the narrative of "The Wakened Sleeper," found in several different accounts of a supposedly real episode, and in *The Arabian Nights,* as well as in some late ballads,[43] and that this is a didactic, not a clown's, tradition: a rich lord finds a sleeping peasant lying on the ground, dresses him like a lord, and treats him like a lord when he awakes; then the deception ends and the poor man finds himself a beggar again, while the lord may laugh at the joke or, more often, propose a moral about the vanity of worldly success and pleasure.

But there may be more lowly origins for Sly's story than the didactic; Shakespeare's version of the Awakened Sleeper resembles several older clown routines and jigs. The clown who suddenly comes into wealth was a standard comic plot (Shakespeare used it when his clownish shepherd and son are made "gentlemen born" in *Winter's Tale*). And sketches about drunken clowns were even more popular, associated with Tarlton in his jestbook and with a long line of clowns from the moralities, like the drunken Hance in *Like Will to Like* (1562–68 [1568]).[44] Baskerville's study of *The Elizabethan Jig* cites jigs about drunken sleepers which resemble Sly's adventure. In one singspiel, for example, a clever girl overhears the drunkard's plan to get her drunk and seduce her and pretends to go along with him to teach him a lesson. She lets him drink heavily while she merely sips her wine, and when he finally falls into a drunken sleep, she pours raw eggs in his lap. He wakes in amazement at this condition until he realizes that she has made him a butt.[45] His frustration is rather more crudely expressed than Sly's disappointment when his noble "wife" refuses her favors, but they belong to the same genre.

To the Wakened Sleeper and the Drunken Clown, Shakespeare added an experience which all his players were to have: being invited by a paternal lord to put on a play at his house. Sly's story is closer than any other version of the Awakened Sleeper story to a family narrative that will be elaborated more fully in *Dream* and *Henry IV*—one that recalls some of the modern actor's regressive concerns: Sly is ousted by the no longer maternal Hostess, who won't give him anything more to drink, ignores his claims of gentility, and threatens to turn him over to the paternal Law in the person of the local Constable. Shakespeare's is the only version of the Awakened Sleeper which makes Sly's adventure grow out of a woman's rejection. (Most versions pay no attention to how the beggar came to be lying where the lord could find him; a male tapster ousts Slie in *A Shrew* and a male Host appears in *Histriomastix*.) The Hostess is not only a "shrew" herself (could the original audience have thought that Sly's was the taming plot?) but a bad mother.[46] And Sly has more of the Shakespearean clown's childlike appeal than any of his analogues. Even in the middle of his rant he is harmless, and our sympathy grows as his humility manifests itself and—unlike *A Shrew*'s Slie—attempts, with some dignity, to maintain his own identity after his transformation: "I am Christophero Sly, call me not 'honour' nor 'lordship.' I ne'er drank sack in my life" (*Shr.* Ind. 2.5–6).

It is to this relatively agreeable "beggar" that a dream is given. Instead of being arrested, Sly is taken up into a world where dreams come true. His is a Hansel and Gretel story: starved and thrown out by his cruel Hostess, Sly finds himself awakened "wrapp'd in sweet clothes," in a "fairest chamber," with music playing to "make a dulcet and heavenly sound," and, of course,

" a most delicious banquet" by his bed (*Shr.* Ind. 1.36, 44, 49, 37). Just as important, he finds himself attended by obsequious servants, among them a new "hostess" who tells him she is his own beautiful and noble wife. And—not least, if this is a dream dreamt by an actor—the players themselves (his own players!) are here to put on a performance for him. It is a poor man's dream, the dream of the powerless, a dream of grandeur like the one Sly had already announced before the drunken stupor had overtaken him, when he told the Hostess that "the Slys are no rogues. Look in the Chronicles. We came in with Richard Conqueror" (*Shr.* Ind. 1.3–4).[47] Geoffrey Bullough even suggests that Shakespeare lifts Sly out of farce for a moment and into romance, combining the moralistic Awakened Sleeper tradition with the romance of Thomas of Erceldoune's dream of the Fairy Queen.[48] Or perhaps we might see it as the beggar's comic version of Romeo's dream:

> I dreamt my lady came and found me dead . . .
> And breath'd such life with kisses in my lips
> That I reviv'd and was an emperor.
>
> (*Rom.* 5.1.6–9)

In his dream, Sly is surrounded by Ovidian lushness and eroticism (at least in the "wanton" pictures and the wife offered to him).

Unlike Thomas's though, Sly's dream of maternal nurturance is directed by a powerful lord, like Navarre and like the master of revels who will preside over all of Shakespeare's later inner plays as well. This lord is what every father should be: an aristocrat, a manly hunter (with the purebred dogs who mark such men in the plays), a man who knows right from wrong and tells others what to think (no one contradicts him about his dogs). He provides the instruction which contains and justifies Sly's delight in the performance. Though he initiates the jest, or "passtime passing excellent," he is also disgusted by the sight of Sly's drunkenness, and uses it as a memento mori: "O monstrous beast, how like a swine he lies! / Grim death, how foul and loathsome is thine image!" (*Shr.* Ind. 1.32–33).[49] In S. Goulart's version of the Awakened Sleeper, the Prince's motive was "to make triall of the vanity of our life," and Goulart added his own lesson at the end: "O man, this stately usage of the above named Artisan, is like unto a dreame that passeth. And his goodly day, and the years of a wicked life differ nothing but in more and lesse. . . . It is a little or a great dreame: and nothing more."[50] Characteristically, Shakespeare makes the episode into something more like a practical joke, but the moralizing colors the *Shrew* Lord's first reaction to Sly. Even later in the midst of his sport, the lord injects four separate warnings about the need for "modesty," so that it will not provoke "over-merry spleen" or "grow to extremes" (*Shr.* Ind. 1.66, 135–36). Under his well-tempered auspices Sly can indulge himself without guilt, regress to infantile bliss without offending this spokesman for paternal Law. In the Lord's play Sly can even achieve the actor's dream of bringing the dead to life: he is resurrected from the image of "grim death" to become a new man.

It is significant that Sly's happy relation to the Lord emerges only through the medium of theater. Sly's transformation was effected by the lord as director manipulating Sly like an actor to fit into a script. This first "play," however, does not entirely indulge Sly. Sly's "wife" refuses him the favor he most wants when she will not come to bed with him. Neither his longing for the services of the rejecting hostess and wife, nor his yearning to be identified with a manly father (the missing "Richard Conqueror" whom he invoked to protect him against the hostess) are satisfied. But the theatrical relation between him and the Lord is further elaborated by the second play, which the Lord stages *for* the tinker. In that twice-distanced play-within-the-dream, Sly finally sees a strong, happy Petruchio[51] subdue a woman and demand the service from her which Sly has been refused. If the Hostess has left Sly for dead, Sly gains vicarious revenge when Petruchio "kill[s his] wife with kindness."[52]

The presentation of the play unites Sly and the Lord, despite their unequal status, in complicity against the "shrew." The inner play about a heterosexual union turns out to be a gift from one man to another. It implies a bond like the one Freud describes between the teller of a dirty joke and his audience, a bond which links the two men more closely than it links either of them to the woman who is usually the butt of the joke. The Lord does not offer Sly his own wife, but he offers him a funny play about a wife to laugh at. Actually, the Lord does offer Sly a sort of "wife," and since that wife is a page in drag—reminding us that "Katherine" in the inner play is also a boy actor—the suggestion of male bonding permeating heterosexual union is even stronger. There may also be a suggestion that Sly and the Lord do in some sense share the "wife" after all, because the Lord takes unusual interest in this page. He seems to know already that "the boy will well usurp the grace, / Voice, gait and action of a gentlewoman"—something he longs to hear (*Shr.* Ind. 1.129–31). Such remarks on an Elizabethan stage would have been heard in the context of the gossip about erotic encounters between players and the boy players thought to serve as "ingles." The Lord's little joke is not very different from the offstage games which Jonson would later describe in *The Devil's Law Case,* where one of the players' boys gives an offstage performance as a woman. Perhaps not only is the Lord necessary to realize Sly's fantasies, but Sly is also necessary for the Lord to work out his own;[53] at any rate, the performance—like all theatrical performances—draws the two together even while it marks the boundary between them.

In the end, the Lord's gift to Sly is only a sport, and the dream vanishes. Or so we assume, for at this point Sly himself disappears from Shakespeare's text, never to be disillusioned on stage, at least in the Folio. A possible lost ending for his story is suggested by *A Shrew,* where Sly awakens a beggar again and announces that he will put into practice the lesson he's learned about taming shrews in his dream. As Karl P. Wentersdorf has argued, this possibility is supported by the fact that Shakespeare's text allows for—and at one point even seems to demand—interruptions by scenes inserted as Sly's would be.[54] Sly is so closely related to Bottom that it is tempting to believe he too must have had an opportunity to comment on his most rare vision. Whether or not he did, however, the implication is that awake he must, even if Shakespeare minimized the necessity by refusing to show the awakening on stage. *Shrew* is a fantasy about disillusionment as well as fulfillment. What the Lord does is finally in its way a repetition of what the Hostess had done: Sly is allowed into the house, cared for—then thrown out again. For Sly, the story of the King and the Beggar merges with the flattering dream of kingship that overwhelms so many better men and women. In their cases—in the case of Margaret in *Richard III,* of Richard II, of Queen Katherine in *Henry VIII,* true royalty proves as insubstantial as any man's dream. Sly was not born a king; his dreams of royalty derive from having received the attention of a powerful lord who stages them for him.

Of course this is a far from complete account of what is happening in Shakespeare's play. In the inner play about the two sisters which forms the main body of the play, the motives for playing, the relation among players, the subtle effects of playing are far more complex, and are more grounded in the realities of social life. The relation to hunting and "the special ability of acting to embrace and give form to violence," are worked out more thoroughly.[55] The transformations which Katherine undergoes are not nearly so much a matter of purely private regressive fantasy as they are a matter of learning to integrate private and public experience, desire and its socially acceptable modes of expression. Indeed, one of the ways in which Shakespeare encourages us to see the importance of Katherine's playing is to contrast it with Sly's much more superficial experience. And yet, strictly speaking, Sly's is the only real experience in the play. It is or course a joke to make the clown frame "real" and the main plot into a "play"—a joke which Shakespeare never repeated. But Sly's story is prior to Katherine's; it is the ground out of which hers emerges as more compelling, more complex, though from one point less substantial. Shakespeare's first comedy (if it is that) emerges as the dream of a beggar playing in a great man's house.

* * *

Stage history of the play is unknown, but one wonders whether it could have been produced at a great house near Stratford.[56] Sly's plot is certainly autobiographical in its setting. Says Arden editor Brian Morris, "Shakespeare's tinker goes out of his way to establish his origins at Burton Heath and Wincot, with Marian and Cicely Hacket, Peter Turph and old John Naps of Greece. . . . The whole atmosphere—with its lord, its country house, its hunting, its pedlars, cardmakers and bear-herds—is redolent of the countryside around Stratford. . . . No other play in the canon refers so specifically and extensively to the county of his birth."[57] This needn't indicate that, as Morris argues, *Shrew* was one of Shakespeare's earliest plays—such memories do not disappear—but it is odd, not only for Shakespeare, but also for the drama of the period, to be so specific. Local names like this in an interlude text are thought to be references to performance sites; perhaps those in *Shrew* indicate a self-referential performance at some manor in the country around Stratford.[58] If so, the joke about the unappreciated importance of a clownish and beggarly player like Sly may have had a special point in the circumstances, and may have called attention to the actual exchange between the dominant lord and the servile players performing *Shrew* for him. The Induction includes another quasi-joke on Shakespeare's audience, the only other sign here of the kind of teasing which would predominate in *Love's Labour's Lost's*—and, as we'll see, in *Dream's*—self-consciousness about its status as a play. The Lord greets one of the players with compliments about his earlier performance as "Soto," and audiences would recognize the remark as reference to the play *Woman Pleased* (ca. 1620 but perhaps existing in an earlier version) in which Soto appears.[59] Reference to that play, a version of *The Wife of Bath's Tale,* would have roused expectations in *Shrew's* audience that they were about to see another story in which women tame men.[60] But, having prompted such associations, the Lord then provides a play on exactly the opposite theme.[61] He plays with their expectations just as Shakespeare does at the end of *Love's Labour's Lost.*

Apart from the geography, the play's concern with social mobility may have had a personal meaning for Shakespeare that added to the charged relation between *Shrew's* actors and their aristocratic audience. Playing allows Sly to be taken into a great house where he will not only be pampered but will finally become a "gentleman born" (*WT* 5.2.128–39, passim). Shakespeare's family had its own dreams of gentility—John Shakespeare had applied, unsuccessfully, for a coat of arms. One basis for the application was John's claim that his late grandfather had done faithful service for Henry VII—like Sly's claim that his ancestors had come over with "Richard Conqueror." Another basis was Mary Arden's inheritance, now lost to Shakespeare's uncle Edmund from Sly's own Barton-on-the-Heath. If Sly's story does draw on Shakespeare's class ambitions, perhaps there is an answer to Morris's editorial query about one of Shakespeare's sources. Gerard Legh's *Accedens of Armory* (1562), seems to be the source for the episode in *Shrew*'s main plot where Petruchio rants against the tailor who slashed Katherine's gown. But the *Accedens* is a treatise on the science of armorial bearings: why, asks Morris, was Shakespeare reading a book like that at the time? [62] Shakespeare's armorial ambitions may provide an answer: Legh's tale describes the perils of an upwardly mobile shoemaker. The shoemaker asked his tailor to make a gown for him of the same style and material the tailor was using for Sir Caulthrop's gown. When Sir Caulthrop came to the tailor's, saw the imitation and discovered the shoemaker's intent, he ordered the tailor to slash his own gown to shreds. Of course the tailor then slashed the shoemaker's gown as well—and the shoemaker's furious tirade followed. In any case, although the anecdote turns up in Katherine's plot, it was more appropriate to Shakespeare's—or at least to Sly's—social transformation than to Katherine's psychological transformation.

Finally, as we have noted, Sly's relation to the noble Lord who welcomes him into his home and then rejects him may also have had special significance for the poet of the sonnets—the poet whom Simon Callow recognized as an actor "at the root of his being." Like Sly, though more conscious of what was going on, the poet was sustained by a great man's attentions which proved to be illusory. And he too describes himself as a kind of Awakened Sleeper:

> Thus have I had thee as a dream doth flatter:
> In sleep a king, but waking no such matter.
>
> (Son. 87, 13–14).

Bottom in Theseus's Palace: Player as Little Boy

In *Midsummer Night's Dream* Shakespeare again combines the inner play with the clown's plot, and the result is comedy that—unlike that in some other clown scenes—still works effortlessly for modern audiences. The uncertain balance between theatrical self-deprecation and theatrical pride in *Shrew*'s Induction gives way in *Dream*—temporarily—to a moment of perfect poise. *Dream*'s amateur players are even more important inside this play then Sly was in the framing context for *Shrew*. Bottom, who leads them (though Quince is their nominal chief), is a metropolitan reincarnation of Christopher Sly and goes through a similarly delusive dream. A notch or two above the strolling tinker—he is established in the city (like the London players) and no longer a loner—still, like Sly he is optimistic, ignorant of his ignorance, self-confident and possessed of considerable dignity in the face of his absurd good fortune. And he is still mechanical, rude, and a figure of fun. But important differences make his experience as player richer and more significant than Sly's, though no less ridiculous. Shakespeare's

Athens is a world devoted on one level to producing heirs as a stay against mortality. Theseus's wedding is the occasion for the plot (as, most likely, some noble wedding was the occasion for the play), and appropriately he banishes melancholy forth "to funerals" in order to celebrate the new life which marriage symbolizes. The play's action moves from the betrothal to the fairy's wedding-bed blessing intended to ensure children without "blot" or mark. Bottom, whose play is the culmination of the wedding ceremony, has no children—like the "Athenian eunuch" who offered to sing for Theseus's wedding—but he becomes a child in Titania's arms. This experience "in the cradle of the fairy queen" not only provides a model of happy union towards which the play's more fertile lovers struggle, but also inspires him to embellish his performance. With it, Shakespeare gives us something like a portrait of the actor as a young child—appropriately enough in a play so centered on the players' performance.

The structural similarities between Sly's experience and Bottom's are striking. Sly, ejected from the tavern to the ground outside, is taken up into the Lord's "play." When Bottom and his fellow mechanicals go into the forest outside Athens to rehearse a play for the Duke's wedding, Bottom, too, unwittingly becomes part of a play which Oberon, the Fairy King, is staging to punish his wife Titania, making her fall in love with the first creature she sees. Once again a clown leaves behind a difficult life and unwittingly becomes part of a dream of fulfillment. The dream is orchestrated, again, by an arrogant aristocrat to teach a lesson about the evils of self-indulgence. As in *Shrew,* the union promised in the dream—Sly's with his page-wife and Bottom's with Titania—is frustrated, and the dream gives way to a theatrical production which redirects the player's fears and desires. Like Sly's play it is also, more directly, a way of making contact with the father who runs the show, and of substituting this contact for the lost dream of maternal embrace. It helps Bottom to move, as mortal changelings must, from the static enclosure of Titania's "bower" to the mobile thrust of Oberon's "train,"[63] or more literally, to Theseus's company of players, on retainer of "six pence a day during his life" (*MND* 4.2.19–20).

Though Bottom is not literally evicted from Athens as Sly was from the Hostess's tavern, Athens is "hell" (*MND* 1.1.207) on its children, who run from it to the dreamworld of the forest. The harsh realities of Athens's patriarchal fathers have been well explored recently, but Athens is a world of harsh matriarchal mothers as well—insofar as it has room for mothers at all.[64] Its one mature female presence is Hippolyta the Amazon, for Elizabethans a subversive woman who threatens civilization as they see it and must be conquered—as Theseus has wooed her with sword and won her by doing injuries (*MND* 1.1.16–17). Whatever sympathy we may have for her position, when the play opens, Hippolyta is a queen as cold as the waning Athenian moon, and as tight as the drawn bow it resembles.[65] Hippolyta, unlike Sly's Hostess, does not literally throw Bottom out but like all Amazons has regularly thrown out all her baby sons, if indeed she hasn't killed them. A breastless woman in a moonless city, she is a Volumnia in the making, or a mother like Thisbe's, appropriately played by "Starveling" (MND 1.2.56).[66] Her coldness becomes more evident later when she reacts to the players. Though she can accept irrationality (she finds constancy in the lovers' reports which Theseus dismisses), she does not suffer fools at all. She twice rejects the mechanicals' play, once in the offing, and once, less forgivably, in performance. Even the tough Princess in Love's Labour's Lost is more gentle, more generous at a similar moment. Hippolyta remains aloof from the players even at the end, when she seems to achieve a more open and mutual relation with Theseus.

Appropriately enough, above her kingdom shines a harsh moon-mother—as Theseus describes it, "a step-dame or a dowager / Long withering out a young man's revenue" (MND 1.1.5–6).[67] The children of Athens escape to the forest where a more lovingly generous dowager dotes and one needn't either compete or wait for her bounty: the "dowager / Of great revenue," as Lysander tells Hermia, who "respects me as her only son" (MND 1.1.157–60). The moon that shines over Athens is a "cold fruitless moon" (MND 1.1.73), enforcing chastity in a convent where virgins chant faint hymns to her, not actually even shining, or quickly disappearing when it does. By contrast the forest moon weeps "lamenting some enforced chastity" and provides her light throughout (MND 3.1.192).[68]

The contrast between the two moons is matched by that between the two queens, as Bottom discovers when Titania finds him in the forest and takes him for an "angel," despite his magical translation into an ass (MND 3.1.124). If Hippolyta is cold, Titania is warmly sensual, fertile and child-loving. If Hippolyta threw out baby boys, Titania has adopted one. While Hippolyta scorns Bottom's play and his class, Titania finds his deplorable song angelic and calls him a gentleman. We are constantly reminded that Hippolyta is a warrior and huntress, but we forget Titania's origins in Ovid's Titania or Diana, goddess of the hunt. Ovid's Diana had banished her pregnant votress, while this one adores hers.[69] When Actaeon stumbled accidentally into her bower, Ovid's Diana (called Titania) turned him into a stag so that his own dogs attacked and killed him. This Titania welcomes Bottom into her bower, ass's head and all.[70] And there, far from criticizing him, she cherishes him with a mother's perfect love, entwining him in her arms, feeding him honeybags, singing him lullabies, and doting on his every word and move.[71] There is no one else, no husband, no other child: she loves him as the dowager loves Lysander, as her "only son."[72] We do hear about the little "changeling child" to whom Titania had been so devoted and whom Oberon has taken away. But we never see that Indian boy, and the asinine Bottom, who has taken that lovely child's place in her lap, is the only literal changeling in the play. Bottom is the boy's ugly substitute—the replacement child—and he is loved anyway. Wish fulfillment indeed.[73]

As in Sly's experience, the movement from one world, one moon, one mother, to another is effected by a master of ceremonies—a father-director who is both a hunter and a moralizer. Here the master's role is shared by Theseus and Oberon. Theseus's Athenian wedding provides the occasion for Bottom's dream, and his hunting excursion marks its boundaries when he discovers the sleeping lovers in the forest—as Sly's Lord had come upon Sly—in the midst of his disquisition on his hounds. Oberon arranges the dream and comments on it. Together the two men officiate over what will be for Bottom a far more extensive transformation than Sly's. Sly's dream was merely a practical joke, but Bottom's, while it lasts, is real—Titania does love him. Sly's dream of fulfillment was manifested largely in sensual pleasure and social status. While Bottom enjoys both these perquisites, his dream exceeds a merely mechanical imagination to incorporate the stuff of romance and of Ovidian metamorphosis. Sly's adventure may have been partly inspired by that of Thomas of Erceldoune who saw the Fairy Queen, but Bottom sees the lady herself, in the flesh. The Ovidian atmosphere, which in Sly's case was confined to "wanton pictures" (*Shr.* Ind.1.45), here takes over to more happy effect as Sly's pictures come to life. While Sly saw a painting of Daphne, in Bottom's dark forest Puck makes Daphne chase Apollo (*MND* 2.1.231). Sly was offered a picture of Venus and Adonis, but Bottom actually becomes an Adonis and lives out a happier version of Shakespeare's own "Venus and Adonis."[74] Shakespeare's Venus had stroked Adonis, coyed his cheeks and offered to dance like a fairy on the grass—but she then overpowered him, turned him into a bleeding flower, and tucked him in her bosom to wilt there forever (*Ven.* 45, 146, 1166–88). Bottom, stroked and coyed, goes on refreshed from his fairy's lap (*MND* 4.1.2); in *Dream* the flower provides the magic for a happier metamorphosis.[75]

Bottom's dream in "the cradle of the Fairy Queen" (*MND* 3.1.74) is not simply a regressive end in itself. When he wakes to describe his "most rare vision" (*MND* 4.1.203), Bottom's childlike "blur of sensation"[76] is transformed into St. Paul's mysterious vision of the things God has prepared for "them that love him": "The eye of man hath not heard, the ear of man hath not seen, man's hand is not able to taste, his tongue to conceive, nor his heart to report, what my dream was" (*MND* 4.1.209–12). The regression which facilitates the religious vision also gives Bottom a sense of what the erotic union so hotly pursued elsewhere in the forest might be. His night with the Fairy Queen suggests the mysterious marriage of "the turtle and his queen" in the *Phoenix and the Turtle*. The fairies' lullaby in *Dream* is echoed suggestively by the rites in the later poem, both songs designed to ward off intruders from the mystery ("Come not near"); as is Puck's final blessing on all the couples.[77] Bottom's understanding that "reason and love keep little company together nowadays" (*MND* 3.1.138–39), becomes a mystery in *Phoenix:*

> Reason, in itself confounded. . . .
> That it cried, How true a twain
> Seemeth this concordant one!
> Love hath reason, reason none,
> If what parts, can so remain.[78]

                                          (*PhT* 41, 45–48)

This loss of boundaries, I would suggest, also facilitates Bottom's histrionic talent, or is another version of it. With Titania he experiences the billing and cooing exchange that Weisman describes as the earliest experiences of identification in a young actor-to-be. Having once so much enjoyed being close to a woman, Bottom is ready to play Thisbe, unlike poor Flute, whose incipient manhood is threatened by the very thought of cross-dressing (*MND* 1.2.43–50).[79] Nonetheless, as in the case of Sly, beneficial as the regressive dream might be, it cannot last forever; Sly's "wife" had refused him, and Bottom's Fairy Queen now recoils when the spell ends. Like Sly's Lord disgusted by drunkenness, Oberon has no patience with the oral satisfactions of infancy; he designed his play precisely because he wanted Titania's child to move on to more manly occupations, and he wanted Titania to move on to more manly men. Once that goal is achieved, he undoes his magic.

As a result, Bottom, like Sly, progresses from being an unwitting player in his own dream to participating in an actual performance on a stage. He too exchanges consummation with his lady for consummation in a play—but in this case with a difference. For Sly, an unwitting actor in one play and mere audience to the second, the theatrical experience was entirely passive. Bottom's unwitting stint as an actor, however, rouses him to command a ballad of his own choosing and to offer to sing it during his performance of Pyramus. For Sly the play was a continuation of the illusory dream; for Bottom it is a return to reality. Bottom never for a moment considers looking for the Fairy Queen—unlike Slie in *A Shrew*, who vows to make his dream come true; and unlike Spenser's Arthur—or the comic Sir Thomas of Erceldoune—who woke from a dream of the Fairy Queen to seek her duplicate in the real world. Bottom makes his lost dream into art for the Duke; he discovers the only way to make dreams come true: "I will get Peter Quince to write a ballad of this dream: it shall be called 'Bottom's Dream' . . . and I will sing it in the latter end of a play, before the Duke.

Peradventure, to make it the more gracious, I shall sing it at her death" (*MND* 4.1.212–17). No one would make too much of Bottom's motives here; he is simply staking out his claim to a piece of the main action, unlike a jig-maker who comes in only "at the latter end of a play." His ballad will no doubt be a poor thing, if it is anything in the style of "Pyramus and Thisbe." But Bottom's instincts are sound. The dream loss of Titania blends imperceptibly into the art loss of Thisbe, both made "more gracious" by Bottom's creation.[80]

Shrew's players had made the standard claims for drama's curative properties and its ability to lengthen life. But from Sly's point of view the play was at best an escape from frustration and a displacement of desire. Bottom's play works as a displacement too—for him and for the newly-married Athenians who use it to "wear away this long age of three hours" before bedtime (*MND* 5.1.33). But it is something more as well. The mechanicals may have created an esthetic failure, and they may not only rehearse but also present it "most obscenely" (*MND* 1.2.100–1); nonetheless their tragic mirth has redeeming social value. When Bottom as player gains entry into this Athenian great house, he brings with him a glimpse of the "melancholy" facts of life which Theseus thought he had banned from his wedding (*MND* 1.1.14). He reminds the wedding guests of the nightmare variations possible in a midsummer dream. Bottom's play gives local habitation and a name to the destructive erotic forces which Theseus thinks he can control by selecting some of them to solemnize in a legal wedding ceremony—just as he thinks he can control murderous violence by sanctioning some of it in the aristocratic ritual of the hunt.[81] Theseus rejects two of the offered wedding entertainments—"The battle with the Centaurs" and "The riot of the tipsy Bacchanals,/ Tearing the Thracian singer in their rage" (*MND* 5.1.45, 48–49)—each of which records the violence which frustrated male or female erotic desire can inflict.[82] But Bottom's play, which passed the censor, reveals the destructive sexuality even in mutual desire, when the lovers—at least consciously—want only to love one another. The young Athenian lovers blame their parents and the harsh world for their crosses, like viewers blaming Athens's flaws wholly on its patriarchal structure—"O hell! to choose love by another's eyes!" (*MND* 1.1.40). But Pyramus, as Quince says, is by definition "a lover who kills himself" (*MND* 1.2.20). Love is always already doomed before the parents even discover it.

Bottom wants to write a prologue explaining that "Pyramus is not killed" (*MND* 3.1.17–18), and he believes in a world where he can have his Thisbe and Lion can eat her too; but as the play shows, there is no such world. Pyramus and Thisbe meet at Ninny's tomb partly because of parental restraint—as Romeo and Juliet met at the Capulet's tomb—but just partly. The tomb is the only appropriate site for their rendezvous with destiny: this kind of love *is* death. Tearing down the wall between the genders is catastrophic. In Bottom's play Lion materializes absurdly out of nowhere to symbolize the devouring, deflowering erotic violence no one wants to hear about in Athens (though Hermia does dream about it). The play may not represent what actually happened in the forest, only its potential; but Lion's attack is an unhappily accurate figure for what will happen to Hippolytus, the child born of Theseus's and Hippolyta's union.[83] For the time being, however, Bottom's play exorcises these forces—as they were so often exorcised in the folk plays which "Pyramus and Thisbe" resembles.[84] Bottom, though killed for love, bounces up again like the fool in the mummer's play, ready to dance a bergomask. Sly, an image of "grim death" (*Shr.* Ind. 1.32), was passively resurrected by the Lord's play in *Shrew* when he was dressed in new clothes and made a new man; but Bottom revives himself.

It would no more occur to Bottom to expound his play as I have just done than to expound his dream; he simply considers it a "very good piece of work" (*MND* 1.2.13). It is Shakespeare who shapes Bottom's playing here, as he shaped Bottom's dream earlier, to be a much more respectable enterprise than Sly's. From Bottom's point of view, the play is primarily a means of pleasing the Duke; and as in *Shrew,* the performance does effect an otherwise impossible meeting between them. One of the most amusing aspects of "Pyramus and Thisbe" is the unnecessary lengths to which the players are prepared to go in order to please the Duke. The mechanicals' compliance should be seen in the context of widespread artisan efforts to accommodate to the aristocracy during the period of the rebellions of the 1590s.[85] But although Bottom's desire to please may be aimed primarily at facilitating a relation with the entire class of nobles who could either "hang us every mother's son" (*MND* 1.2.73) or provide "six pence a day during . . . life" (*MND* 4.2.19–20), he also seems more personally involved with the Duke, just as Armado was with Navarre.

Bottom's "intents," as Philostrate describes them to the Duke, are "Extremely stretch'd and conn'd with cruel pain / To do you service" (*MND* 5.1.79–81)—as if the service itself, even without reward, were satisfying. There is an element of childish narcissistic delight in showing off for a parent when Bottom offers to play every part and can't bear to give up any opportunity to shine for Theseus. Bottom is concerned not to "fright the ladies" with either a live lion or with a dead Pyramus (*MND* 1.2.74), but most of all he wants to please the Duke; and in this patriarchal world the mechanicals think of themselves as providing entertainment for "his wedding," as they say (*MND* 1.2.6–7). That's why Theseus's rudeness to the players is telling, though it is less vicious than Navarre's or Berowne's in *Love's Labour's Lost.* Once again the nobles insult, or even merely analyze the players as if they were not there—like children, or slaves, or animals. The aristocrats, women as well as men this time, use the mechanicals' performance as an occasion to show off their own wit, ironically turning the clowns' own weapon against them and resorting to word-play for subversion. So they turn Bottom's "tragic" death into an opportunity to call him an ass:

> *Bottom:* Out sword, and wound /. . . . Thus die, I, thus, thus, thus, / Now am I
> dead, / Now am I fled. . . . / Now die, die, die, die, die.
> *Demetrius:* No die [i.e., singular of dice], but an ace for him. . . .
> *Lysander:* Less than an ace, man for he is dead, he is nothing.
> *Theseus:* With the help of a surgeon he might yet recover and prove an ass.
>
> (*MND* 5.1.285–99)

Bottom is oblivious to the attack and the occasion remains less painful than its parallel in *Love's Labour's Lost*. But the potentially dangerous—or at least humiliating—confrontation is similar. "Bottom is gored by an audience, not by a boar," Staton says, comparing the play to Shakespeare's *Venus and Adonis*, but the scent of the hunt remains.[86] Even Theseus's famous defense of "Pyramus and Thisbe," after Hippolyta calls it "the silliest stuff that I ever heard," is no more than faint praise (*MND* 5.1.207); and he goes on to a patronizing dismissal of playing which extends to all professionals as well as to the tacky amateurs on stage at the moment.

* * *

As Barber notes, the pointed reference to sixpence a day for life would not go unremarked by the (presumably) aristocratic audience for *A Midsummer Night's Dream*.[87] Shakespeare's metadramatic self-reference is more obtrusive here than in *Shrew*. All that linked play to author in Sly's case was the beggar's general resemblance to a strolling player and the insistently Shakespearean environs of Stratford. Here we have an audaciously detailed allusion to the play's actual condition of performance. Bottom is a lowly artisan invited into a great lord's house to put on the play "Pyramus and Thisbe," full of tragic mirth, at an aristocratic wedding. Shakespeare is also a lowly artisan, coming to a great lord's house, to put on the play *A Midsummer Night's Dream,* full of tragic mirth, for that wedding. Bottom, like Shakespeare, is theatrically gifted. How "gracious" of Shakespeare, then, to make Bottom foolish, lowly, an ass, a bumbler, and of course entirely well-meaning: all service and eagerness and willingness to work hard, if also eagerness for a duly appreciated reward. How very much the performance—its reception rather—means to him. No offense, no offense in the world, as the prologue says, or seems to say. The offense, as we have noted, comes entirely from the audience.

But when Chaucer told the story of Theseus and Hippolyta in *The Knight's Tale,* one of the main sources for Shakespeare's play, he too accom-

panied it by a story of a silly bumbling image of himself, Chaucer the pilgrim, telling his ridiculously inept and old fashioned story of the Fairy
Queen.[88] That notoriously ironic portrait suggests that "Chaucer's naïveté
is wiser and more humane than the sophistication of the noblest pilgrims.
The equally gentle ironies in the presentation of Bottom suggest that Shakespeare might have had a similar perspective on the social divisions within
his play. Bottom, as nearly every commentator notes, is at the visionary
center of the play. Bottom is *deep*. He is portrayed with some sense of the
appealing richness Shakespeare later gave to that other player, Rosalind,
so many fathoms in love ("My affection hath an unknown bottom";
AYL 4.1.197–98). The nobility, by contrast, are shown to misunderstand
both love and drama, to be neither generous or noble in their treatment of
the players, beyond the minimal and patronizing noblesse oblige.

Shakespeare triumphs over his audience even in the midst of the self-
deprecatory portrayal of players; "Pyramus and Thisbe" is the culmination
of *Dream;* it is a total success in its failure. And, although the Duke announces "No epilogue" for Bottom's play (*MND* 5.1.341), Shakespeare includes one for his own play that gently insults the audience. As Puck takes
his leave with the Epilogue's usual obsequious gesture toward the audience,
his words belie his posture, and he manages to do what the "Pyramus" Prologue had ineptly promised: to "offend . . . with good will" (*MND* 5.1.108):

> If we shadows have offended,
> Think but this and all is mended,
> That you have but slumber'd here
> While these visions did appear.
> And this weak and idle theme,
> No more yielding but a dream.
>
> (*MND* 5.1.409–14)

"It's only an idle dream" might pass as modest self-depreciation in any other
epilogue, but this entire play has been devoted to the power both of "love-
in-idleness" (*MND* 2.1.168) and of "dreams." Anyone who accepts their
devaluation now has missed the point of the play—or, as Puck says, has
slept through the play. The resentment Bottom never feels—at least never
expresses—energizes Puck's address to the audience (as it perhaps fuels his
"mistake" in carrying out the orders of his master-within-the-play, Oberon).
But it is after all Puck and not Shakespeare speaking. Despite the ironies, in *Dream* Shakespeare creates his most affectionate portrait of the
player, representing himself with an urbane self-mockery that will become
self-loathing only in later plays.

Chapter Five

Player King as Beggar in Great Men's Houses—II

Falstaff in the House of Lancaster: Player as Dog

*F*alstaff has only the briefest stint as a harlotry player, to use Mistress Quickly's term (*1H4* 2.4.391), and, strictly speaking, the second *Henriad*'s informal theatrics do not belong with the true inner plays in *Love's Labour's Lost, Shrew* and *Dream*.[1] But the material from the earlier plays returns in Falstaff's scenes, as if there were a connection in Shakespeare's mind between the more literal occasions of playing and this one. The beggarly player subordinated in *Shrew,* then recreated briefly as a cherished child in *Dream,* now appears at his aged best to invade the main action in the *Henriad* before being banished to justified ignominy. Falstaff, indifferent to his version of the fairy queen, Doll Tearsheet,[2] concentrates single-mindedly on playing his way into the greatest house of all, the royal House of Lancaster, where the Prince presides over Falstaff's dreams of greatness—and occasionally plays them out with him. Falstaff's relation to Hal allows him a kind of temporary comic resurrection like Sly's or Bottom's before he is finally awakened from his dream. But by now the dissatisfactions of playing emerge more clearly, and Falstaff's scenes reveal for the first time the darker aspects of service to a great lord who is a soldier and a hunter. The inner play and the player's experience serve a new and different function in the play's overall structure, at once more important and less tolerable than in *Love's Labour's Lost, Shrew,* and *Dream.* Falstaff the player is finally eliminated from the *Henriad* and replaced by a formal apparatus of Prologue, Epilogue, and Chorus who mark the play as play.

* * *

Despite Sir John's title Prince Hal, boasting that he can "drink with any tinker in his language," would probably include Falstaff among the "tinkers" he descends to; and Falstaff, knight though he may be, is no less a savvy reincarnation of Sly dreaming on better days. Like Sly he is most at home in a tavern, and he is also deeply in debt to his hostess. By the end of the second part of *Henry IV* he is threatened with arrest for a bill that reveals drinking habits similar to Sly's, both in the amount consumed and in the breakage of mugs. Falstaff may claim the prerogatives of class (like Armado, largely to the woman in his life), but with Hal he plays the beggarly servant

115

by instinct, a role W. H. Auden identified as "the prince's dog."[3] The story of the beggar Lazarus and the glutton Dives comes easily to Falstaff's lips (he identifies with the beggar; 1H4 3.3.30–32, 4.2.25).

Falstaff's "insouciant mastery"[4] in Henry IV, Part One allies him even more closely to Bottom than to Sly.[5] Though he is more the prince's jester, especially in Henry IV, Part One, where he appears only at Hal's side, Falstaff is clownish like Bottom. Shakespeare drew on the clown Cob in The Famous Victories of Henry V, as well as on "Oldcastle" in creating Falstaff, originally named Oldcastle himself. J. Dover Wilson argued that Falstaff was played by the Chamberlain's clown Kempe (there is no other identified "clown" in the Henry IV plays), and it is possible that he was modeled on the clown-actor Tarlton.[6] But clown or not, he is histrionic to the core. Both he and Bottom come alive pretending, and can slip weasellike from role to role, recovering with undiminished self-respect after being made victim of a practical joke—like Tarlton goaded by his audience.

Their primary medium for recovery is drama. When the dream evaporates both turn to a play, whether much rehearsed in Bottom's case or extempore in Falstaff's.[7] After Bottom recovers after his night of asshood in the forest, he next enters calling "Where are these lads? Where are these hearts? . . . every man look o'er his part: for the short and long is, our play is preferred" (MND 4.1.25, 35). Likewise, as soon as Falstaff recovers himself—and, he believes, the money—after his embarrassment on Gad's Hill, he calls "Gallants, lads, boys, hearts of gold . . . What, shall we be merry, shall we have a play extempore?" (1H4 2.4.273–76). Falstaff will not be put off by the king's messenger who arrives just then summoning Hal to war. He insists on a play to "practice" Hal's answer to the king, with himself of course playing the King. The Boarshead, we should remember, was an actual playing site in Shakespeare's London. Falstaff's preparations for this play sound like the mechanicals' rehearsal, and Shakespeare must have had it in mind, consciously or otherwise: "This green plot shall be our stage," says Quince (MND 3.1.3); says Falstaff, "This chair shall be my state, this dagger my sceptre" (1H4 2.4.243–44). Falstaff is quite conscious of flowing "in King Cambyses' vein" (1H4 2.4.382), while Bottom unwittingly echoes that general vein in his tragic climax. Like a true player, Falstaff can weep on demand and can change roles in an instant and play the son to Hal's "father"—just as Bottom can play Lion, Hercules, or even, joyously, Thisbe herself. We don't see Falstaff play a woman until Merry Wives of Windsor, but Hal seems confident that he could. Carried away by his own dramatic sketch of Hotspur at breakfast, Hal wants to take it further: "I'll play Percey, and that damned brawn [Falstaff] shall play his wife." (1H4 2.4.107).

"Playing" in a general sense is a chronic condition for Falstaff. "From an actor's point of view," as Auden observed, "the role of Falstaff thus has the enormous advantage that he only has to think of one thing—playing to an audience."[8] He addresses them directly at moments throughout the play, especially when flaunting his rebellions against honor, society, and other constraints.[9] But like Sly and Bottom, Falstaff is also an *unwitting* player in a dream of greatness, facilitated by an aristocratic master of ceremonies who will interrupt the play and discard the player. The notorious banishment scene, which Shakespeare's design requires at the end of *Henry IV, Part Two,* has been seen as specific to the history plays and to Falstaff. It is, to be sure, an essential part of the morality and epic traditions which shape Hal's story. But the tone is pure Shakespeare and the scene a reworking of the lesser but related "banishments" in the two earlier great house plays. The overdetermined banishment is even more complex when seen in the context of Shakespeare's continuing myth about the player's fate.

Sly's banishment from nobility we cannot discuss, unless we assume it resembled that in *A Shrew.* There the tinker wakes a beggar again but believes he is enlightened, and he is able, one feels, to absorb the inevitable disillusionment as cheerfully as ever. Bottom's banishment from Titania's lap is also relatively painless. It occurs at the midpoint of his experience, a prelude to greater participation in his Lord's world—and, it seems likely, in the Lord's grant of sixpence a day. But Falstaff's awakening comes at the very end of his experience in *Henry IV, Part Two;* the next we hear of him he has died offstage in *Henry V.* The audience's response to his dismissal is far more complex than in the other plays. It is not so much the banishment itself that pains audiences: Falstaff is ousted, but only until he reforms; and he will be paid a knight's equivalent of "six pence a day during . . . life" (*MND* 4.2.19–20). But Hal's tone is withering. The original detachment of Hal's private calculations in the tavern—"I know you all"—is nothing compared to Hal—now Henry—'s "I know thee not, old man," at the end of the play (*1H4* 1.2.190, 5.5.47). He annuls his play with Falstaff by reducing it to "a dream"—and unlike Puck in the epilogue to *Dream,* he means it. Hal gives Falstaff what, according to morality tradition, he needs, but not what he desires. The unpaid emotional debt is externalized as the thousand pounds payment to which Falstaff's mind first turned when he heard about Hal's coronation. ("A thousand pound, Hal? A million, thy love is worth a million, thou owest me thy love"; *1H4* 3.3.135–37.) Falstaff is not spared, as the others were, full recognition of the discrepancy between his dream of acceptance and his patron's disgust. Hal confronts Falstaff with the self-righteous moralizing which Sly's lord had uttered only when Sly couldn't hear. He conveys the loathing Titania felt when she awakened from her dream, but he speaks it to Falstaff's face.

Falstaff's difference from his predecessors and his new function in the play emerge most obviously at the level of character, in his relation to Hal, which is both more intimate and more ambivalent than the other players' relation to their Lords.[10] Sly's play and Bottom's had been preceded by dreams of maternal nurturance—a noble wife for Sly, a fairy queen for Bottom—in each case staged by the presiding lord. But there is no page-wife here, and only Doll Tearsheet to take the place of a fairy queen. With her, Falstaff goes through a pathetic replay of Bottom's dream in the tavern where Hal, like Oberon, stands back to watch. Like Titania caressing Bottom, Doll scratches Falstaff's head ("clawing like a parrot," says Hal, as disgusted as Oberon was; 2H4 2.4.256–57). But while Titania cradled Bottom in her arms, Doll has no choice but to sit on top of Falstaff; and while Bottom was simply an "elm" (MND 4.1.43), Falstaff is a "withered elder" tree and a "dead elm" (2H4 2.4.256, 328). Rather than feeding him dainties Doll advises him to give up his indulgences; rather than promising to purge him of mortal grossness she capitulates to mortality and tells him to think on his end. "Do not speak like a death's-head," he says, but then adds, "I am old, I am old" (2H4 2.4.231, 268). Oberon had seen Titania and Bottom as monstrous, but most audiences find their coupling attractive in its own way. We come much closer to sharing Hal's view of Falstaff's dalliance, especially after Hal reveals himself and Falstaff coolly repudiates Doll along with the lies he had been telling her about Hal. Titania's devotion to Bottom had evoked an emotional center for the adult lovers in the rest of the play, an ideal of closeness that is immature and limited, but still to be desired. Falstaff, however, embodies infantile passions against which Hal's entire world is marshaling itself; it presents them with the distaste reserved for old people trying to be young. While Titania's votress was pregnant, here Doll's pregnancy is specious: Quickly's "votress" has nothing to show for all the foining. She is a sterile fertility goddess.

Most important, she means very little to Falstaff.[11] Bottom was centered by his affair with the Fairy Queen, goddess of the moon, but Falstaff's life revolves around his affair with the sun king Henry, clouded though he may be at this stage. And an affair it is. Shakespeare was supposed to have deviated from the Falstaff of the histories when he created Falstaff in love in Merry Wives of Windsor to please Queen Elizabeth. But in Henry IV, Part Two he had already shown Falstaff as much in love as he will ever be. The knight has designs on the prince, but he also needs and adores Hal, and in contrast to Merry Wives, the need is the first note sounded by Falstaff in this play. It's a joke, but with truth in it: "I have forsworn his company hourly any time this two and twenty years, and yet I am bewitched with the rogue's company." (1H4 2.2.15–17). The dream of nurturance, as Sly and Bottom knew it, is further reversed. Not only does Falstaff look to the father rather than the mother for satisfaction. In addition, rather than being a child cared for by a parent-lord, he becomes the parent caring for the child-lord. Aged visibly by the end of the second play, Falstaff feels old even in *Henry IV, Part One,* and twice he mentions Hal's age, twenty-two, in contrast to his own; in the play extempore, he plays Hal's father. In *Dream,* Bottom was the "changeling child" Oberon and Titania were fighting about; here Falstaff is competing with King Henry IV for possession of the changeling Hal (*1H4* 1.1.85–88). This is no longer a child's dream but an old man's dream of vicariously recapturing the pleasures of being an adored child, by adoring someone younger. Falstaff's satisfactions are indirect, as the sonnet poet's are, when he urges the fair young man to marry.

For a time Hal too is more implicated in the relation than either of the two earlier lords. The tavern life is more important to Hal than he admits; and even after he aligns himself with the serious politicians, he remains loyal enough to gild Falstaff's lies about service in battle. Hal is also more democratic than either Sly's or Bottom's lord; he and Falstaff actually take turns directing. Falstaff even casts Hal momentarily as "dog": "The young Prince hath misled me. I am the fellow with the great belly, and he my dog" (*2H4* 1.2.144–45). But Hal nonetheless establishes his superior status as early as the end of their first scene, when he stands back coldly—like the *Shrew* Lord and *Dream*'s Oberon—to comment on the action. A manipulator like them, he sees Falstaff as a pawn, and he rationalizes his manipulations, this time not as a lesson for the participants but as a good career move for himself ("My reformation, glitt'ring o'er my fault, / Shall show more goodly"; *1H4* 1.2.208–9) or a useful education in the vernacular ("I can drink with any tinker in his language"; *1H4* 2.4.18–19). In the first scenes of the *Henriad,* the closeness between Falstaff and Hal is a rehearsal for banishment even before the play extempore where Hal as King Henry announces that he will "banish . . . Jack" Falstaff (*1H4* 2.4.473–74). Hal's life with Falstaff consists of a series of practical jokes—thefts, actually—in which he lets Falstaff believe he has gotten away with something only to catch him in the act, call down the law, and take it all back.

Shakespeare's thematic purpose in all this is clear; but at the level of character in this psychologically realistic play there are signs of strain and conflicting purposes. For example, as Theodore Reik asked in his analysis of this play, where is Falstaff's anger? Why doesn't he resent his subordination and humiliation? This question makes less sense in the case of Sly and Bottom who are much more subordinated to the play's design. But Falstaff's plenitude invites analysis. Reik suggests that the anger is there, but not consciously, and that Falstaff's "jolly fat man" pose helps ward off aggression. Falstaff turns to infantile pleasures of the table instead of competing with formidable adult rivals, and incorporates the world in order not to destroy it with his anger.[12] As Reik's argument predicts, Falstaff's anger emerges openly once Falstaff's oral defenses begin to fail. In *Part Two,* instead of taking things in by eating and drinking, he loses them and leaks; *Part One*'s images of eating are balanced by *Part Two*'s images of urination, vomit, and sweat. He dwindles, or says he does, and as he shrinks he gets aggressive. By the end of *Part One* he is already bullying the people most available, his famished recruits. Like Bottom greeting the fairies newly at his service in *Dream*, Falstaff reviews the potential recruits, but he takes advantage of his authority to prey on their helplessness and manipulates them far more extensively than Hal had manipulated him.[13]

Whatever his unconscious defenses, Falstaff's lack of aggression is also a conscious strategy—on both his part and Shakespeare's—that makes sense in the play's own terms. It's a strategy not all that different from Hal's own calculated performance of "the prodigal son" for his father, the narrative core of the *Henriad* which Shakespeare repeated in both parts of *Henry IV*.[14] Falstaff knows there are benefits in being a loser. He doesn't merely become "the prince's dog"; he plays it for all it's worth—just as he plays dead on the battlefield. The posture brings safety, material gain, and, most of all, what Falstaff needs even more than food: an appreciative audience. So long as the exchange holds ("I'll make a fool of myself if only you'll laugh"), his resentment is kept at bay. It's an actor's bargain. In fact Falstaff's greatest moments are triumphs of recovery from humiliation; he succeeds by lying or charming his way out of traps. In *Part Two,* Poins has caught on to the strategy: "My lord, he will drive you out of your revenge and turn all to merriment, if you take not the heat" (*2H4* 2.4.295–96). The moments we most remember when we think of Falstaff's vitality are escapes, rather than escapades: Falstaff claiming he was a coward by instinct when Hal sees through his boasting, but not Falstaff capturing Coleville.

Yet, however well we understand Falstaff and the play's design, audience discomfort still grows as Hal inevitably reneges on the supposed bargain. Hal had already begun to fail as audience in *Part One,* when he interrupted the play extempore to respond to the king's messenger, and again when he rebuffed Falstaff's battlefield joke: "What, is it a time to jest and dally now?" (*1H4* 5.3.55).[15] In *Part Two,* Hal all but disappears. Falstaff is a jester without a prince, a player without an audience. He acquires a page, as if to fill the empty other half of his habitual playing space, but it isn't the same. At first, although he is forced to spend time with substitutes like Justice Shallow, Falstaff keeps thinking about the Prince as his absent audience: "I will devise matter enough out of this Shallow to keep Prince Harry in continual laughter the wearing out of six fashions . . . and 'a shall laugh without intervallums. . . . O, you shall see him laugh till his face be like a wet cloak ill laid up!" (*2H4* 5.1.75–82). But as it becomes clearer that the Prince's appearance will be deferred for some time, Falstaff has to find another way of getting what he wants.

As he sets out to exercise his power more directly, the resentment merely latent in Sly and Bottom emerges more openly. By the time he meets Shallow in *Part Two,* Falstaff is overtly driven by the greed and envy which had

never surfaced when he was with Hal: "And now is this Vice's dagger become a squire . . . now has he lands and beefs" (*2H4* 3.2.313–14, 22).
Reversing the roles of prince and jester, Falstaff now plays with Shallow as
Hal had played with him. Shallow himself tells us that he had played Sir
Arthur's Fool Dagonet as a youth, and now he plays Falstaff's Fool. Falstaff
makes Shallow into the debased "minion" who appears so often in Renaissance drama. While Falstaff had toadied to Hal, who would one day be king,
now Shallow toadies to Falstaff who will, they all believe, one day be the
king's familiar. Hal had laughed indulgently at Falstaff's self-aggrandizing
lies; now Falstaff sneers at Shallow's: "Lord, how subject we old men are to
this vice of lying! This same starved justice hath done nothing but prate to
me of the wildness of his youth . . . and every third word a lie" (*2H4*
3.2.297–302). Even while participating in the tavern society, Hal had
stepped aside to plot his strategy: "I know you all" (*1H4* 1.2.190). Now
Falstaff stands back to manipulate Shallow. "I will fetch off these justices. I
do see the bottom of justice Shallow" (*2H4* 3.2.295–96). Hal had "stolen"
one thousand pounds from Falstaff; now Falstaff borrows that exact sum
from Shallow with no more intent of returning it than hope of getting it
back from Hal.

The exploitative elements in Falstaff's relation to Hal were only one part
of a complex relation between two men, evoking parental care for an infant
and fatherly concern for a growing boy, as well as analogues in homosocial
and homoerotic attachments on the battlefield and in the tavern. But in the
reenactment with Shallow the sexuality is more sadistic and no longer attractive. The scene begins innocently enough, with some homoerotically
suggestive joking among the recruits. It is a traditional moment for such
all-male humor, which is part of the ritual of separating from heterosexual
civic life. Falstaff asks a tailor, one of the potential recruits, "Wilt thou make
as many holes in an enemy's battle as thou hast done in a woman's petti-
coat?" (*2H4* 3.2.152–54). When one of the recruits begs off because of his
marriage—an infallible source of humor in such scenes—Bardolph tells
him that "a soldier is better accommodated than with a wife" (*2H4* 3.2.65–
66), alluding perhaps to accommodations by his fellow soldiers as well as
by the prostitute camp-follower.

However, Falstaff's jesting turns nastier when directed at Shallow. Having sneered at the Justice's portrait of himself as a ladies' man, Falstaff criti-
cizes more than Shallow's choice of clothing when he claims that the justice
"was ever in the rearward of the fashion" (*2H4* 3.2.309–10). Such euphe-
misms for sodomy, James M. Saslow suggests in his study of sixteenth-
century homoerotic relationships, were common coin. Ariosto's sixth satire
characterizes one poet by saying it was dangerous to turn your back when
sleeping with him.[16] Falstaff accuses Shallow to his face of something like
sodomy when he sees the servant boy Davy and snidely remarks that "this

Davy serves you for good uses; he is your serving man and your husband" (2H4 5.3.10–11). Unlike Sly's page—or Bottom's mate Flute beneath Thisbe's dress—this boy is "husband," not wife. But in an age when servants and pages were notorious objects of homoerotic attention, the conjunction is nonetheless suggestive. Driven by a combination of anger at Hal and disgust with his own role (he is after all an "old man" like Shallow), Falstaff seems to be accusing Shallow of the relation which he might have had with Hal—or indeed with his own page, now that Hal is gone. It is a demystified version of their friendship, or perhaps merely an older version, as the adult Capulets' marriage is an older version of Romeo and Juliet's young love. Falstaff leaves Shallow threatening "it shall go hard but I'll make him a philosopher's two stones to me" (2H4 3.2.323–24). In other words, "I'll have his balls." Falstaff is not promising to rape Shallow so much as to "fuck him over," but the scene comes as close to overt allusions to homoeroticism as any in the canon apart from Patroclus's scene with Achilles in *Troilus and Cressida,* except that here Shakespeare writes with the satire confined to scurrilous Thersites in the later play. This is the last we see of Falstaff before Hal's rejection.

In fact, to detour briefly, Patroclus is a version of the male friend who epitomizes (by exaggerating) Falstaff's combination of the roles of house jester and "male varlet." Patroclus, the one character in Shakespeare's plays explicitly engaged in same-sex love, is very much a player. With Falstaff's gift for mimicry, he makes his way into Achilles' tent explicitly as an entertainer. With Achilles he lies "upon a lazy bed the livelong day" and "breaks scurril jests" (*Tro.* 1.3.146, 147). He makes Achilles laugh by making fun of the Greek leaders, just as Falstaff had made Hal laugh by making fun of Hal's father, King Henry. "He pageants us," Ulysses complains,

> Sometime, great Agamemnon,
> Thy topless deputation he puts on,
> And like a strutting player, whose conceit
> Lies in his hamstring and does think it rich
> To hear the wooden dialogue and sound
> 'Twixt his stretch'd footing and the scaffoldage,
> Such to-be-pitied and o'er-wrested seeming
> He acts thy greatness in.
>
> (*Tro.* 1.3.151–58)

It is this actor who is called "parasite," "boy," or, more explicitly, Achilles' "male varlet" and "masculine whore" (*Tro.* 5.1.14, 16). Shakespeare's presentation of Patroclus is restrained, given the context of general degradation in *Troilus.* Though not the hero he was in *The Iliad* (he has "little stomach to the war"; *Tro.* 3.3.219), he speaks to Achilles of "your great love to me"

(*Tro.* 3.3.220) and they call each other "sweet," in a matter-of-fact way which makes their attachment seem much more real than Helen and Menelaeus's, though more low-keyed than Troilus and Cressida's. But they are hardly ever together without Thersites' corrosive presence to suggest a less attractive view of the relationship. When Thersites speaks, Patroclus becomes the epitome of the antitheatricalist's nightmare, a degenerate "hang-bye," as Stephen Gosson had called the players, who diverts his audience from the proper business of war, who brings "Patriarkes and kings [like Nestor and Agamemnon] on stage to be derided, hist and laught at" in his ridiculously strutting fusty style,[17] and who includes sexual along with histrionic services.[18]

Falstaff is not a Patroclus. But as a more self-conscious player than either Sly or Bottom, he is most pained by playing, and his encounter with "death" is correspondingly more complex. Sly had momentarily become the "image of grim death," and Bottom as Pyramus killed himself for love, but both were resurrected through theater's magic. In *Henry IV, Part One,* where Falstaff can swallow danger as well as humiliation, he too springs back from death. Early in the play we see him lying like Sly in a drunken sleep, while Hal stands over him—like the Lord moralizing over Sly—coldly assessing his flaws and assigning him a charge of foot that will kill him for sure (*1H4* 2.4.521–40; *Shr.* Ind.1.29–34). Then we see Falstaff "dead" on the battlefield while Hal eulogizes him fondly but with detachment—"death hath not struck so fat a deer today" (*1H4* 5.4.106)—as though Falstaff was simply one more obstacle now conveniently cleared away from Hal's ascent to the throne. But then in one of the most famous of Shakespearean scenes, Falstaff pops up once the coast is clear and walks away with the mortal Hotspur on his back—even more strikingly reincarnated than either Sly or Bottom. Falstaff can even rouse "dead" men to fill the ranks when ordered to impress foot soldiers: "A mad fellow met me on the way and told me I had unloaded all the gibbets and pressed the dead bodies" (*1H4* 4.2.36–38). These men are dead, we assume, because they are thin; they are "scarecrows" (*2H4* 4.2.38) or skeletons who have succumbed to the fate Falstaff's gluttony safely precludes here.[19]

But in *Part Two,* death turns and stalks Falstaff, first in the form of thinness, and then in the form of a "starved bloodhound" of a beadle who arrests his tavern companions—"Goodman death, goodman bones," they call him, "atomy" or skeleton (*2H4* 5.4.27, 28, 29)—the "fell sergeant" death who is strict in his arrest (*Ham.* 5.2.341). It is as if one of Falstaff's own corpse recruits had escaped to do the job. Though he himself does not die yet, Falstaff is more aware of the dangers he escapes than Sly or Bottom were; he is the only one who knows it is his own death he postpones. The lord in *Shrew* likened Sly to an "image of grim death," but it's Falstaff here who sees Bardolph as a death's head, and then, after the battle, sees the thing itself in Sir Walter's "grinning honor" (*1H4* 5.4.59). Even in Doll's arms he thinks on a memento mori.

* * *

Bottom's private performance for the Duke invited comparison with the performance of Shakespeare's *Midsummer Night's Dream* itself. Falstaff's "performances" for Hal—so much more private that they can no longer even be considered pure performances—have also invited biographical speculation. Falstaff has been compared to the poet Shakespeare, writing sonnets to his version of Hal;[20] but Falstaff is also very much a figure for the actor, and like Bottom, he is potentially a figure for actor-dramatist Shakespeare. Even more so: not only is he, like Bottom, a player within the play, but he also addresses the audience directly, reminding them that they are watching a play about playing. Indeed the three *Henry* plays are in other ways notably self-conscious about their status as plays. All through the *Henriad*—beginning in *Richard II*—there are suggestions of a parallel between the king's role in creating order in his country and the dramatist's role in ordering the play.[21] Then Shakespeare introduces a Prologue and Epilogue for *Henry IV, Part Two,* and finally in *Henry V* a Chorus who introduces each act and whose Epilogue closes not only this play but the entire sequence of eight plays which make up the two *Henriads*.[22] In other words, as Falstaff is cut off from his patron within the play and increasingly from his audience outside it, Shakespeare's relation to the audience changes as well.

In *Henry IV, Part One,* where Falstaff is in touch with Hal, Shakespeare uses him as the audience's main contact with the play. Hal never addresses us as "you," as Falstaff does, or speaks in the first-person plural. He may be speaking in part to us in his "I know you all" speech, when he coldly announces his plans to use his tavern friends for his own purposes, but this calculating hypocrisy does not endear him to us and we are not even sure we are meant to overhear him. By contrast, not only does Falstaff engage us in the action; in *Henry IV, Part One,* the action is structured to create and satisfy an audience's predictable expectations for a story about Hal and a patriotic victory; it builds toward battle and provides a resoundingly enjoyable one, capped by Falstaff's happy resurrection. The play keeps us engaged by promising that the fun will continue; King Henry's closing speech moves immediately from acknowledging the current triumph to forecasting the future—which includes, presumably, a further play:

> Rebellion in this land shall lose his sway,
> Meeting the check of *such another* day.
> And since this business is so fair done,
> *Let us not leave* until all our own be won.
>
> (*1H4* 5.5.41–end; italics added)

He will not leave, and that means we will not have to leave. Our theatrical holiday is still in progress.

In *Henry IV, Part Two* Hal withdraws from Falstaff and finally banishes him, reducing him from "all the world" to a scapegoat banished in order to cleanse the kingdom. Shakespeare similarly closes the play to us. The audience had already begun to withdraw sympathy from the diseased and now unforgivably flappable Falstaff—just as we withdraw sympathy from Richard III at the end of his *Henriad* when he gets too involved in his role to remember that he is only playing—to remember us. Though Falstaff still has moments of direct contact, his disquisition on "sherris-sack" the most notable of these (*2H4* 4.3.94–123), he has none after he is banished—from our presence as well as from Hal's. The play offers us less engaging intermediaries to substitute for Falstaff, surrounding itself with a formal apparatus that distances even as it addresses us. The action is introduced by Rumor, "full of tongues" (*2H4* Ind., stage direction), who tells a different kind of lie than Falstaff—with his "whole school of tongues in this belly" (*2H4* 4.3.18)— and in a very different spirit. Rumor announces that he will confuse the characters with false rumors of peace, and he makes us coconspirators by assimilating the crowd in the theater to the "blunt monster with uncounted heads" who spreads rumors for him: "But what need I thus / My well-known body to anatomize / Among my household?" (*2H4* Ind.18, 20–22). What we soon discover however is that the play misleads us too, the household retainers creating expectations for the audience, making promises and then disappointing them. We are led to expect a cleansing climactic battle, but are given only John's trick at Gaultree; we wait for Hal's reformation but get more than we bargained for when his growth forces Falstaff out of the play.[23]

The play finally ends with a strange Epilogue who reminds us of debts between himself and the audience,[24] and who continues the vaguely alienating effect created by the prologue Rumor. He *seems* nice enough. He apologizes not only for the present play—which was customary—but also for an earlier one. He offers to pay us back with *Henry IV, Part Two*, and, if the play fails to redeem the debt, he asks forgiveness (as was the fashion of obsequious Epilogues):

> I was lately here in the end of a displeasing play,[25] to pray your patience for it and to promise you a better. I meant indeed to pay you with this; which if like an ill venture it come unluckily home, I break, and you, my gentle creditors, lose. Here I promised you I would be, and here I commit my body to your mercies. Bate me some, and I will pay you some, and, as most debtors do, promise you infinitely: and so I kneel down before you—but indeed, to pray for the Queen. (*2H4* Epi.8–17)[26]

But in offering such a reconciliation he suggests antagonism. Using language of "payment," "debt," "creditors," "venturing," "coming unluckily home," and "breaking," he recalls the mercantile atmosphere of *The Merchant of Venice*, which had played about a year earlier. And going further than Rumor, who had merely "anatomized" his body for us, the Epilogue, like Antonio offering his body to Shylock's knife, offers his body to his "gentle creditors": "Here I commit my body to your mercies" (*2H4* Epi.14). The Epilogue sounds humble but he has managed to taint us with a Shylockian potential for collecting debts. The player's seeming graciousness here, like Antonio's self-sacrifice in *Merchant,* is perhaps more complex than it might seem at first.[27] Certainly the Epilogue's kneeling obeisance is ambiguously offered—and then quickly retracted—when he "waggishly," as J. Dover Wilson says, protests that he is really kneeling only for the Queen.[28] We know that modern players who "strive to please you every day," as Feste says (*TN* 5.1.407; "strife to please," the *All's Well That Ends Well* Epilogue calls his effort, *AWW* Epi.4), are highly ambivalent about the process; this Epilogue seems ambivalent as well. In an alternate or added section, the Epilogue reminds us about Falstaff's mortality even within the play's fiction, by promising to kill him in a forthcoming play—"unless a be killed with your hard opinion" (*2H4* Epi.30–31). He also alludes to "Falstaff's" reversal in the real world by distinguishing him from Sir John Oldcastle, his original and politically incorrect name which Shakespeare was compelled to change. Thus the second part of *Henry IV,* which began with a speech by an openly deceptive Rumor, ends with the slyly deceptive Epilogue who defers to us but refuses to meet all his debts ("I will pay you some, and, as most debtors do, promise you infinitely"; *2H4* Epi.15–16).

The Chorus who introduces the next and final play in the *Henriad, Henry V,* also defers to us, but with equally ambiguous and alienating effect. Here the Chorus takes over completely as audience liaison—Falstaff's role is limited to an offstage death—speaking as Prologue before every act and ending the play with his epilogue. This Chorus presents himself with the combined authority of a dramatic prologue and an epic invocation; with grand flourishes he leads us through the drama, filling in unstaged episodes and preparing us for the events in each new act; but he proves so untrustworthy a guide that readers have taken him to be an alien intrusion, added after the play was composed.[29] He is both more enthusiastic about Henry and the war, and less enthusiastic about the actors, than is justified by what we see.

But nonetheless he is more in charge of the action than our previous guide, Falstaff, had been. Falstaff had been controlled by Prince Hal; here the Chorus all but subdues King Henry to a play-within-a-play, just as Hal had cast Falstaff in inner plays of his own direction. It is true that King Henry is enough in control to stage his own "inner inner play" for the lower classes when he puts on his commoner's cloak the night before Agincourt to eavesdrop on his soldiers. But such practices are always framed by the Chorus's competing descriptions of them, by the Chorus's disillusionment with all theater, and, finally, by the Chorus's reminder in the epilogue that Henry V has not only been confined "in little room" onstage, but lived only "small time" before everything he won was lost again (*H5* Epi.3, 5). The Chorus has become a protagonist in his own right, coaching us as Henry coaches his soldiers.[30] He moves the here and now from the story to the frame, to our story. He makes the story of Henry's war into a story of telling that story. He is the culmination of the reversible actor-soldier metaphor from *Henry VI, Part One* and *Love's Labour's Lost*,[31] as the play successively presents soldiers who are actors ("*imitate* the action of the tiger," Henry tells his men; *H5* 3.1.6, italics added), and this actor who is as active as soldier and general ("Work, work your thoughts," the Chorus tells his audience, distancing us from the action even as he tries to make us responsible for it, just as Henry tries to make his soldiers responsible for their war; *H5* 3.Pro.25). No doubt the chronicle material itself demanded the changing stance with which it is presented to its audience in the *Henriad*. The parallels between the politics of state and the politics of theater emerge almost inevitably in Shakespeare's exploration of kingship, ceremony and the relation between illusion and power. But as in *Dream,* theatrical self-consciousness came also out of the nature of Shakespeare's theater as well as out of the epic material it presented. Falstaff in the *Henriad* is, like any player, a figure for the player Shakespeare, always aware of his dependence on patron and audience.

Shakespeare's relation to his audience, for better or for worse, was especially important at this time. *Dream* was written at a high point in Shakespeare's career, after he had become a sharer in the Lord Chamberlain's company; it was a moment when he could consolidate his early dramatic experiments in *Dream*'s exquisite balance, and could claim large powers for the inner play *Dream* contained. *Henry IV, Part One,* where Falstaff was called Oldcastle, was probably written not long after *Dream* in 1596, perhaps even before *The Merchant of Venice,* and performed in the winter season of 1596–97.[32] That season, however, was a time of significant reversals for Shakespeare, both private and professional. That the rest of the Henry (and Falstaff) plays were written in very different circumstances may have contributed to their diminished optimism and increased distance from the audience.[33]

Lord Cobham's objection to Oldcastle's name in *Henry IV, Part One* (and perhaps *Part Two,* if it was already on stage) had the effect of altering Oldcastle's name to Falstaff both in the existing and future plays, and perhaps of adding the last of *Part Two*'s odd epilogue. Censorship was a common enough experience for the Lord Chamberlain's men; but Cobham's objection would have had special power if it came, as is thought, in the spring of 1597. In July 1596 Shakespeare's patron, Sir Henry Carey, Lord Hunsdon and Lord Chamberlain, had died. Carey's son George Carey took over as Shakespeare's patron but not as Lord Chamberlain, so Shakespeare's company lost its title. If Cobham's complaint was made between July 1596 and his death in March 1597, Cobham would himself have been Lord Chamberlain, and Shakespeare's company therefore censored by the very office which had once protected them. Their new untitled patron demonstrated his unreliability in other ways too. In November 1596, Carey's neighbors signed a petition to prevent Shakespeare's troupe from occupying the Blackfriar's Theater which James Burbage had purchased for winter playing; George Carey made no effort to prevent them—or if he did, he left no record and had no effect. The players were now out both a playing space and a good chunk of their capital. Nashe's letter, cited earlier, about the players' insecurity dates from just this moment, when they were being "piteously persecuted by the Lord Mayor and the Aldermen; and however in their old Lord's time they thought their estate settled, it is now so uncertain they cannot build upon it."[34] Shakespeare's troupe was now merely Hunsdon's Men, with no direct tie to the court. It was a comedown in some ways like the one Shakespeare had suffered when John Shakespeare lost his title and power. The Cobham episode produced Falstaff's new name and the sacrificial hints in the *Henry IV, Part Two* epilogue; did it also contribute to that play's inhospitableness to both the player Falstaff and to its own audience?

In addition to professional vulnerability generated by the general uncertainty of players and the specific loss of his patron, Shakespeare was also aware of more personal vulnerabilities. His only son, Hamnet, age 11, had died just two weeks before Lord Hunsdon. Shakespeare had lost no children before this, though his sister Anne had died when he was fifteen. Hamnet's death would have been painful whenever it happened, but issues of inheritance and lineage were perhaps even more important at that moment because William Shakespeare had just renewed his father's application for a coat of arms—and finally succeeded in winning one.[35] The Shakespeares were now to be considered gentry, their sign to be a falcon shaking its spear; but there was no male heir to inherit the honor.

No biographical event, whether the death of a patron or the death of a son, determines a text or simply reproduces itself in a text. But all events become part of the conditions for creating texts. Shakespeare had begun the *Henriad* before either Hamnet or Hunsdon died, and the historical record demanded that the *Henry* plays include an exploration of father-son relations writ large as the struggles for succession to the English throne. But the death of his patron, Lord Cobham's aristocratic censorship, and especially the loss of his only son could not have been far from his thoughts as he continued. Perhaps that is one reason Shakespeare departed from his chronicle source when he chose to open *Henry IV, Part Two* with Rumor's cruel trick on Northumberland: Rumor sends the old man false news about his son Hotspur's victory when, as Northumberland soon learns, Hotspur is already dead. Rumor was also busy earlier, he brags, spreading false news about war when the land was actually "swoll'n with some other grief" (*2H4* Ind.13). Sigurd Burckhardt asked what that unidentified "other grief" is, and though there are answers enough in the play's troubled fiction, perhaps Shakespeare's real grief about Hamnet contributed to it.[36]

Falstaff in Ford's House: Player as Deer

I have sent and bene all thys morning huntyng for players Juglers & such kinde of Creaturs, but fynde them harde to finde.

Walter Cope

The flight of Hawkes and chase of wilde beastes, either of them are delights noble: but some think this sport [acting] of men the worthier, despight all calumny.

Webster, An Excellent Actor

When the Epilogue predicts Falstaff's death in *Henry IV, Part Two* he looks ahead to Falstaff's sacrificial role in *Merry Wives of Windsor,* as the offer of his own body looked backward to Antonio's sacrifice in *Merchant.* Falstaff, in fact, dies more often and in more modes than any other Shakespearean character: a counterfeit death in *Henry IV,* a real death in *Henry V* (foreseen by the *Henry IV* epilogue), and between these a symbolic death in Shakespeare's notorious detour from the histories, *The Merry Wives of Windsor.* Those who find the *Wives'* version of Falstaff defective have blamed Queen Elizabeth. Tradition has it that, on two weeks' notice, she ordered a play about Falstaff in love, and because Shakespeare was forced to write to specifications, he just wasn't deeply engaged. But blame may not be so easy to assign. Even if the Queen did order such a play, Shakespeare needn't have felt compelled to write it; Falstaff in *Wives* is not in love but in "rut" at best, and most likely not even that. He decides to "make love to Ford's wife" not only because he "sp[ies] entertainment in her," but because he is out of money and she "has all the rule of her husband's purse" (*Wiv.* 1.3.49–50). The problem with *Wives* (if there is a problem—the play works splendidly as theater) may not be that Shakespeare wasn't engaged but that he was too deeply engaged. The play draws on unassimilated fantasies which had been contextualized in the *Henriad,* but are foregrounded here. Though he is not nearly so attractive as he was earlier, this Falstaff merely continues a trend

Ateone mutato in Cerbio da Diana. 42

Dati, sete e'l calor cacciando vinto
Cerca Ateon pel bosco vna fontana,
Hallo si ben fer destino in parte sfinto,
Co' mal per lui vi trona entr' Diana.
La Dea, col viso di vergogna tinto,
Gli muta in ceruio la sembianza humana,
Et dice, ne gettar quell' onda cruda,
Non lice à ognino veder Diana ignuda.

Ateone lacerato da suoi Cani. 43

Il miser cacciator cangiar di faccia
Come si sente, affretta tosto il corso,
Che vede ben se quindi non si spaccia,
Ch' hauer potrebbe lacerato il dosso.
Ma poco vals, che i cani gli dan la caccia:
Et d'ogni parte l'han trafitto e morso,
Eì benche eì gridi, e i can per nome chiamê,
Si tra gon dal padron l'ingrata fame.

Actaeon, hunter and hunted. From *La Vita et Metamorfoseo d'Ouidio Figurato e Abbreuiato in* begun in the *Henriad,* where he was already the butt of Hal's jokes and was finally cast out of his life.

The continuity between *Wives* and the other great house plays is suggested by the way *Wives* has inherited from *Shrew* a world strongly reminiscent of the English countryside, complete with talk of specific hunting dogs in the first scene, and from *Dream* the context of thwarted young lovers, confusion in the woods, and holiday, in the form of Anne Page, her several suitors, and the Fairy Queen and train.[37] Even though Bully Bottom's conviviality has been largely displaced onto Windsor's Host rather than Falstaff,[38] and though the tavern world of the *Henriad* appears only in diminished form, the evocation of the earlier plays is clear enough. Down on his luck like Sly, Bottom, and his earlier self at the beginning of the *Henriad,* the difference is that Falstaff is more active in setting out to "shift" (*Wiv.* 1.3.31), and he has neither great house to beg at nor great lord to make his wishes come true. The only remnant of that heroic and aristocratic world is a bit of talk about the approaching ceremony for initiation into the Order of the Garter, which defined heroism in the first *Henriad.* Falstaff is reduced to stage-managing his own dream and to drafting his own middle-class male audience, and the play turns on the way in which his plans backfire and the trickster ends up tricked. Mistress Ford (and Mistress Page, whom he has decided also to seduce for good measure) sees what he is up to and goes along with him only to trap him;[39] meanwhile Ford, who has been alerted to the plot, disguises himself as Master Brook to "sound Falstaff" (*Wiv.* 2.1.227), and Falstaff, who always needs an audience, is easily duped into providing Ford, alias Brook, with a running commentary on his progress seducing Ford's own wife. Thus like Sly's and Bottom's, Falstaff's pursuit of a woman takes place not only in her husband's house but also—though he doesn't know it—under the husband's auspices. Ford as Brook oversees the seduction procedure, just as Sly's Lord and Oberon had watched Sly and Bottom, all biding their time for steely purposes of their own.

Falstaff sets out not once but three times to make his dream come true, and each time he is almost caught in the act—or, rather more frustratingly, caught on the verge of the act—and threatened with public exposure when Ford bursts in on the scene. His dream turns into theater as he resorts to increasingly humiliating disguises and increasingly theatrical deception, unaware that he is part of the wives' own larger play ("Mistress Page," says Mistress Ford, "remember you your cue"; *Wiv.* 3.3.33). The disguises appear first as desperate escapes: Falstaff squeezes into a basket of foul-smelling dirty laundry, in which he is barely able to "'scape suffocation," is carried out of the house, and dumped in the river like "a blind bitch's puppies" (*Wiv.* 3.5.108, 15) and almost drowned. He then dresses as old

Mother Pratt, "counterfeiting the action of an old woman" (*Wiv.* 4.5.113), and is beaten out of the house by Ford. The third time, in the midst of the woods where the young lovers have agreed to meet, he enacts his own version of Bottom's dream, this time replayed as comic nightmare where he is made the butt of an entire society.[40] Mistress Ford, who has by now joined forces with her husband, has gotten Falstaff to disguise himself in stag horns as Herne the Hunter, and to wait in the forest for what the two wives promise him will be a double tryst. But it turns instead into a comic revenge masque when Falstaff encounters Mistress Quickly playing the Fairy Queen, accompanied by a "fairy train" of local schoolboys. Willy-nilly, "fat Falstaff" is made an actor and "hath a great scene" (*Wiv.* 4.6.16–17). Like Bottom with his ass's head, Falstaff with his buck's head has stumbled into the Fairy Queen's bower, but instead of welcoming him as Titania welcomed Bottom, she turns on him. The fairies surround him, pinch him, burn him with their tapers, and then chide the frustrated lover before finally "dis-horn[ing]" him in front of the entire community and having him "publically shamed" (*Wiv.* 4.4.63, 4.2.222).

Falstaff ends up feeling like an ass, but the stronger faunal impression is of a stag. Falstaff's prominent horns link him with the hunting exchanges present in the other great house plays, but this time in a new way. Falstaff entered the play as a poacher who had killed one of Shallow's deer, and his amorous hunt in the preceding scenes made him a stalker of other men's "deer."[41] Now, though disguised as a hunter, his costume—stag's horns (or possibly an entire stag's head)—marks him instead as the prey (he had already confined himself inside a "buck" basket). He completes the transition into a hunted animal, a deer held at bay, as "a noise of [hunting] horns" is heard and he is "pinched" by the citizens of Windsor before they go off to feast on venison (*Wiv.* 5.5.30, 103). While Sly in *Shrew* and Bottom in *Dream* had been accidental intruders into a royal forest where the Lord was hunting, Falstaff in *Wives* becomes the object of the hunt. Falstaff's transformation to stag had already begun in the *Henriad,* when Hal called him a "rascal" (that is, a deer too young or old to endure the chase; *1H4* 2.2.5, 2.4.347, 3.3.156),[42] and then stood over Falstaff's "dead" body on the battlefield. Noting dispassionately that "death has not struck so fat a deer today," Hal had then gone on ambiguously to promise he would see Falstaff "embowell'd" (*1H4* 5.4.106, 108): Hal is probably referring to the embalming process reserved for aristocrats, which he presumably will secure for Falstaff in one last act of illegitimate patronage; but emboweling refers more immediately to the ritual undoing or dismemberment of a hunted stag, and therefore marks Falstaff as so much dead meat.[43]

In another context, of course, the stag could be an aristocratic beast himself, taking on the stature of the great lords and princes who alone were allowed to hunt him.[44] Even in *As You Like It,* despite Shakespeare's satiric thrust and preoccupation with cuckoldry in presenting Arden's outlaw huntsmen, the ceremonial splendor of the hunt can be glimpsed:

> *Jaques:* Which is he that killed the deer? . . . Let's present him to the Duke like a Roman conqueror; and it would do well to set the deer's horns upon his head for a branch of victory. (*AYL* 4.2.1–5)[45]

Just as commonly, the royal stag, impaled, or "surrounded," and perhaps also impaled or "pierced" with arrows, was a figure for Christ.[46] Shakespeare assigns his own heroes staglike deaths throughout the canon. In the first *Henriad,* Henry VI is literally caught like a deer in a forest by two Keepers: "Aye, here's a deer whose skin's a keeper's fee./ This is the quondam king. Let's seize upon him" (*3H6* 3.1.22–23). And we have seen how Henry's brave defender, Talbot, meets death like a deer "ring'd about with bold adversity" (*1H6* 4.4.14):

> How are we parked and bounded in a *pale,*
> A little herd of England's timorous *deer,*
> Maz'd with a yelping kennel of French curs!
> If we be English *deer,* be then in blood;
> Not *rascal-like* to fall down with a *pinch,*
> But rather, moody-mad and desperate stags,
> Turn on the bloody hounds with heads of steel . . .
> And they shall find dear deer of us, my friends.
> God and Saint George, Talbot and England's right,
> Prosper our colors in this dangerous fight!
>
> (*1H6* 4.2.45–56; italics added)

In Talbot's call to "turn on the bloody hounds," Shakespeare manages to make the deer at once heroic and pitiful. Antony in *Julius Caesar* will later exploit that combination in the most well known use of the trope, when he first sees Caesar's body:

> Here was thou bayed, brave hart. . . .
> O world, thou wast the forest to this hart,
> And this, indeed, O world, the heart of thee.
> How like a deer, strucken by many princes,
> Dost thou here lie!
>
> (*JC* 3.1.204–10)[47]

But unlike these serious moments in the other plays, in *Wives,* the ceremony is mock heroic, perhaps even enabling a tacit contrast, in this Garter play, between Falstaff and these earlier heroic warriors—like the contrast between Talbot and the original cowardly Falstolfe in *Henry VI, Part One,* who was stripped of his Garter. Here in fact the hunt is more a matter of poaching than a princely ritual, and Falstaff himself reminds us of its merely appetitive dimension when he sees the two wives and imagines himself a deer's carcass, sharing out his "haunch[es]" (*Wiv.* 5.5.24) to both. For him it is a matter of butchery, not sacrifice. In fact Falstaff's adventure may be based not so much on actual hunting as on the mock stag hunt, or skimmingtonlike ritual, still practiced in nineteenth-century Devon. In this version of rough justice or mob punishment, a man was dressed as a stag and hunted down for a realistic "kill" in front of the house of the offender, who was often chased himself and "thrown into the nearest pond or stream."[48] Shakespeare appropriated the already theatricalized humiliation ritual along with the stag hunting itself.

Just as important for Falstaff as the mock heroic implications of the ritual hunt and its transformation into pageantry, is the stag's connection with Actaeon and the force of that hunter's myth in *Wives* as a figure for histrionic display. The Windsor citizens themselves are aware only of Actaeon's association with cuckolds, and they noisily enjoy the irony of Falstaff's winding up with horns after starting out to cuckold Ford, or, as Pistol had said earlier, to make Ford an Actaeon (*Wiv.* 2.1.115). But the Actaeon myth itself has nothing to do with cuckolds; a second set of associations links Actaeon instead to sexual arousal per se or to sexual initiation.[49] Thus Actaeon's story (in contrast to his name) has lent itself not only to the portrayal of adultery but to the exploration of all sexuality, particularly of the erotics of the gaze.[50] The ocular eroticism associated with the hunt in general in *Love's Labour's Lost* is here epitomized in Actaeon and Diana's specific version of the hunt. Ovid's bachelor-Actaeon, at rest and off guard, innocently penetrated Diana's ("Titiana's" in Ovid) secret bower, whose hidden recesses, arching tufa, lush underbrush, and central fountain are suggestive of the goddess's secret anatomy and of the extent of Actaeon's crime. Furious at the invasion, Diana splashes Actaeon with her magical water. He becomes a stag and is torn apart by his own dogs. Actaeon's enemy here is not a rival male; instead he is the victim of the woman's retaliatory attack and of his own savage dogs of desire. Actaeon's experience figures the sudden reversals of prey and predator, and of antagonism and identification, which are mediated by the lovers' mirroring gaze, whatever their marital status.[51]

Actaeon's story of sexual initiation lends itself to the triangularities—and humiliations—of cuckoldry, if with Freud we assume that *all* sexual awakening takes place in the context of the family: the first woman a child desires is always another man's woman, and his initiation is always already a betrayal of another man.[52] Shakespeare's most extensive use of the Actaeon myth, in *Titus Andronicus,* explores both sexual initiation and cuckoldry. *Titus,* Richard Marienstras argues, is entirely structured by Actaeon's reversal from hunter to hunted.[53] Its central scene is a hunt which takes place in a forest where the hills echo back the hunter's trumpet at him, "as if a double hunt were heard at once" (*Tit.* 2.3.19), Titus observes, just before his daughter is raped and her husband and his sons killed. *Titus's* forest is a savage world where the unstable structure of violent opposition—between male and male, male and female—matters more than one's position in it. Thus "Actaeon" is used indiscriminately both for Bassanio, the inadvertent intruder into Tamora's bower, and for the husband whom Tamora is there cuckolding with Aaron. The relation between victim and prey, or actor and witness, is further confused when Bassanio is himself cuckolded as punishment for his forbidden glimpse of Tamora.

Shakespeare follows tradition elsewhere too by evoking Actaeon in representing erotic love's antagonism and ambivalence. But for him the Actaeon story, colored by the cuckold's humiliation, can also suggest the complexities of the difficult "love" between player and audience, who are linked by their own mirroring gaze of desire and destruction—"buck fever," as Sergel calls it in modern actors.[54] Shakespeare's usage suggests that what links the two otherwise incompatible interpretations of Actaeon's fate (Actaeon as old cuckold revealed and Actaeon as innocent intruder punished for sexual hubris) are the elements of public exposure and reversibility that are also the actor's obsession. Actaeon's is a crime of the eye rather than of the hand (or any other part of the body), and once he sees her, Diana's revenge takes the form of making him the object of what Elias Canetti called the pack's "rapacious looks."[55] He becomes the center of attention for the dogs and hunters who converge on him. He becomes a body on display, purely an object, losing all ability to speak or to define himself as one of them. Similarly, when Actaeon as cuckold suspects his wife's crime, he hides to watch for "ocular proof" (*Oth.* 3.3.366), but inevitably suffers a reversal when the whole world stares and laughs at him.[56]

Falstaff's is an ocular humiliation on both counts, as lustful voyeur and as cuckolder. In the play's first scene, he defines the parameters of his adventure as visual when he announces that he "sp[ies] entertainment in" Mistress Ford (*Wiv.* 1.3.41). He even tries to reverse the guilt by claiming that she was eyeing him. Mistress Ford, he tells Pistol, "gives the leer of invitation," and Page's wife "gave me good eyes too, examin'd my parts with most judicious œillades" and "did so course o'er my exteriors with such a greedy intention that the appetite of her eye did seem to scorch me up like a burning-glass!" (*Wiv.* 1.3.42, 55–56, 65–67). But it is Falstaff who is the voyeur, and the female gaze is not an invitation, as it seemed, but a poetically just punishment. What Falstaff sees reflected in the "glass" of Page's eye is not, as he thought, a flattering reflection of his own desire but rather a voracious attack from a woman who has been watching him. Appropriately enough, given the theatrics of his supposedly secret meetings with the wives, each of Falstaff's would-be intimacies is also overseen by Ford and the crowd of hostile witnesses who arrive to expose him. Falstaff comes closest to Actaeon's fate at the end of *Wives* when Ford finds him in the Fairy Queen's bower—"They are fairies," Falstaff says, frightened by attackers. "He that speaks to them shall die. / I'll wink and couch: *no man their works must eye*" (*Wiv.* 5.5.48–49; italics added). Fairies, like displaced versions of Diana's nymphs, traditionally punished their victims for voyeurism.[57] Falstaff is not only pinched and burned by the fairies—punishment for playing with fire—but also spied on and exposed as the fairies close in "like to the Garter's compass, in a ring" (*Wiv.* 5.5.102, 67). For eyeing the forbidden he is exposed to the destructive gaze of others. Not only does the hunter become the hunted; the voyeur becomes the object of the hunting pack's voracious gaze.

The baying of the deer as the dogs encircle him, its psychological elaboration in Actaeon's story of reversals, the theatrics of the Garter Ceremony, the theatrics of Evans's pageant celebrating that ceremony with a ring of punitive fairies, and the skimmington ritual it embodies: all are apt figures for the actor caught in the "wooden O" of an amphitheater. Webster would describe the "excellent actor" charming attention "by a full and significant action of his body," so that when you "sit in a full Theatre . . . you will think you see so many lines drawn from the circumference of so many eares, whiles the *Actor* is the *Centre*."[58] For Actaeon there is a circumference of mouths, barking and slavering.

Falstaff's humiliating exposure is a resonant moment in the canon, and has drawn to itself pieces of another Shakespearean image cluster also associated with "pinching," which here leads to thoughts of death.[59] It too can suggest an actor's sensitivity to the hostile gaze, and it too emerges directly from the hunt. Golding uses "pinch," in fact, in translating the literally heartrending moment in Ovid's Actaeon's story, when the youth is attacked by his own dogs:

> First Slo did *pinch* him by the haunch, and next came Kildeere in,
> And Hylbred fastned on his shoulder, bote him through the skinne. . . .
> They did gainecope him as he came, and helde their Master still,
> Untill that all the rest came in, and fastned on him to.
> No part of him was free from wound. He could none other do
> But sigh, and in the shape of Hart with voyce as Hartes are woont,
> (For voyce of man was none now lefte to helpe him at the brunt)
> By braying show his secret grief among the Mountaynes hie,
> And kneeling sadly on his knees with dreerie tears in eye,
> As one by humbling of himselfe that mercy seemde to crave,
> With piteous looke in stead of handes his head about to wave.
>
> (*Met.* bk. 3, lines 280–91)[60]

Golding, like Ovid, dwells on the pathos of Actaeon's enforced and unnatural silence—"for voyce of man was none now lefte to help him at the brunt"—as he kneels begging for mercy with piteous looks, only his body left now that his voice is gone. Actaeon, like a frightened player, is paralyzed and mute with fear, forced to beg (or "crave . . . mercy") from those he had commanded.

Other "Actaeons" are exposed and pinched throughout the Shakespearean canon beginning in *The Comedy of Errors,* the first of Shakespeare's "fairy" plays. There it is Egeon who has transgressed by crossing into the forbidden territory of Diana's Ephesus. Somewhat illogically it is Egeon's son, Antipholus of Ephesus, who is the "unruly deer" strayed from the "pale" (*Err.* 2.1.100) to the house of a courtesan and who becomes "horn-mad" or "mad as a buck" (*Err.* 3.1.72) when he thinks his wife is cuckolding him. Dr. Pinch himself materializes at the end of the play to close in on Antipholus, bind him and shame him in public. Meanwhile Antipholus's twin and alterego, has risked not only pinching but also suffocation at the hands of Ephesus's fairies ("They'll suck our breath, or pinch us black and blue"; *Err.* 2.2.192).[61] An even closer version of Falstaff's pinching reappears in the canon some years later, when Parolles in *All's Well That Ends Well,* a braggart soldier like Falstaff,[62] suffers a demythologized version of Falstaff's midnight "dis-horn[ing]" in Windsor forest. Parolles is "crushed with a plot" (*AWW* 4.3.360) when his fellow soldiers, tired of the coward's lies, trick him into making good on his promise to recover his drum from enemy territory. Like the Fords, they have him secretly surrounded, then ambushed and blindfolded on his mission. His captors, like Falstaff's fairies, taunt and "pinch" him: "If ye pinch me like a pasty I can say no more," he finally cries (*AWW* 4.3.119–20). They bring his master, Bertram, to look on as they stage a scene they entitle the "dialogue between the Fool and the Soldier" (*AWW* 4.3.95), in which Parolles betrays Bertram to save himself. At last the "counterfeit," who has already been de-drummed if not dis-horned, is unmasked (*AWW* 4.3.96).[63] It is Bertram who has violated the Diana in this play—indeed Shakespeare arranges the scenes so that Bertram gains entrance to Diana's chamber at the very moment when Parolles is ambushed. But rather than blaming the young man himself, everyone, including Diana, blames Parolles for misleading Bertram, and it is Parolles, like Falstaff, who must be scapegoated by living through another version of Actaeon's fate.[64]

All these Actaeon-like encounters suggest Shakespeare's fear of women and sexuality, and of the dangers of penetrating the female, ultimately the maternal, body.[65] But they are also related to the actor's experience when he steps into the center of the stage before a similarly maternal audience, whose acceptance he desires and whose retaliatory punishment he fears.

* * *

Wives, more so than the other Falstaff plays, is very much an occasional play, and the Folio text includes references to its immediate dramatic circumstances. Shakespeare's patron, George Carey, had just been named Lord Chamberlain, and it is Hunsdon's installment into the Order of the Garter that we think occasioned the play. Shakespeare's troupe had thus been restored to its former status, but not without the year of uncertainty described earlier. *Wives* is not so obviously self-referential as *Dream;* unlike Bottom, Falstaff does not set out to entertain aristocrats at a Garter installation ceremony like the one Shakespeare was writing for, nor does Shakespeare invite, as he does in *Dream,* even an ironic identification of his own dramatic efforts with Falstaff's. But Falstaff does star in an inner masque, directed by Ford and Page and staged by the schoolmaster Evans; and the final chorus of that masque refers unmistakably to preparations at Windsor for the Garter ceremony.[66] Sly had been tricked into sharing the cross-dressed page with the great Lord in *The Taming of the Shrew* as prelude to a performance which proved harmless to him; Bottom had been tricked into sharing Titania with Oberon in *Dream* as a prelude to a performance which left him no worse for the experience either. But Falstaff has unknowingly helped trick himself into trying to steal Ford's wife as prelude to playing the victim in Shakespeare's only comic revenge masque.

Falstaff's histrionic bent links him not only to the great house players but, as many have noted, to Shakespeare's first "player," Richard III, with whom he shares other traits that usually escape notice but which are important here. Richard and Falstaff, Shakespeare's two most grossly misshapen characters, could not be more different in most ways, but each is defined in part by his reaction to his bodily presence—and to the ways others see it.[67] The repeated iconography of the swollen hump or stomach is striking, especially since his physical liability stops neither Richard nor Falstaff from pursuing women. Richard began his play by courting Anne and succeeded in that improbable goal. Falstaff is not a direct suitor for the Anne in this play,[68] but he does preen himself when he thinks that Anne's mother, Mistress Ford, will accommodate him and provide a burning "glass" for him: "Says't thou so, old Jack? Go thy ways; I'll make more of thy old body than I have done. Will they yet look after thee? . . . Good body, I thank thee" (*Wiv.* 2.2.133–36).[69] Richard's confusion between seeking heaven in a "lady's lap" and seeking Elysium within the golden circuit of the crown ultimately proves disastrous to him: he finds himself both "smothered" and "impaled" by the crown.[70] Falstaff's ambitions also prove (at least symbolically) fatal to him, when he is "smothered" in laundry and finally impaled and hunted down like a deer. Perhaps the most telling resemblance lies in their similar contributions to the social order when each is made scapegoat. Richard's death exorcises the evils of the *Henriad*'s aggression and civil war, so that both sides can feel innocent as they unite to foresee the birth of Queen Elizabeth. In his own smaller world, Falstaff is made scapegoat for Windsor's jealousies, appetites, and shames.[71] Part of the hilarity of the last act is the double contrivance whereby Falstaff's punishment becomes the means of freeing Anne Page to marry her true love, Fenton. In the poetic logic of the play, Falstaff is killed off three times so that Anne and Fenton may thrive and renew the world, harmony is restored among the community's married couples, and the play ends with the promise of a communal feast. Finally, perhaps entirely accidentally but interestingly so, given Richard's potentially autobiographical significance, Falstaff's play, as current opinion has it, was produced on 23 April 1597, Shakespeare's thirty-third (and Christological) birthday. Years before, Shakespeare's sister Anne had died just before he celebrated his birthday; the birthday in 1597 would be the first since his son's and his patron's recent deaths.[72] It would be appropriate (however accidental), if among the several reversals which the play effects (between hunter and hunted, cuckold and cuckolder) were one in which Falstaff, figure for Shakespeare the survivor of his sister, should now be sacrificed, so that this time young Anne could live happily ever after.

Whether or not Falstaff, the old player dying in his boots, locates Shakespeare in this play, there is a more obvious autobiographical reference in young William, Anne's brother. William Page, like Falstaff, is a player in *Wives'* inner play. "Williams" turn up elsewhere in the plays, ironically self-deprecating cameos like Alfred Hitchcock's brief appearances in his films, and the sonnets contain another debasing play on the name when "Will" refers both to Shakespeare himself and to sexual anatomy. In *Wives,* young William Page, who did not appear in any of the sources, combines both sorts of inconsequence in a clearly Shakespearean addition. Little Will's primary purpose in the play, one assumes, is to err suggestively in his Latin lesson (*Wiv.* 4.1)—which takes place, improbably, on the very day he and the other boys have been given a holiday from school—and to provoke Mistress Quickly into mistakes even bawdier than his. Like Bottom and company rehearsing most "obscenely" in *Dream,* they charge the language with sexual significance and provide a similar kind of humor.[73] But Will serves another function when he takes part in the masque of the Fairy Queen. There he plays one of the hobgoblins or elves—"ouphs" (or changelings, like the little changeling boy in *Dream*)—along with his sister Anne. We do not know which boy (in addition to the "postmaster's boy"; *Wiv.* 5.5.188, 198) in the fairy train was dressed up and passed off as substitute (or replacement child?) for Anne when the would-be suitors came to claim her. But if it was William, then not only would the old player Falstaff have been sacrificed for Anne, but young William would also have been offered up as a most unsatisfactory[74] substitute for her, as perhaps Shakespeare was a replacement for his dead sisters. Slender, one of Anne's would-be husbands, sums up the disappointment such a replacement implies: "I came yonder at Eton to marry Mistress Anne Page, and she's a great lubberly boy" (*Wiv.* 5.5.183–84).

Tragedians at Elsinore: Great Man as Player

The lord who had directed the prominent players in *Shrew, Love's Labour's Lost,* and *Dream* moves to the center of the metadramatic plays in the figures of Hamlet, Duke Vincentio in *Measure for Measure,* and Prospero in *The Tempest.* And with his repositioning, the problematics of theater are combined with questions about government as well as about selfhood. In *Hamlet,* for example, probably the most theatrically self-conscious of all the plays, the arrival of the players at Elsinore recalls the similar arrival in *Shrew,* and Hamlet's greeting recalls the *Shrew* Lord's delighted response to his players. Both men know and welcome the players, and each makes his authority clear by demanding that the players treat with respect an audience who does not really deserve it—Sly in *Shrew* and Polonius in *Hamlet.* Each lectures the players about their own jobs, as if a better judge than they of such things. But in the earlier play the focus was on Sly, as much an actor as the players, and it is Sly's transformation that is mirrored in the inner play when Petruchio transforms Kate from shrew to perfect wife. In the latter the focus is on Hamlet, who is not only an actor but also master of ceremonies, playwright, and prince; it is his story that is mirrored in the inner play, "The Murder of Gonzago." And Hamlet's story, of course, is Denmark's story. Hamlet's refusal of the deceptives roles he finds himself forced to play is part of his recoil from all seeming in a world where hypocrisy taints even love and friendship, and where all human achievement is illusory.[75] His theatrical self-consciousness corresponds to our sense of Denmark as *theatrum mundi,* where "there's a divinity that shapes our ends, / Rough-hew them how we will" (5.2.10–11). Amidst *Hamlet's* encompassing theatricality, a professional actor's psychological concerns, like his financial concerns now that the boy actors are competing in the capital, remain tangential. We need no actor come from the stage to tell us what every sensitive adult should feel in this Denmark.

But just as an actor has private stakes in the play he serves, Hamlet has his own reasons for his obsession with Denmark's playing. Just as the theater serves an actor, the *theatrum mundi* metaphor, as true as Shakespeare has made it here, serves Hamlet; and theater itself provides a way out of his melancholic paralysis. When the Lord in *Shrew* turned from contemplating the image of "grim death" in Sly's drunkenness, to thinking about staging his own play the conjunction seemed accidental. For Hamlet the movement from thoughts of death to "The Murder of Gonzago" seems inevitable in a play where the play-within-a-play marks a turning point for the entire action; but it nonetheless reveals something about him as well as about Denmark. The players deflect Hamlet from suicide, and they allow him to take control over the situation which has made him powerless.[76] In "The Murder of Gonzago" Hamlet brings his dead father to life again; more importantly, the play gives life to Hamlet's own dead emotions. Simply by revealing the truth, the play serves as the act of aggression Hamlet could not bring himself otherwise to perform.[77] But in his role as the play's presenter or chorus and interpreter, Hamlet also changes the revelation into a threat, the history into a prediction. Hamlet makes "Gonzago's" murderer Lucianus into the "nephew to the King," and he cues the actor playing Lucianus with, "the croaking raven doth bellow for revenge" (*Ham.* 3.2.239, 248). But Lucianus is about to commit regicide not revenge—it's Hamlet who is thinking of revenge.[78] Hamlet's passionate involvement in the play emerges in his frenzied remarks to Ophelia ("Lady, shall I lie in your lap?"; *Ham.* 3.2.110–11), as well as to Claudius, alternating like Richard III between a "lady's lap" (*3H6* 3.2.148) and the crown.[79]

In particular, Hamlet becomes as emotionally involved with his audience as any actor does. The performance becomes a hunt, and Claudius the wounded deer. Hamlet's manic crow of delight after Claudius leaves makes the analogy: "Why, let the stricken deer go weep, / The hart ungalled play; / For some must watch while some must sleep, / Thus runs the world away" (*Ham.* 3.2.265–68). The tables have been turned since the *Shrew* Lord found Sly while hunting, and Ford held Falstaff at bay to dis-horn him. Now Hamlet is the hunter who stalks deer with the players, and he boasts to Horatio that his hit in "Gonzago" would earn him "a fellowship in a *cry* of players" (3.2.271–72)—a cry being a canine hunting pack, so-called after the yelping of dogs on a scent.[80] For the moment at least, Hamlet sees the actors as dogs, or as "the 'hounds' in a skimmington-like 'stag-hunt'"—like the one in *Wives* that made Falstaff its object—"of which the object is to flush and publically pursue an offender against sexual morals."[81] He has gotten into the spirit of the playing he had once disdained. By the end of the play Hamlet has accepted his actor status not only as a willing "seemer," but also as one who depends on the dangerously venal vicissitudes of performance before an audience. Throughout the play he had recoiled from being watched and been on guard against unseen witnesses. Now Hamlet freely acknowledges his audience: "You that look pale and tremble at this chance, / That are but mutes or audience to this act" (*Ham.* 5.2.339–40). The man whose first words had rejected all seeming for "that within which passeth show," dies concerned about how he seems to others: "O God, Horatio, what a wounded name, / Things standing thus unknown, shall I leave behind me" (*Ham.* 5.2.349–50). Appropriately enough when Fortinbras arrives to take over he first likens the death scene to a hunt ("This quarry cries on havoc"; *Ham.* 5.2.375); he ends by making Hamlet into a triumphant actor ("Bear Hamlet like a soldier to the stage"; *Ham.* 5.2.401).

The two later directorial plays, *Measure* and *Tempest,* are even less concerned, it would seem, with the parochialism of an actor than *Hamlet* is. The plays staged by Duke Vincentio in *Measure* and by Prospero in *Tempest* are real; the later dukes' control over life and death is less like Hamlet's than like the saving power given to holy friars in *Romeo and Juliet* and *Much Ado About Nothing.* As Francis Fergusson says, these men use drama primarily to heal the world (not to act out their own wishes, as Hamlet does), "to purify the spiritual atmosphere of their societies through significant shows."[82] Theater, for example, serves both a social function in Duke Vincentio's Vienna and a structural function in Shakespeare's *Measure for Measure.* But more so than in *Hamlet,* it is also a questionable strategy, as it was not in *Romeo* or *Much Ado.* And it serves a psychic function for the "mad fantastical" Duke, just as it does for the "antic" Hamlet.

Duke Vincentio comes to theater with a past. Like Hamlet he suffers a paralysis of will, signaled by his ducal permissiveness and his nine-year inability either to free or to execute the drunken murderer Barnadine; he too is overcome with disgust at the rampant sexuality he sees around him and with thoughts about grim death. The Duke's Hamletian melancholia emerges only indirectly, in his stoic advice to Claudio, who is to be killed for getting Juliet with child. "Be absolute for death," he tells the boy (*MM* 3.1.5). But as Richard Wheeler points out, the Duke's personal nihilism speaks through the passionately felt sermon, more passionately felt, in fact, than most of the Duke's pronouncements. He lapses into the first person as he tells Claudio to "reason thus with life":[83] "If *I* do lose thee, *I* do lose a thing / That none but fools would keep. A breath thou art, / . . . Merely, thou art Death's fool" (*MM* 3.1.7–11; italics added).[84] Hamlet finds relief from such thoughts by sending Lucianus on stage in "The Murder of Gonzago" to do his dirty work "tropically" ("This play is an image of a murder done in Vienna. . . . 'Tis a knavish piece of work, but what of that? Your Majesty, and we that have free souls, it touches us not"; *Ham.* 3.2.232–36). Similarly the Duke finds his relief by appointing Angelo to clean up Vienna: "Who may, in th' ambush of my name, strike home, / And yet my nature never in the fight / To do in slander" (*MM* 1.3.41–43).[85]

To be sure Shakespeare's primary goal here is to examine the general "enigma of authority vested in flesh and blood."[86] In the Duke's disguise Shakespeare glances at divine authority and the mystery of incarnation—

or to secular authority and the mystery of the king's two bodies, to King James's authority to rule sublunary England and Scotland by divine right. The play scrutinizes "proud man, / Dress'd in a little brief authority" and the superficiality of every "ceremony that to great ones longs" (*MM* 2.2.119, 59), betrayed by the mere man underneath—like Lear's justice who hotly lusts to use the whore he whips. Duke Vincentio's withdrawal and return in friar disguise is like Henry's disguise, walking among his men as a common soldier on the eve of Agincourt, hearing such attacks on the king that he is prompted to his only soliloquy, about the emptiness of "ceremony" and the loneliness at the top (*H54* 4.1.245–50). The theatrics in *Measure for Measure* belong not so much to a professional player as to a ruler who uses theater to organize his state.[87]

The issues at stake, however, are also ones that obsess professionals on the more literal stage. The play is an exploration of dramatic (as well as political) authority and the ways in which it is compromised by less than professional motives. Vincentio as playwright, though supposedly independent of the play, turns out to resemble the *Shrew* Lord providing Sly with a new life and wife, Oberon sending Bottom to Titania's bower, Hal spying on Falstaff and Mistress Quickly, or Ford watching Falstaff cuckold him with Mrs. Ford. The playwright hides safely behind the curtain saying "tsk-tsk," while his private fantasies are acted out by others.[88] Is the Duke too closely identified with the actor Angelo, too much in love with the actress Isabella whom he sends to Angelo's bed, too tempted to become an actor himself so that he not only interprets between the puppets but manipulates them for his own ends? Is he too much like Lucio, who goads the others in their parts—or betrays them—for his own purposes? "Craft against vice I must apply," chants the Duke (*MM* 3.2.270), as if Shakespeare were trying to create a benign form of that charismatic actor, the Vice, a "Virtue" who manipulates characters, supposedly for the right reasons only.

Such a playwright-actor, whose fortunes can only issue forth in the characters' actions, is, like the actors themselves, alert to his audience. Accordingly it makes sense that the Duke's often-cited aversion to crowds turns out to be the other side of a flair for ostentation. Just as Hamlet died caring about his "wounded name" (*Ham.* 5.2.349), the Duke's directorial vision of the world—and of the necessary cure for it—is bound up with an actor's concerns about displaying himself to an audience. The Duke claims to have no need for approval. The whole problem in Vienna has arisen because he disdains (rightly, we think) the gaudy public display which is as inherent in a duke's role as in a player's. "I have ever loved the life remov'd," he explains to the friar after turning over his government to Angelo (*MM* 1.3.8). He had already told Angelo:

> I love the people,
> But do not like to stage me to their eyes:
> Though it do well, I do not relish well
> Their loud applause and *Aves* vehement;
> Nor do I think the man of safe discretion
> That does affect it.
>
> (*MM* 1.1.67–72)

Yet at the end, Vincentio makes an elaborate plan to stage himself to the people's eyes in a spectacular ritual which unmasks Mariana, Angelo, Claudio, and, climactically, the Duke himself, at last safe from "slander." It is not the staging that the Duke avoids, but the vulnerability to slander that attends any public action. Perhaps that's why the Duke's final anger is reserved for Lucio alone among Vienna's sinners: "Slandering a prince deserves it" (*MM* 5.1.521). Lucio's slurs loom so large in the Duke's imagination that this one petty rogue's gossip becomes multiplied into "millions of false eyes" that are "stuck upon" him,[89] their gaze comparable to the threat of the hunt:

> Volumes of report
> Run with these false, and most contrarious quest
> Upon thy doings: thousand escapes of wit
> Make thee the father of their idle dream
> And rack thee in their fancies.
>
> (*MM* 4.1.60–65)

Lucio's accusations proliferate into a pack of hounds who "run" and "chase or give tongue to *quest* what these false eyes see."[90] Vincentio is not an actor; nor is he here describing appearances on a literal stage. But part of his sense of what is at stake should he "stage me to their eyes" as a functioning Duke, both the possible reward ("*Aves* vehement") and the danger (the "most contrarious quest" of a hunting pack), is an actor's sense of what is at stake when he comes on stage. That Shakespeare assigned the description to such an autobiographical character, and that he himself was both drawn to and repelled by a career on stage, are facts which cannot help but illuminate one another.[91]

Lear Outside His Daughter's House: The King and the Player-Beggar

The actor's combined power over and dependence on the audience watching him was made explicit in any performance after the play when he came forward to kneel and ask for applause. ("The King's a beggar, now the play is done," the Player King says in the epilogue to Shakespeare's *All's Well;*

AWW Epi.1.) Within the plays, the actor's dependence, thematized in the great house inner plays we have been examining here, also finds its way into the narratives of a surprising number of Shakespeare's plays which are not about actors at all. Whatever led Shakespeare to become an actor was of a piece with his ability to imagine the story of other "beggars," from Titus Andronicus to Lear, who find that their tongues cannot move their stony-hearted auditors. The reversal from king to beggar that every player knew, like the reversal from hunter to hunted, is so important for Shakespeare that it comes close to defining *the* tragic situation in the early *Titus Andronicus,* already heavily colored by the dynamics of the hunt.[92] The action in *Titus* unfolds from the moment when the conquered queen, Tamora, kneels to beg the conqueror Titus for her son's life.[93] When Titus refuses her, the play's logic leads to a sequence of horrors in which Titus and his family find themselves begging pity from people who turn out to be as pitiless as Titus was to Tamora. As the hunter becomes the hunted in the forest outside Rome, the conqueror turns beggar.

Reversed begging scenes recur elsewhere in the plays; a king to whom everyone has bowed suddenly finds that he must kneel to someone—often a woman—who had kneeled to him before and been turned away.[94] Although it extends throughout the plays following *Titus,* however, the topos is most completely realized in *King Lear,* which Maynard Mack sees as an elaboration of the ancient tale, "The Abasement of the Proud King."[95] King Lear's "darker purpose" (*Lr.* 1.1.35) in dividing his kingdom is precisely to avoid the beggary attendant on what Shakespeare earlier called "unregarded age in corners thrown" (*AYL* 2.3.42). Lear wants total devotion from his Cordelia; he wants to be loved for himself alone, though he no longer can claim such devotion, from either his married daughters or his abandoned subjects. To avoid even the semblance of owing Cordelia anything for her love, Lear pays for it by promising "all" his kingdom once she professes her love. But she refuses to love him "all," and he feels as if he has nothing. He is reduced lower than "our basest beggars" (*Lr.* 2.4.262) and soon acts out sarcastically the role in which his daughters have cast him after all:

> Do you but mark how this becomes the house:
> "Dear daughter, I confess that I am old;
> Age is unnecessary: on my knees I beg
> That you'll vouchsafe me raiment, bed, and food."
> (*Lr.* 2.4.150–53)

The old *King Leir* play, Shakespeare's source, contained several scenes of melodramatic begging which Shakespeare had already borrowed for other plays—probably *Titus* among them—even before he repeated them in his own full-length version of the play.[96] The begging remains central in his own version.

The begging in *Lear* is only a symptom of the radical vulnerability of characters dependent on one another in a godless world. The play, Stanley Cavell has argued, explores the equal terrors of rejecting and accepting love and the lengths to which people will go to avoid recognizing one another rather than risking those terrors.[97] For Cavell the theater audience's distance from the tragedy it watches is recreated within the play, as characters hide behind disguises or watch each other unseen. This is the defense actors know best—to display the self and ask for love, but only by pretending to be someone else. In other ways too, though Lear is obviously not an actor, what he wants and what he suffers when he puts himself on the line and asks for love, are what actors always want and always dread on stage. In fact *Lear* is a transfiguration of Sly's story at the beginning of the great house sequence. The concerns relegated to the comedy at the edges of *Shrew,* however, have here become the core of tragic suffering.[98] In *Shrew* nothing was at stake except Sly's resilient sense of himself. He is thrown out by the Hostess because he can't pay his bill, rants bravely about his injured innocence ("Third, or fourth, or fifth borough, I'll answer him by law. I'll not budge an inch, boy"; *Shr.* Ind. 1.11–12) and collapses on the cold ground. Then he wakes, as if resurrected ("What's here? One dead, or drunk?" asks the Lord, "See doth he breathe"; *Shr.* Ind.1.29), and he finds his life's a miracle. Now Sly is a lord, surrounded by grandeur and the love of a newly adoring Hostess, and he watches a play about taming shrews who won't behave.[99] In *Lear,* by contrast, everything is at stake. Ousted by his own daughters, Lear endures the tempest and proclaims his innocence to an indifferent audience on the heath; in his madness he even stages what we might call an "arraigning of the shrew" in his life, working out his pain vicariously before he finally collapses.[100] ("Arraign her first; 'tis Goneril . . . she kick'd the poor King her father"; *Lr.* 3.6.46–48). When he awakes, Lear is miraculously restored to authority and, at last, to the kind nursery of a newly devoted Cordelia. But while Sly's adventure was open-ended, Lear's brings on the promised end. The *Shrew* Lord's question, "See, doth he breathe?" has become Lear's desperate "Lend me a looking-glass; / If that her breath will mist or stain the stone, / Why then she lives" (*Lr.* 5.3.260–62). The difference is that Cordelia doesn't live.

Despite the crude plot similarities to Sly's story, Lear is not a literal actor and not even a literal beggar. The real beggar in *King Lear* is Edgar, and on the heath it is Edgar, not Lear, who echoes Sly's lines outside the tavern in *Shrew* ("Go to thy cold bed and warm thee"; *Shr.* Ind.1.7–8). Victimized by his brother, disowned by his father, and hunted down while Lear is still at Goneril's house organizing hunts for sport,[101] Edgar chooses the way opposite from Lear's to beg for love. Instead of commanding love as his due, the way Lear does even on the heath, Edgar gives up everything to become "Poor Tom," the mad Bedlam beggar who can command nothing. But it is precisely through Edgar's experience as Tom O'Bedlam that literal theatricality is reintroduced into *King Lear* after all. The mad beggar was already an actor on two counts: Bedlam beggars were assumed to be able-bodied con men engaged in a seventeenth-century version of a welfare scam,[102] and "mad" victims of satanic possession were, according to Samuel Harsnett's then-recent *Declaration of Egregious Popish Impostures,* fakes. Certainly the "mad beggar" in *Lear* is a mere disguise. Edgar tells us that his "*presented nakedness*" is intended for display (*Lr.* 2.3.11; italics added); he strips before our eyes, grimes his face, and strikes "wooden pricks" in his "mortified bare arms" as he talks about traveling with his own sort of road show through "pelting villages" and "sheep-cotes" to display himself to the country people and "enforce their charity" (*Lr.* 2.3.15–20, passim). But it's Tom, not Edgar, who begs. Edgar's disguise protects him from giving or receiving charity not only from strangers but also from those closest to him; he is there to watch the suffering of both Lear and his father Gloucester, but they never know it. Instead, as Tom, Edgar takes part in the play-trial Lear stages on the heath; he stages a play of his own for his father when he lets the blinded and suicidal Gloucester think he has jumped from a cliff. Throughout, Edgar occupies the no-man's-land between characters and audience, admitting full membership in neither. He moves in the stage space that belonged to the Vice and his descendants—including Edgar's bastard brother Edmund, whose roles as audience confidant and "illegitimate son" Edgar takes up along with his disguise. In other words, when King Lear meets Poor Tom, "the thing itself," at the center of his play (*Lr.* 3.4.104), he meets a Player-Beggar just as Hamlet meets a Player-King at the center of his, when he decides "the play's the thing" (*Ham.* 2.2.600). Like Hamlet's presentation of his play, Lear's meeting with Edgar opens a dizzying sequence of reversals, as it dissolves the boundary between actor and witness, passion and sympathy, as well as between reality and pretense.

Although *King Lear* is not about acting, then, Lear's experience recalls the story of the player-beggar Sly thrown out by the Hostess in *Shrew.* Edgar's experience as well as Lear's makes this of all the plays most focused on the actor's instrument, his body, and on his hunger for recognition. Finally, the play addresses most powerfully the experience of spectatorship and response, not only for the characters but for their offstage audience as well.[103] No Epilogue steps forward at the end of *Lear* to beg our approval, although audiences may have recognized that Lear's Fool had taken up a song from Feste's epilogue to *Twelfth Night.* But the action of the whole play has compelled our charity as effectively as any Bedlam beggar, "so repellent, nasty, and noisy that you pay him to go away."[104] We, like Edgar with Lear and his father, are drawn despite ourselves. Gloucester begins the play as a shallow old man who mistreats his son, but he is kind to Lear, and we can't help identifying too closely with him when his eyes are torn out on stage. We condemn Lear too, at first, watching Cordelia suffer from his selfish tyranny in the opening scene. Still we cannot help but respond with him when she forgives him and sacrifices herself to him after all.[105]

In *Lear,* finally, the confrontation between Beggar and King, both on-stage and between actors and audience, reaches out to the audience because it takes on more than personal or local theatrical significance to generate a wider social consciousness: "This play alone, of all the major "tragedies," Annabel Patterson argues, "is clearly and profoundly engaged . . . with socioeconomic issues, feudal rights and obligations, and something that verges on class analysis."[106] Jonathan Dollimore goes so far as to argue that the play is "*above all* . . . about power, property, and inheritance" and the fate of poor naked wretches.[107] This is true. But for Shakespeare, private and public concerns are versions and reinforcements of one another.[108] What matters is their constant interaction—the cyclical dynamic in which the fresh eruption of one conflict reproduces the other. Lear's recognition of the poor naked wretches, responsive though it is to its historical circumstances, is also a continuation of the identification with beggars which was so important in Shakespeare's earlier players. *King Lear* thus provides an especially clear example of the ways in which personal fantasies engage with social and economic realities, and the ways in which Shakespeare's actor identity might influence more than the literal or figurative players in the plays.[109]

Chapter Six

Theater as Reflecting Glass:
The Two-way Mirror

*A*ny study of Elizabethan players must take account of the way in which playing was theorized at the time, and should note the connection between Actaeon's reversal—or Falstaff's or Lear's— and the prevailing notion of theater as mirror or reflecting glass. The sixteenth-century English were a mirror-hungry people, to judge by the steady flow of such widely read (and in many cases often-reprinted) titles as a *Mirror for Magistrates* (1559–1620) or *A Looking Glass for Lovers* (1576).[1] Apologists for the theater claimed that drama in particular was the most effective kind of mirror. The very purpose of playing as Hamlet said, is "to hold the mirror up to Nature" (*Ham.* 3.2.22). But theatrical optics were not simple, and throughout the canon Shakespeare evokes a variety of mirroring relations between player and audience which suggest that drama had more purposes than the one Hamlet describes.

When Elizabethan spectators asked for a mirror they most often wanted something like a pattern or exemplar.[2] Hamlet's advice to the players comes in the midst of warning them not to ham it up unnaturally, but he assumes an idealistic rather than naturalistic notion of truth. To hold a (truth-revealing) mirror up to Nature was to reveal something the unaided eye could not see—an absent ideal (thus Hamlet was "the *glass* of fashion and the *mould* of form"; *Ham.* 3.1.155, italics, added) a hidden evil, the unflattering truth *beneath* the surface. When Hamlet "set[s] up a glass" for his mother, "where you may see the inmost part of you" (*Ham.* 3.4.18, 19), she finds that he "turns't my eyes into my very soul, / And there I see such black and grained spots / As will not leave their tinct." (*Ham.* 3.4.89–91). A mirror may "show virtue her feature" or "scorn her own image" (*Ham.* 3.2.22–23) but should not reflect mere perceptual reality.[3] Shakespeare's Richard II smashes his mirror because it reflects physical reality—the same face he'd seen when he was king—rather than reflecting the metaphysical reality of his new unkinged identity as mere subject. A mirror was expected to show things you did not already know and could not already see.

The important question for a sixteenth-century mirror-gazer was not whether but why the image in the glass differed from the subject's ordinary impression. Was it dictated by a higher truth (moral judgment or superior models) or only by the subject's own distorting wishes? In the latter case he would be looking at a flattering glass rather than a true glass (the subject of the next chapter)—like Vanity in the emblem books, misled by worldly beauty.[4] The important question about a dramatic mirror was like the one Hamlet found himself asking about the ghost: is this "thing" strange because it is revealing a hidden truth—or because some power is trying to deceive me?[5] Is my father truly being murdered again on stage—(or, as Claudius might ask, "my brother")—or is it only a maliciously fictionalized version of that murder? Even if the spectators for Shakespeare's *Henry VI* were sophisticated enough—as we know most of them were—not to wonder "Is this really Talbot risen from the grave?" they might well ask, "Is this Essex in the current French wars or only his party's propaganda? Is this really to be believed?" Tropes, as Hamlet implies in his commentary on "The Murder of Gonzago," or "The Mousetrap," could be traps.

Playwrights—including Hamlet in his capacity as collaborator on "The Murder of Gonzago"—could also have designs upon their beholders more palpable even than cognitive deception. Rather than trying to hold the mirror up to nature, a playwright could attempt, through his play, to make nature mirror his own will, just as Tamburlaine, standing victorious over the bleeding bodies of conquered kings, claims proudly that nature mirrors his:

> Such are objects fit for *Tamburlaine,*
> Wherein, *as in a mirrour,* may be seene
> His honor, that consists in sheading blood.
> (*Tamburlaine* 5.1.475–77; italics added)[6]

Shakespeare's Richard III certainly used playing to impose his will on the audience and make the world mirror his desire:

> I'll slay more gazers than the basilisk;
> I'll play the orator as well as Nestor, . . .
> And, like a Sinon, take another Troy.
> (3H6 3.2.187–90)

Richard, like a modern actor, realizes about playing that, "It is power; and it is beyond power."[7]

We do not know much about the intended functions of actual plays, of playing, or of writing plays, beyond those of making a profit and affecting the audience's opinion. But if we take the fictional inner plays represented in Renaissance drama as our sample, the functions would certainly seem to include aggression like Richard III's. As we noted in chapter 4, few of the period's inner plays were performed by players like Bottom or those who perform at Elsinore. Instead, more often the ordinary characters are briefly and secondarily "actors," and the production is a masque rather than an inner play proper.[8] The result of this resolute amateurization of playing—the focus on what we might call "illegitimate theater"—was its association with deception and hostility, or even violence. Most masques were revenge masques, meant not only to reveal the truth about the past but to repeat it in the present, reversed in form. They hold the mirror up to nature, giving measure for measure, exacting an eye for an eye. They create a punishment that mirrors the crime rather than merely reflecting the status quo. As a result, whenever an audience in Shakespeare's day saw preparations for playmaking on stage, they could expect to see an exchange in which the main characters dressed up to entertain their friends and family, and they knew that the sole purpose of the production often would be to murder that audience or the players—though, in a comedy like Munday's *John a Kent* or Shakespeare's *Merry Wives of Windsor*, the goal might merely be to cheat, rob or punish.[9]

The Elizabethan player might be a beggar in the great man's house, but he could be dangerous. The assassins in *Woodstock*, for example, gain entrance to their victim's hall disguised as masquers. As Simon in Middleton's *Mayor of Queenborough* (1619) sagely observes, just before he is robbed by the "players" performing in his house, "I have seen a great man poisoned in a play." This is poison in jest—or "gest," as interludes were called.[10] Laurence Olivier stood behind the curtain in the twentieth century and whispered "You bastards!" to the audience, but that's as far as he went. Kyd's Hieronimo left real corpses on stage, and Tourner's Vindice left them in the audience. Hamlet's "Murder of Gonzago" is very nearly a revenge play itself. "Gonzago" holds the mirror up to Claudius by presenting a murderer poisoning a king in a garden as he poisoned his brother, but it simultaneously threatens him, because the murderer in "Gonzago" is the victim's nephew as Hamlet is Claudius's. In *Titus Andronicus*, Tamora's appearance with her sons in a masque of Revenge, Rape, and Murder—she calls it a "jest"—has similar predatory designs.[11] Aggression also prevails in a larger subcategory of self-conscious drama, the induction plays.[12] Here a "frame" plot involving observers distances the inner action as if it were a play. In the inductions as in real life, acting was associated with deception, dramatic license was often a license to kill, and spying on ("audiencing") an unwitting "actor" was a means of dominating or even attacking him.[13] The hostility thus moves from audience to player—as it moves from Kyd's Andrea, in the *Spanish Tragedy* frame, to the characters he sees in the main action. In the later induction plays, written largely for the boys' companies, it extended more or less playfully to include the offstage audience.[14] Hostility of some sort seemed at least as natural to the induction as obsequiousness did to the epilogues.

Whatever the valence of the exchange between audience and player, however, exchange there was, and even Hamlet acknowledged it. His pompous "mirror" speech about the "purpose of playing" ignored the interaction, but his earlier, more informal response to the players was more telling. Hamlet recalled a play they had once performed about the fall of Troy, *the* most tragic subject in Renaissance literature. Within that play, the speech he says he "chiefly loved" is Aeneas's tale told to Dido and, within that, the part about "Priam's slaughter" (*Ham.* 2.2.442, 444). Hamlet asks the First Player to recite the speech but becomes so involved that he runs on for some dozen or sixteen lines before he allows the Player to take over. Hamlet has tendentious motives for this particular choice, but his enthusiasm for the play suggests that he was attracted to its passionate melodrama even before Claudius made its murder especially significant for him.[15] Hamlet's taste in plays shows that something else is at stake in "The Murder of Gonzago"—as it always was for players in Shakespeare's day: the player's ability to move his audience. The purpose of playing, it turns out, is not only to hold the mirror up to nature, but also "to cleave the general ear" (*Ham.* 2.2.557) or rouse the audience's passion—to "make mad the guilty and appal the free" (*Ham.* 2.2.558), as Hamlet says. The play must not only make the audience see its reflection in the mirror but must make them feel. One could not take place without the other.[16]

Given these expectations we might say that the Player's speech, "Aeneas's tale to Dido," is—for Shakespeare—*the* player's speech, the archetype (or mirror) of all acting, because it is the epitome of witnessed and shared passion. It maps the dynamic and emotional interdependence of player and audience. Harry Levin has described the "dizzying hierarchy of externalized emotion" even within the speech, as the First Player, playing Aeneas, conveys the pathos of Priam's death only indirectly, by noting Hecuba's distress as she watches him killed; her suffering, in turn, is conveyed only by describing its audience, the gods.[17] The resulting "triangulation" of grief, as we might call it, emerges not via its original sufferer, Priam, but as Aeneas observes it being observed.[18] Equally striking is the fact that Aeneas's tale of displacements itself depends on a displacement, for its passion is conveyed only through Dido's response to him. Just as Othello depends on Desdemona's "greedy ear" to ratify his sad tale ("She lov'd me for the dangers I had pass'd, / and I lov'd her that she did pity them"; *Oth.* 1.3.167–68), just as Berowne must learn that "a jest's prosperity lies in the ear / Of him that hears it" (*LLL* 5.2.853–54),[19] so the actor needs his audience.

Dido as audience was already present in the nondramatic text of the *Aeniad*. But in Shakespeare's play the mutuality of performer and audience onstage (Aeneas and Dido) is further complicated because it is relayed outward by means of its audience, Hamlet and Polonius. Even the philistine

Polonius is impressed by the player's tears; Hamlet is completely changed by them and discovers in them his own "motive and cue for passion" (*Ham.* 2.2.555).[20] What the player gets in return for his effect on the audience is not entirely clear, but he seems to be getting something—and something that is not legitimate. Hamlet, even while being affected by the performance, condemns the player's perverse achievement:

> Is it not monstrous that this player here,
> But in a fiction, in a dream of passion,
> Could force his soul so to his own conceit
> That from her working all his visage wann'd;
> *Tears in his eyes,* distraction in his aspect,
> A broken voice, and his whole function suiting
> With forms to his conceit? *And all for nothing!*
> *For Hecuba!*
>
> (*Ham.* 2.2.545–552; italics added)

Although Hamlet is not explicit about whose "monstrousness" he's disgusted at, these lines directly echo another "player's" description of acting in which the object is clearer.[21] Richard III, as we have seen, knows that the actor's pride lies in moving the audience so as to confirm his own sense of himself.[22] Because Richard *is* a monster, he takes delight in this histrionic process rather than recoiling from it:

> Was ever woman in this humor woo'd?
> Was ever woman in this humor won? . . .
> What, I that kill'd her husband and her father:
> To take her in her heart's extremest hate,
> With curses in her mouth, *tears in her eyes,*
> The bleeding witness of her hatred by . . .
> And yet to win her, *all the world to nothing!*
> *Ha!*
>
> (*R3* 1.2.232–43; italics added)

Both Richard and Hamlet exclaim on the "tears in [his or her] eyes" without proper justification—"all for nothing!" Both end with an aspirated snort of disbelief at the way emotion can be so "unnaturally" summoned up or dispelled by the actor's powers. But while Richard sees in such powers a sign of the actor's superiority, Hamlet finds it a sign of spiritual deviation like Richard's physical deformity.

Despite his glance at the player, Hamlet is finally interested in the relay of passion in one direction only, outward from stage to audience. The First Player is not affected by the audience, who seem rather at his mercy than he at theirs. But this was not Shakespeare's only version of the relation

between actor and audience. In *Troilus and Cressida*, written within a year
or so of *Hamlet*, Ulysses describes an exchange which moves even more
obviously in the other direction, from audience to actor, and reverses the
dependence.[23] The "actor" here is the soldier Achilles, but a literal player
would find special relevance in Ulysses' words. His advice to Achilles at the
center of this play in fact parallels Hamlet's advice to the players at the
center of his.[24] The difference is that while Hamlet, idealist that he is, told
the players to hold the mirror up to nature, Ulysses, the wily pragmatist,
tells Achilles that his audience holds the mirror up to him. Achilles, who
thought himself above any need to join his fellow Greeks in battle, had
noticed the Greeks slighting him, passing him by "as misers do by beggars"
(*Tro.* 3.3.141–44). He insists defensively that he doesn't need "these men's
looks" (*Tro.* 3.3.90), but Ulysses shows him that he does, that he is a "hero"
only in the eyes of those who watch and validate his identity. The audience
not only holds the mirror up to Achilles, but unless they keep seeing a
satisfactory image there, Achilles does not exist (as a modern actor would
say, you are only as good as your last performance):[25]

> Man, how dearly ever parted,
> Cannot make boast to have that which he hath,
> Nor feels not what he owes, but by reflection.

This is not the literal truism about eyesight which Achilles would reduce
it to:

> Speculation [i.e., sight] turns not to itself
> Till it hath travell'd and is mirror'd there
> Where it may see itself. This is not strange at all.

Ulysses means something more general:

> No man is lord of *anything*,
> Till he communicate his parts to others;
> Nor doth he of himself know them for aught,
> Till he behold them form'd in the applause,
> Where th'are extended; who [i.e., the applauders] . . .
> . . . like a gate of steel[26]
> Fronting the sun, receives and renders back
> His figure and his heat.
>   (*Tro.* 3.3.96–123, *passim;* italics added)

Even the sun needs a reflecting glass to know his own "figure and his heat."
Hamlet as audience needs the player to mirror or mediate his own pas-

sion—his "form and pressure" (*Ham.* 3.2.24); but Achilles-as-player needs an *audience* to mirror and maintain his own identity.[27] Without it, as he says, he is like "beggars" (*Tro.* 3.3.143), little better than Armado's Worthies or Quince's mechanicals snubbed on stage. Ulysses' theory of "speculation" thus coincides with the epilogues' repeated insistence that the player does not know his parts until he beholds them in the audience's "applause."

A Mirror for Monsters

If Hamlet thought it was "monstrous" that his Player could weep for nothing, Ben Jonson objected to the many "monsters" who insisted on overacting on his stage. To Jonson and Hamlet actors are "unnatural," as was the "monstrous" traitor Jack Cade (*2H6* 4.10.65) or Othello's "monstrous" vision of Desdemona in bed with Cassio (*Oth.* 5.2.191)—and as was Proteus, who could transform himself into new shapes. Sixteenth-century theories of rhetoric gave currency to the belief in a player's ability to defy nature,[28] as did critics like William Rankins in his *Mirrour of Monsters, wherein is plainly described the manifold vices, & spotted enormities, that are caused by the infectious sight of playes* . . . (1587), which purported to reveal the actor's deviance from proper Christian behavior.

But the actor, defined by his audience, is like a monster in another sense, a "painted monster," Greene called him,[29] for he, like the literal "monsters" and fairground freaks at whom crowds paid to gape, earned his keep by putting himself on display. A "monster" for Shakespeare was not only someone unnatural and inhuman, but someone whose unnaturalness was witnessed and held up to the common view. The monster was the obverse of the successful hunter or warrior who rode in triumph through Persepolis. He was one of the prisoners or slain animals at the back of the parade, a souvenir or trophy, a deflated enemy, like Talbot exposed as a mere "scarecrow" to the French (discussed in chapter 4). Worse still for any would-be hero like Talbot in *Henry VI, Part One,* monsters could even seem pitiable or puppyish; Viola compares herself to a monster in *Twelfth Night* because she is so hopelessly in love with Orsino: "[He] loves her dearly; / And I, poor monster, fond as much on him" (*TN* 2.2.32–33). Caliban in *The Tempest,* "half man and half fish," dotes pitifully first on Prospero and then on the shipwrecked mariners who capitalize on his servility by making him their "servant-monster" and planning to put him on show back in England (*Tem.* 3.2.28, 3ff.).[30] Fear of being made such a monster overwhelms Macbeth's bravery, once Macduff threatens to let him live so that Macduff can "have thee, as our rarer monsters are, / Painted on a stick and underwrit, / 'Here may you see the tyrant'" (*Mac.* 5.9.25–27).[31] In *Antony and Cleopatra,*

Antony, furious that Cleopatra has deserted their cause in battle, predicts the particularly female form of this shame that will follow their defeat at Caesar's hands:

> Let him take thee,
> And hoist thee up to shouting plebeians
> Follow his chariot, like the greatest spot
> Of all thy sex. Most monster-like be shown
> For poor'st diminutives, for doits.
>
> (*Ant.* 4.12.33–37)

She will not merely be shown, but shown cheap to the rude masses, the "poor'st diminutives." Later, in her better-known restatement of Antony's prediction, Cleopatra elaborates her fear to Iras and makes the connection explicit between such degradations and the stage:

> Thou, an Egyptian *puppet,* shall be shown
> In Rome, as well as I: mechanic slaves
> With greasy aprons, rules and hammers, shall
> Uplift us to the view. In their thick breaths,
> Rank of gross diet, shall we be enclouded. . . .
> saucy lictors
> Will catch at us like *strumpets,* and scald rhymers
> *Ballad* us out o'tune. The quick comedians
> Extemporally will *stage* us and present
> Our Alexandrian revels . . .
> and I shall see
> Some squeaking Cleopatra boy my greatness
> I' the posture of a whore.
>
> (*Ant.* 5.2.207–19; italics added)

Cleopatra foresees an increasingly debased series of public displays. The series culminates in a performance representing her, but it begins in her own forced performance, when she herself is "uplift[ed] to the view" for an audience even more rudely mechanical than the lowly players in *A Midsummer Night's Dream.*

The eroticization of shame for those on display is suggested by the fact that Shakespeare's monsters included those who had been defeated in love as well as in war; in particular they included the horned cuckold ("wise men know well enough what monsters you make them," says Hamlet to Ophelia before accusing her of woman's "wantonness"; *Ham.* 3.1.141–42, 147). Benedick in *Much Ado About Nothing* has only to think about getting married—that is, about becoming a potential cuckold—to imagine for himself a fate like Macbeth's: If I ever fall in love, he says, pick out mine eyes with a ballad-maker's pen, and hang me up at the door of a brothel-house for the sign of blind Cupid. . . . Hang me in a bottle like a cat and shoot at me. . . . And let me be vilely painted, and in such great letters as they write "Here is good horse to hire" let them signify under my sign, "Here you may see Benedick, the married man." (*Ado* 1.1.233–48, *passim*)[32]

Love makes Benedick into a target for archery practice and reduces him to a painted sign (first the Cupid marking a brothel, then The Married Man) for everyone to stare at. Indeed, in one of the reversals inherent in these ocular relationships, he is not only to be stared at but to be blinded. Shakespeare's imaginary cuckolds all predict similarly humiliating exposures for themselves. Othello sees "the time of scorn / [pointing] his slow unmoving fingers" (*Oth.* 4.2.55–56); Leontes hears the whispers that "Sicilia is a so-forth" (*WT* 1.2.218).[33] For women, the equivalent is the humiliation of being publicly accused of unchastity, like Cleopatra, or like Hermione on trial for adultery in *The Winter's Tale*. Hermione finds having "to prate and talk for life and honour 'fore / Who please to come and hear me" as painful and degrading a part of her trial as the accusation itself (*WT* 3.2.41–42).[34]

People are all too likely to become monsters in love, both unnatural beasts and public laughingstocks. Thus Troilus is simply wrong when he tries to calm Cressida's anxiety about their love by assuring her that, "in all Cupid's pageant there is presented no monster" (*Tro.* 3.2.72–73). He is more accurate when he goes on to refine his claim: "This is the monstruosity in love, lady: that the will is infinite, and the execution confined: that the desire is boundless and the act a slave to limit" (*Tro.* 3.2.79–82). The "monstruosity" Troilus acknowledges is not, he says, part of a play like Cupid's pageant. But Troilus's paradox could serve well as a rationalization for what the histrionic Richard III takes to be his uniquely loveless psyche. Richard's monstrosity lies in the fact that he is so deformed that no woman can love him: "And am I then a man to be belov'd?/ O monstrous fault to harbour such a thought!" (*3H6* 3.2.163–64). In Richard's case at least, the monstrosity, as we have seen, is part of what it means to him to be a player.[35]

Among Shakespeare's literal players, only Sly and Bottom are actually described as monsters. They are monstrous, presumably, because each is the kind of creature who makes a spectacle of himself—a motley to the view—even before he turns to the stage. Sly is monstrously transformed by drink ("Oh, monstrous beast!" cries the Lord on discovering him, "How like a swine he lies!" *Shr.* Ind.1.34), and Bottom, by his ass's head ("My mistress with a monster is in love!" Puck tells Oberon; *MND* 3.2.6). But their predicament has more general implications. It gives us a sense of what Shakespeare thought about display and raises questions about why someone who could represent display as so monstrously demeaning should nonetheless continue to display himself onstage.

Two Gentlemen of Verona: Woman's Part, Dog's Part

The assumption that the actor as well as the audience is affected by their mutual exchange lies behind Shakespeare's only extended discussion of acting outside Hamlet and Troilus, in Two Gentlemen of Verona, where the mirroring relationship is so complex that one literally cannot distinguish between player and audience. The discussion is initiated by lovesick Julia, an early version of the "poor monster" Viola, who dotes on Orsino in Twelfth Night. The most obvious figure for the player in Two Gentlemen is the aptly named male deceiver, Proteus, but his dependence on Silvia as audience is repeated in Julia's still more abject dependence on him; and it is her position which prompts the discussion of playing.[36]

When Julia speaks, she has already been secretly playing the role of Proteus's page, Sebastian, in order to be near Proteus. When Proteus asks Sebastian (i.e., Julia) to court another woman, Silvia, for him, Sebastian agrees—and does so by telling Silvia about a role "he" had once played. Sebastian's description resembles "Aeneas' tale to Dido," the speech Hamlet asked the First Player to recite, and we might even call it "Julia's tale to Silvia." Hamlet's player, as Aeneas, stood by watching Hecuba, a woman lamenting her loss; Julia describes playing Ariadne, a similarly "lamentable" role (TGV 4.4.64). Disguised in Proteus's household, Julia cannot openly express her sorrow or rage at Proteus's betrayal, like Hamlet on guard in Claudius's court, unable to express his rage at Claudius. Unlike Hamlet, however, she does not have access to any players to act out an analogous mythic situation for her. Instead she, speaking as the page, pretends to have acted one out herself—and for herself:

> Our youth got me to play the woman's part,
> And I was trimm'd in Madam Julia's gown. . . .
> And at that time I made her weep agood,
> For I did play a lamentable part.
> Madam, 'twas Ariadne, passioning
> For Theseus' perjury, and unjust flight;
> Which I so lively acted with my tears,
> That my poor mistress [i.e., Julia], moved therewithal,
> Wept bitterly; and would I might be dead,
> If I in thought felt not her very sorrow.
>
> (TGV 4.4.158–70)

At this double distance from her own emotion (Julia playing Sebastian-playing-Ariadne), she can at last acknowledge it as her own, but only

Launce and his dog. Cruikshank frontispiece to the Cumberland edition of *Two Gentlemen of Verona* (London, 1821?). Library of Congress.

by imagining herself being moved by watching herself playing it. Julia/ Sebastian-Ariadne as player moves Julia as audience; then, in a responsive moment, Julia as audience moves Julia/Sebastian-Ariadne as player (says the latter, "would I might be dead,/ If I in thought felt not her [i.e., Julia's] very sorrow"; *TGV* 4.4.169–70). Here the player, Julia/Sebastian-Ariadne, does not merely hold the mirror up to her audience, Julia by wearing Julia's gown; she also moralizes the audience, by representing Julia as Ariadne, and engages in a dynamic exchange with it. Finally, Julia uses the report of this dizzying prior exchange to affect her present audience, Proteus's new mistress Silvia. Silvia's response to the description is to sympathize with Julia: "Alas, poor lady . . . I weep myself to think upon thy words" (*TGV* 4.4.172–73). Thus Julia finds her part—the "woman's part" (*TGV* 4.4.158)— only when, as Ulysses told Achilles, she sees it "receive[d] and render[ed] back" (*Tro.* 3.3.122) by Silvia.

Julia seems to have plumbed the depths of selflessness made possible by the lover's identification with the beloved and by the complex identifications among actor, audience, and character in the theater. But the posture first appears in *Two Gentlemen* in an even lower-than-female form, in the clown Launce (who, like Julia, is Proteus's servant). Launce has willingly "sat in the stocks," "stood on the pillory," and taken whippings for his beloved, but unloving, dog Crab (*TGV* 4.4.30, 32). Crab is a "cruel hearted cur" (*TGV* 2.3.9), as cold as any Petrarchan mistress or Elizabethan cad.[37] Launce first enters the play quite independently of its plot to tell us about the cur.[38] Like any typical Elizabethan clown speaking his introductory monologue, Launce is a kind of comic Aeneas, stepping forth to tell his sad tale to the only Dido he has: to us, the spectators in the audience. He still weeps as he remembers leaving home:

> Nay, I'll show you the manner of it. This shoe is my father. No, this left shoe is my father; no, no. . . . This hat is Nan our maid. I am the dog. No, the dog is himself, and I am the dog. O, the dog is me, and I am myself. . . . Now the dog all this while sheds not a tear . . . but see how I lay the dust with my tears. (*TGV* 2.3.13–32)

In soliciting our response, Launce's soliloquy foregrounds his ambiguous relation to the audience, who both are and are not there; he calls attention to the precariousness of the actor's position and to the audience's multiple roles in validating it. Bert O. States cites Launce's scene to epitomize theater's defining ontological frisson, which he says depends on the actor's unsettled status.[39] Crab, States insists, is a real dog in an imaginary setting, and thus reminds us of the strange process by which all props and actors are transformed into theater. In *Midsummer Night's Dream,* Shakespeare makes a point about the paradox of live theater when Quince declares ponderously at rehearsal that "this green plot shall be our stage" (*MND* 3.1.3)—in other words, "this stage, which I have asked you to pretend is a green plot, shall be our stage" or, "that which I have asked you to transform into something else is really only itself after all." Here, less explicitly but just as paradoxically, Shakespeare announces that "this dog shall be a dog." The excitement audiences always feel at theater, States argues, depends on a condition epitomized by the fact that at any moment a real dog can misbehave drastically. Even if Crab doesn't misbehave, he reminds us of the tenuousness of performance and the fact that it is always dependent on its "real" material ground, which at any moment can be foregrounded as such. Launce's words express our own "ontological queasiness"[40] when identifying with characters on stage who supposedly mirror us: "I am the dog. No, the dog is himself, and I am the dog. O, the dog is me, and I am myself" (*TGV* 2.3.21–23). Even when Launce doesn't think he is confused, he unsettles the rules of the language game to produce confusion: Crab is so cruel, Launce says, "he has no more pity than a dog" (*TGV* 2.3.10–11).[41] That is, Crab is "dog" as *symbol* or *sign* of cruelty; of course he is also and more immediately "dog" as dog or *referent*. When Launce calls attention to both entities in the same breath, the vast expanse between the two opens up. The clown, who lives always at the edge where the illusional world falls off into the audience's, makes his position even more precarious with the dog. It becomes impossible to tell the mirror from Nature.

Robert Weimann also finds Launce an epitome of theatrical precariousness—at least in Shakespeare. But instead of dwelling on the merely cognitive dissonance induced by Crab's presence, Weimann shows the social use to which Shakespeare puts this dissonance. In an appendix to his book on popular theater Weimann examines Launce (and his fellow Speed) as perfect examples of the Elizabethan popular actor, mediating between play and audience by commenting on it from the (audience's) popular point of view. Here, Weimann argues, Launce's mediation achieves structural significance in the plays, and indeed in the canon, for with Launce Shakespeare seems to discover a new mode of comedy, defined by the actor's relation to the audience rather than by the shape of the plot or the tone of the experience. The audience, Weimann says, laughs with, not at, both Speed and Launce, and therefore gains a wider perspective from which to view the romance characters. The audience's response thus becomes part of the play. Weimann goes on to distinguish between Speed and Launce and to suggest that Launce is more deeply implicated in this effect. While Speed merely laughs with the audience at other characters, Launce laughs with the audience at himself, and thus becomes both the object and the subject of his own mirth—subject, as Weimann explains, "in the sense of *Subjekt,* or ego, or self. His, indeed, is what Hegel called the 'blessed ease of a subjectivity, which, as it is sure of itself, can bear the dissolution of its own ends.'"[42] Private subjectivity, Weimann argues, is therefore (paradoxically) made possible by the social or public position of the actor. That position helps resolve the tension within the fictional character Launce (between Launce the mocker and Launce the mocked), by assimilating it to the tension between fictional character and real actor. The character Launce's ridiculousness within the play's world—his shame and isolation—are thus mitigated by the actor Kempe's connection to the laughing spectators.[43] They laugh at Launce but identify with Kempe. This unity between audience and actor, Weimann argues, "has its ultimate origins in the rituals of a less divided society," and generates "the laughter of solidarity rather than that [like Ben Jonson's] of satire." The social context of Shakespeare's theater which places the comic actor this way, Weimann says, "points to a state of society, or, more likely, to a vision of Utopia, that precludes any *Entzweiung* or alienation between self and the social."[44]

Weimann's optimistic account of the dynamic he identifies, however, might be qualified by considering the individual—subjective or psychic—cost of the clown's offering, the use the clown makes of himself in order to secure unity with society, and the degree to which union depends on a reminder of difference. The union of self and society does not eliminate the alienation between self and self, or the "monstrousness" which that alienation can create in a player. When Launce takes on the role of "dog" and makes light of his humiliations—makes use of them—he is not unlike Richard III taking on the role of currish "villain" for similar motives. Both "willingly" assume uncongenial roles and distance them; but neither is completely successful. Launce's mild dismay at the role confusion ("I am the dog. No, the dog is himself, and I am the dog . . .") takes more troubling form in Richard's confusion at the end of his play, in his final nightmare confrontation with himself:

> Is there a murderer here? No. Yes, I am!
> Then fly. What, from myself? Great reason why,
> Lest I revenge? What, myself upon myself?
> . . . I am a villain—yet I lie, I am not!

> (*R3* 5.3.185–87, 192)

The two soliloquies were written within a year or two of each other, perhaps less, and show two sides of the same experience.[45]

Nor is the cost purely psychic. It registers at the social level as well. Launce creates the festive humor of a classless Utopian world, but only by evoking a very class-conscious gallows humor. Freud describes gallows humor by citing the joke about a rogue on his way to execution who asks for a scarf for his bare throat so as not to catch cold—"an otherwise laudable precaution," Freud notes, "but one which, in view of what lay in store so shortly for the neck, was remarkably superfluous and unimportant."[46] Freud admits of the rogue that, "It must be confessed that there is magnanimity in . . . the man's tendentious hold upon his customary self and his disregard of what might overthrow that self and drive it to despair"; here Freud sounds like Hegel on a Subjectivity so "sure of itself" that "it can bear the dissolution of its own ends."[47] But unlike Hegel or Weimann, Freud also stresses the fact that the self *is* to be overthrown, and that that, as the audience knows, is a high price to pay for magnanimity. Indeed in some gallows humor the victim displays more stupidity than magnanimity, and the audience's laughter is tinged with sadism even in its solidarity. The player embodied as Launce has nothing except self-deprecating humor with which to establish solidarity. He is a self-consuming artifact.

Launce's, in other words, is a typically Shakespearean detour on the royal road to social Utopia, one of a series of positions, not all of which are cost free, along the line from obedient Uncle Tom to defiant camp compliance. Some of Shakespeare's clowns display even more literal gallows humor. The nearly contemporary "clown" in *Titus Andronicus,* who hears that he is to be hanged, shrugs ironically, "Then I have brought up a neck to a fair end!" (*Tit.* 4.4.48–49).[48] But Launce embodies the uniquely Shakespearean tone, more sinned against than sinning, which will reappear in Feste's unfestive sadness and in Lear's Fool.[49] It appears as well in the sonnet poet, who can accept his mistress's imperfections with Launce-like equanimity, in what Stephen Booth aptly calls the poet's "clown act." The comic anti-Petrarchanism in "My mistress' eyes are nothing like the sun," according to Booth, "appears to have no target and no aim except to be funny."[50] We might ask, however, why a poet would choose to be funny at such a moment, and what the humor implies about the quality of his love.

Weimann avoids these dystopian implications of clowning by confining his analysis to Launce's first monologue, where Launce reveals nothing shameful, and where his self-division is projected outward onto his props: "I am the dog. No, the dog is himself, and I am the dog . . ." But in Launce's later monologue such comedy covers over a more painful confusion between self and other. "In his 'I am the dogge,'" as Barbara Everett neatly puts it, "the clown is wrestling, in words of one syllable, with the issues that give the Sonnets all their love-metaphysics."[51] Not only the sonnets; Launce—like other Shakespearean performance-oriented clowns—provides an early vehicle for material whose tragic potential is more fully developed later on.[52] Launce's hopeless love for Crab, for example, is a grotesque analogy for Antonio's devotion to Sebastian in *Twelfth Night.* Launce has rescued his beloved Crab from drowning only to have the ungrateful dog ignore him.[53] Antonio too rescued his beloved Sebastian from drowning, only to have the boy deny knowing him:

> That most ingrateful boy there by your side,
> From the rude sea's enrag'd and foamy mouth
> Did I redeem. A wrack past hope he was.
> His life I gave him, and did thereto add
> My love, without retention or restraint,
> All in his dedication. For his sake
> Did I expose myself (pure for his love)
> Into the danger of this adverse town.
>
> (*TN* 5.1.75–82)[54]

Later, when telling us about Crab's adventure at Silvia's house, Launce literally takes on the dog's identity—at least takes on his sins—and thereby exposes himself to what would be one of the most degrading moments in the plays, if Launce did not resolutely ignore what would, as Freud wrote, "drive [him] to despair." The monologue is Launce's tour de force, an account of his physical humiliation when he takes responsibility for Crab's odorous indiscretions and is whipped out of the chamber for his offense. Proteus had told Launce to give Silvia a lapdog as a gift, but Launce substitutes his own oversized Crab (a dog for a dog) and brings him to Silvia at dinner, where Crab promptly misbehaves by relieving himself under the table.

> O, 'tis a foul thing [says Launce], when a cur cannot keep himself in all companies. . . . If I had not had more wit than he, to take a fault upon me that he did, I think verily he had been hanged for't; sure as I live he had suffered for't. You shall judge: he thrusts me himself into the company of three or four gentleman-like dogs, under the Duke's table: he had not been there (bless the mark) a pissing while, but all the chamber smelt him. "Out with the dog," says one; "What cur is that?" says another, "Whip him out," says a third; "Hang him up," says the Duke. I, having been acquainted with the smell before, knew it was Crab; and goes me to the fellow that whips the dogs: "Friend," quoth I, "you mean to whip the dog?" "Ay, marry do I," quoth he. "You do him the more wrong," quoth I; "'twas I did the thing you wot of." He makes no more ado, but whips me out of the chamber. How many masters would do this for his servant? (*TGV* 4.4.10–30)

There is a kind of triumph here, to be sure—Launce allows himself to identify with the dog's uninhibited freedom. But only at the price of vicariously living out the actor's fear of exposing himself and "messing up" on stage, here reduced to its most primitive physical embodiment—as in the vision of the defecating horse which came to William Redfield when he panicked about his role in *Hamlet* (see chapter 2). Launce takes on not only Crab's sins, but his punishments as well—and, as for the actor, the punishment is always public humiliation, the shame that announces deflated fame. Launce has already suffered public humiliation by sitting in the stocks for his dog—an ordeal Shakespeare associated with the bad smells which would be inescapable after a day's confinement—and with being publicly whipped.[55] Now he exposes himself at a private performance in the hall of a great house by publicly "confessing" and offering himself up for the punishment in place of his dog.

As if that weren't enough, Launce simultaneously repeats the humiliation by acting it out for the audience once again, just as he had acted out his leave-taking before. "You shall judge," he says to us. Then he stages the scene by taking on all roles himself and ends by showing how Crab left the table to "make water" on Silvia. "When didst thou see me heave up my leg, and make water against a gentlewoman's farthingale?" he asks Crab in irritation, even repeating, "Didst thou ever see me do such a trick?" (*TGV* 4.4.37–39). Clearly the joke depends on our seeing him do that very trick even as he denies it. Having humiliated himself for love at Julia's house, he now humiliates himself for our amusement in the public theater—like Falstaff unwittingly putting on his own horns in Windsor. Weimann sees our response as the "laughter of solidarity" reminiscent of a less divided society, one, presumably, in which Polonius may condescend to players by trying to keep them in their place but in which Hamlet's magnanimity finally prevails: "Use every man after his own desert," Hamlet reminds Polonius, "and who should scape whipping?" (*Ham.* 2.2.524–25).[56] Launce himself counters any vision of solidarity by describing his whipping for us and by stubbornly recalling social divisions between master and servant at the end of his speech: "How many masters would do this for a servant?" he asks (*TGV* 4.4.29–30). Launce has not only switched roles within the play's fiction to become Crab and then Crab's servant; but, in making us laugh at that self-abasement, he is *our* servant as well, like a player "playing the fool," as Thomas Nashe sneered, to earn a few pennies—and our laughter.

Chapter Seven

"Dogs, Licking, Candy, Melting" and the Flatterer's False Glass

And I profess now the courtly philosophy,
To crouch, to speak fair, myself I apply,
To feed the king's humour with pleasant devices,
For which I am called Regius canis.
But wot ye who named me first the king's dog?

Edwards, Damon and Pithias (1564)

*I*t is not surprising that an actor would write plays in which his profession is narratized as it is in *Dream* or discussed as it is in *Hamlet,* or in which theatricality provides a frequent figure for other experience. For Shakespeare, however, the dynamics of reciprocal identification in playing extended their influence further, into the details of his language throughout.[1] In particular they help generate Shakespeare's most famous image cluster, identified by Walter Whiter in 1765 and singled out a century and a half later by Caroline Spurgeon as "by far the clearest and most striking example" of Shakespeare's habit of clustering. Spurgeon named this "curious group" of images the "dog, licking, candy, melting group, called up . . . by the thought of false friends or flatterers" and found it pervading the canon.[2] The cluster is a node, like the dream nodes Freud identified, the umbilical cord of the dream, the mycelium from which signifiers spread metaphorically and metonymically outward into a network of signifiers. "Candy" thus leads not only to "sweet," for example, but, because "candied" means "covered over in crystals," it also leads to "ice" and "glass"—and thus to the disreputable double of the mirror in dramatic theory: the untrustworthy "flattering glass."

This network of signifiers is called up not by the thought of flattery alone, but rather by a group of overlapping thoughts which include the stage and its audience. Like distant stars which the telescope resolves into groups of stars, Spurgeon's cluster is actually a cluster of clusters. The "thought of flattery" moves in one direction towards the cosmic flattery implied by the cluster of *dream, sleep, sweet, king, queen,* joined in later plays by *tears* and *weeping,* in another direction to the intimate flattery implied by the cluster *glass, face, hair, eyes, knee,* and in yet another to the

166

phenomenologically descriptive cluster *sweet/candy, poison/venom, winter, ice/hail, cold, melt/thaw, sun, brook/stream, drop, tears, stone.* Any of these can then lead to the more "familiar combination of *dog* (especially *spaniel* or *cur*), *fawning, sweet* or *candy, melt,* and *knee* or *kneel.*"[3] The cluster is thus related via "kneel" to the motif of beggars who fawn and kneel before kings and might at any moment change places with them. Even this is not a complete account, for the flattery network is only half of a larger complex in which the fawning spaniel becomes a circling cur (or circle of curs) who attack. Most important for our purposes, it merges with the "pinch" imagery of the surrounded and helpless victim, and with Actaeon and the imagery of the hunt, all of which, as we have seen, Shakespeare associated with being on stage or being "uplift[ed] to the view," as Cleopatra put it (*Ant.* 5.2.210).[4]

The cluster, in other words, is informed by a player's sense of being surrounded by a fawning audience who might at any moment turn on him—an audience conceived both as intimately maternal and dangerously fickle. It is enriched by, though it does not necessarily either begin or end in, experiences onstage like the one Robert Wilson's clown described:

> But yonder is a fellow that gapes to bite me,
>   or else to eat that which I sing.
> Why, thou art a fool; canst thou not
>   keep thy mouth strait together?
> And when it comes, snap at it, as
>   my father's dog would do at a liver.
>   (*Three Ladies of London* 6:327)

And, as in the case of the Actaeon myth, the cluster predicates a mirroring reversal that implicates the player himself in the audience's violence. The actor's scorn for the flattering audience is inseparable from his dependence on them and on their flattery. An actor hates flattery because he himself is one of the "flattering Gnatoes," as Phillip Stubbes said, courting the audience's favor.[5] His hostility toward the flattering crowd is derived in part from his own need to fawn and flatter them. He hates himself for playing to them, he hates them for "making" him do it, and he hates them when he fails. Like Talbot captured and put on display in France, the actor would gladly dig up stones to hurl at his beholders.[6]

Shakespeare, we should remember, for all his scorn of sweet words and candied tongues, was the poet whom Francis Meres called "honey-tongued," and he was praised by Richard Barnfield for his "hony-flowing Vaine."[7] It was, after all, in the flattering sonnets—the poetry of "praise," in which Joel Fineman saw the origins of poetic subjectivity—that Callow heard an actor speaking. Shakespeare's recoil from flattery, in other words, need not be simply a fastidious recoil from a false friend's betrayal. It might also project his own conflicted desire to flatter the Other, and it might suggest how central that desire was in producing his sense of himself. Rather than calling it the "flattery" cluster I would call it, after Freud's paper on beating fantasies, "An adult is being flattered."[8] The manifest fantasy Spurgeon describes—"I, an adult, am being flattered by them, and I hate it"—gains its power in conjunction with others, of which it is a transformed version and to which it might at any moment revert. Behind it are others: "I, an adult, am being flattered by them, and I love it"; and, "I, an adult, am being attacked by them." And then, reversing itself, "I, an adult, am flattering them," and "I, an adult, am attacking them." Finally the "I" becomes a child and the audience a maternal presence: "I am flattering my mother" and, ultimately, "I am attacking her." Richard III, Shakespeare's arch player, may claim innocently that he "cannot flatter, and look fair,/ Smile in men's faces, smooth, deceive and cog" (R3 1.3.47–48), but he smoothly flatters Lady Anne into becoming a flattering glass for him, and Queen Margaret knows what lies behind such flattery: "Beware of yonder dog/ Look when he fawns, he bites" (R3 1.3.289–90).[9]

"Flattery" constitutes one of the few core topics to which Shakespeare returned repeatedly, along with another not unrelated preoccupation, sexual jealousy.[10] Shakespeare's first inner play, in Love's Labour's Lost, is set in a world oiled by flattery and peopled with comic parasites from Boyet in the Princess's train to Armado and Nathaniel among the clowns. Flattery turns up in the other great house plays as well when the humble players flatter their patrons, and it permeates King Lear, which retains some of the old Leir's emphasis on the evils of flattery, and incorporates a speech from Jonson's scathing anatomy of flattery in Sejanus (1603).[11] Lear himself, in his madness, associates his fall with flattery: "They flatter'd me like a dog. . . . Go to, they are not men o' their words: they told me I was everything. 'Tis a lie, I am not ague-proof" (Lr. 4.6.96–105, passim). And Shakespeare had treated "slander," the other side of the flattery coin, at some length in Measure for Measure (1603–4 [1604]), where Duke Vincentio's histrionic tendencies are intricately bound up with his concern about slander and what people are saying about him.[12]

By the time Shakespeare began writing romances, he had explored flattery at some length in a series of plays about politics, which in their own way turn out to be as much about theater as the great house plays. Of the six standard examples cited by William Rankins in his 1587 diatribe against flattery, three became important figures in Shakespeare's plays (Julius Caesar, Timon, and Alcibiades—whose association with the tradition may help to explain his somewhat puzzling presence in Timon of Athens); and a fourth appears at a telling moment in *Lucrece* (Sinon, who "flattered" his way past the gates of Troy, like Tarquin trying to invade Lucrece). Shakespeare adds Richard II, an English example of the flattered prince, and Coriolanus as his own contributions to the sequence. These are plays about kings and great men who hate the fawning flattery which Spurgeon described, but who also feel its erotic tug and fall prey to its lurking violence. Each play presents a group of courtiers surrounding and fawning on a central political figure. The man at the center claims to despise the flattery of fickle crowds who bow to Pompey one moment and to Caesar the next— like the fickle crowd at a public theater. But he nonetheless responds to flattery's temptations—often associating them with the more intimate flattery between lovers or close friends. He finds in fact that he himself must stoop to flattery and court the courtiers—or, worse, the masses. In the end, despite their caution, such figures wind up literally flattered to death.

The following sections first sketch the problematics of flattery in Elizabethan culture and then examine the victims of flattery in *Richard II, Julius Caesar, Coriolanus,* and *Timon of Athens* as figures whose fates would be of particular interest to an actor. These four plays may reflect more immediately on the theatricality of Elizabethan and Jacobean princes in their power over—and dependence on—their fickle "audience" than they do on the day-to-day lives of the Lord Chamberlain's men. But the plays also reveal what Shakespeare means by "theatricality." They suggest not only that princes—Elizabeth as well as Richard II—are like actors, but also that an actor can feel like a prince when he pleases the audience and like a savaged god when he doesn't. We have considered that it was Shakespeare's play which prompted Queen Elizabeth to say, "I am Richard II." But we tend to forget the significance—wider than we may so far have guessed—of the player who also said, "I am Richard II."

Elizabethan Moths and Fawns

Spurgeon assumed that the "curious" flattery cluster originated in Shakespeare's fastidious dislike of servile courtiers, scornful portraits of whom appear in several plays: in *Richard III,* when Richard describes the flatterer he cannot be; in *King John,* when the bastard turns his wit on an overcourtly soldier; in *Henry IV,* when Hotspur recoils from another one on the battlefield; in *Hamlet's* fop Osric; in Coriolanus's contempt for the "parasite" in silk; and in *Timon of Athens.* The fastidious Shakespeare, Spurgeon explained, would naturally associate these flatterers with dogs, whose slobbering was the physical equivalent of the psychological slobbering of the courtiers:

> It was the habit in Elizabethan times to have dogs, which were chiefly of the spaniel and greyhound type, at table, licking the hands of the guests, fawning and begging for sweetmeats with which they were fed, and of which, if they were like dogs today, they ate too many, dropping them in a semi-melting condition all over the place.[13]

It is the sort of undisciplined behavior we associated with Launce's dog Crab. Spurgeon assumed that the cluster's significance was personal and saw it as a function of Shakespeare's unique experience:

> He who values so intensely—above all else in human life—devoted and disinterested love, turns almost sick when he watches flatterers and sycophants bowing and cringing to the rich and powerful in order to get something out of them for themselves. It is as certain as anything can be that he had been hurt . . . in this particular way.[14]

Our subsequent recognition of the importance of cultural context might suggest that the flattery cluster is not so curious after all. The link between flattery, fawning courtiers, sweets, and fawning dogs was already well established in Elizabethan culture. "As fawning as a spaniel" was a catch phrase;[15] Shakespeare did not need personal betrayal to create an Osric. Recently we have become aware of how thoroughly flattery characterized a hierarchical world run by patronage and bribery, where "the gathering of flatterers was a mark of arrival."[16] It was a common topic in the books of statesmanship consulted by Elizabethan readers; Holinshed, Machiavelli, Plutarch, and Elyot all included monitory sections on flattery among their lessons. The ambitious generation of overeducated gentlemen, whose ascent into courtly circles was well mapped by poetry manuals and courtesy manuals alike, were alert to signs of flattery in others. Despite—or perhaps because of—its advocation by slick descendants of Castiglione, flattery "was decried as the most pernicious of courtly vices."[17] Hubris brought down the Greek tragic heroes, but the first English tragedy, *Gorboduc,* traced the fatal effects of flattery. This chronic interest in royal "parasites" was reinforced at the end of the 1580s by titillating gossip from Scotland about the flattery rife in the court of James VI.[18]

But if the cluster of associations with flattery did not originate in a unique event in Shakespeare's experience, it is nonetheless far more curious than even the cultural revisions of Spurgeon suggest. Both Spurgeon and recent critics treat flattery—private or public—as a coolly conscious strategy. But, on the contrary, flattery was then as now charged with ambivalence which made it more than merely a practical technique for getting ahead. Even the spaniel was already an ambiguous beast, not just the lowdown hound Burton refers to ("fawning like a spaniel, with lying and feigned obsequiousness") but the sympathetic dog whom Lyly cites ("the more he is beaten the fonder he is") and whom Erasmus includes among the true "fools."[19] The dog's double valence led William Empson to devote two chapters in his *Complex Words* to this creature at once despised by his countrymen and elevated to the status of the English national animal.[20] No less than the spaniel—though in different ways—the human fawner is ambiguous; Falstaff as the "Prince's dog" is a complex creature indeed. Burdened by the very contradiction he uses to get ahead, the flatterer is seen not only as a hypocritical knave ready to savage you even as he smiles, but also as a groveling slave beneath contempt, even though the latter was supposed to be a mere disguise. In the words of Jonson's Mosca in *Volpone* (1605–6 [1606]), one of the archflatterers in Renaissance drama, he can "*rise / And stoop* (almost together) like an arrow" (3.1.24; italics added):

> Oh! Your parasite
> Is a most precious thing . . .
> All the wise world is little else, in nature,
> But parasites, or sub-parasites. And yet,
> I mean not those who have your bare town-art,
> To know who's fit to feed 'em
> . . . nor those,
> With their court-dog-tricks, that can fawn and fleer,
> Make their revenue out of legs and faces,
> Echo my Lord, and lick away a moth.
> But your fine, elegant rascal, that can rise
> And stoop (almost together) like an arrow.
>   (*Volpone* 3.1.7–24, *passim*)

Or, as another Jonsonian toad put it, "The way to rise, is to obey, and please" (*Sejanus* 3.735).

No wonder Mosca is such a brilliant actor. He has much in common with the professional players who "strive to please you every day" (*TN* 5.1.407), those "proud beggars" who knew how to rise and stoop at once, and—not for nothing—were also known as parasites and flatterers. Players in general were also at times called dogs, as in William Vaughan's complaint that "all kinds of persons, without respect of sexe or degree are nickt and nipped, rayled and reviled by these snarling curre-dogs [players]." And David Wiles argues that the clown actor Robert Armin's "shape and size gave point to the recurrent image of the cringing dog" associated with his comic roles.[21] In any case, both the flatterer and the player were self-servers masking in selflessness. Mosca gets what he wants by seeming to give his masters what they want; the player proudly secures the spotlight for himself and gets what he wants by being obsequious to the audience.

But Mosca's balance between rising and stooping was not so easily achieved, whether on stage or off. Flattery entails an erotically tinged intimacy not entirely subject to rational control. To fully understand it, we need to pay attention not only to more public experience but rather to what are usually considered even more private realms than those Spurgeon referred to.

Even political flattery always maintained contact with private relationships—with "friendship" and the friendship tradition. Outside courtly circles as well as in them the mistrust of "a flatterer's tongue with sugared words" was incorporated into the literature; private men as well as princes knew to "beware a flattering Gnatho."[22] The roots of this political vice in intimate experience are observable in the sequence of political flatterers spanning both politics and intimacy who appeared in drama. With striking regularity, and long before 1604, when an entire play was devoted to *The Fawn,* the type had come alive on the English stage. The flattering parasite appeared both in popular drama, growing out of the morality play character Vice, whose pernicious weapons included flattery; and in the amoral creatures in Plautus and Terence who were known for appetite, self-interest, and pandering as well as obsequiousness.[23] The Elizabethan hybrid parasite combined the Roman parasite's amoral sleaziness with the Vice's immorality. He was usually portrayed as one of those "caterpillars as corrupt the commonwealth" (*A Knack to Know a Knave* [1592]),[24] a dangerous royal sycophant like Herman and Tyndar in *Gorboduc* (1562), whose evil counsel could bring kingdoms to a tragic end.[25]

The flatterer's political destructiveness, however, consisted largely of dubious personal services which corrupted the king's mortal as well as divine body. He not only fed the king's narcissism with unctuous flattery, but worked in other ways to "smooth" or "flatten"—etymologically the origin of "flatter"—his master's path. The parasite counseled and facilitated self-indulgence, and typically served as a pander procuring illegal liaisons for his master. Perin, the parasite villain of *A Knack to Know a Knave,* brags to his father on his death bed,

> Father, I live as Aristippus did,
> And use my wits to flatter with the king. . . .
> Did Sinon live, with all his subtlety
> He could not tell a flattering tale more cunningly.
> Sometime I move the king to be effeminate,
> And spend his time with some coy courtesan.
> Thus with the king I curry favor still,
> Though in my heart I wish him any ill.

> (*Knack* 518)

The move is swift and smooth from "Sinon," the famous hypocrite who insinuated the fatal horse into Troy, to "pander." The transition is natural because traditionally flattery was a necessary component to seduction. As Marlowe's Tamburlaine says, excusing his uncharacteristically effeminate praise of Zenocrate, "women must be flattered" (*Tamburlaine* 1.2.107).

Adept as the parasite is at seduction, it is not surprising that his "devotion" to the king itself often verged on the erotic, its extravagance almost sensual. (To "stroke with the hand, caress," is among the etymological roots and subsidiary meanings of "flatter.") The recoil from flatterers as enemies to a kingdom was also recoil from the threat of personal and sexual betrayal. Another flatterer in *Knave* was "bedfellow to the king," who says he "loved thee as my second self" (*Knave* 526); Peter Pleaseman, dressed as a parson in *The Three Ladies of London* (1581), is also known as "pleasewoman too, now and then": as he says, "*homo* is indifferent."[26] Ateukin, the parasite in Greene's *James IV* (1592), expresses his devotion just after swearing to arrange an adulterous match for the king:

> Did not your grace suppose I flatter you,
> Believe me, I would boldly publish this:
> Was never eye that saw a sweeter face,
> Nor never ear that heard a deeper wit—
> O God, how I am ravished in your worth!
> . . . I'll kiss your highness' feet.
>
> (*James IV* 1.1.272–78)

Mosca's talents prompt a similar outburst from his master Volpone:

> My witty mischief!
> Let me embrace thee! Oh, that I could now
> Transform thee to a Venus.
>
> (*Volpone* 5.3.102–4)

The best-known of these parasitical "friends" are Gaveston in Marlowe's *Edward II,* Edward's overtly homosexual lover;[27] Bushy, Bagot, and Green in Shakespeare's *Richard II,* which is partly based on Marlowe's play; and Jonson's Sejanus, a male prostitute, "the noted pathic of the time" (*Sejanus* 1.1.216), who rose to become Tiberius's (traitorous) advisor. Despite the many ways in which male homosocial and even homoerotic friendship was accepted in the Renaissance, this kind of male friendship—unlike the love for young boys—was always suspect, a traitorous color inseparable from an eroticism that was consistently portrayed as sexual perversity. The parasite embodied the dark side of male attachment, the section on "The Flatterer" that was inevitably appended to the chapters on "Friendship" in

Renaissance manuals. He lurked as potential destroyer in male attachments, his betrayal equivalent to cuckoldry in heterosexual attachments and as greatly feared and loathed. What Vandiver calls the age's general "repugnance" to the parasite is due at least in part to the same kind of emotional and erotic paranoia which generated the hatred of women.[28] Even the imagery is similar. Shakespeare used the tainted cup as emblem of tainted marriage. Claudius fouled the wine in his cup with a poisoned "union" (*Ham.* 5.2.331), and when Leontes "discovers" Hermione's adultery, "he cracks his gorge" thinking he has drunk "the spider" in the cup (*WT* 2.1.39–45). But the poisoned cup signaled the contamination of other intimacies as well: in *Gorboduc,* when the king drinks poison from a golden cup and drops dead, the Chorus explains, "The delightful gold filled with poison betokeneth flattery, which under fair seeming of pleasant words beareth deadly poison" (*Gorboduc* 2.1.17–19).[29]

Still more relevant, Shakespeare describes the "monarch's plague, this flattery," as a "poison'd" cup (Son. 114.2, 13) and finds it inherent in love's most intimate alchemy:

> Or whether doth my mind, being crown'd with you,
> Drink up the monarch's plague, this flattery?
> Or whether shall I say mine eye saith true,
> And that your love taught it this alchemy—
> To make of monsters and things indigest[30]
> Such cherubins as your sweet self resemble,
> Creating every bad a perfect best
> As fast as objects to his beams assemble?
> O 'tis the first, 'tis flatt'ry in my seeing,
> And my great mind most kingly drinks it up.
> Mine eye well knows what with his gust is greeing,
> And to his palate doth prepare the cup.
>   If it be poison'd, 'tis the lesser sin
>   That mine eye loves it and doth first begin.
>
>   (Son. 114)

The poet drinks his poisoned cup but knows full well that it is poison.

Not surprisingly, the other notorious "flatterer" in Elizabethan literature is the prostitute. Alcibiades, as traditional a victim of flattery as Caesar and Timon, succumbed to the harlot Timandra's flattery; as William Rankins put it, Alcibiades lay lulled in the lap "of that filthie strumpet" and so allowed his enemies to set fire to his house. Rankins, who includes Timandra in his 1587 list of pernicious flatterers, caps the list with an emblematic Concubine attempting to lead Christian astray with her "ambracings and sweete perswasions."[31] Shakespeare may have drawn on the association between prostitution and flattery in the final couplet of sonnet 138, which begins "When my love lies and swears she is made of truth":

> Therefore I lie with her, and she with me,
> And in our faults by lies we flattered be.
>
> (Son. 138.13–14)

The link between prostitutes and dogs was proverbial: "Whores and dogs fawn upon a man no longer than they are fed."[32] The two groups of flatterers—parasites and prostitutes—are further linked in the use of word "dog" to refer to a male prostitute:

> hee, who condemneth the female hoore and male, and, detesting speciallie the male by terming him a *dogge;* might well controll likewise the meanes and occasions whereby men are transformed into dogges, the sooner, to cutt of all incitements to that beastlie filthines, or rather more then beastlie.[33]

It is clear that Elizabethan spaniels, both canine and human, were capable of doing more dirty mischief under the table than Spurgeon suspected.[34] Indeed, the complex of forces encompassed by flattery can reverse itself and become a savage attack. Spurgeon's dogs licked and then just turned their backs, but Elizabethans knew that flattering dogs can turn ferocious. Rankins warns, "beware of such pernicious Gnatonists, who taking us friendlie by the one hand, have in the other a naked blade to shed out bloud." The wisdom was proverbial: "He can both fawne like a spaniell, and bite like a Mastive."[35]

In Shakespeare, the origin of the flattery cluster in intimate experience, and its gradual accretion of public, and theatrical, meaning becomes clear if we trace its evolution and watch the various elements congeal. Just as Simon Callow found an actor speaking in the sonnets' love story, the flattery cluster emerges first in Shakespeare's love scenes. At first, "flattery" was associated not so much with the wiles of a devious hypocrite but rather with one's own flattering dreams, with internal rather than external deception. Hobday in fact finds Christopher Sly to be the earliest occasion for the image cluster, a creature as far from court and ambitious courtiers as one might imagine, though not so far from players and playing. "On finding Sly asleep," Hobday notes,

> one of the huntsmen remarks: "This were a bed but cold to *sleep* so soundly", and the lord orders him to be put to bed and "wrapped in *sweet* clothes". He suggests that on waking Sly will think it "a *flattering dream*", and adds an order to "burn *sweet* wood to make the lodging sweet".[36]

Some of these flattering dreams are illusions like Sly's; some refer to the real but transitory grandeur of actual princes (e.g., Queen Elizabeth in *Richard III*). What is important is that the dream of kingship is nearly always a dream of love as well. The elevation in status derives from the love, and is perhaps only a figure for love. Thus Romeo:

> If I may trust the flattering truth of sleep. . . .
> I dreamt my lady came and found me dead . . .
> And breathed such life with kisses in my lips
> That I reviv'd and was an emperor.
>
> (*Rom.* 5.1.1–9, *passim*)

Thus the poet's disillusionment at the end of sonnet 87:

> Thus I have had thee as a dream doth flatter:
> In sleep a king, but waking no such matter.[37]

The other components of the cluster also originate in private rather than political relationships. The "fawning," "spaniels," and "melting" each appear separately in the early plays, and each emerges in the context of love, most often an intense and impossible courtship—like Richard III's for Anne. Only later do they become associated with political power over and dependence on a mass of subjects. Ambiguities continue to accrue—the "sweets," for example, soon start to be accompanied by "poison." But throughout, this "political" vice is always associated with more private experience. The "melting" associated with flattery, for example, refers not only to Spurgeon's doggie treats but also to the emotional changes wrought by love and even to the physiology of erotic excitement, as in our contemporary "true romance" formulae ("Her heart melted when she saw him")—though Shakespeare tended to associate this dissolution with male response. Timon, in Shakespeare's most flattery-conscious and dog-ridden play, imagines that Apemantus would have "melted down thy youth / In different beds of lust" (*Tim.* 4.3.258–59). Even in *The Tempest,* where marriage is redeemed, Ferdinand promises prenuptial chastity by swearing that he "shall never melt / Mine honour into lust" (*Tem.* 4.1.26–27) and Antony's grand renunciation, "let Rome in Tiber melt" (*Ant.* 1.1.33), has among its implications the purely physiological.

Just as the first flatterers in the canon are those persuading the dreamer he is loved, so too the first "spaniels" are pining lovers who indulge their abject infatuations to neurotic extremes. The devotion often outweighs or displaces the hypocrisy which Spurgeon associated with flattery. Here is Helena in *A Midsummer Night's Dream,* who, though a woman, is certainly no self-serving hypocritical whore, groveling before Demetrius:

> I am your *spaniel;* and, Demetrius,
> The more you beat me, I will *fawn* on you.
> Use me but as your *spaniel,* spurn me, strike me,
> Neglect me, lose me; only give me leave,
> Unworthy as I am, to follow you.
> What worser place can I beg in your love—
> And yet a place of high respect with me—
> Than to be used as you use your *dog?*
>   (*MND* 2.1.203–10; italics added)

Shakespeare's later Helena in *All's Well* repeats the posture though without the language—quite the opposite of Helen of Troy. But it is not only women who act this way. The very earliest Shakespearean spaniel is Proteus in *Two Gentlemen of Verona,* whose love for the unobtainable Silvia reduces him, as we have seen, to a melting inconstancy. He describes his servile passion in lines which introduce the "spaniel" into the flattery cluster for the first time in the canon: "Yet, spaniel-like, the more she spurns my love, / The more it grows, and fawneth on her still" (*TGV* 4.2.14–15).[38] Rather than a dog's or prostitute's knavish detachment, these young people are experiencing the extremes of what we might call puppy love.

More to the point, servile flattery can be associated with a human infant's helpless dependency as well as a puppy's.[39] Hamlet's condemnation of foppish courtiers draws on several elements of Spurgeon's cluster to suggest pre-oedipal devotion: "let the *candied* tongue lick absurd pomp, / And *crook* the pregnant hinges of the *knee* / Where thrift may follow *fawning*" (*Ham.* 3.2.60–62; italics added). In this description of what we might call "licking up,"[40] John Hunt has seen "an indictment of the flatterer so suggestively lewd that even the compleat courtier might blush to hear it."[41] The lewdness, however, derives not only from the context of courtly politics (which suggests an encounter in which one adult male licks another), but also from the taint of untimely regression. Hamlet's words evoke the mother-child relation ("pregnant") and the first object one licks or sucks up to, the breast. Hamlet's contempt for Elsinore's resident fop, Osric, later leads him to picture that water fly at the breast: "A did comply with his dug before a sucked it" (*Ham.* 5.2.184). Hamlet's association was not unique; it reminds Arden editor Harold Jenkins that Ulpian Fulwell includes in his introduction to *The Arte of Flattery* (1567) the claim that "the very sucking babes hath a kind of adulation toward their nurses for the dug."[42] Like the Roman parasite, known not only for his obsequious flattery but also for his ravenous appetite and umbilically suggestive "belly ties" to his patron, as Plautus called them,[43] the flatterer here is pictured at feed. Osric is not only a knavish hypocrite but also an obsequious fool, like a babe at the breast—a sucker, as it were. The Machiavellian politics of flattery has its roots in the polymorphous perversity of infantile infatuation. The political language of flattery is also the private language of the nursery.

The flattery cluster first congeals in a scene which, like Richard III's courtship of Anne, is one in which the politics of state are inseparable from sexual politics. It is a typically Shakespearean scene, though located in the apocryphal *Edward III*. It is so typical in fact that its presence strengthens the already impressive case for including this part of *Edward III*, if not also the entire play, in the canon.[44] What's at stake is not merely the resolution of a debate about authorship but the landscape of Shakespeare's early development and the shape of the imaginative world he was creating. Edward III's courtship of the Countess of Salisbury (*E3* 1.4–2.end) is the fifth version of the outrageous courtship whose ties to the flattery cluster we have traced through Shakespeare's early plays. The first version took place in *Henry VI, Part Three* (*3H6* 3.2), when Edward IV found he could not purchase the favors of the widow Lady Jane Grey but had to marry her. Richard III, who had watched and commented nastily on that scene, acts out the second version when he proposes an equally tendentious marriage to the widowed Lady Anne at her father's funeral. Proteus in *Two Gentlemen of Verona*, echoing Richard, courts Silvia in a third version of the scene. The fourth version is Tarquin's Sinon-like rape of Lucrece in Shakespeare's poem, to which *Edward III* apparently alludes.[45]

In this play *Edward III*, who has arrived with his troops to protect the Countess of Salisbury's castle from a Scottish siege, falls in love with the Countess and sets out to make her his mistress. Edward takes it for granted that he can command what he wishes from the Countess: she is his social inferior and has just been kneeling to him. But she refuses; her eyes "are like a glas" (*E3* 2.1.118) but one that reflects the burning sun on him rather than returning his own flattering self-image.[46] Though she "thaws" cold water she will not melt for him. Now Edward, who would be flattered himself, must hire a poet to flatter the Countess for him. Though Edward reassures his scribe, "For flattery feare thou not to be convicted" (*E3* 2.1.88), the script he asks for consists precisely of flattery. Edward's poem offers the Countess his estate like "a footstoole where shee treads," and the King admits feeling himself melting away on a "ground of shame" for having adopted such a posture even in writing (*E3* 2.1.102, 198). Eventually the Countess makes it clear that their union would mean murdering both their spouses[47]—and that she would first kill herself. At last Edward recognizes her virtue and awakes from his "idle dreame" to carry on his duties as king and warrior (*E3* 2.2.201). Here is the "Shakespearean" flattery cluster—melting, thawing, sun, glass, sweet, and kneeling—and, whether the sequence was written by Shakespeare, influenced by him, or contains the familiar elements only by some freak coincidence, the play locates the cluster in a sexual encounter. It is also a scene in which the Countess's first lines announce a Cleopatra-like sensitivity about seeing herself represented on the stage. Like the defeated Egyptian queen, who scorns the thought of her conqueror's quick comedians putting on a play about her, the Countess foresees the Scots making a "skipping jig" about her if they should defeat her forces:

> How much they will deride vs in the North,
> And, in their vild, vnseuill, skipping giggs,
> Bray foorth their Conquest and our ouerthrow.
>
> (E3 1.2.11–13)

Presumably she fears seeing some squeaking Countess "boy [her] greatness/ I' the posture of a whore" (*Ant.* 5.2.218–19).

Whether Shakespeare's or not, Edward's experience with the Countess defines the subtext for the histrionically colored flattery narratives in the canonical plays. Like his players, Shakespeare's victims of flattery each enjoy a "dream" of kingship maintained by the flattering ministrations of their followers; all the while, of course, they loathe "fawners" and "flatterers." Each then suddenly realizes that it was only flattery after all and fears that he must now turn and flatter the others. The later flattering dreams have little to do with actual women like the Countess; they are more likely to concern the king's relation to Lady Luck (or Dame Fortune, as Timon calls her), to Rome imaged as a voluminous matron, or to England, "this nurse, this teeming womb of royal kings" (*R2* 2.1.51) rather than to a merely mortal mistress. Nonetheless they are often sustained by assumptions about female ministrations, like the Countess's properly asexual love for Edward III, or Titania's maternal attentions to Bottom.[48] The most obvious expression of such total devotion, however, always takes the form of male flatterers, or minions, who pretend to love their king as only a mother can, then turn on him like a dog. Each is part of a mirror play, a structure of reversal in which an enemy twin rises as the king falls: Richard and Bolingbroke, Caesar and Brutus, Coriolanus and Aufidius, and Timon and Alcibiades. Only two of these flattered men are explicitly called actors, but all experience an actor's fantasies of regression to infantile intimacy with a mother and an actor's agonies of presentation before a fickle crowd. And all are subject to the dizzying reversals of dominance that hold actor and audience together in the theatrical exchange.

Richard II: The "Tedious" Actor

To the Elizabethans, Hobday notes, "Richard II was the classical example of a king ruined by flatterers."[49] Shakespeare continues and even exaggerates the association, drawing on the period's most notorious minion, Marlowe's Gaveston, as model for his flatterers.⁵⁰ Richard's sense of himself as a divinely sanctioned king depends on his vision of an inviolable bond between him and a sustaining maternal presence, the English earth.⁵¹ Gaunt describes her as this "teeming womb of royal kings" in his famous patriotic purple, the "cradle" where peace "draws the sweet infant breath of gentle sleep" (R2 1.3.132–33);⁵² and Richard himself kneels down to greet his mother earth in terms which make it sound like Titania's cradle for Bottom.⁵³ But the overt flatterers in England are his male minions, Bushy, Bagot, and Green, whose names locate them in the onstage garden which figures mother England. When Richard feels his "mother" desert him, he perceives his fall as the result of his flatterers' betrayal, exaggerating their actual sins before he knows anything about what really happened. "Dogs!" he calls them, "easily won to fawn on any man!" and he goes on to reject all comfort as "flattery" (R2 3.2.130, 216).⁵⁴

Although Richard never appears in an actual inner play, this classical example of a king ruined by flatterers is a "born actor," "a poseur" who spends his life "not living, but playing parts."⁵⁵ Richard II, unlike Richard III, is a bad actor who cannot pick up cues from any audience except flatterers. Bolingbroke, his challenger, is on the contrary a supreme actor, playing to every "oyster-wench" in the crowd who watches him ride into banishment (R2 1.4.31). The frequently quoted comparison between Richard and Bolinbroke is thus aptly phrased as one between dull and charismatic actors:

> As in a theater the eyes of men,
> After a well-grac'd actor leaves the stage,
> Are idly bent on him that enters next,
> Thinking his prattle to be tedious;
> Even so, or with much more contempt, men's eyes
> Did scowl on Richard.
>
> (R2 5.2.23–28)⁵⁶

As the play unfolds we see how appropriate it is that Shakespeare portray the known victim of flattery as a natural player. Oblivious at first to his own role-playing, Richard becomes increasingly self-conscious about the process.⁵⁷ We might even call the central scene in which he stages his usurpation, the "antic deposition," to accord with the Hamletian "antic disposition," which Richard assumes, playing martyr to the hilt.⁵⁸ This scene reveals just how enmeshed theatrical self-consciousness is with the recoil from flattery—and from the underlying attraction to it. Richard, who had defined himself in the first scene by announcing, "We were not born to sue, but to command" (R2 1.1.196), begins his deposition by elaborating on how it feels to be forced to sue to another. He enters pitying himself: "I hardly yet have learn'd / To insinuate, flatter, bow, and bend my knee" (*R2* 4.1.164–65). When he is most pressed to bend—to read out his crimes "in common view" (*R2* 4.1.155)—he refuses. But it is at this moment that the flattery cluster emerges, as if to speak his desire in imagery even while he denies it in rhetoric. I cannot flatter, he insists, but then cries out:

> O that I were a mockery king of *snow*,
> Standing before the *sun* of Bolingbroke,
> To *melt* myself away in water drops!
>   (*R2* 4.1.260–62; italics added)[59]

He wants to melt like the fawning spaniels, and, simultaneously, he is alerted to the disgrace of being uplifted to the view in this "woeful pageant," as the Abbot calls it (*R2* 4.1.321). Richard turns away from those "that stand and look upon me" in his shame and says he'll "turn my eyes upon myself" instead (*R2* 4.1.237, 247). Deprived of his human flattering glass— Bushy, Bagot, Green, and the thousand other "flatterers" who "s[a]t within the circle of [his] crown," he says he will play audience to himself (*R2* 2.1.100). He will observe his own shadow in the mirror—just as Julia played audience to herself as Ariadne. But, like Julia's, Richard's supposedly solitary self-reflection is played out for an audience after all—for the successful rival who has displaced him. Julia had lost Proteus to Silvia but told her sad tale to that same Silvia; Richard has lost England and acts out a sad tale of the death of his kingship for Bolingbroke.[60]

The last king who had called for a mirror was Richard's chronological heir (but canonical precursor), Richard III. Richard III, who had avoided mirrors, called for one only after he had won Anne's admiration, after she had mirrored back to him a satisfying image of himself. Richard II has lost the image of himself that was once generated by flatterers and by a fantasized identification with an Edenic England; consequently he has no use for the image which a literal mirror reflects. Mirrors are "true" for him only if they reflect the distortion of another's assessment—whether it be the distortion of a flatterer's beautification or of a usurper's diminution. Richard II's mirror merely reflects his uninterpreted face—not the beggar Bolingbroke has made him. The discrepancy between what he expects (a beggar's face to match his new identity) and what he sees (the king's face of his old identity) is intolerable. He shatters the glass in a last effort to deny the vertigo of being it suggests. More mindful than ever of his shame at being on view, Richard's last request is to be allowed offstage: "then give me leave to go. . . . so I were from your sights" (*R2* 4.1.313–15).

When Marlowe's Dr. Faustus is defeated in the scene on which Shakespeare partly based Richard's final soliloquy, he confronts his terror at being damned. Richard, however, echoing Faustus, fears only being made a beggar. It is perhaps inevitable that Richard's consciousness about role-playing ultimately takes the familiar form of consciousness about beggars and kings:[61]

> Thus play I in one person many people,
> . . . Sometimes I am a king,
> Then treasons make me wish myself a beggar,
> And so I am.
>
> (R2 5.5.31–34)

Part of Richard's "antics" is his ironic play with the slippery reversals between the two. Even his request to go from sight toys with the reversals of "commanding" and "suing," the two extremes his career has spanned, by first taking up the beggar's position and then rejecting it. Richard, like Jonson's Mosca, is learning how to rise and stoop at once: "I'll beg one boon," he had said (R2 4.1.302), and when Bolingbroke responded compliantly— "Name it, fair cousin"—Richard elaborated baroquely on Bolingbroke's politeness:

> When I was a king, my flatterers
> Were then but subjects; being now a subject,
> I have a king here to my flatterer.
> Being so great, I have no need to beg.
>
> (R2 4.1.304–9)

Richard's hierarchical mind is obsessed with rising and stooping. When Lear uncrowns himself, he fantasizes being God's spy, watching the court to see "who's in and who's out." Richard is more interested in discovering who's up and who's down, and his all-or-nothing thinking easily narratizes itself as a reversible story of kneeling obeisances, like the ones in the old *King Leir* play. Our impression of the play's rise-and-fall structure derives in part from Richard's imagery of buckets in wells, his staging a descent from the top of Flint Castle to the "base court," and his strict account of who is kneeling to whom. When he enters on the walls of Flint castle to give himself up to Bolingbroke he begins by scolding Northumberland for not kneeling to him:

> We are amaz'd, and thus long have we stood
> To watch the fearful bending of thy knee.
>
> (R2 3.3.72–73)[62]

After his descent, he ends the scene by telling Bolingbroke *not* to kneel to him:

> Fair cousin, you debase your princely knee
> To make the base earth proud with kissing it.
> . . . Up, cousin, up; your heart is up, I know.
>
> (*R2* 3.3.190–94)

However Richard may soliloquize about playing the beggar, he manages to avoid actually playing out the role; he never does kneel before the king. The role of beggar is displaced onto the Duchess of York, who comes, later in the play, to beg Bolingbroke for her son's life, kneeling until he is exasperated. ("Stand up, good aunt," he says some six times in the scene, before he gives in to her pleas.) Irritated with her tactics he blurts out, "Our scene is alt'red from a serious thing,/ And now chang'd to 'The Beggar and the King'" (*R2* 5.3.77–78). In a figurative sense, as James Black suggests, the deposition scene itself, as well as the description of Richard and Bolingbroke coming into London, might each be called "The Beggar and the King."[63] But the displacement of the literal onstage kneeling and begging to the Duchess, a mother, is not random. It means that the wheel has come full circle. The one time Richard had kneeled, unavailingly, was when he returned from Ireland and bowed his knee to mother England herself, begging the very ground to sustain him against his enemies. Now Shakespeare has a mother kneel to beg for her son ("A beggar begs that never begg'd before," she says; *R2* 5.3.76). It is a pattern we recognize from *Richard III*, who had kneeled to his own mother, asking a blessing she would not give. By the end of the play, his mother was on the ground before him, impeding his progress through the strength of her vulnerability.[64] It is a pattern we will see again in the other flattery plays.

Julius Caesar: "People Clap Him and Hiss Him"

Julius Caesar was an even more famous example than *Richard II* of a "prince ruined by flattery." Like Richard's, Caesar's flatterers fed his sense of himself as born to command, not sue; unlike Richard, Caesar admits no external source for his status. As Shakespeare tells it, Caesar's story, like Richard's, follows from a confrontation resembling that between actor and audience. It is true that Caesar never thinks of himself as an actor. He never plays roles ("Always I am Caesar"; *JC* 1.2.209); and he despises the crowd's opinion. ("When I tell him he hates flatterers," says Decius, "He says he does, being then most flattered"; *JC* 2.1.207–8)[65] Instead it is Brutus and Cassius who liken themselves to actors, and it is through them that Shakespeare brings the theatrical subtext to bear. They see themselves as glorious players on the stage of history, and they frame the assassination with references to the success of their plot and their roles in it. Brutus is the first

to cite the players. He offers them as a model for the conspirators concealing their deadly plan: "[Let's] bear it as our Roman actors do,/ With untir'd
spirits and formal constancy" (*JC* 2.1.226–27). The Roman actor, in Brutus's grandiose fantasy, is not an inconstant Proteus. Quite the opposite; he
is a model of "formal constancy," and formal constancy is *the* Roman ideal.
It is Caesar's last hubristic claim ("But I am as constant as the northern
star"; *JC* 3.1.60) and the accolade Portia wounded herself in the thigh to
secure ("strong proof of my constancy"; *JC* 2.1.299); it is all that is represented by Rome: fortitude, stoicism, appearing "like a colossus." As one
critic said, "it is the dream of every male Roman to be a statue of himself."[66]
Immediately after the murder, once Brutus has issued precise stage directions choreographing the senators' movements, Cassius makes an even
more grandiose comparison. Now the conspirators are not only immutable
but immortal players: "How many ages hence/ Shall this lofty scene be
acted over,/ In states unborn and accents yet unknown" (*JC* 3.1.111–13).[67]
It is one of the most strikingly metadramatic moments in the canon.[68]

But while Brutus and Cassius see themselves as triumphant actors, Caesar repeatedly becomes subject to an actor's defeats. He assumes he bears
his fate "with untir'd spirits and formal constancy," but in reality he can
control neither the script prepared for him nor the audience who watches.
Caesar is introduced as a man of monstrous ego, for whom even the triumphal march through Rome is not enough (*JC* 1.1, 1.2)—"even a full-
dress parade through Times Square with . . . cheering crowds" would not
be enough, as Little said of the twentieth-century actor.[69] Caesar wants
more. He wants the crown, but unlike Tamburlaine he does not want to
seize it himself; he wants it to be given to him. In a curiously passive dream
of narcissistic glory, "He would be crowned" (*JC* 2.1.12). Caesar first hopes
to be crowned in the public theater of the market place, when Antony offers
the crown and he coyly refuses it three times, as "the rag-tag people . . .
clap him and hiss him . . . as they use to do the players in the theatre"
(*JC* 1.2.255–58). Buckingham had called this "play[ing] the maid's part,"
when Richard III staged a similar sham reluctance to accept the crown
(*R3* 3.7.50). And, like Richard rejected by Lady Anne, when Caesar hears
the crowd cheering him for refusing the crown, "he pluck'd me ope his
doublet and offer'd them his throat to cut" (*JC* 1.2.261–63).[70]

J. L. Simmons argues that "of all the Roman actors, Caesar is by far the
greatest," and he takes Casca's description of Caesar's "performance" for the
people to be the "major presentational image of the play," repeated several
times before our eyes.[71] Caesar's second "performance"—again in search of
the crown—again takes place on a stage, but this time on the more private
stage of the senate house floor. Here the audience is aristocratic and, instead of clapping and hissing, they begin with flattery and end by literally
cutting his throat. It is here that Spurgeon finds the "most striking [sic]

example" of the flattery cluster in all the plays.[72] Caesar, who has come to the capitol because he has been flattered into believing that he will be crowned there, prides himself that he will not be flattered into pardoning Metullus's brother. But the conspirators step forward anyway to kneel fawningly in a circle around Caesar and beg for the pardon. First Metullus kneels to Caesar, then Cassius ("as low as to thy foot doth Cassius fall"; *JC* 3.1.56), then Cinna, Decius, and Brutus—"but not in flattery," Brutus protests tellingly (*JC* 3.1.52). Meanwhile Casca circles to the rear to be ready for the first attack. When Caesar sees them kneel, he is disgusted, and the flattery cluster emerges. "Doth not Brutus bootless kneel?" Caesar asks; he had earlier explained:

> These couchings and *lowly courtesies*
> Might fire the blood of ordinary men,
> And turn pre-ordinance and first decree
> Into the law of children. Be not fond,
> To think that Caesar bears such rebel blood
> That will be *thaw'd* from the true quality
> With that which *melteth* fools—I mean *sweet* words,
> *Low-crooked curtesies,* and *base spaniel-fawning.*
> Thy brother by decree is banished:
> If thou dost bend and pray and *fawn* for him,
> I spurn thee like a *cur* out of my way.
>
> (*JC* 3.1.36–46; italics added)

Caesar, spokesman for the disgust which Spurgeon finds to be the main object of the cluster, sees himself as constant, unmeltable, and thus above responding to fawning prayers.

But Caesar dies protesting too much. His speech, like Richard II's at a similar moment, dwells on flattery and embraces the elements of Spurgeon's cluster—"spaniel," "thaw," "sweet," "melt"—associated predictably with "low-crooked curtesies." The very language Caesar uses suggests how deeply moved he is, and how seductive is the flatterers' power. He begins by denying his susceptibility: flattery might "fire the blood" of "ordinary" men, he says, but not mine.[73] It is as if the fawners—whom Caesar calls "suitors"—were threatening to arouse him ("fire the blood" and "rebel blood" suggest lust) and he were denying such vulnerability.[74] Their "low-crooked" posture even recalls Hamlet's disgust with the "candied tongue" that will "lick absurd pomp, / and *crook* the pregnant hinges of the knee." (*Ham.* 3.2.60–61; italics added) And then, of course, the flatterers attack, fulfilling the movement from "spaniel" to "cur" in Caesar's own speech.[75] The intimate betrayal explodes into mob violence, and the "dogs of war" (Antony's phrase; *JC* 3.1.273) are unleashed. Caesar has become a hunted deer, like Talbot "bounded in a pale" outside Bordeaux, or like Fal-

staff playing dead on Hal's battlefield and then encircled and "dis-horned"
in Windsor.[76]

> Here wast thou bay'd, brave hart;
> Here dids't thou fall; and here thy hunters stand. . . .
> O world, thou wast the forest to this hart;
> And this indeed, O world, the heart of thee.
> How like a deer, strucken by many princes,
> Dost thou here lie!
>
> (*JC* 3.1.204–10)

Antony's funeral oration later describes the murder as if it were the ritual
curée after the hunt, when the animal's body is carved by designated officers
of the hunt, as a sacrificial ceremony instead of a preparation of meat. This
is of course what Brutus had done when he had tried to rationalize Caesar's
murder: "Let's carve him as a dish fit for the gods, / Not hew him as a carcass
fit for hounds" (*JC* 2.1.173–74). What Brutus does not see is that the aristocratic hunt is, like any performance, both sacrifice and butchery.[77]

Caesar does not live to endure the reversal from King to Beggar which
Richard II feared. But the assassination scene is replayed in one last "performance" on the public stage of the forum, a performance which demands
a posthumous appearance from Caesar—unique in the canon—in which
he is made to beg after all. Caesar is brought before the Roman people once
more, this time reduced to a body on display—just as Talbot, to his shame,
was made into a "scarecrow" in the French market. Richard II, histrionic
though he was, shrank from reading his sins aloud in the "base court," and
Coriolanus will shrink from displaying his wounds in the marketplace. The
double valence of such display is implied by the way in which Antony's
current performance both idolizes Caesar and recreates the assassination,
as he invites the crowd to make "a ring around the corpse of Caesar" and
focuses their attention on Caesar's wounds (*JC* 3.2.160). The group comes
forward, just as the conspirators had, and listens to Antony's verbal reconstruction of the murder. Antony appeals to their "love and pity" for their
fallen leader; Caesar, who would not deign to ask for favors when alive, is
now made to beg for the audience's tears. Then, having earlier suggested
that the Romans "kiss dead Caesar's wounds," Antony offers to "put a
tongue / In every wound of Caesar that should move / The stones of Rome
to rise and mutiny" (*JC* 3.2.134, 230–32). He means of course that he will
interpret the wounds in such a way as to move the crowd,[78] but his imagery
of tongues in wounds suggests a gesture as lewd as Hamlet's fiat about the
candied tongue licking absurd pomp. When Calpurnia dreamed that Caesar's statue was spouting blood, Decius hastily reinterpreted the omen to
mean that "great Rome shall suck reviving blood" from Caesar (*JC* 2.2.87–
88)—evoking the medieval oddity of lactating wounds.[79] But Antony sup-

plements that anomaly with his own baroque imagery of erotic wounds.[80] Antony invokes the invisible hole in Caesar's heart, and then the holes in Caesar's mantle, before performing a vicarious strip tease by removing the mantle and then finally revealing the holes in the naked body itself:

> Kind souls, what weep you when you but behold
> Our Caesar's vesture wounded? Look you here!
> Here is himself, marred as you see, with traitors.
>
> (*JC* 3.2.197–99)

"Shakespeare," notes the Arden editor of the passage in an unintended pun, "provides a powerful and moving climax with the uncovering of the body."[81]

Understandably, such treatment has provoked modern commentary on the Roman figuration of Caesar's weakness in terms of femaleness and on what such discourse implies about the construction of "woman" in Shakespeare's time. We could even see Caesar, the "brave hart" as Antony called him earlier, not only as a stag but also as the female deer in an erotic love hunt.[82] Thus the murder is a rape, with Casca, as Shakespeare tells us, striking first from behind, the betrayal of male intimacy suggested by Caesar's famous "Et tu, Brute." Henry Ebel in fact argues that the assassination has been assimilated to Shakespeare's myth or vision of Roman masculinity as predicated on the prior violation of a woman.[83] The myth is overt in Shakespeare's earliest visions of Rome, with Lavinia's rape in *Titus Andronicus,* and Lucrece's in *The Rape of Lucrece.*[84] Appropriately enough in this context, the play's most immediate parallel to Caesar's wounds is Portia's wounded thigh. That wound, though self-inflicted to prove that Portia is "stronger than my sex" (*JC* 2.1.296), ironically calls attention to the other "wound" associated with castration and the female genitalia. The parallel between these two wounds is made explicit in "The Passionate Pilgrim"— (which Shakespeare, if he did not write it, would have read)—when Venus warns Adonis from the dangers of hunting the boar. Telling Adonis that she has seen the boar gore another youth, Venus exposes her own thigh to show how:

> "See in my thigh," quoth she, "here was the sore."
> She showed hers: he saw more wounds than one,
> And blushing fled, and left her all alone.
>
> (Pil. 19.12–14)

In Shakespeare's own version of the story, it was Adonis who suffered the ambiguously multiplying wound "in his soft groin" (Ven. 1116) while Venus saw "more wounds than one."[85] Here, as with Caesar, the stress is on the feminization of the male body as the alternative to violation of the woman's body.[86]

But Caesar's vulnerability is figured by more than anatomy, and his "feminine" weakness is not only a matter of castration. When Antony takes up Caesar's body and brings it to the forum to put tongues in its wounds, we might even recall Shakespeare's first play about Roman sacrifice and butchery (and kings and beggars), *Titus Andronicus*. There the villainous Aaron describes another possible analogue to Caesar, in addition to the "castrated" Lavinia still alive and spouting blood onstage. After he is caught, Aaron boasts about his many crimes, and he spends most time elaborating lovingly on a macabre practical joke in which he too used a dead body to make an audience mourn:

> Oft have I digg'd up dead men from their graves,
> And set them upright at their dear friends' door,
> Even when their sorrows almost was forgot,
> And on their skins, as on the bark of trees,
> Have with my knife carved in Roman letters,
> "Let not your sorrow die, though I am dead."
>
> (*Tit.* 5.1.135–40)

Wounds, as Aaron knows, are not only genitalia but also mouths that need to be heard as well as fed; they are signs that need to be read. Woman's weakness in Rome arises from her position as well as from her "castration" and from her assigned role in the scene of the king and the beggar. The women in this play are, to reverse Richard II's declaration, not born to command, but to sue—as Portia sues Brutus to come back to bed and Calpurnia sues Caesar to stay home. When Cassius bad-mouths Caesar to Brutus he not only likens him to a girl but says that the great man had begged for water "as a sick girl" (*JC* 1.2.127). In the Senate, Caesar's male flatterers signal their subordination by taking the woman's position at his feet, kneeling to him in the stage configuration that we have seen twice before—when Portia and Calpurnia had kneeled. The flaws in Roman integrity in *Caesar*, as in *Titus Andronicus* and the early poems, are manifested not only in the physical wounds prominent in each text but also in the narrative emphasis on fawning and begging—and on the psychological humiliations which the wounds imply. Lavinia and Lucrece beg to save their chastity, and Venus makes a fool of herself begging Adonis to give up his. These characters are not only feminized, they are reduced to speaking wounds. They are, in other words, caught in what I would call the actor's nightmare.[87]

By the end of his life Richard II was fully conscious of his role as actor; in this play Caesar remains oblivious. But Shakespeare does sharpen the audience's awareness of Caesar and Brutus as actors by forcing its awareness of itself as audience. As soon as the play begins, several characters walk onstage and, before the audience can learn who they are, one of them (well-

dressed, official-looking) calls out haughtily, "Hence! home, you idle creatures, get you home: / Is this a holiday? (*JC* 1.1.1–2). The actual audience
might well think, at least momentarily, "Does he mean us? Does he mean
that we shouldn't be here watching a play, that we ought to feel guilty for
taking a holiday from work?" Of course he means no such thing. The tri-
bune is speaking to the crowd onstage, who have come, as they later explain, "to see Caesar" (*JC* 1.1.30–31).[88] But for a moment the audience is
uncertain; after all, they too have come "to see Caesar." Casca had assumed
that the "rag-tag" crowd who clapped for Caesar is the same crowd who
claps for the Roman actors; soon that Roman crowd will be assimilated to
the real English crowd clapping at that moment for the English actors who
play the Romans. Shakespeare forces the assimilation in the forum scene.
As Kenneth Burke suggests in the "speech" which he imagines Antony offering to Shakespeare's real audience, Antony manipulates both crowds at
once, both onstage Romans and offstage Englishmen. "My Elizabethan audience," Burke's Antony begins,

> under the guise of facing a Roman mob I confront you at a most complicated
> moment. . . . Your author has kept you in as vacillating a condition as this very
> Roman mob you have been watching with so little respect. I doubt if he distin-
> guishes between the two of you. All that I as Antony do to this play-mob, as a
> character-recipe I do to you. He [i.e., Shakespeare via the character-recipe, or
> actor] would play upon you; he would seem to know your stops; he would
> sound you from your lowest note to the top of your compass. He thinks you as
> easy to be played upon as a pipe.[89]

Antony transforms the Elizabethans in the audience—along with the Roman mob—into "dogs of war" (*JC* 3.1.273). The Elizabethans are horrified
when the Roman mob surges forward and attacks a passerby who identifies
himself as Cinna the poet and not Cinna the conspirator. But, as Burke
argues, the Elizabethan audience itself, stirred up by Antony's rhetoric, has
just "lynched" Brutus in an analogous fashion. Earlier they had identified
with Brutus and the conspirators; now Antony wins their sympathies for
poor mutilated Caesar.[90] Joining Antony, they turn against their former hero
Brutus—and therefore also against their own identification with Caesar's
murderer. This is not, Antony reminds us, a comfortable position to be in:

> You have been made conspirators in a murder. For this transgression, there
> must be some expiative beast brought up for sacrifice. . . . it is Brutus that must
> die to absolve you of your stabbing an emperor who was deaf in one ear and
> whose wife was sterile.[91]

The Elizabethan audience—and the modern one as well—must now get
rid of Brutus. The dynamics onstage between mob and victim thus extend

outward to encompass our own exchange with the characters and perhaps with the actors as well. Stephen Booth has written about "the actor as kamikaze pilot," suicidal whenever he takes on an uncharismatic role that inevitably disappoints audiences no matter how well he performs. Brutus is one of Booth's examples.[92]

Having explored Caesar's role as the victim of flattery who suffers the fate all actors fear, it is useful to remember that this play offers another exemplary tale of fatal flattery, in the would-be Roman actor, Brutus himself. This one is less political and is played out in the private register of friendship. But the political conspiracy would never have occurred had not Brutus first succumbed to Cassius's flattery and offer to be the mirror wherein Brutus could see himself as others see him:

> Since you cannot see yourself
> So well as by reflection, I, your glass,
> Will modestly discover to yourself
> That of yourself which you yet know not of.
>
> (*JC* 1.2.66–69)

What Cassius shows him is his desire to be Caesar, and, though this is not made explicit, "being Caesar" means having a flattering audience like Cassius, who is most flattering when he says Caesar hates flattery. But later Cassius fails to supply Brutus with the devoted support he needs, and the two find themselves quarreling in an odd scene which Shakespeare expands from the historical record. Brutus makes excuses for his anger, but ends with a telling outburst: "Must I stand and crouch / Under your testy humour?" (*JC* 4.3.45–46)—that is, "must I kneel to the very man who was supposed to be flattering me?" It is as if the single moment of Caesar's "Et tu, Brute?" were expanded into an entire scene between Brutus and Cassius.[93] The context of flattery and betrayal is underscored a few lines later; when Cassius complains about Brutus' faultfinding, Brutus unwittingly echoes Caesar's spurning of the conspirators' flattery—"Wilt thou lift up Olympus?" (*JC* 3.1.74):

> *Cassius:* A friendly eye could never see such faults.
> *Brutus:* A flatterer's would not, though they do appear
>   As huge as high Olympus.
>
> (*JC* 4.3.89–91)

But Brutus's real grievance is that he had to fawn on Cassius: "I did send to you / For certain sums of gold, which you denied me" (*JC* 4.3.69–70). In other words, Cassius made him beg.

Cassius would not sustain him—as the earth (along with Bushy, Bagot, and Green) would not sustain Richard II. The quarrel is made up only after Cassius reverses the relationship again by abjectly offering both his gold and his heart to Brutus (as Caesar had offered his to the crowd):

> There is my dagger,
> And here my naked breast; within, a heart
> Dearer than Pluto's mine, richer than gold:
> If that thou be'st a Roman, take it forth.
> I, that denied thee gold, will give my heart:
> Strike, as thou didst at Caesar; for I know,
> When thou didst hate him worst, thou lov'dst him better
> Than ever thou lov'dst Cassius.
>
> (*JC* 4.3.99–106)

The real issue is "love." This play is often taught in high schools because it has no sex in it—nothing like Antony and Cleopatra's love play. G. Wilson Knight argues that the word "love," which appears here more often than in any other play, refers solely to spiritual and not fleshly love.[94] But, on the contrary, the love between men in this play is based on the erotic tie they deny, and on a vision of devotion as intimate as Richard II's fantasy about England, nurse of kings. When the two men are reconciled here, the mother whom Caesar never acknowledged makes an appearance after all; Cassius asks forgiveness for the "rash humor which my mother gave me" (*JC* 4.3.119)—the mother is Shakespeare's own invention—and Brutus replies that he will forgive, because: "When you are over-earnest with your Brutus, / He'll think your mother chides, and leave you so" (*JC* 4.3.121–22). That high-minded Brutus should quarrel about money is not wholly ironic.[95] It is perfectly in keeping with his ideal of total loyalty between friends. The emotional debts circulating between men and figured by gold had already been made evident in *Merchant of Venice,* where Antony's "ancient Roman honour" led him to offer both "my purse, my person" to Bassanio "with all [his] heart" (*MV* 3.2.294, 1.1.138, 4.1.277). Debt will move to the center of Shakespeare's *Timon,* but it is already at work here, as it was in Falstaff's thousand pounds. Debt is implied in the story of the intense tie between the narcissistic figure on display and the audience—of one or many—which seems at first to be feeding his grandest image of himself with "golden opinions" (*Mac.* 1.7.33) but who may suddenly demand that he serve them.[96]

Coriolanus: "It Is a Part That I Shall Blush in Acting"

I equally dislike the favor of a public with the love of a woman—they are both cloying treacle to the wings of independence.

—John Keats, *Letters*

Although Coriolanus was not traditionally associated with flattery, Shakespeare made the dynamics of flattery essential to his play about the man. Coriolanus hates not only flattery but even the well-deserved praise ("He would not flatter Neptune for his trident"; *Cor.* 3.1.254) which follows his miraculous success against the Corioli:[97] "Pray now, no more. My mother, . . . / When she doth praise me, grieves me" (*Cor.* 1.9.13–15). Spurgeon's flattery cluster does not appear here in its canine entirety, though a number of variants do.[98] But the play's action revolves around relationships which define the intimate origin ("My mother, . . ./ When she doth praise me, grieves me") and multiple transformations of flattery. For Coriolanus, as for Richard II and Caesar, the disgust with flattery dissolves into a hidden desire for it, the fawning flatterer leaps to attack like a hunter seizing his prey, and finally the flatterer and his victim reverse their roles. As before, the reversals occur in a context that reproduces, even though it is not intended to represent, the actor's role before an audience.

Coriolanus's mother, Volumnia, little given either to praise or to feed her son, had taught him that "Better it is to die, better to starve, / Than crave the hire which first we do deserve" (*Cor.* 2.3.112–13). Coriolanus learned his lesson well enough to deny any craven hunger—even for praise—but he did not learn to eliminate the desire he denies. Just as Richard's image of himself as king was sustained by the image of mother England, "teeming womb of royal kings," so Coriolanus depends on the devoted approval of Rome, that "unnatural dam," and of his mother Volumnia (*Cor.* 3.1.290). Volumnia is his "nurse," as Aufidius sneers, whose name and personality expand her mere bodily presence to Roman proportions. She is a kind of female "colossus," as Cassius might say, like the huge Caesar he had enviously conjured up for Brutus. She is figured by the political leviathan in Menenius's "Fable of the Belly": Coriolanus is (in?) her belly and the plebeians are her toes. Even those plebeians recognize her importance to him: "He did it [fought well] to please his mother" (*Cor.* 1.1.37–38), they say, not out of concern for us.

Coriolanus will not do anything to please the ragtag plebeian crowd—not because they are too unimportant, as he suggests, but because he cannot depend on them for nurturance any more than he can depend on his Roman-hearted mother. They are changeable, fickle; they might not praise him. If he consents to be a "sweet" for the "multitudinous tongue" to "lick" (*Cor.* 3.1.155–56), he puts himself in real danger.[99] Like Rome, the "unnatural dam" who eats her children, the plebeians have "teeth" (*Cor.* 3.1.35), and they might turn on him to "devour" (*Cor.* 2.1.8) him, when they "put [their] tongue in those wounds" (*Cor.* 2.3.7). In the end they do turn, and it is a reversal so important that John Holloway saw in it the clearest example of a pattern he finds in all Shakespearean tragedy, in which the protagonist is "'the observed of all observers,' the man sought by everyone, the saviour of the state, the centre of its ceremony," but then "ceremonial and deference turn into a pursuit, a hunt; . . . [and] the transformation is of cynosure at once into a victim and a monster."[100] Coriolanus enters the center of "all gaze" (*Cor.* 1.3.7):

> All tongues speak of him, and the bleared sights
> Are spectacled to see him.
>
> (*Cor.* 1.203–4)

> I have seen the dumb men throng to see him, and
> The blind to hear him speak.
>
> (*Cor.* 2.2.260–61)

But he is soon set upon; the movement from mob worship to mob attack is embodied in the play's characteristic choreography, repeated in scene after scene, of a crowd swirling around the central figure, whether friend or enemy (and probably played by the same minor actors in both cases).[101] The crowd raises Coriolanus high in triumph on the battlefield in act 1, then surges around him to tear him to pieces, just as the crowd in *Caesar* turns from adoration of Caesar to an attack on Cinna the poet; when the crowd raises Coriolanus again to carry him out in act 5, he is a battered corpse.[102]

Imagery of the hunt suggests the savagery of the conflict. Laurence Olivier's Coriolanus looked like "one man lynching a mob," as he threatened the wild slaughter of an unrestricted hunt:[103] "I'd make a quarry [a pile of dead prey] / With thousands of these quarter'd slaves" (*Cor.* 1.1.197–98). But the "slaves" themselves are a "common cry of curs" (*Cor.* 3.3.120)—a hunting pack ready to tear him apart. Menenius implies as much when he tries to deflect their attack on Coriolanus: "Do not *cry havoc* where you should but *hunt* / With modest warrant" (*Cor.* 3.1.272; italics added). Finally Coriolanus offers his countrymen his throat (*Cor.* 4.5.93–94)—as did Richard III, Caesar, and any hunted animal brought to bay. To the enemy Volscians he says, "Cut me to pieces" (*Cor.* 5.6.111), and they do.

Coriolanus is like an actor insofar as he faces not only a fickle crowd but also the specter of maternal power behind them. Gary Wills noted a link between Coriolanus's mob and a femme fatale, if not literally a mother, when he suggested that Coriolanus, in a recent production, "is like a rock star whose most ardent fans can turn and rend him if their enthusiasms are frustrated" and went on to note, "It is interesting that the two great impersonators of Coriolanus put themselves in the rock star's position of power and vulnerability—Olivier by marrying the movies and Vivien Leigh, Burton by his marriages to Elizabeth Taylor."[104] The Shakespearean play most dominated by the mob is also his most mother-dominated play, uniting an actor's two nightmares. Indeed, Volumnia, the mother of all stage mothers, whose love for her son is inseparable from her desire to show him off, materializes immediately after the currish plebeians have surrounded him threateningly (*Cor.* 3.1.2).[105] Coriolanus of course hates acting. He refuses to put his scars on display for the Roman plebeians; he does not want to "mountebank their loves" (*Cor.* 3.2.130) "It is a part," he says, "that I shall blush in acting" (*Cor.* 2.2.144–45): "Would you have me / False to my nature? Rather say I play / The man I am" (*Cor.* 3.2.14–16). (As Caesar said, "Always I am Caesar.") But Volumnia wants Coriolanus to take the part. She reminds him coldly that he has been acting all along and that he has not been doing a very good job.[106] The man he is, it turns out, is the man she made him: "my praises made thee first a soldier" (*Cor.* 3.2.108). Volumnia has cast her son in the dashing role of Soldier.[107] Now she wants to recast him: "To have my praise for this, perform a part / Thou hast not done before" (*Cor.* 3.2.109–10). Coriolanus is Volumnia's puppet; no wonder he thinks of himself as a machine.[108] She tells Coriolanus to learn his lines by rote, shows him how to hold his bonnet in his hand ("thus far having stretch'd it"), and, most of all, directs him to kneel down.[109] She even assures him she'll be by his side during the performance: "we'll prompt you" (*Cor.* 3.2.55, 74, 106).[110] Richard III's mother had disapproved of her son's arrival with teeth and feet first, armed like a male rather than bearing "resemblance to the dam." This mother, having insisted too soon that Coriolanus be a man, now insists that he beg like a woman or a child. As soon as Coriolanus realizes that he must do as she says—must beg like a schoolgirl, as Cassius had put it—he himself draws the analogies: "possess me / Of some harlot's spirit . . . my throat . . . a pipe / Small as a eunuch, or a virgin voice / That babies lull asleep" (*Cor.* 3.2.111–19). All this it is to submit to her. Literally, of course, she is telling him to kneel to them, the plebeians, but the kneeling role represents all role-playing here; it represents the agreement to play at all. He is really kneeling to his mother and he knows it.

The kneeling suggests Coriolanus's underlying wish—which he must deny—to beg for the flattery he says he hates, and to flatter his audience into providing it. The flattery cluster in this play is called up when Coriolanus feels himself softening (or "melting," as he will call it later when he gives in to his mother's prayers); (*Cor.* 5.3.28) into someone who cares about his audience's reaction.[111] One reason that Coriolanus, who is an inverse "braggart soldier," refuses to boast about his scars or "badges of merit," is that the scar is not only a badge of merit but a sign of vulnerability. To flaunt it would make him like Portia in *Caesar*, bragging about a wound which, as he says, should be kept private. To display such a badge he must "appear i' th' market place" in the "napless vesture of humility," like Caesar's wounded body on display in the market, offering his vulnerability as drawing card (*Cor.* 2.1.230–31). As in *Caesar*, vulnerability is signified not only by physical wounds but also by the begging that goes with their display. Coriolanus is afraid that people will believe he got his wounds only in order to beg with them, that he did his deeds of valor "for hire."

This is an elitist's disdain for money and vulgar commercialism—Coriolanus is a proud beggar indeed, but the horror at working for hire also comes from the emotional implications of money, as in Brutus' quarrel over gold with Cassius in *Caesar*. Money is love, and "working for hire" is another way of admitting that he needs their voices, their "breath," their love. To expose his wounds is to offer up his breast, like Cassius offering his heart "dearer than Pluto's mine" to pay his debt to Cassius. Thomas Dekker used the same monetary metaphor to describe the playwright's more-than-financial dependence on popular approval, when he complained that "Muses" are "now turned to Merchants" and "barter away that light commodity of words for a lighter ware than words, plaudites and the *breath* of that great *Beast,* which . . . vanish all into air."[112] Michael Redgrave assumed a link between the character of Coriolanus and that of the actor in general when he warned against giving in to the audience's demand for melodrama. "Of course you can't be a Coriolanus about it either," he concluded—as if Coriolanus were a benchmark for the actor calibrating his relation to the audience.[113]

Coriolanus never does manage to beg; instead he joins Rome's enemy, the Volscians, and marches with them to attack his own city. Like that of the other heroes, however, his story ends with a begging mother intercepting his forward march, his one mode of self-assertion in the face of a world that has rejected him. As Coriolanus moves toward Rome, Volumnia comes to him flanked by two other women to make a mythic threesome, like the three old queens who had blocked Richard III's way. He tries to act the Roman warrior, but, by now, even he sees that that is only a role: "Like a dull actor now / I have forgot my part and I am out / Even to a full disgrace" (*Cor.* 5.3.40–42). Then he kneels to his mother, as he had kneeled to her after his victory at Corioli (*Cor.* 2.1.169). But she makes him rise and kneels herself instead, then kneels again (*Cor.* 5.3.29, 169) until he agrees to give up his attack on Rome. "The gods look down, and this unnatural scene / They laugh at," he says (*Cor.* 5.3.184–85).[114] Or, as Bolingbroke complained when the Duchess planted herself to kneel in front of him, "Our scene is alt'red from a serious thing, / And now chang'd to 'The Beggar and the King'" (*R2* 5.3.77–78). None of the kneeling was in Shakespeare's source for the Coriolanus story; he added it all.

Timon of Athens: Playing Host

Timon of Athens provides the culminating example of the flattery cluster, not only because it makes flattery most central to its rhetoric and narrative and is the most dog-ridden of Shakespeare's plays, nor only because it was (probably) written last. Equally important, the private elements of Shakespeare's flattery cluster remain awkwardly prominent in this play, not yet subordinated to a more comprehensive design. Most critics accept E. K. Chambers's suggestion that the extant play is a rough draft, its language still uneven, and its structure incomplete.[115] There is, Ellis-Fermor argues, a sense of "passages . . . missing, containing such essential parts of the story as would have made the structure of the last three acts solid by relating Timon clearly to Alcibiades and both to Athenian politics."[116] Bullough calls the play "our chief glance at Shakespeare in his dramatic workshop."[117] If the play is truly our one example of material hot from the forge, its obsessive concern with flattery is both a telling indicator of the topic's importance to Shakespeare and a revealing glimpse into its intricacies. Viewed as a private fantasy, the play is complete. The details which Ellis-Fermor describes as missing are "essential" only for logical consistency and social significance, two Shakespearean goals which, in this case, seem to have been secondary to the expression of the personal myth ringing changes on the scene in which someone is being flattered.

The fantasy Timon presents is perfectly consistent with its better-integrated versions elsewhere in the canon. Timon's generosity is a more extreme version of the commanding self-sufficiency (and supposed selflessness) which the earlier heroes flaunted. If Caesar won't listen to a prophecy concerning himself, Timon refuses to receive repayment of debts. If Coriolanus didn't need to eat, Timon feeds others, a still more energetic denial of neediness.[118] But as in the earlier plays, the denial masks the importance of a maternal presence like Richard II's England or Coriolanus's Roman mater. Timon's fantasized wholeness depends on Fortune, the bounteous lady who favors him and with whom he identifies. The allegory of Fortune on a Hill, which the Poet offers Timon in the play's opening scene, is like another version of the fable of the Belly, which Menenius offered to explain Coriolanus's position in Rome—except that Timon is pictured at the breast of his patroness rather than in her belly. The poet begins the allegory by describing Timon's generosity to others (which will be called his "plenteous bosom"; *Tim.* 1.2.120–21) and the "large fortune/ Upon [Timon's] good and gracious nature hanging" (*Tim.* 1.1.56–57) which makes everyone kneel to him—as if they truly were licking up to Timon's great pendant breast.[119] But tellingly, this image shifts to become an image of Timon on Fortune's "plenteous bosom" (*Tim.* 4.3.188), the chosen one out of the many who climb her "high and pleasant hill" (*Tim.* 1.1.65), the female version of Caesar's Mount Olympus. Fortune may not be a "womb of royal kings" (*R2* 2.1.51), but like the "dear earth" (*R2* 3.2.6) Richard II greets on his return from Ireland, who had "sweets" for Richard but "venom" for his rivals (*R2* 3.2.13–14), Fortune wafts Timon to her and translates his rivals into slaves (*Tim.* 1.1.72–74). When Timon later flees Athens for the woods, he all but literalizes the opening description of climbing on Fortune's bosom. Down on his knees, he digs into mother earth and calls her by name, demanding the sustenance he had previously assumed Fortune—with a little help from his friends—would provide. This time he is far more aware of the presence of rivals and of the earth's potential for betrayal:

> Common mother, thou
> Whose womb unmeasurable and infinite breast
> Teems and feeds all ["thou common whore of
>   mankind," he says elsewhere (*Tim.* 4.3.36)]; whose self-same mettle,
> Whereof thy proud child, arrogant man, is puff'd,
> Engenders the black *toad* and *adder* blue,
> The gilded newt and eyeless *venom*'d worm . . .
> Yield him, who all the human sons do hate,
> From forth thy plenteous bosom, one poor root.
>
> (*Tim.* 4.3.179–88; italics added)

Richard II greeting his mother earth had used the same rhetoric and vocabulary: [120]

> Feed not thy sovereign's foe . . .
> But let thy spiders that suck up thy *venom*
> And heavy-gaited *toads* lie in their way . . .
> And when they from thy bosom pluck a flower,
> Guard it, I pray thee, with a lurking *adder.*
>
> (*R2* 3.2.12–20; italics added)

Timon's prayers (like Richard's) don't work. Flatterers will turn on you. Fortune on her hill, like golden-haired Portia, who drops undeserved portions of manna from her "beautiful mountain," Belmont, is fickle. Those who depend on her are sure to be disappointed. At best they may find gold, but not love; Timon's problems arose because he could not tell one from the other. Unlike love, golden treasure, Timon learns, is not always satisfactory. Treasure must be dug out of the earth by force and, once exposed, can turn to dust. The good food becomes excrement ("composture stol'n / From gen'ral excrement"; *Tim.* 4.3.443–44), the apples of Paradise become ashes in the mouth; or in this case, the glittering stuff turns out to be mere gold, a metal.[121] As Aaron in *Titus Andronicus* put it when he buried a cache of gold to incriminate Titus in murder and adultery: "And so repose, sweet gold, for their unrest / For all who seek their alms out of the empress' chest" (*Tit.* 2.3.8–9). The "empress' chest" refers literally to the casket in which Aaron has hidden the telltale gold. But the chest (as Freud suggested in his analysis of the casket scene in *Merchant of Venice*) becomes assimilated to woman's body, to what Aaron elsewhere calls Lavinia's "treasury" (*Tit.* 2.1.131). Aaron is punishing the Andronici for intruding on Tamora's territory and her forbidden bower. Pertinent as they are to the rampant sexual rivalry in the play, his lines may also be read as a warning that anyone who looks for "alms" or nurturance at the breast of an unnatural mother like Tamora (or Rome or Volumnia or Fortune) will find death instead.[122]

Poor Timon of course remains too long oblivious to the dangerous reversibility of such favors. In this case it is particularly clear that Timon's maternal fantasy is supported by the flatterers who recreate a mother's doting attention, because it is one of the flatterers, the Poet, who quite literally creates and presents the allegory of Fortune on a Hill. As always in all these plays, the bond established with such friends is erotic, though not necessarily physical. In the words of Timon's most appreciative critic, the play begins in "transcendent love," as in *Antony and Cleopatra,* and shows "the true erotic richness of Timon's soul." His love for his friends is "the love of Othello for Desdemona . . . of Shakespeare for the fair boy of the sonnets . . . the . . . love of one lover for another, physical and spiritual, of the senses as of the soul."[123] What Richard II found in Bushy, Bagot, and Green; what Caesar thought he had in Brutus, and Brutus in Cassius; what Coriolanus looked for by idealizing Aufidius and making that self-serving enemy into a twin, Timon sees in all his friends. Timon's generosity is, as Empson, put it, "a way of begging for affection, and it makes him the same kind of dog as the spaniels he could hire."[124] Timon betrays the unacknowledged begging in his contradictory statements about friendship during his opening banquet. At one moment he rules out any return of his favors: "there's none/ Can truly say he gives, if he receives," but, soon after, he defines friends precisely as those who give: "what need we have any friends, if we should ne'er have need of 'em?" The thought moves him to tears (*Tim.* 1.2.10–11, 93–94).[125]

Fortune of course deserts Timon. At first he seems absurdly eager to accept his fall and embraces poverty as maniacally as Richard II had embraced his deposition.[126] But his flattering friends are no more reliable than mother earth, and they too desert him, as did Richard's friends when his fortune disappeared. Timon's unacknowledged bargain with his unacknowledged flatterers doesn't work. He had given them love in the form of gold and food, but, from their point of view, they had already paid their debt to him in flattery. Now they owe him nothing. At last his former friends deny him even "what charitable men afford to beggars" (*Tim.* 3.2.77). They send servants to lie in wait outside his house to ambush him, demanding repayment of loans smaller than his least gifts to them. No longer licking up to him but dining on him, as Apemantus had warned (*Tim.* 1.1.204), the friends who had "smile[d], and fawn[ed] upon his debts,/ And take[n] down int'rest into their glutt'nous maws" now come to take him down (*Tim.* 3.4.51–52). They who had given him their praises—their "breath" (*Tim.* 2.2.174)—now come to stifle him. Even Timon recognizes what is happening:

> *Timon:* Cut my heart in sums.
> *Titus:* Mine, fifty talents.
> *Timon:* Tell out my blood.
> *Lucius's servant:* Five thousand crowns, my lord.
> *Timon:* Five thousand drops pays that. What yours? And yours?
> *First Varro Servant:* My lord—
> *Second Varro Servant:* My lord—
> *Timon:* Tear me, take me, and the gods fall upon you! . . . They have e'en put
>   my breath from me, the slaves.
>   (*Tim.* 3.4.91–102)

They have come to eat him alive, to take his heart, like Cassius's "dearer than Pluto's mine" (*JC* 4.3.101), to suffocate him, and, though he does not make the connection explicit as Richard did, nearly to crucify him.[127]

At a similar point in their careers, each of the other flattered princes had to confront the possibility of having to beg and flatter the very men who had served him before. Apemantus cynically advises Timon to do just that. As in the other plays it is at this moment that the flattery cluster emerges:

> Be thou a *flatterer* now, and seek to thrive
> By that which has undone thee. Hinge thy *knee*,
> And let his very breath whom thou'lt observe
> Blow off thy cap.
>   (*Tim.* 4.3.212–15, italics added)[128]

Sounding like Caesar at the capitol resisting his flatterers, Timon recoils from the very suggestion, and lashes out at Apemantus:

> Thou art a slave . . . but bred a *dog.*
> . . . thou wouldst have plunged thyself
> In general riot, *melted* down thy youth
> In different beds of lust, and never learn'd
> The *icy* precepts of respect, but followed
> The *sugar'd* game before thee. But myself—
> Who had the world as my *confectionary,*
> . . . I, to bear this,
> That never knew but better, is some burthen.
>   (*Tim.* 4.3.252–69; italics added)

You ordinary men might respond to such things, but not I, Caesar had said.

Where is the theater in all this flattery? *Timon* is in a sense the last of the great house plays, complete with its own inner play—here a masque of Amazons, presented, at the opening banquet, for (or by) Timon.[129] The masque is very much part of the play's flattery exchanges (masques are "tied to rules / Of flattery," as someone says in Fletcher's *Maid's Tragedy;* 1.1.10–11). But occurring at Timon's banquet, the masque is also a version of culinary theater, in which the five senses "come freely to gratulate thy [Titus's] plenteous bosom" and to "feast thine eyes" (*Tim.* 1.2.120–21, 123).[130] Heralded by Cupid, the players offer sexual as well as edible gratification. These players are not merely feminized in their tantalizing display of their bodies; they are real women, "Ladies as Amazons," singing and dancing on stage and then moving into the audience. The stage directions specify that the lords rise "*with much adoring of Timon, and to show their loves each single out an Amazon, and all dance*" (*Tim.* stage direction after 1.2.141). Lucillus had already pointed the moral: "You see, my lord, how ample y'are belov'd" (*Tim.* 1.2.126). Amply indeed. This is the work of an all-providing mother, who gratifies Timon's senses and then multiplies herself so that every lord has a partner, and, by the very act of selecting a lady for himself also shows his love to Timon—no rivalry here!

But "Ladies as Amazons" are little better than wolves in wolves' clothing, taken for sheep only because the theatrical context says "it's not real." Just as audiences can turn on players, players can turn on their audience.[131] Women do return "one day," in the form of the prostitutes who accompany Alcibiades to visit Timon in the woods. Although they do not "stamp on" Timon they do show their untrustworthiness: they will do, or play, anything for gold. They are not (one assumes) the same women who appeared in the masque, but this play hardly makes such distinctions, and "Amazon" was a cant term for prostitute so it could apply to both sets of women. Timon is the greatest of great house lords, a "father" (*Tim.* 3.2.69) to his friends and a source of almost mythic hospitality. As in the other late great house plays, *Hamlet* and *Lear,* we see the performance through the lord's eyes, not the players'. In the earlier great houses, the players had indulged in flattering dreams of kingship, but here it is the great man, not the players, who is living in what his servants call a "dream of friendship" (*Tim.* 4.2.34), and the masque is only part of that dream.

Unlike Richard II or Coriolanus, Timon never thinks of himself as an actor. But he does stage a performance of sorts when he is "brilliantly and histrionically revenged in a mock banquet" for his friends.[132] Like the masque itself, Timon's theater is a false feast. It is Shakespeare's own version of the traditional revenge play masque, like Hieronimo's playlet in *The Spanish Tragedy,* where the scripted murders are inflicted on the real players and Hieronimio gets rid of all his enemies. Shakespeare's version of the revenge masque is a revenge banquet, a staged feast in which the director is a cook dishing out revenge, and, as the Mayor of Queenborough said, "a great man [is] poysond in a play" (*Mayor of Queenborough* 5.1.148). This version of the revenge masque perverts the feeding process which, for Shakespeare, is so closely associated with the staging of plays and watching them. In *Titus Andronicus,* Titus says, "I'll play the cook" (*Tit.* 5.2.204), and he feeds Tamora a pastry "coffin" filled with her sons (*Tit.* 5.3.60–63). It is a poetically just revenge, not only because Tamora's sons have killed Titus's sons, but also because Titus thus forces Tamora to ingest what her body once emitted, the fruit of her loins. In *Timon's* similarly reversed banquet, Timon offers his guests an excrementally suggestive two-course meal of "lukewarm water" (*Tim.* 3.6.85; a unique Shakespearean detail)[133] and stones, both of which he throws at them. He used to feed his "mouth-friends" rich and nourishing food, but now he throws something more like excrement and forces them to eat what the body emits (*Tim.* 3.6.85). It is only a kind of joke, but as effectively as Hamlet's jokes it delivers poison in jest.[134] Later, Prospero, the last of the great house lords, will stage a similarly frustrating banquet offered up by actors dressed as harpies, his educational revenge culminating with a masque promising Edenic provisions offered by mother Ceres but frustratingly interrupted.

The ambivalent motives behind Timon's masquelike revenge banquet are further suggested by Alcibiades' trial, another "performance," which intrudes between Timon's dinner invitation and the dinner itself. The trial has bothered many critics; it "tumbles suddenly into the action with the bewildering inconsequence of an episode in a dream, and its power and vividness only strengthen this impression."[135] But the trial has a dream logic of its own that further aligns *Timon* with the other flattery plays. We see Timon in act 3, scene 4, outwardly gracious toward his friends, but inwardly seething with murderous rage and planning to attack them at dinner. Enter Alcibiades in scene 5 announcing that *someone* has committed murder out of a sense of outraged honor, and that Alcibiades has come to beg the Senate for his friend's pardon.[136] In speaking both for his murderous friend and for himself ("the law shall bruise 'em" both, the Senators say; *Tim.* 3.5.4), the humble petitioner Alcibiades enacts the conflict which Timon feels between wanting to earn back his friends' love by begging for it, and wanting to revenge himself on them. Richard II acted out the conflict by offering to depose himself and then fighting the ceremony; Coriolanus acted it out by agreeing to show his wounds and beg for the people's voices, then insulting them instead. Alcibiades, more like Coriolanus than anyone in Shakespeare's sources for *Timon,* invokes the wounds he himself has suffered in the state's wars. "My wounds ache at you" (*Tim.* 3.5.96), he says. "Is this the balsam that the usuring Senate/ Pours into captains' wounds?" (*Tim.* 3.5.111–12). Then, banished like Coriolanus, he leaves to join his city's enemy and returns to attack it. The warrior who fought for the city fights against it; the man who fed his friends poisons them.

Timon has what may be seen as one more theatrical moment at the very end of the play, when not he but his self-composed epitaph (as if a man were author of himself) returns like an Epilogue offering a final prayer for the audience—or in this case, a curse, and a "corse" to end his banquet. There is no accommodation here:

> Here lies a wretched corse, of wretched soul bereft:
> Seek not my name. A plague consume you, wicked catiffs left!
> Here lie I, Timon, who, alive, all living men did hate.
> Pass by and curse thy fill, but pass and stay not here thy gait.
> (*Tim.* 5.4.70–73)[137]

No more than Timon are Richard II, Caesar, or Coriolanus literally actors. But, like an actor, each enjoys a dream of greatness maintained by the flattering ministrations of unreliable followers, both intimate friends who serve him and the public which admires him. And each discovers that both intimates and the public betray him—in scenes like those in a modern actor's fantasies about showing off for a doting but dangerous mother and performing for an adoring but fickle mob.

Chapter Eight

"Every Man Must Play a Part, and Mine a Sad One": The Player's Passion

The actor is not there for us but instead of us.

Grotowski

[Actors] are like victims signaling through the flames.

Artaud

I am a tainted wether of the flock,
Meetest for death.

Antonio, Merchant of Venice

s an Elizabethan actor Shakespeare could draw on an actor's vulnerability to portray the princely victims of flattery described in the last chapter. Accustomed as we are to gentler modes of entertainment, the comparison between Caesar attacked by conspirators and Roman (or Elizabethan) actors hissed by their audience may seem farfetched. But Elizabethans participated enthusiastically in publicly sanctioned attacks on victims of the scaffold, the stocks, and the whipping post.[1] More importantly they were familiar with two popular entertainments—bearbaiting and the Christian mystery plays—that culminated in sacrifice or butchery. Part of the fascination was that the performance was deadly to the performer and that the audience was itself implicated in the violence. In each event the central figure is singled out, surrounded, and exposed to the public gaze as well as to their attack—like Talbot made a scarecrow for the jeering French, or Falstaff pinched and dis-horned by the ring of fairies. Each is structured around a baiting scene that recalls the reversals in Actaeon's story or the fawning admirer's sudden attacks in the flattery plays. Each is analogous to the modern actor's fantasies about mass adoration and the baiting crowd, but each takes a specifically Elizabethan form. The bloody sport of bearbaiting and the cycle of mystery plays culminating in the baiting and crucifixion of Christ each provided a spectacle in some ways similar to the ones available in London theaters, and each left significant traces in Shakespeare's plays and his portrayals of histrionic heroes. Together they suggest another way in which a player's perspective influenced

203

Shakespeare's plays, this time by making him sensitive to something which everyone else took for granted.

Bearbaiting, along with cockfighting and bullbaiting, was a well established sport by the mid-sixteenth century, both in London and in the provinces. Neither cocks nor bears were popular enough actually to put the players out of business (the well-known law forbidding plays on Thursday was made to protect the bears, not the actors), but they did create competition for audiences who saw little difference between the two sorts of entertainment.[2] In bearbaiting, the bear was chained or tied to a stake at the center of a circular ring, and several mastiffs—the most vicious of dogs—were loosed to bait him. The dogs initiated a frenzy of encounters as they moved in to "pinch" or nip the bear and the bear struck back, often killing several dogs before he was beaten or killed himself. The act was often accompanied by what we might call a bear-garden version of the stage jig, in which a chimp rode in on horseback, screaming as he too was attacked by the dogs.[3] What strikes the modern observer is the cruelty of the sport, but Elizabethan crowds roared enthusiastically. A visitor to Henry VIII's court in 1544 thought the dog and pony show "very laughable," and Dekker tells how Harry Hunks, the blind bear, was whipped "till the blood ran down his old shoulders"[4]—a fate threatening the players, as Hamlet knew (*Ham.* 2.2.525; 3.2.13). Slender, one of Anne's foolish suitors in *Merry Wives of Windsor,* "love[s] the sport well" (*Wiv.* 1.1.266) and caps his display of fatuousness by bragging that he has caught Sackerson "twenty times" when the bear escaped.[5] Despite the violence, however, bearbaiting was not raw savagery but a kind of ceremony or game not wholly unlike drama. The audience participated vicariously by betting on (or rather against) the animals; they admired the bears' courage, and they apparently identified in other ways with the anthropoid creatures, who also appeared outside the ring for more peaceful performances.[6] Individual bears like Sackerson, Harry Hunks, and Samson—or Moll Cutpurse and Mad Besse—attracted fans, and on occasion had poems written about them; King James knighted a bearward in 1603.[7] "At the end of the sixteenth century," Sir Sidney Lee wrote, fighting bears like "George Stone, Harry Hunks, Tom of Lincoln, and, above all, Sackerson were for the sporting public of London vulgar idols."[8]

Some bears, or imitation bears at any rate, actually appeared along with the actors in plays during the brief vogue they had on the Elizabethan stage;[9] but in their own ring they could be associated with the players too. Thomas Dekker sarcastically reports that while the playhouses stand empty, "the company of the *Beares* hold together still; they play their *Tragi-Comedies* as lively as ever they did."[10] Elizabethan clowns may have been imitating the bears when they engaged in their popular comic trick of "fighting with a Masty [mastiff]."[11] Perhaps actors in general were also associated with bears or other fighting animals; the Prologue's call for "a muse of fire" in *Henry V,* for example, locates that self-consciously theatrical action in a space described both as "this wooden O" and as a "cockpit" (*H5* Pro. 1, 14, 11).[12] Certainly it was common to wager on a competition between actors as well as on a competition between the bear and the mastiffs.[13]

We have already seen the lasting impression made on Shakespeare by the plight of the deer pinched by surrounding dogs. Edward Armstrong suggests that much of Shakespeare's "pinch" imagery originated in bear-baiting, where the victim was not only pinched but chained. While the stag's plight is a humanist commonplace, Shakespeare's interest in bears is unusual among contemporary dramatists and suggests his own reading of the sport.[14] Just as the deer hunt lent itself to sacred and erotic allegories, Shakespeare's bearbaiting references often carry symbolic weight, even in the comedies. In *The Comedy of Errors,* for example, Antipholus walks about wearing a golden chain that has come to symbolize the confinements of marriage. Suddenly his wife appears with Dr. Pinch himself, the "minion" Antipholus believes is cuckolding him (*Err.* 4.4.58). Pinch, promptly declares Antipholus "possess'd" and calls helpers to have him "bound and laid in some dark room" (*Err.* 4.4.90, 92) so that Pinch can exorcise Antipholus's evil spirits. Here the image of a bear maddened by pinching dogs becomes a figure for a husband at the mercy of a nagging, jealous, "pinching" wife.[15] As the Abbess tells Adriana: "The venom clamours of a jealous woman / Poisons more deadly than a mad dog's tooth" (*Err.* 5.1.69–70). By the end of the play the same image has come to suggest also the pinch of death, which Shakespeare elsewhere associates with women but here locates in the cadaverous person of Pinch: "A mere anatomy, a mountebank . . . / A needy-hollow-ey'd-sharp-looking-wretch; / A living dead man" (*Err.* 5.1.239–42). But whatever domestic or metaphysical torments are implied in Pinch's attack, they also impose an actor's torment as Antipholus, like Talbot and Falstaff, is surrounded and put on display. Humiliated by the public arrest, by his frustrating powerlessness, and by his sexual defeat, Antipholus accuses his wife of collecting a vicious audience, "a damned *pack* / To make an loathesome abject scorn of me" (*Err.* 4.4.100– 101; italics added). As we might anticipate, he threatens to get back at her—and perhaps at the larger audience as well—through a specular attack: "with these nails I'll pluck out these false eyes / That would behold in me this shameful sport" (*Err.* 102–3). Like the actor's torment, Antipholus's is reversible, at least onstage; for, as we hear later, he gives Pinch as good as he gets—binds him, "nicks him like a fool" with scissors, and alternately singes his beard and douses it with filthy water (*Err.* 5.1.169– 75).[16] Despite this onstage attack, however, he never retaliates against *us.*

By the time the bears reappear in *Twelfth Night* the theater audience is implicated even more directly in the bearbaiting.[17] Orsino, bearish by name, begins the play complaining that his "desires, like fell and cruel hounds . . . pursue me" (*TN* 1.1.21–22), and Olivia's equally painful erotic adventures make her fear that Sebastian has "set mine honour at the stake / And baited it with all th'unmuzzled thoughts / That tyrannous heart can think" (*TN* 3.1.118–20). But in this play the baiting is displaced onto a scapegoat, Malvolio, golden chain and all, who is even more meanspirited, pinched, possessive, and grasping than Antipholus imagines his wife to be (or, indeed, than he turns out to be himself). Spoilsport Malvolio, who had gotten Olivia's followers in trouble, over a bearbaiting among other things, has finally provoked "the lighter people" (*TN* 5.1.338) to retaliate by exposing him to "some notable shame" (*TN* 2.5.5). Planting a forged letter from Olivia, they trick the steward into wearing yellow stockings, cross garters, and a foolish leer to woo his supposedly lovesick mistress. Malvolio is made even more ludicrous than the horned Falstaff, waiting in vain for his merry wives, or the frenzied Antipholus locked out of his house and calling for his wife. So ludicrous, in fact, that he is taken for a madman and locked in a dark cell. There is no Dr. Pinch here, but Malvolio finds his exorcist in Feste (alias Sir Topas), who keeps him confined until he changes his unholy spiritual beliefs. Yet this is a comedy, and when the practical joke begins to turn sadistic, Shakespeare seems to let the audience off the hook with Fabian's reminder, just before Malvolio is locked up, that this is after all only a play: "If this were played upon a stage now, I could condemn it as an improbable fiction" (*TN* 3.4.128–29). But at the end of the play we realize that we cannot detach ourselves so easily. Even more abused than Antipholus, Malvolio walks off for the last time with Antipholus's words, vowing to be "revenged on the whole pack of you."[18] "At pack," Ralph Berry argues, "the subliminal metaphor discloses itself. It is a bearbaiting." As Malvolio pivots to address the onstage tormentors surrounding him, he clearly sees the audience as well as the characters as part of the pack. "It is theatre as blood sport, theatre that celebrates its own dark origins."[19] It reminds us in fact not only of distant roots but also of our own current appetites. It foregrounds the less festive possibilities of doing "what you will," whether licensed by Twelfth Night or by the holiday atmosphere of the theater. The spectator is roused from passivity to both run with the deer and hunt with the hounds—made to feel in his bones the ambiguities which the actor's position epitomizes, the antagonisms and identifications in powerful emotion.

These "comic" figures suggest that, although sixteenth-century audiences laughed at bearbaitings, Shakespeare could create enough sympathy for the performing "bear" (or "poor fool," as Olivia calls Malvolio) to make spectators feel guilty about the blood.[20] Elsewhere the bear's perspective predominates as it figures the tragic fate of men like Gloucester and Macbeth who have their own "dark roots." Here the language of the bear ring refers not only to the violence its protagonists suffer, but to the claustrophobic nightmare of being tied down in the midst of circling enemies, of being exposed helpless before a hostile mob. Even before his defeat, Macbeth, like Richard III at the end of his play, had begun to feel trapped by his conscience:

> I am cabin'd, cribb'd, confin'd, bound in
> To saucy doubts and fears.
>
> (*Mac.* 3.4.23–24)

Once he begins to "doubt th'equivocation of the fiend / That lies like truth" (*Mac.* 5.5.43–44)—a kind of passive exorcism—his external enemies close in, and the image of the bear comes to mind:

> They have tied me to the stake: I cannot fly,
> But, bear-like, I must fight the course.
>
> (*Mac.* 5.7.1–2)

Macbeth dies fighting, rather than yielding to being displayed like "our rarer monsters" and "baited with the rabble's curse" (*Mac.* 5.8.25, 29). Though we despise his crime we identify with Macbeth as much as with his politically-correct attackers, implicated despite ourselves. We are left equivocating with ourselves even after the "juggling" fiend's riddles are resolved.

In *King Lear,* the balance of sympathy shifts almost entirely toward the "guilty" victim, making the audience's moral positions even less secure. Gloucester, who is undeniably guilty of casual adultery and cruelty toward the son it produced, is betrayed so cruelly by his bastard son (and by Lear's "dog-hearted daughters"; *Lr.* 4.3.45) it is almost impossible to remember his long-past guilt.[21] He is tied to a chair while his enemies circle him, bait him by reciting his "crimes," and move in to tear out his eyes. Gloucester makes the analogy himself: "I am tied to th'stake, and I must stand the course" (*Lr.* 3.7.53). Edgar, the "good" son, later moralizes the attack for his bastard brother:

> The Gods are just, and of our pleasant vices
> Make instruments to plague us:
> The dark and vicious place where thee he [Gloucester] got
> Cost him his eyes.
>
> (*Lr.* 5.3.169–73)

Lear, driven mad by his own suffering, recalls Gloucester's sin for us when
he "pardons" Gloucester on the heath, calling him simply "blind Cupid"
(*Lr.* 4.6.9, 136). But in addition to the talion law as old as Oedipus's blinding, what operates here is the kind of human ritual Shakespeare imposed
on men who are surrounded and publicly shamed for their passion: Antipholus for his jealousy, Malvolio and Falstaff for their misplaced lusts. Each
is surrounded and put in the dark or literally blinded,[22] in an imposition of
justice which Gloucester however sees as nothing more than mob violence:
"As flies to wanton boys, are we to th' Gods; / They kill us for their sport"
(*Lr.* 4.1.38–39).[23] The implications for the theater audience are not as clear
as they are in Malvolio's baiting. But here too, as we watch—with curiosity
despite our horror—the ritual punishment, we are made to feel the de facto
cruelty of our detached participation in theatrical "sport," in tragedy as well
as bearbaiting. There's no immediate exorcism for Gloucester during his
punishment, as there was for Antipholus and Malvolio. But later Edgar exorcises his father's demon by staging a false suicide, leading Gloucester to
the edge of a "high cliff," letting him jump, then meeting Gloucester at the
"bottom" and pretending to see a fiend leave the top.[24]

Even earlier in the canon, in what might appear merely an automatic
reference to Warwick's badge, the "muzzled bear rampant and ragged
staff,"[25] Shakespeare goes on at a length suggesting both an interest in the
sport for its own right and the tragic significance which bearbaiting will
later acquire. The man who invokes the bears, Richard, Duke of York, is
interesting to us as the flamboyant father of Shakespeare's player, Richard III. When Clifford threatens York, York retaliates by summoning his
"bears":

> Call hither to the stake my two brave bears [Salisbury and his son Warwick],
> That with the very shaking of their chains
> They may astonish these fell lurking curs.
>
> (*2H6* 5.1.144–46)

Clifford counters with a threat that reduces York to a bearward, an entertainer even more despised than players:

> We'll bait thy bears to death,
> And manacle the bear'ard in their chains.
>
> (*2H6* 5.1.147–48)

Then York's son, our Richard III-to-be and apparently a connoisseur of
bearbaiting, elaborates the metaphor still further by mocking Clifford's
"dogs":

Oft have I seen a hot o'erweening cur
Run back and bite, because he was withheld;
Who, being suffer'd with the bear's fell paw
Hath clapp'd his tail, between his legs and cried:
And such a piece of service will you do.

(2H6 5.1.151–55)

The Yorkists, says Richard, are brave bears and their enemies cowardly curs, all bark and no bite. Finally, in the last *Henry VI* play, Richard, separated from York, imagines his father himself as the bear fighting bravely in another part of the battlefield. "Methought," says Richard,

he bore him in the thickest troup
As doth a lion in a herd of neat;
Or as a bear, encompass'd round with dogs,
Who having pinch'd a few and made them cry,
The rest stand all aloof and bark at him.
So far'd our father with his enemies . . .
Methinks 'tis prize enough to be his son.
See how the morning opes her golden gates,
And takes her farewell of the glorious sun.

(3H6 2.1.13–22; italics added)

Richard sees the paternal bear as a heroic warrior, a kingly lion who can make his son a glorious sun, someone with whom he can proudly identify. It is the first of Richard's untrustworthy dreams.

Bearlike though Richard believes his father to be, we have already seen York die, his death shaped more by our second precedent for Shakespeare's mobbed and baited victims, the Christ of the passion plays. The biblical narrative of Christ's passion can be said to lie behind any scene of tragic suffering, but Emrys Jones argues that the specific version of the story found in all extant mystery plays seems to have had a particular effect on Shakespeare.[26] Unlike the Bible, the plays elaborate on the entrapment and humiliation leading up to the crucifixion. In each of the cycles Christ's enemies, led by Caiaphas and Annas, are represented as "monsters of hate and malice" who plot against him under the guise of legal righteousness.[27] Their physical attack on Jesus is preceded by at least two "baiting" scenes in which they surround him, examine him and taunt him. They move smoothly from ceremonious interrogation to savagery, like the flattering spaniel who suddenly turns cur. York's death scene in *Henry VI, Part Three* condenses this repeated baiting from the Passion play into a single scene, where he is surrounded by his enemies Queen Margaret and young Clifford. They make York, "that raught at mountains," stand on a molehill; they put a paper crown on the head of the man who thought to be king and "pale his head in Henry's [usurped] glory" (*3H6* 1.4.68, 103). The paper crown makes histrionic York, whose rhetoric already stands out against the pragmatics in the *Henriad* like the player's speech in *Hamlet,* into a player Christ as well as a player king. York's enemies go on to announce the murder of his youngest son, offering to wipe his tears with a napkin stained in the boy's blood. Though he is on the wrong side, York is the sole representative of Talbot's heroism in the play, and his death is made momentous as he exhibits a Christ-like patience before he answers his attackers.

York is the only Shakespearean figure who is both a bear and a Christ. But the baiting of Christ is evoked elsewhere in the canon, frequently in the plays about players. Like bearbaiting, the baiting of Christ appears first in the first *Henriad,* most extensively in the fall of noble Humphrey, Duke of Gloucester.[28] We watch Gloucester's enemies, Queen Margaret and Cardinal Beaufort, plot against him as the high priests had conspired against Christ. Twice they circle him, interrogating him sadistically about his presumptions as Protector. Despite the violence, ceremoniousness prevails during the baiting and makes it, Jones suggests, a "formalized group-act of execration."[29] Finally they take the old man offstage and he is suffocated in his bed.

The rest of Shakespeare's baited Christs are associated with the performative aspects of flattery and its reversals. In *King Lear,* the physical violence is reserved for Humphrey's namesake, the Duke of Gloucester, who, as we have seen, is "staked," baited, and blinded, more like a bear than like Christ.[30] But Lear himself suffers the psychological baiting which both York and Humphrey endured. Like Christ in the passion plays he is twice baited and humiliated for presuming a king's prerogatives (*Lr.* 1.4, 2.4). Goneril and Regan viciously mock Lear's request for a train of knights, concealing their malice beneath a legalistic rationale for treating him like a beggar. ("O, *reason* not the need," he cries, when they coolly arrange to take away his last vestige of royal estate; *Lr.* 2.4.262; italics added.) Lear, in his madness, associates his reversals with flattery: "They flatter'd me like a dog . . . To say 'ay' and 'no' to everything that I said! . . . Go to, they are not men o' their words: they told me I was every thing; 'tis a lie, I am not ague-proof" (*Lr.* 4.6.96–105, *passim*). The other baiting scenes appear in the flattery plays, where the physical violence surfaces. In *Richard II,* Northumberland "torments" Richard (4.1.270) by forcing him to confess to crimes that will make his deposition legal, and then he is carried off to prison and assassination. In *Julius Caesar* it is Brutus, not Caesar, who feels baited: "Bait not me," he tells Cassius when he feels sorry for himself during their quarrel (*JC* 4.3.38). But Caesar is surrounded by the hypocritical conspirators who provoke his anger with their nagging just before they attack. Coriolanus is baited by the two tribunes and Timon by his creditors, before each falls victim to the crowd's righteous violence.[31] Each of these baited victims is set upon by crowds and violently but ceremoniously attacked. Several of these baitings recall Gloucester's in *Henry VI, Part Two*: Lear suffers an attack of the "mother," or suffocation; Coriolanus has been desperate for the voices and "breath" of the crowd; and Timon is so crowded that the creditors who besiege him and "e'en put my breath from me"—as if Gloucester's suffocation were still on Shakespeare's mind.

A somewhat different aspect of the passion play suggests one more resemblance between Jesus' passion and what Hamlet called the player's passion. Christ in the plays, the Man of Sorrows, accepts his fate, subordinating himself to the necessity of his sacrifice and to the Father who has forsaken him—to his role and to his audience. Yet even as he is forsaken, he is the center of attention. Jesus is dramatically singled out from the crowd and forced to display his body and his wounds. He is the object of the murderous gaze of his enemies and the devoted gaze of his disciples—"Jesus Christ, Superstar," as Broadway has restyled him. Like an actor's passion, Jesus' passion must be witnessed if it is finally to be effective; it must move its audience. "Christ died for us" not only as a token in a divine exchange behind the scenes, but as an eternally visible example which we can now have before our eyes.[32] It is a part actors would die for.

Besides being a rewarding role, "Christ" is one actors can identify with. "The actor is not there for us but instead of us," Grotowsky says—to live out the conflict we would otherwise have to endure ourselves. Actors "are like victims signaling through the flames," says Artaud, with an equally expansive vision of the function of theater in our time. Nor is it only theorists who find the actor Christ-like. Denys Arcand's recent film *Jesus of Montreal* provides an almost embarassing elaboration of the fantasy. The film is about Daniel, an actor who bravely revives the parish passion play to incorporate scandalous evidence of Jesus' mortality—and as a result is himself all but literally crucified for his efforts to bring this new gospel truth to the people through drama. (He dies on the stage cross, though accidentally, when the mob surges forward to protest his midperformance arrest.)[33] Arcand's is hardly a sixteenth-century perspective on the actor;[34] not even Marlowe would have seen Jesus as a superstar, though he did create a star martyr of sorts in *Edward II*. But three seventeenth-century playwrights in France and Spain each found the actor-martyr St. Genest fascinating, and each wrote a play about Genest's martyrdom after a conversion onstage while playing a martyr in a performance for Emperor Diocletian.[35] And one figure in the Shakespearean canon suggests an attitude toward histrionic Christ-like sacrifice at least as complex, if not as self-indulgent, as Arcand's. Antonio in *Merchant of Venice*, Shakespeare's self-styled man of sorrows, chooses the sacrificial role himself in a posture as unintentionally histrionic as Daniel's in *Jesus of Montreal*. Antonio is not an actor, any more than the flattered kings were actors. But his experience—like Christ's—can provide an analogy for what actors feel about their ordeal before an audience and about what makes it worthwhile.

By the end of the play, it is the moneylender Shylock who will be "sacrificed," or at least scapegoated, and Bassanio's hard-won Portia who will actually say "I stand for sacrifice" (*MV* 3.2.57), likening herself to Hesione waiting for her herculean savior (in the unlikely form of Bassanio) to rescue her. But despite the poetry straining to give sacrificial significance to Bassanio's choice in the casket scene, Antonio preempts the role of sacrificial lamb for himself, by financing Bassanio's courtship and offering his pound of flesh when Shylock insists on his bond and Antonio cannot pay: "I am a tainted wether of the flock, / Meetest for death" (*MV* 4.1.114–15). It is Antonio's sacrifice that comes most dramatically to life when, Christ-like, he is put on trial to face his version of Caiaphas in Shylock, and the Jew sharpens his knife as he insists that he is merely asking for justice.

Nonetheless, Antonio is not Christ. His selflessness conceals its own kind of demand for exchange, and his devotion to Bassanio is two-edged. Antonio is no Caesar or Coriolanus either, but his "ancient Roman honor" (and his ancient Roman name, along with Portia's) links his ambiguous fate to that of the central figures in the Roman and Greek flattery plays.[36] Antonio of Venice, like Timon of Athens, gives all, but with hidden strings attached. "Debts are clear'd between you and I, if I might see you at my death," he writes Bassanio, summoning him from Portia's side when the debt comes due (*MV* 3.2.317–18); and then, as he prepares for the knife:

> Commend me to your honorable wife,
> Tell her the process of Antonio's end,
> Say how I lov'd you, speak me fair in death:
> And when the tale is told, bid her be judge
> Whether Bassanio had not once a love.
>
> (*MV* 4.1.269–73)

I will die for you, he says, but you must tell your wife that my death makes me, not her, your true lover.[37] I give you up in order to secure you more profoundly.

As in Timon's predicament, the emotional debts are signaled by the circulation of money; like gold, love can be hoarded, borrowed, or given freely. This is a sophisticated, if "natural," symbolism for what has been called "love's wealth,"[38] but it is grounded in a child's unsophisticated concrete imagination, where mother's love is inseparable from mother's milk. Both precious substances are gold, the "alms out of the empress' chest" (*Tit.* 2.3.9), as Aaron describes his buried gold[39]—or Portia's "golden fleece" (*MV* 1.1.170), as Bassanio calls it, locked up in the lead chest with her portrait. Like all unreliable nurturers, Portia can either sustain or starve her favored son. If Bassanio is good, Portia's golden fortune will flow like her mercy: it "droppeth as the gentle rain from heaven" (*MV* 4.1.181), or at least from her beautiful mountain. But if he is bad—chooses the wrong casket—he is doomed. Antonio, by contrast, makes no conditions for Bassanio, and puts no restraints on his love: "My purse, my person, my extremest means, / Lie all unlock'd to your occasions" (*MV* 1.1.138–39).[40] He has given himself heart and soul to Bassanio, which is precisely why (though he himself "knows not why") he is so sad (*MV* 1.1.1). As Mahood argues, Antonio has wisely diversified his financial investments:

> My ventures are not in one bottom [ship] trusted,
> Nor to one place; nor is my whole estate
> Upon the fortune of this present year:
> Therefore my merchandise makes me not sad.
>
> (*MV* 1.1.42–45)

But he has invested all his love—garnered up his heart, as Othello would say—in one young man, and he fears it is not safe.

In offering to pay Bassanio's debt "with all my heart" Antonio repeats Cassius's extravagance when he gave Brutus a knife during their quarrel, opened his robes and offered "a heart dearer than Pluto's mine" for Brutus's forgiveness (*JC* 4.3.100–101). Or Timon's sarcastic offer to the crowd of creditors presenting their bills, "cut my heart out in sums" and "tell out my blood" (*Tim.* 3.4.91, 93). As in those plays, the wound, which here remains a merely verbal threat, implies an emotional loss—like Shylock's loss of his own "flesh and blood," his daughter Jessica. But Shakespeare's insistence on the physicality of the loss is essential to convey the pain it inflicts. At the trial Shylock's knife and the extended discussion of scales to weigh the flesh make Antonio's wounds imaginatively real; even the subtly begging letter he writes to Bassanio is "every word a gaping wound" (*MV* 3.2.264). Caesar's wounds were paralleled by Portia's wound in the thigh, but *Merchant's* Portia has no wound.[41] The wounds here, like the sacrifice, are all Antonio's.

Though not a player, the fatalistic Antonio associates himself with the stage through his self-consciousness about his assigned role and his willingness to play it:

> I hold this world but as the world, Gratiano,
> A stage, where every man must play a part,
> And mine a sad one.
>
> (*MV* 1.1.77–79)

Later at the trial, while Shylock sharpens his knife, Antonio accepts his death so willingly, so nobly, so eloquently, and so often, that he commands the whole audience's breathless attention. "There is still," as Herbert Blau reports old actors saying, "nothing more dramatic than a trial."[42] It's not quite that Antonio stages a love death like Cleopatra's or plays "industrious scenes and acts of death" like King John (*KJ* 2.1.376), and it would be unkind to compare his lingering leave-taking to Bottom's protracted "Thus die I, thus, thus, thus! . . . Now die, die, die, die, die!" (*MND* 5.1.289, 295) as he bleeds to death through his left pap in "Pyramus and Thisbe." But, as the Player in Tom Stoppard's twentieth-century version of Hamlet says, "Dying is what we do best," and Antonio is every inch a player as he prepares to die center stage here. We know that many Elizabethan players died well; it was Talbot's death scene that Nashe recalled from *Henry VI, Part One;*[43] and a death scene helped make Burbage famous:

> Oft have I seene him, leap into the Graue
> Suiting the person, which he seem'd to have
> Of a sadd Lover, with soe true an Eye
> That ther I would have sworne, he meant to dye,
> Oft have I seene him, play this part in ieast,
> Soe livly, that Spectators, and the rest
> Of his sad Crew, whilst he but seem'd to bleed,
> Amazed, thought even then he dyed in deed.[44]

"A death speech," as Muriel Bradbrook argues, "was the big finale for any [Elizabethan] actor, demanding complete identification."[45]

The sacrificial stance is not always as overtly histrionic as it is in *Merchant*, but its appearance elsewhere in Shakespeare's plays illuminates the emotional context to which both self-sacrifice and playing are responses. In particular, Antonio's histrionic sacrifice is poised between two others which suggest the range of relationships recreated by the player's ambivalent relation to the audience for whom he sacrifices himself. Each is located in one of the plays where a scapegoat is baited like a bear and vows revenge: *The Comedy of Errors*, where Antipholus is baited, and *Twelfth Night*, where Malvolio is baited. The first is a father's sacrifice for his son, the second a lover's sacrifice for his beloved. In the opening lines of *The Comedy of Errors*, a "hint of a sacrifice"[46] colors Egeon's almost melodramatic longing for the "doom of death," after he has voyaged into enemy territory to search for his sons (*Err.* 1.1.2).[47] But Egeon's selfless devotion is tainted with melancholy when his son "sham'st to acknowledge me in misery" and will not "pay the sum that may deliver me" (*Err.* 5.1.322, 285). Then in *Twelfth Night*, another Antonio sacrifices himself for a friend, a youth named after

Sebastian, the saint most closely associated with homoerotic love.[48] This time the underlying possessiveness and melancholy acceptance of betrayal are still more open. Here, as in Venice, a male villain (Malvolio), like Shylock, is singled out as scapegoat, and Duke Orsino threatens to "sacrifice" a woman (Viola disguised as his "page" Cesario), because Olivia prefers the page to him. But it is an Antonio who actually puts his life in danger to be near and help Sebastian. Having risked his life to save Sebastian from drowning, and given the boy his purse and person, Antonio now steps in to rescue him in a duel—only to hear "Sebastian" deny knowing him. More offended than Egeon, this Antonio also rebukes his love: "Thou hast, Sebastian, done good feature shame. . . . None can be call'd deform'd but the unkind" (*TN* 3.4.375–77). Sacrifice is bearable only when recognized and appreciated, witnessed, and, even if silently, applauded.

* * *

The self-sacrificing stance, whether before a crowd or before the one significant other who counts for all the world, also characterizes the texts in which Shakespeare comes closest—though by no means all the way—to speaking in his own voice. The first group of these consists of dedicatory texts: the prose dedications to "Venus and Adonis" and "The Rape of Lucrece," and two sonnets, one (sonnet 26) written to accompany an unidentified "written ambassage," and another (sonnet 23) to accompany some "books." The second group is the entire body of the sonnets with their characteristic voice of effacement.

The dedications are in many ways unremarkable. Self-abasement was customary on occasions of public homage; the dedication was one of the nondramatic genres in which the ancient Roman Gnatho remained alive and well. Shakespeare's are typical of their kind, and their self-denial alone does not necessarily reveal anything about his "real" attitude. But the dedications to the two narrative poems do differ from one another, and from those differences we may perhaps see something about Shakespeare's unique use of the convention. Readers have often noted that the first dedication, the 1593 preface to "Venus and Adonis," is more formal and distant in tone, while the second, the 1594 preface to "Lucrece," written (presumably) after the first poem had gained public recognition and after Shakespeare's relation to his patron had been more well established, sounds more assured and familiar.

What has not been noticed is that as Shakespeare the poet becomes more intimate he becomes more self-effacing. The "Venus" dedication, however formal, is written by a poet of aspiring mind. Though he uses the conventional language of humility, this poet admits a desire to be "highly praised," and takes for granted his ability to honor the patron with "some graver labour" in the future if this "first heir" of his invention pleases. The dedication's epigraph, scorning any offer of caviare to the general, might have been written by Tamburlaine:

> Vilia miretur vulgus: mihi flavus Apollo
> Pocula Castalia plena ministret aqua.
> (Let the mob admire base things; may golden Apollo
> Serve me full cups from the Castalian spring.)
> (Ovid, Amores I.15.35–36, Ven. Ded.)

By contrast, the "Rape" dedication focuses on Southampton and on Shakespeare's relation to him as mediated by the poem. The poet's self-assurance has nothing to do with his own merit; it depends instead on the patron's "disposition": "The *warrant I have* of your Honorable disposition, not the worth of my untutored lines, makes it assured of acceptance" (*Luc.* Ded. 2–4; italics added). While the first dedication reminded its reader of the poet's Apollonian springs and his independent ability to create new poems, this one completely subordinates the poet to his patron: "What I have done is yours, what I have to do is yours, being part in all I have devoted yours" (*Luc.* Ded. 4–6). *I am the dog and the dog is me.* It is as if the closer Shakespeare came to the honorable lord in question, the more intensely self-denying was his service, and the more he identified with the object of his devotion.

All the sonnets are in some sense dedications, and the Petrarchan selflessness which pervades them in places reaches extremes which have reminded readers of Antonio's sacrifice for Bassanio in *The Merchant of Venice.*[49] But two of the sonnets seem to have been written more literally to present the poet's work and to dedicate it to the beloved. Shakespeare's sonnet 26, which refers to an accompanying "written ambassage," employs an even more self-deprecatory version of the usual dedicatory rhetoric. But here the poet can "rise and stoop at once," displaying himself by offering his duty, and flaunting a witty conceit to show his lack of wit. The poet's paradoxically selfless self-assertion in love, or his achievement of subjectivity through serving the other, always resembles the actor's achievement onstage. What connects the poet's with a player's offering more specifically in this sonnet is the "series of variations on the idea of showing"—that is, on the actor's forte—which runs as subtext throughout.[50] In the course of proclaiming his duty, the poet speaks of showing his wit, wanting words to show it, being naked (though possibly it is the lord's thought which is, or is also, naked), being shown worthy, but at the last not yet daring to show his head:

Lord of my love, to whom in vassalage
Thy merit hath my duty strongly knit,
To thee I send this written ambassage,
To witness duty, not *to show my wit.*
Duty so great, which wit so poor as mine
May make seem bare in *wanting words to show it,*
But that I hope some good conceit of thine
In thy soul's thought, *all naked,* will bestow it;
Till whatsoever star that guides my moving
Points on me graciously *with fair aspéct,*
And puts apparel on my tottered [tattered] loving,
To show me worthy of thy sweet respect.
    Then may I dare to boast how I do love thee;
    Till then, *not show my head* where thou mayst prove me.
                    (Son. 26; italics added)

Paradoxically, in his very humility, the poet manages to show himself in a sonnet of self-effacement—"show" in two senses, for, as Booth notes, the emphasis on showing and nakedness carries additional "overtones of witty—though puerile—obscenity."[51] Such ironies, barred from dedications proper, are allowable and even expectable in sonnets, as they are in dramatic epilogues on stage. Finally the poet's offering, whether poetic or dramatic, is also to be a means of entrance into the lord's elevated presence and thus of being transformed himself: the poem begins in vassalage but ends with hope that that poet will be made "worthy" and can be "prove[d]." Lines 7–12 may even evoke a faint recollection of Sly's dramatic elevation out of service in *The Taming of the Shrew*, where another lord's "conceit" "bestowed" and "put apparel on" the "tattered" Sly.[52] Is this the sort of thing Callow meant when he discovered that the sonnet poet was "at the root of his being an actor"?

Sonnet 23 seems also to have been written to accompany, or perhaps simply to interpret, a text: here, the poet's "books" or "leaves of poems."[53] This time the poet's dedicatory gesture immediately evokes the theatrical context, and "the theme of *eloquentia* runs through the sonnet":[54]

As an unperfect actor on the stage,
Who with his fear is put beside his part,
Or some fierce thing replete with too much rage,
Whose strength's abundance weakens his own heart;
So I for fear of trust forget to say
The perfect ceremony of love's rite,
And in mine own love's strength seem to decay,
O'er-charged with burthen of mine own love's might.

> O let my books [looks?] be then the eloquence
> And dumb presagers of my speaking breast,
> Who plead for love and look for recompense
> More than that tongue hath more expressed.
>   O learn to read what silent love hath writ.
>   To hear with eyes belongs to love's fine wit.
>
> (Son. 23)

Here, of course, the poet is speaking about his love, not about theater. He is saying something like, "I love you, but I am so overcome, both by the importance of expressing this and by the intensity of my emotion, that I cannot express my love verbally or in person. Let my poems speak for me; let them win more of your love (and be better rewarded) than others do who speak to you openly about such things." The opening theatrical image seems merely to be a figure for the poet's prior concern with his tongue-tied love. He is "unperfect" and cannot perform the perfect ceremony of love's rite; mere word play or analogy leads him to the image of the "unperfect actor," one who has forgotten his lines, is not "word perfect" as we would say now—or "parfit" as Costard would say; "unperfect" may convey additional self-deprecatory connotations as well.[55] As elaborated in lines 5 and 6, the image perhaps also recalls the tongue-tied amateur actors, Moth in *Love's Labour's Lost* and the clerks whom Theseus recalls in *A Midsummer Night's Dream*. The poet says he is overwhelmed by his ceremonial responsibility and cannot trust himself—just as Moth forgets his part because "presence majestical put him out" (*LLL* 5.2.102), and Theseus's clerks, overwhelmed by "fears" "dumbly" broke off their premeditated welcomes (*MND* 5.1.97, 98).

But although theater seems peripheral, as the sonnet moves out from the opening theatrical figure to elaborate on the emotion which is its primary concern, it also moves towards the theatrical relation we have seen between Shakespeare's actors and audience. Like the actor's, for example, the poet's love may be tinged with hostility. He is not only silent like an "unperfect actor . . . who with his *fear* is put beside his part" but also silent like "some *fierce* thing replete with too much rage" (italics added)—too much anger, or perhaps too much thoughtless predatory "lust." The poet no doubt means simply to convey the magnitude of his love: the very excess of love stifles its expression. But "rage" necessarily leaves its mark on that love. It suggests the reversible hunt; and the poet's humility suggests the hostility of a "fierce thing," Actaeon-like, made dumb in the midst of its approach. The excess which prevents the poet from expressing his love is not only love itself, but its opposite.

The next quatrain continues the overt paradox of a love so excessive it undoes itself; but it also elaborates on the covert paradox of a devotion inseparable from its opposite, rage and mistrust. Here the "fear," likened to the actor's fear, is "fear of trust." But it is not clear who fears what: the poet may not trust himself to perform the ceremony correctly; or he may be afraid that even if he does, the beloved will not trust him. Or he may also mistrust his "love's strength"—his own "rage" which could lead him to love not wisely but too well. The expression of such intensely self-denying love, in other words, is ambivalent and can also be too self-assertive or willful. In any case the conjunction between "fear" and "trust" works against any profession of "perfect" love, and continues the analogy to acting.[56] The paradox is not resolved but only evaded in the sestet, where the poet asks to be understood through his poems, which can be seen with eyes, or looked at: "And let my books be then the eloquence / And dumb presagers of my *speaking breast*" (Son. 23, 9–10; italics added). He asks to be understood through the kind visual "showing" which colored sonnet 26, one more associated with the entire body ("speaking breast") than with the tongue specifically as organ of speech.[57] The sense of showing is even stronger if we accept the emendation of "looks" for "books" in line 9. In either case, what the books (or looks) say is not, "I love you," but rather, "Please love me": they "plead for love and look for recompense."

The poet, in other words, begins by apologizing for not expressing his love, but suggests that the love is somehow like rage, and he goes on instead to ask to be loved. The throwaway metaphor about actors in the first line begins a drama in which shyness belies ferocity, and the speaker avoids expressing active love in favor of asking for it passively. Love is tinged with hostility; the would-be expression of love amounts to a desire for love and "recompense." This is precisely the kind of ambivalent relation to audiences which lies behind an actor's experience and generates stage fright in the first place. The poet's predicament may seem entirely removed from any but superficial connections with the unperfect actor's fear in the opening line, but it nonetheless takes us back to the dynamics in which the actor's fear is generated and which it recalls.

Not only in the dedications but throughout the sonnets, the poet recreates the actor's stance before an audience, suggested by his vacillation between grandiose claims (about his love and his verse) on one hand, and on the other his self-abasement before the aristocratic young man and his dependence on the young man's mirroring love.[58] In addition, the sonnets contain a number of provocative references to the stage itself. There are not many of these; the stage is not what the poet was writing "about." But they are important because they are all negative. And though some are trivial, several are more central in their own way. The stage metaphor, which seems at first to be merely a figure for a sonnet's ultimate concern with something else, can turn out to be more important than it seems, or at least more implicated in that ultimate concern. The remaining sonnet references to the stage are largely confined to the notorious lines in sonnets 110–12 where many readers have heard the poet overtly likening himself to an actor, although others have strongly denied the connection. These sonnets constitute the most suggestive, if also the most controversial, clues we have about Shakespeare the actor. That the allusion to playing, if such it is, would be oblique enough to cause diverse interpretation should not surprise us. But, inconclusive as the lines are, it may be possible to resolve part of the controversy by carefully comparing them to Shakespeare's portrayal of actors elsewhere in the canon as proud beggars, first flattered and then attacked or wounded, and always exposed to the judgmental crowd.

As in sonnet 23, the sonnets in question deal primarily not with playing but rather with some other shameful action. The playing enters only as gloss, as figuration of something else; but as it does in sonnet 23, the "something else" returns us to the ground of acting. The sonnets are part of a sequence (109–12) which deals with the poet's recent absence from the young man when he had become involved with someone else, perhaps purposely to make the youth jealous, perhaps not. Now he returns, ashamed, and the posture calls up a series of stage metaphors. The most famous occurs in the first quartet of sonnet 110, where the poet says he has "made myself a motley to the view":

> Alas 'tis true, I have gone here and there,
> And made myself a motley to the view.
> Gored mine own thoughts, sold cheap what is most dear,
> Made old offences of affections new.
>
> (Son. 110, 1–4)

In 1811 Charles Lamb claimed that Shakespeare here "alludes to his profession as a player."[59] Many readers have since agreed, but others see the allusion as irrelevant or possibly misleading.[60] Sonnet editor Stephen Booth, assessing the debate, argues convincingly that the primary meaning of "made myself a motley to the view" is "behaved like an idiot" and that the phrase merely uses one meaning for "play" and "fool" ("perform the role of professional clown") to stand for another ("behave like an idiot"). "If this poem were not by a professional actor," Booth argues, "the line would simply say 'I have made myself a public laughingstock.'" The fact that Shakespeare actually was an actor, and that all readers know it, "operates to give a witty, pun-like extra dimension to the lines," Booth says, but the knowledge adds very little to the sonnet. "Unfortunately," he adds, disapprovingly, "scholarly craving for biographical knowledge has led to

readings of this poem as an expression of Shakespeare's opinion of his profession and to correspondingly extravagant counterdistortions."[61] Critics
have exaggerated the importance of the motley.

Even if the reference to acting is not primary, however, it might still be
operative as an opinion of Shakespeare's profession, particularly in its emphasis on the *public* exposure, if not on "playing" per se. Shakespeare may
not be saying "Being a player is the same thing as being a fool or motley,
and that's what I'm ashamed of here," but he is saying, "I've done something
shameful, and the first thing that comes to mind to describe my shame is
the feeling an actor has when acting"—that is to say, "acting is shameful."
In any case, it is never easy, we have learned, to separate the supplementary,
random, or "extra" from the primary meaning. Booth's justification for
separating "made myself a motley" into theatrical and nontheatrical meanings depends on his analogy with the phrase, "play the fool." But it may not
be possible to separate the theatrical and nontheatrical meanings in "play
the fool" either. On the contrary, the phrase is already thoroughly implicated in what Booth calls an "extra" bit of witty, punlike meaning. The
author of *Theses Martianae,* or *Martin Junior,* for example, confounds the
two meanings when he writes about players who "for one poor penny" play
"ignominious fools for an hour or two together."[62] The primary meaning of
"play the fool" here is "behave like an idiot," and not "behave like a professional fool," or "take the role of clown onstage." But the primary meaning
is not complete until we see that it means "behave like an idiot *by going on
the stage.*" In this case the "extra" meaning ("behave like a professional fool"
or "take the role of clown onstage") reinforces the primary one. In other
words, here "play the fool" already means "to be a stage clown," and is
already a theater expression. This use of the phrase is not unique. In the
early play *Misogonus,* the clown Cacurgus, a servant, is fired by his master
in the middle of the play. At that point he steps forward, turns to the audience, asks them (in vain) for another job, then shrugs his shoulders and
goes off, saying, "I'll play the fool still." The "accident" of Shakespeare's
including stage reference in the phrase "play the fool" was not an accident
at all, but rather it was already a tradition essential to the word; any reference to "playing the fool" or "making myself a motley" would prompt the
listener to be alert for stage reference whether the author were really an
actor or not.

Even apart from the verbal association between playing and "made myself a motley to the view," the humiliation described in this sonnet resembles the player's discomfort described in the great houses and in the flattery
plays: a shame at being on display, exposed, vulnerable. The poet goes on
in the sonnet to equate exposure specifically with the "wounds" exhibited

by the central figures in the flattery plays. He has not only "made myself a motley to the view" but has damaged his self-image, or "gor'd mine own thoughts." "Gore" means "to wound" (one's reputation), as in Hamlet's "To keep my name ungor'd" (*Ham.* 5.2.261). It might also allude to the "shaped piece of material" creating "the parti-colouring in a buffoon's breeches"; "gor'd mine own thoughts" would then mean "made myself a motley to the view *internally* as well as externally."[63] Or it could mean "besmirched, sullied," as with dried blood.[64] But the basic sense of "to gore" is "to pierce," and, specifically of horned animals, "to pierce with horns."[65] It thus carries the sense of a real wound like Coriolanus's or Antonio's.[66]

The "poor dappled creatures . . . with forked heads" in *As You Like It* "have their haunches gor'd" (*AYL* 2.1.22–25); that is why Jaques weeps for them. Given this sonnet's origin in a lover's betrayal "gor'd" can also carry suggestions of "horned" or "cuckolded," as in, "Paris is gor'd with Menelaus' horn" (*Tro.* 1.1.112).[67] "Besmirch," "wound," and "cuckold," together implicate "gore" in a shameful, perhaps even feminizing, visible wound. When Achilles discovers that his audience is gone, he says, "I see my reputation is at stake; my fame is shrewdly gor'd" (*Tro.* 3.3.226–27).[68] His fame (like Menelaus's reputation) is gored because he will not fight, and would rather spend the time watching his male varlet Patroclus mimic the Greeks. The sonnet springs up at the crossroads where thoughts of sexual betrayal, hunting, and stage playing meet.

In sonnet 111 the supposedly "secondary" or "extra" theatrical meaning of sonnet 110 becomes even more primary:

> O for my sake do you wish fortune chide,
> The guilty goddess of my harmful deeds,
> That did not better for my life provide
> Than public means which public manners breeds.
> Thence comes it that my name receives a brand,
> And almost thence my nature is subdued
> To what it works in, like the dyer's hand.
>
> (Son. 111, 1–7)

Now instead of referring to some isolated occasion or occasions in which he figuratively "made myself a motley to the view," the poet concerns himself at greater length with a permanent condition. He speaks in general of the "public means" with which he must provide for himself, and the "public manners" which that means breeds. It is from "thence"—and not from some other isolated action, as sonnet 110 had implied—that his name receives a "brand," just as it had earlier been "gor'd." Like the flattered Roman heroes, the poet has suffered a wound which he must now display.[69] It is hard to resist the idea that Shakespeare is referring here to his profession, and that he associates its drawbacks with those of the flattered kings and Roman heroes. His "dyer's hand" may even implicate the poet in the violence he suffers, as the dyed hands do in *King John:* "like a jolly troop of huntsmen. . . . all with purple'd hands / Dyed in the dying slaughter of their foes" (*KJ* 2.1.321–23).

To "receive a brand," Booth explains, conflates the two Roman practices of marking guilty citizens' names with a *nota,* or mark of censure, and marking bad slaves with a *nota* or brand; both of these are linked with the Elizabethan practice, still current in Shakespeare's time, of branding criminals and prostitutes. Thus Laertes in *Hamlet* resists the appellation "bastard," which "brands the harlot . . . between the chaste unsmirched brow" (*Ham.* 4.5.115–16); and Lucrece feels so tainted that even the sun will mark her crime: "Brand not my forehead with thy piercing light" (*Luc.* 1091).[70] The one Shakespearean character who is most notably branded or stigmatized is Richard III. Queen Elizabeth says that Richard should be branded like Cain: "Hid'st thou that forehead with a golden crown, / Where should be branded . . . / The slaughter of the Prince that ow'd that crown?" (*R3* 4.4.140–42).[71] Young Clifford calls Richard a "foul stigmatic" (*2H6* 5.1.216), and Queen Margaret later tells him "thou art neither like thy sire nor dam, / But like a *foul misshapen stigmatic,* / Marked by the Destinies to be avoided" (*3H6* 2.2.135–37; italics added).[72] They of course mean that Richard is branded as a murderer; but it is suggestive that this archplayer is thus implicated in the wounding so closely associated elsewhere with "players."

The next sonnet, 112, makes no reference to motley, public means, or the theater. But the "brand" or stigma has now moved forward into the opening lines. There it acquires depth and becomes an "impression" to be "fill[ed]." The sense of a gaping hole lingers over this sonnet, brought forward also by the pun on "pit" in "pity" and by the later mentions of "well" and "profound abysm."[73]

> Your love and pity doth th'impression fill,
> Which vulgar scandal stamped upon my brow;
> For what care I who calls me well or ill,
> So you o'er-green my bad, my good allow?
> You are my all the world, and I must strive
> To know my shames and praises from your tongue;
> None else to me, nor I to none alive,
> That my steeled sense or changes right or wrong.
> In so profound abysm I throw all care
> Of others' voices that my adder's sense
> To critic and to flatterer stopped are.
>
> (Son. 112, 1–11)

The poet says, "your love and pity outweigh all the public shame I have suffered; I don't care about being gored or branded anymore, I don't care about being criticized or even flattered by anyone except you. You are all my world; the only thing that matters is your opinion." Just as Coriolanus turned away from the people to his "all my world," his mother, the poet turns to the young man. Here, then, the equivalence between the collective audience of "voices" who might criticize or flatter—like those Coriolanus had to seek—and the single beloved voice is made explicit. Then with line 10, perhaps inevitably, the poet moves from the misbehavior and wounded notoriety associated with playing in sonnets 110 and 111 to the inseparable issue of flattery which we have already seen associated with the theatrical experience.[74]

Booth finds sonnet 112 incomprehensible, with its convoluted examination of the "impression . . . which vulgar scandal stamped upon my brow." He surmises that it is "an unfinished poem or one that Shakespeare abandoned in frustration."[75] If Booth is correct, then the sonnet provides a fitting conclusion to the sequence of texts we have been considering. Like the others, its text is marked by the special sensitivites of a player surrounded by a potentially hostile crowd threatening to attack him and expose his wounds. Shakespeare's one unfinished sonnet, if it is that, deals with the same difficult topic of flattery and its reversals that we find in his one "unfinished" play, Timon of Athens. Shakespeare's "frustration" or inability to take control of that material, testifies to its power and to its ability to defy rational or aesthetic constraint.

Circles and Centers

he previous chapters have elaborated on some implications of the Elizabethan player's dual status as someone who not only plays roles, but who is also exquisitely aware of the audience surrounding him. While those chapters worked from clues about performance found in Shakespeare's verbal scripts, what follows is concerned instead with the physical locus for Elizabethan performance. It is less a conclusion drawn from earlier chapters than a gathering of Shakespeare's several variations on "the wooden O" (*H5* Pro. 13), the charmed circle in which an audience enshrines or entraps a player, and is itself enclosed. The examples suggest one final way in which the phenomenology of playing helped shape both plays and performance.

Despite theater-in-the-round and other twentieth-century innovations, we still tend to think of the theatrical encounter in terms of two planes facing one another across the stage; but Elizabethans thought in terms of circles and centers. The circle was a more familiar spatial configuration then, institutionalized in other displays like bearbaiting and cockfighting, and almost inevitable on the numerous informal occasions when ballad makers and mountebanks collected crowds around them. In an arena theater the radius moved up into three dimensions as well. The circularity of the theater's external perimeter, its internal span—small enough for any spectator to take in the entire circumference at one glance—and the literal thrust of the platform into the center of a surrounding crowd, all made the sense of a circle physically more available to audience as well as to actors.[1] In his portrait of "The Excellent Actor," John Webster suggests that if you "sit in a full Theater," the configuration will be obvious: "You will thinke you see so many lines drawne from the circumference of so many eares, whiles the *Actor* is the *Center*."[2] Thomas Middleton's less complimentary picture is equally circular when he likens a "ring" of ants surrounding one of their number to "a dull audience of stinkards sitting in the penny-galleries of a theater and yawning upon the players."[3] Michael Drayton—as author sharing the actor's perspective only vicariously—described the same configuration:

> With those the thronged Theaters that presse,
> I in the Circuit for the Lawrell strove: . . .
> With Showts and Claps at ev'ry little pawse,
> When the proud Round on ev'ry side hath rung.[4]

Encircled actors. Albrecht Dürer's frontispiece for an unpublished series of illuminations for *The Comedies of Terrence* (c. 1492). Kupferstich Kabinett, Basel.

In *The Roaring Girl* (1608), Dekker and Middleton, "inspired by the audience of the Fortune," allude to the proud round as seen from the stage, so that the audience becomes a wall of faces surrounding the players. The words are spoken by Sir Alexander Wengrave early in the play.[5] He is showing off his parlour, its galleries so crammed with portraits that they look like an amphitheater. Of course, since the actor playing Sir Alexander was then standing in the middle of just such an amphitheater and seeing the audience's surrounding faces, the speech provided an opportunity for a moment of metadramatic comedy:

> Nay when you look into my galleries,
> How bravely they are trimmed up, you all shall swear
> Y'are highly pleased to see what's set down there . . .
> Within one square a thousand heads are laid
> So close that all of heads the room seems made;
> As many faces there, filled with blithe looks,
> Show like the promising titles of new books
> Writ merrily, the readers being their own eyes,
> Which seem to move and to give plaudities;
> And here and there, whilst with obsequious ears
> Thronged heaps do listen, a cutpurse thrusts and leers
> With hawk's eyes for his prey: I need not show him,
> By a hanging, villainous look yourselves may know him,
> The face is drawn so rarely. Then sir, below,
> The very floor, as 'twere, waves to and fro,
> And like a floating island seems to move
> Upon a sea bound in with shores above.
>   (*The Roaring Girl* 1.2.14–16, 19–32)

Sir Alexander ends by comparing the galleries to a ship's gallery, which corresponds neither to the fictional location (his private gallery) nor to the real location (the public theater), but does describe the way both appear. The playful reversal of real and fictional mise-en-scène is typical of the Shakespearean stage.

The placement of stage and audience lent itself to self-consciousness on the part of audience as well as player. Elias Canetti describes the self-contained excitement of a twentieth-century crowd rounded on itself much like the Fortune audience in Middleton and Dekker's description:

> The seats are arranged in tiers around the arena, so that everyone can see what is happening below. The consequence of this is that the crowd is seated [or standing] opposite itself. Every spectator has a thousand in front of him, a thousand heads. . . . Whatever excites him, excites them; and he sees it. . . . There is no break in the crowd which sits like this, exhibiting itself to itself. It forms a closed ring from which nothing can escape.[6]

The experience of this closed ring remained available to early modern audiences and actors even as the "breaking of the circle" progressed outside
the theater; and the theater's circularity was an important part of the equation between world and stage:[7] "the world a theater present[s], / As by the
roundnes it appears most fit."[8] The world is like a theater, and the theater
like a world, not only because all humans act roles but because both round
on themselves.

The circle, which could become a "wooden O" and had already gone
through several other metamorphoses in the European imagination,[9] had
its own associations for Shakespeare. They ranged from private ones, the
circle of a mother's arms and the imagined enclosure of her womb, to the
public image shared by all Englishmen of their country as an island strong-
hold surrounded by the sea, and they included other associations in which
these extremes of privacy and plenitude met, as in the familiar trope of
mother England, "this nurse, this teeming womb of royal kings," as Gaunt
calls it (R2 2.1.51). Shakespeare's references to wombs and islands, or to
other enclosed spaces, were neither primarily allusions to the stage, nor,
most often, to one another. Nevertheless, Shakespeare's experience in the
theater—standing onstage in it as well as writing for it—gave him a unique
awareness of the ways in which both intimacy and community could be
mediated by the physical facts of London performance, which was always
both private and public.

Begin with the private circles. The experience of an enclosed or surrounded space, isolated from the public world, was part of the development
of privacy well under way when Shakespeare wrote, and at times Shakespeare presents the circle as this sort of retreat from all social roles. When
Hamlet tells Rosencrantz and Guildenstern that he has no political ambitions, for example, he swears, "O God, I could be bounded in a nutshell
and count myself king of infinite space—were it not that I have bad
dreams" (Ham. 2.2.254–56). But most often for Shakespeare enclosure implies intimacy rather than isolation; it is the spatial equivalent of merging
with one other person. As such it can be warm, reassuring, and sustaining,
or it can be claustrophobic. Encirclement in Shakespeare's early plays is
sometimes associated with a child's passivity in its mother's arms, in an
embrace that can either nurture or kill. In the earliest histories, when the
evil Queen Margaret holds Suffolk in an adulterous embrace before he is
banished, he feels like a suckling child; when she next appears she is cradling his severed head in her arms, as if she herself had decapitated him.[10]
The image melds with the imagined enclosure of a mother's womb—a myth
of origin—in Margaret's description of Richard in the "kennel" of his mother's womb (R3 4.4.46).[11] Elsewhere the maternal is replaced by a sexual
surround, like the anatomical ring to which Gratiano refers obscenely in
The Merchant of Venice in his prescription for keeping his wife chaste:

"while I live, I'll fear no other thing / So sore as keeping safe Nerissa's ring" (*MV* 5.1.306–7). Or in Mercutio's bawdy suggestion that lovesick Romeo will "raise a spirit in his mistress' circle" (*Rom.* 2.1.24).[12]

As Mercutio's remark implies, female enclosure is also associated with the sorcery of witches' circles, like the one Mother Jourdain creates in *Henry VI, Part Two* when she calls up her evil spirits for the Duchess of Gloucester (*2H6* 1.4.15–25), or later like the circle of witches around their cauldron in *Macbeth*. Shakespeare's circle, following tradition, can also be a city which soldiers besiege, or rape—and into which some are absorbed fatally or nearly so. Talbot's story in *Henry VI, Part One* is a fairy tale of towers and circles, consisting of a single adventure repeated three times: he attacks a walled city, penetrates to its "middle centre" (*1H6* 2.2.6), and finds that he is surrounded by a hostile audience who threaten to kill him—first Joan of Arc on the walls of Rouen, then the Countess of Auvergne, who traps him in her castle, and the Governor of Bordeaux, who has him "girded with a waist of iron" (*1H6* 4.3.20). Years later the siege of the circle reappears when Henry V goads his men into the famous attack at Harfleur, seen in the play retrospectively as a rape: "Once more unto the breach" (*H5* 3.1.1).[13] In *Coriolanus,* the walled city of the Corioli nearly kills Martius when it swallows him up, but he hews his way out with a bloody sword and takes its name as his own.

All these circles are implicitly contrasted with the benevolent circle of a father's arms, as in the scene which Shakespeare invented for *Henry VI, Part One,* where the dying Mortimer encircles York in his withered arms and names him his heir (*1H6* 2.5.37–114). Talbot himself begins that play by encircling the dying Salisbury in his arms (*1H6* 1.4.71–110), and he ends encircling his son (*1H6* 4.7.1–32) though, as he says, he had wished rather himself to die with his son's arms around him. On the social level, the male equivalent of the witch's circle is the sacred ring of the garter in *Henry VI, Part One* and in the ceremonial circle dance celebrating it in *The Merry Wives of Windsor;* Prospero's magic circle at the center of his island, where he decides to forgive rather than to cast spells over his subjects; or the great globe itself, enclosed within a paternal God's cosmic spheres. When we are told in the histories that

> Glory is like a circle in the water,
> Which never ceaseth to enlarge itself
> Till by broad spreading it disperse to nought.
> (*1H6* 1.2.133–35)

it is in the context of hearing that "with Henry [V]'s death the English circle ends" (*1H6* 1.3.136). It is when the father dies that the circle is broken and one may fall prey to maternal enclosure.

Among Shakespeare's female circles, the most traditional is the enclosed garden, for him an ambiguous retreat. The garden can be a fertile, nurturing bower, a park or pale, like the flowered "cradle of the Fairy Queen" in *A Midsummer Night's Dream* (*MND* 2.1.4), but it can become a tangled forest and thorny wood which impales (both "claustrophobically imprisons" and "tears through") anyone caught inside. When Venus tries to seduce Adonis, she tells him

> I have hemm'd thee here
> Within the circuit of this ivory pale [the circle of her white arms],
> I'll be a park, and thou shalt be my deer:
> Feed where thou wilt.
>
> (*Ven.* 229–32)

Though Adonis escapes her suffocating kisses for the moment, ultimately the boar's tusk gores him, and Venus realizes, "Had I been tooth'd like him, I must confess, / With kissing him I should have kill'd him first" (*Ven.* 1117–18). Mother England itself, which Gaunt describes figuratively as an "other Eden, demi-paradise" (*R2* 2.1.42) turns into a literal garden run to seed, a pale "choked up" with weeds, as the gardeners working within its compass describe it.[14] Elsewhere Shakespeare's pales encircle a male deer, surrounded by hunters who have brought him to bay.[15] The deer itself appears only once in the flesh, but its figurative presence is felt in the battle scenes when soldiers are impaled, as we have seen in *Henry VI, Part One,* when Talbot is circled by the enemy, "park'd and bounded in a pale— / A little herd of England's timorous deer, / Maz'd with a yelping kennel of French curs!" (*1H6* 4.2.45–47).[16] Or when Henry VI himself is caught like a deer in a park.[17]

In a final Shakespearean transformation, the garden pale becomes the golden circuit that impales a king's head. If England's garden is another Eden (*R2* 2.1.42), the crown itself is the "Elysium" (*3H6* 1.2.30) which Richard, Duke of Gloucester, thinks to win by having himself crowned King Richard III. His father York had been killed because he "would *pale* [his] head in Henry's *glory*" (*3H6* 1.4.103; italics added). Then, when Gloucester announces his own ambition that "this head / Be round *impaled* with a *glorious* crown" (*3H6* 3.2.170–71), he sees the glorious crown merging with a thorny wood from which he can only escape by hewing his "way out with a bloody axe" (*3H6* 3.2.181; italics added).

Unlike the garden, however, the crown can be populated. The golden circuit which isolates the King from the crowds of people thronging outside, also contains a crowd of inner persons and voices. At times the crown in fact mediates between the two crowds, one out there and one inside, which—for better or for worse—become indistinguishable. Richard III's final nightmare, for example, is brought on by the ghosts who came "thronging to the bar" (*R3* 5.3.200) to accuse him, and who are internalized as his conscience. "My conscience hath a thousand several tongues," he says (*R3* 5.3.194); "shadows tonight have struck more terror / Than can the substance of ten thousand soldiers (*R3* 5.3.217–19). Fortunately he can be cured once he calls up a friendly throng; as soon as he sees his army massed before him in the morning he revives: "A thousand hearts are great within my bosom" (*R3* 5.3.348).

No one more than the histrionic Richard II learns better how insidiously an audience can be internalized. Richard would not listen when the dying John of Gaunt warned him that:

> A thousand flatterers sit within thy crown,
> Whose compass is no bigger than thy head,
> And yet, incaged in so small a verge,
> The waste is no whit lesser than thy land.
>
> (*R2* 2.1.100–103)

But when an army twenty thousand strong deserts him, Richard suddenly pales:[18]

> But now the blood of twenty thousand men
> Did triumph in my face, and they are fled;
> And till so much blood thither come again,
> Have I not reason to look pale and dead?
>
> (*R2* 3.2.76–78)

And once he becomes obsessed with the frailty of office Richard sees himself as a miniature *theatrum mundi* in which he plays "many people, / And none contented. Sometimes am I king, / Then . . . a beggar" (*R2* 5.5.31–33). Like the dying Talbot, who saw the antic Death watching his death scene, Richard reduces his entire reign to a doomed pageant staged within the mental space of the crown:

> Within the hollow crown
> That rounds the mortal temples of a king
> Keeps Death his court, and there the antic sits,
> Scoffing his state and grinning at his pomp,
> Allowing him a breath, a little scene,
> To monarchize, be fear'd, and kill with looks;
> . . . and, humour'd thus,
> Comes at the last, and with a little pin
> Bores thorough his castle wall, and farewell king!
>
> (*R2* 3.2.160–70)

No safer in his English pale than Adonis or Talbot (or old Hamlet), Richard is impaled by Death.

What have these circles to do with theater? Richard's histrionic fantasy suggests that the English pale, or the crown which internalizes it, is also seen as a stage. So too, the stage can be a pale. The physical structure of an amphitheater made the thrust stage literally into a pale where actors were hemmed in by the audience and, very probably, surrounded by a low fence or pale. The gardener in *Richard II* may in fact be alluding playfully to his onstage location when he refers to the contrast between his garden and England:

> Why should we, in the compass of a *pale*,
> Keep law and form and due proportion,
> Showing, as in a model, our firm estate,
> When our sea-walled garden the whole land,
> Is full of weeds. . . ?
>
> (R2 3.4.40–44; italics added) [19]

The gardener's dangerous question in *Richard II* could have provided almost as significant an extradramatic moment as the deposition scene, if the audience heard the actor behind the gardener ask, "why should we actors behave ourselves within the compass of the stage when the real audience's 'whole land is full of weeds.'" It is even more probable that, as J. W. Saunders argued, the porter in *Henry VIII* refers to the stage rails when he threatens the unruly crowd come to see Princess Elizabeth's christening in that play.[20] Because there is no onstage crowd, the porter must speak directly to the Globe audience. He does not feel impaled, though he fears that he might be "torn a-pieces" (H8 5.3.75);[21] but he does refer to the "pales" which may be the railings literally surrounding the stage, and he threatens one of the crowd who seems to be trying to climb over the rails.

> *Porter:* You'll leave your noise anon, ye rascals; do you take the court for
>   Parish-garden? ye rude slaves, leave your gaping. . . . Is this a place to
>   roar in? Fetch me a dozen crab-tree staves. . . . I'll scratch your heads; you
>   must be seeing christenings? do you look for ale and cakes here, you rude
>   rascals? . . . How got they in, and be hang'd? . . . These are the youths that
>   thunder at a playhouse and fight for bitten apples. . . .
> *Lord Chamberlain:* Mercy o'me, what a multitude are here!
>   They grow still too; from all parts they are coming,
>   As if we kept a fair here! where are these porters. . . ?
>   There's a trim rabble let in; are all these
>   Your faithful friends o'th'suburbs? . . .
>   Ye should do service. Hark, the trumpets sound,
>   Th'are come already from the christening
>   Go break among the press, and find a way out
>   To let the troop pass fairly, or I'll find
>   A Marshalsea shall hold ye play these two months.

Porter: Make way there for the princess. . . .
                   You i'th'chamblet, get up o'th'rail,
                   I'll peck you o'er the pales else.

                                              (*H8* 5.3.1–88, passim)

The references to Parish-garden, the suburbs, and youths that thunder at a
playhouse call attention to the stage as stage and assimilate the fictional
crowd to the audience itself, pressed up against the stage rails like "the tide"
(*H8* 5.3.18).

Shakespeare's most extended reference to the physicality of the wooden
O comes from the patriotic Chorus in *Henry V,* who coins the term and
laments the limits imposed by such a stage on his material.[22] He begins the
play by apologizing for trying to contain Henry's army "within the girdle of
these walls" (*H5* Pro.19), asking,

> can this cockpit hold
> The vasty fields of France? or may we cram
> Within this wooden O the very casques
> That did affright the air at Agincourt?

At the end he is still apologizing for theater's failure to encompass its heroic
subject, "in little room confining mighty men" (*H5* Epi.3). Audiences may
note that Shakespeare's ambivalence about theater paradoxically makes the
confinement seem heroic, like the paradoxical grandeur of the tiny English
island and its "inward greatness, / Like little body with a mighty heart"
(*H5* 2.0.16–17).[24] Or perhaps like the larger paradox of God's infinite presence in a finite point, the body encompassing divinity.[25] But as the Chorus
suggests the expansive mystery of theatrical circles, he also sees more mundane images to describe the circles he finds in Henry's story—the walled
city, garden pale, and womb associated with Shakespeare's other circles. In
the prologue to act 4, for example, the Chorus first sets the scene in "the
foul *womb* of night, / . . . who, like a foul and ugly witch, doth limp / So
tediously away" (*H5* 4.0.4, 21–22), before he goes on to describe "How
dread an army hath enrounded" Henry (*H5* 4.0.35–36; italics added).
Then, to describe Henry's victorious return to England before act 5, the
Chorus tells how

> the English beach
> *Pales in* the flood with men, with wives, and boys,
> Whose shouts and claps out-voice the deep-mouth'd sea,
>
>   (*H5* 5.0.9–11; italics added)

as the crowds at Dover throng to greet the King's ship from France.[26] Henry's men burst out of night's womb and the enemy circle, or they appear

triumphantly in the midst of an adoring crowd which pales in the sea, just as the play expands from the midst of its cramped dramatic space. Both the Chorus and Henry, Goldman says, show energy bursting its confines.

They also figure the actor's movement between the actor's inner space and theatrical space, across the boundary that performance defines and defies. With the self-conscious presentation of the Chorus's stage, Shakespeare has moved from Richard's crown, inside which he plays "in one man many people," to the Chorus's public wooden O, in which one actor must represent many people—with the help of the audience:

> Piece out our imperfections with your thoughts [he tells the audience];
> *Into a thousand parts divide one man,*
> And make imaginary puissance.
>
> (*H5* Pro.23–25; italics added)

The Chorus doesn't ask the audience, as one might expect after hearing that there are not enough actors, to multiply one actor to represent many soldiers, but rather to divide him, as Richard had felt divided. The imagination moves both inward and outward, from mental space to theatrical space, from Richard II's bone O to the Chorus's wooden O, with the actor's body as the pivot, divided into a thousand parts.[27] It is as if one plenitude created another, the multitudinous inner world conditional upon the multitude thronging to see it externalized on the peopled stage.

Notes

Authors' surnames are set boldface in first citation of each text, where bibliographic information is given. For sources of selected sixteenth- and seventeenth-century texts cited, see also the "Sources for Texts Quoted" (pp. xiii–xvi above).

Introduction

1. Simon **Callow**, *Being an Actor* (New York: Grove Press, 1988), 124.

2. For a survey of the contradictory attitudes toward playing and its opposing implications for "homo ludens," see Alvin **Kernan**, "The Plays and the Playwrights," in *The Revels History of Drama in English, 1576–1613,* ed. J. Leeds **Barroll**, Alexander Leggatt, Richard Hosley, and Alvin Kernan (London: Methuen, 1975), 3:237–474, and William B. **Worthen**, *The Idea of the Actor: Drama and the Ethics of Performance* (Princeton: Princeton University Press, 1984).

3. Literary studies of self-fashioning have profited from the intersection of widely varied studies. See, for example, Norbert **Elias**, *The Court Society,* trans. Edmund Jephcott (New York: Pantheon Books, 1983); Erving **Goffman**, *The Presentation of Self in Everyday Life* (Woodstock: Overlook Press, 1973); for an earlier elaboration of courtly fashion and the theatrical, G. K. **Hunter**, *John Lyly: The Humanist as Courtier* (London: Routledge and Kegan Paul, 1962); on the artifices of courtly style, Daniel **Javitch**, *Poetry and Courtliness in Renaissance England* (Princeton: Princeton University Press, 1978); and, a landmark study which initiated a still-thriving discussion, Stephen **Greenblatt**, *Renaissance Self-Fashioning: From More to Shakespeare* (Chicago: University of Chicago Press, 1980).

4. See Joseph Quincy **Adams**, *A Life of William Shakespeare* (Boston and New York: Houghton Mifflin Co., 1923), 423–39, for a summary of the data about his acting. Some recent commentators have noted the importance of Shakespeare's acting experience and actor status. See Muriel C. **Bradbrook**, *The Rise of the Common Player: A Study of Actor and Society in Shakespeare's England* (Cambridge: Harvard University Press, 1962), and Leo **Salingar**, "The Player in the Play," in *Shakespeare and the Tradition of Comedy* (Cambridge: Cambridge University Press, 1974), 257–67, for the effects of the player's social status and self-justification; for psychological implications of being an actor-playwright, see C. L. **Barber** and Richard P. **Wheeler**, *The Whole Journey: Shakespeare's Power of Development* (Berkeley: University of California Press, 1986), and Sherman **Hawkins**, "Aggression and the Project of the Histories," 41–65, and William **Kerrigan**, "The Personal Shakespeare: Three Clues," 176–190, both in *Shakespeare's Personality,* ed. Norman N. **Holland**, Sidney Homan, and Bernard J. **Paris** (Berkeley: University of California Press, 1989).

5. Jonas **Barish**, *The Antitheatrical Prejudice* (Berkeley: University of California Press, 1981).

6. It would not be possible, of course, even to ask such a question without the information about acting styles and conditions provided by theater historians and by general studies of the Elizabethan stage and its origins (see chap. 2). Until recently few works have focused specifically on the actor's experience—Bradbrook, *Common Player,* and Gerald Eades **Bentley,** *The Profession of Player in Shakespeare's Time, 1590–1642* (Princeton: Princeton University Press, 1984), are obvious exceptions. Since I began this book, however, two extremely important books have appeared—David **Wiles,** *Shakespeare's Clown: Actor and Text in the Elizabethan Playhouse* (Cambridge: Cambridge University Press, 1987), and David **Mann,** *The Elizabethan Player: Contemporary Stage Representation* (London: Routledge, 1991)— and the continued interest in performance criticism has generated increasing attention to the actor as well as to the audience's reception of him.

7. Stephen **Booth,** unpublished talk, Folger Shakespeare Library, 1991.

8. Michael **Goldman,** *Shakespeare and the Energies of Drama* (Princeton: Princeton University Press, 1972), "Acting Values and Shakespearean Meaning: Some Suggestions," *Mosaic* 10 (1977): 59–75, and *The Actor's Freedom: Toward a Theory of Drama* (New York: Viking Press, 1975). Goldman's work in general has been a starting point for my own. There will always be a connection, Goldman says, between the "process by which the actor keeps his projection of the character alive and interesting—and the larger action of the play, just as there is a connection between the brushstroke of a painter and the felt significance of his design." Goldman, "Acting Values," 60.

9. Jonas Barish describes Jonson's ambivalence toward the stage in "Jonson and the Loathèd Stage," in Barish, *Antitheatrical Prejudice,* 132–54; see also John Gordon **Sweeney,** *Jonson and the Psychology of Public Theater: "To Coin the Spirit, Send the Soul"* (Princeton: Princeton University Press, 1985). Though far more extreme and expressed in different ways, Jonson's ambivalence was not unlike Shakespeare's. In both cases, I would suggest, such attitudes helped propel the young men into acting before they settled into writing for the stage.

10. Goldman, *Energies of Drama,* 10.

11. Irving **Berlin,** "There's No Business Like Show Business," 1946.

12. T. J. **King,** "Shakespeare to Olivier: A Great Chain of Acting, 1598–1935," *Notes and Queries* 231, n.s., 33 (1986), 397–98.

13. J. **Earle,** *Micro-Cosmography; or, A Piece of the World Discovered in Essayes and Characters* (1628), ed. Gwendolen Murphy (Waltham St. Lawrence: Golden Cockerel Press, 1928), 39.

14. Richard Wheeler's term, personal communication.

15. Caroline **Spurgeon,** *Shakespeare's Imagery and What It Tells Us* (Cambridge: Cambridge University Press, 1935; reprint, 1977), 195.

Chapter One

1. The title of this chapter is drawn from two actors' autobiographies: Callow, *Being an Actor,* and Joshua **Logan,** *Josh: My Up and Down, In and Out Life* (New York: Delacorte Press, 1976).

2. Barish calls them "mimicry" and "ostentation" in Barish, *Antitheatrical Prejudice*. Others use different pairs of terms but seem to be getting at the same distinction: Michel Benamou, for example, speaks of "presentation and re-presentation, Being and absence, presence and play," in *Performance in Postmodern Culture*, ed. Michel **Benamou** and Charles **Caramello** (Madison: Coda Press, 1977), 3.

3. Retold in William **Redfield**, *Letters from an Actor* (New York: Limelight Editions, 1966), 91.

4. J. **Laplanche** and J.-B. **Pontalis**, *The Language of Psychoanalysis*, trans. Donald Nicholson-Smith (New York: W. W. Norton and Co., 1973), 205.

5. *The Actor's Freedom* is Goldman's book on the performance dimension of acting. I refer throughout to the actor as "he" because this study is concerned with male actors. Comparing contemporary female actors to those in Shakespeare's time would be more difficult.

6. Otto **Fenichel**, "On Acting," *Psychoanalytic Quarterly* 15 (1946): 150.

7. Rex **Harrison**, *A Damned Serious Business* (New York: Bantam Books, 1991), 29.

8. W. E. Henry and J. H. Sims found that actors showed fewer symptoms of identity confusion when tested after rehearsing a role for several weeks than when tested at the beginning of rehearsal. Cited in Seymour **Fisher** and Rhoda **Fisher**, *Pretend the World Is Funny and Forever: A Psychological Analysis of Comedians, Clowns, and Actors* (Hillsdale: Lawrence Erlbaum Associates Publications, 1981), 149–50. See also Frank **Langella**, "The Demon Seesaw Actors Ride," *New York Times*, Sunday, 17 September 1989, sec. 2. Langella is primarily concerned with the fear of not getting another job, but his description also captures the actor's more pervasive need to be doing a role.

9. David Cole's terms, in his extended comparison between theater's ability and that of religious ritual to make imaginative life felt as physical presence. David **Cole**, *The Theatrical Event: A Mythos, a Vocabulary, a Perspective* (Middletown: Wesleyan University Press, 1975), 2–57.

10. Konstantin **Stanislavski**, *An Actor Prepares*, trans. Elizabeth Reynolds Hapgood (New York: Theatre Arts Books, 1936), 294; Michael **Redgrave**, *The Actor's Ways and Means* (New York: Theatre Arts Books, 1953), 41; John C. **Gustin**, "Psychology of the Actor," *Psychoanalysis* 4 (1955): 32.

11. Eugène **Ionesco**, "Expérience du théâtre," *Nouvelle Revue Française* 62 (1958), 258. Cited in Martin **Esslin**, *Theater of the Absurd*, rev. ed. (Garden City: Anchor Books, 1969), 113.

12. Fisher and Fisher, *Pretend*, 155.

13. Goldman, *Actor's Freedom*, 9.

14. Cole, *Theatrical Event*, 61.

15. Harley **Granville-Barker**, "The Heritage of the Actor," *Quarterly Review* 240, no. 476 (July 1923): 53–73, esp. 62.

16. Fisher and Fisher, *Pretend*, 161, 165.

17. Richard **Huggett**, *Supernatural on Stage: Ghosts and Superstitions of the Theatre* (New York: Taplinger Publishing Company, 1975), 19, 53. Martin Gardner notes that "the largest single group of professionals in the US today who believe in

astrology are actors, with dancers and people in the fashion business close behind." Martin **Gardner**, "Seeing Stars," *The New York Review of Books,* 30 June 1988, 44; see also Fisher and Fisher, *Pretend,* 161.

18. Fisher and Fisher, *Pretend,* 166; Georgia **Holt** and Phyllis **Quinn**, with Sue **Russell**, *Star Mothers: The Moms Behind the Celebrities* (New York: Simon and Schuster, 1988), 269.

19. Fisher and Fisher, *Pretend,* 165.

20. Interview cited in Antony **Holden**, *Laurence Olivier: A Biography* (New York: Macmillan, 1988), 4.

21. Granville-Barker, "Heritage of the Actor," 63.

22. On the postmodern actor's opacity, see Herbert **Blau**, *Take Up the Bodies: Theater at the Vanishing Point* (Urbana: University of Illinois Press, 1982).

23. Bert O. **States**, "The Dog on the Stage: Theater as Phenomenon," *New Literary History* 14 (1983): 373–88, esp. 373. States's use of an erotic exchange to prove his point is apt.

24. Redfield, *Letters,* 47.

25. Actors quoted in Stuart W. **Little** and Arthur **Cantor**, *The Playmakers* (New York: W. W. Norton and Co., 1970), 88–89; Stephen **Aaron**, *Stage Fright: Its Role in Acting* (Chicago: University of Chicago Press, 1986).

26. Callow, *Being an Actor,* 143.

27. Granville-Barker, "Heritage of the Actor," 59; Redfield, *Letters,* 29.

28. Antonin **Artaud**, *The Theater and Its Double,* trans. Mary Caroline Richards (New York: Grove Press, 1958), 13.

29. Little and Cantor, *Playmakers,* 90. Fenichel describes the desire in more primitive but similar terms. The actor, he says, "wants to be reunited with these persons [the audience], to eat them, to be eaten by them, to rob them of their power, to ingratiate [him]self." Fenichel, "On Acting," 146.

30. Redfield, *Letters,* 122.

31. Sybil **Thorndike**, "I Look at the Audience," in *Theatre Arts Anthology: A Record and a Prophecy,* ed. Rosamond **Gilder**, Hermine Rich Isaacs, Robert M. MacGregor, and Edward Reed (New York: Theatre Arts Books, 1950), 301.

32. Actors cited in Little and Cantor, *Playmakers,* 88, 89, 90.

33. Fenichel, "On Acting," 157.

34. Cited in Little and Cantor, *Playmakers,* 90.

35. Cited in Aaron, *Stage Fright,* 98.

36. Goldman, *Actor's Freedom,* 23, 14–15.

37. Redfield, *Letters,* 30; see the same metaphor in Glen O. **Gabbard**, "Further Contributions to the Understanding of Stage Fright: Narcissistic Issues," *Journal of the American Psychoanalytic Association* 31 (1983): 430.

38. Little and Cantor, *Playmakers,* 92.

39. Timothy J. **Wiles**, *The Theater Event: Modern Theories of Performance* (Chicago: University of Chicago Press, 1980), 82.

40. In our ultratheatricalized age, all discourse has taken on the muscularity that theater terminology has always needed—thus the "drop dead dress" and the need of literary critics to "intervene," "interrogate," and "radically" alter our perceptions.

41. On the difference between benign regression to "normal" childhood narcissism and pathological narcissism, in which the sense of self and others is more driven by rage and envy, see Otto F. **Kernberg**, "Further Contributions to the Treatment of Narcissistic Personalities," *International Journal of Psychoanalysis* 55 (1974), 215–40.

42. Michael **Balint**, *The Basic Fault: Therapeutic Aspects of Regression* (London: Tavistock Publications, 1968); Jacques **Lacan**, "La Signification du phallus," *Ecrits* (Paris: Seuil, 1966); Heinz **Kohut**, *The Analysis of the Self* (New York: International Universities Press, 1971) and *The Restoration of the Self* (New York: International Universities Press, 1977).

43. Evgeny Vakhtangov, cited in Callow, *Being an Actor,* 148.

44. Fisher and Fisher, *Pretend,* 167–68.

45. Holt, Quinn, and Russell, *Star Mothers,* 124. Hoffman, wary of being typecast as the sleazy drifter, Ratso Rizzo, he played in *Midnight Cowboy* (1969), recently told an interviewer: "I've always wanted to play a doctor, a lawyer. . . . I'd love to look handsome before it's too late." He went on to recall a visit to Sir Laurence Olivier, shortly before his death, during which he asked Olivier why he became an actor: "He said, 'You really want to know?' and I said, 'Yes,' and Olivier put his face up against mine and said, 'Look at me, look at me, look at me, look at me.'" Bernard **Weinraub**, "Ratso Rizzo Redux? Not If He Can Help It," *New York Times,* Sunday, 27 September 1992, sec. 2H, p. 13, col. 1.

46. Cited in Aaron, *Stage Fright,* 40.

47. Callow, *Being an Actor,* 1.

48. Holt, Quinn, and Russell, *Star Mothers,* 40.

49. Redfield, *Letters,* 5.

50. Little and Cantor, *Playmakers,* 125.

51. Huggett, *Supernatural on Stage,* 29–30.

52. Little and Cantor, *Playmakers,* 125.

53. Cited in Redfield, *Letters,* 63.

54. Stephen **Booth**, "The Actor as Kamikaze Pilot," *Shakespeare Quarterly* 36 (1985): 553–70. Cibber describes Samuel Sandford, "an excellent actor in disagreeable characters," who "was not the stage villain by choice, but from necessity, for having a low and crooked person, such bodily defects were too strong to be admitted into great or amiable characters. . . . In this disadvantaged light, then, stood Stanford, as an actor. . . . The crowd only praised him by their prejudice." In Colly **Cibber**, *Apology for His Life* (1740; reprint London: Everyman's Library, J. M. Dent and Sons; New York: E. P. Dutton, 1938), cited in *Actors on Acting,* ed. Toby **Cole** and Helen Krech **Chinoy** (New York: Crown Publishers, 1949), 109.

55. Sherman Louis **Sergel**, ed., *The Language of Show Biz: A Dictionary* (Chicago: Dramatic Publishing Company, 1973), 205.

56. Callow, *Being an Actor,* 181.

57. Cited in Marilyn **Berger**, "Still a Perfectionist and Delighted To Hear It" (review of *A Damned Serious Business* by Rex Harrison), *New York Times,* 11 November 1989, sec. 2.

58. "The really creative actor reaches a different and far worse terror." Peter **Brook**, *The Empty Space* (New York: Avon Books, 1969), 104.

59. Donald **Kaplan**, "On Stage Fright," *The Drama Review* 14 (1964): 60–83. Jenny Laird "hypnotizes herself into thinking that it's not her in the part but somebody else, and that she is standing in the wings watching her alter ego; once she has done this, the first night has no further terrors for her." Huggett, *Supernatural on Stage*, 31.

60. Aaron, *Stage Fright*, xvi. See also the accounts of the origins of stage fright in Glen O. **Gabbard**, "Stage Fright," *International Journal of Psychoanalysis* 60 (1979): 383–92, and Gabbard, "Narcissistic Issues."

61. Leo **Rangell**, "The Psychology of Poise with a Special Elaboration on the Psychic Significance of the Snout or Perioral Region," *International Journal of Psychoanalysis* 35 (1954): 313–32.

62. Aaron, *Stage Fright*, 82.

63. Redfield, *Letters*, 7. Or, as Aaron says, by "spoon-feeding," the term directors use to describe coaching helpless actors.

64. Personal communication, 1989.

65. Holt, Quinn, and Russell, *Star Mothers*, 40.

66. Callow, *Being an Actor*, 97, 47.

67. Redfield, *Letters*, 34.

68. Konstantin **Stanislavski**, *Building a Character*, trans. Elizabeth Reynolds Hapgood (New York: Theatre Arts Books, 1949), 27.

69. Redfield, *Letters*, 88.

70. E. Bergler, cited in Aaron, *Stage Fright*, 98; Donald M. **Kaplan**, "Theater Architecture: A Derivation of the Primal Cavity," *The Drama Review* 12 (1968): 105–16.

71. Redfield, *Letters*, 21; Callow, *Being an Actor*, 194.

72. "Ocular identification" is Fenichel's phrase; he cites Freud's essay on the Medusa as visual threat to explain an actor's fantasies of magically influencing the audience. Fenichel, "On Acting," 147.

73. See Heinz **Kohut**, "Narcissism and Narcissistic Rage," *Psychoanalytic Study of the Child* 27 (1972): 360–400, on "the developmental series of demands for immediate mirroring responses to concretely exhibited aspects of the child's body or of his physical or mental functions," 374–75.

74. Cited in Redfield, *Letters*, 70.

75. "Stage fright . . . is the specific fright of an exhibitionist: shame. Unconsciously, it is the shame of an inferiority [which Fenichel defines as castration and I am referring to as a narcissistic wound], which to cover has been the chief motivation in the choice of acting as a profession." Fenichel, "On Acting," 160.

76. Edmund **Wilson**, "Philoctetes: The Wound and the Bow," in *The Wound and the Bow: Seven Studies in Literature* (New York: Oxford University Press, 1929), 272–95.

77. Bruno **Bettelheim**, *Symbolic Wounds: Puberty Rites and the Envious Male* (London: Thames and Hudson, 1955), 29–30.

78. Callow, *Being an Actor*, 177.

79. Fenichel, "On Acting," 160.

80. Nicholas **Craig**, *Nicholas Craig, I an Actor* (London: Pavilion Books, 1988), 11.

81. Sigmund **Freud**, *The Interpretation of Dreams*, in *The Standard Edition of the Complete Psychological Works*, trans. James Strachey (London: Hogarth Press, 1953), 4:216.

82. Harrison, *Damned Serious Business*, 1; Redfield, *Letters*, 25.

83. Little and Cantor, *Playmakers*, 95.

84. Laurence **Olivier**, *Confessions of an Actor* (London: Sceptre, 1987), 312; Huggett, *Supernatural on Stage*, 32. Such personal confessions, like any anecdotal accounts, must be taken with a grain of salt. But even if they are not descriptions of actual practices they testify to the nature of actors' fantasies.

85. The authors of *Star Mothers* "looked at the childhoods of over 150 stars and found a thread of emotional pain running through the majority of them. . . . Absent parents, broken homes, poverty, death, disruption, crop up again and again." Despite finding such disturbances in the backgrounds of three-quarters of the stars they discuss, the generally optimistic authors hesitate to draw any conclusions: "It would be a gross oversimplification . . . to assert that such pain was a necessary ingredient, a prerequisite for stardom." Nonetheless, the prevalence of pain seems significant. Holt, Quinn, and Russell, *Star Mothers*, 18, 36, 35.

86. Fisher and Fisher, *Pretend*, 153; Redgrave, *Ways and Means*, 36.

87. Fisher and Fisher, *Pretend*, 168–70.

88. Olivier, *Confessions*, 22.

89. Benedict **Nightingale**, "Master of the Roles" (review of *Laurence Olivier* by Anthony Holden), *Times Literary Supplement*, 10–16 June 1988, 652.

90. Callow, *Being an Actor*, 15, 17.

91. Holt, Quinn, and Russell, *Star Mothers*, 124.

92. Logan, *Josh*, 4. *Star Mothers* tells of many similar cases: Alec Guinness never knew who his father was, and George Burns, Charlie Chaplin, and Rock Hudson each lost his father to death or desertion before the age of seven. Holt, Quinn, and Russell, *Star Mothers*, 156, 158, 163.

93. Holt, Quinn, and Russell, *Star Mothers*, 52, 57.

94. Harrison, *Damned Serious Business*, 3; Holt, Quinn, and Russell, *Star Mothers*, 179. See also the Fishers' story about the actor whose mother made him try on a dress when shopping, so that she could see whether or not it would fit his sister. Fisher and Fisher, *Pretend*, 176.

95. Philip **Weissman**, *Creativity in the Theater: A Psychoanalytic Study* (New York, London: Basic Books, 1965), 14–16, 19, cited in Marianne **Novy**, "Shakespeare's Female Characters as Actors and Audience," in *The Woman's Part: Feminist Criticism of Shakespeare*, ed. Carolyn Ruth Swift **Lenz**, Gayle **Greene**, and Carol Thomas **Neely** (Urbana: University of Illinois Press, 1980), 265.

96. Novy, "Female Characters," 115, 266.

97. Logan, *Josh*, 1–2.

98. Gabbard, "Narcissistic Issues," 438.

99. Holt, Quinn, and Russell, *Star Mothers*, 50, 68.

100. Holt, Quinn, and Russell, *Star Mothers*, 15.

101. Aaron, *Stage Fright*, 39–40; the material in this paragraph is drawn largely from Aaron, chap. 2.

102. Little and Cantor, *Playmakers*, 94.

103. Fenichel, "On Acting," 156, comparing the audience's attitude toward actors with their attitude toward whores.

104. Barish, *Antitheatrical Prejudice,* 3.

105. Cole, *Theatrical Event,* 69–73.

106. Edith Oliver, "Up from Stratford," *The New Yorker,* 30 January 1984, 83.

107. Bertolt Brecht, "A New Technique of Acting," trans. Eric Bentley, *Theatre Arts* 33 (1949): 38–40, esp. 38.

108. Cited in Redfield, *Letters,* 101–2.

109. Little and Cantor, *Playmakers,* 125.

110. Elias Canetti, *Crowds and Power,* trans. Carol Stewart (New York: Viking Press, 1962), 50, 97, 203.

111. Redfield, *Letters,* 6.

112. Brook, *Empty Space,* 9.

Chapter Two

1. This chapter's title draws on Sir Bounteous's description of players' uncertain lives in Thomas Middleton, *A Mad World, My Masters* (1604–7 [1606]), ed. Standish Henning (Lincoln: University of Nebraska Press, 1965), 5.1.29–30.

2. Recent distinctions between performance and drama suggest such a disappearance.

3. See Alfred Harbage, *Shakespeare's Audience* (New York: Columbia University Press, 1941) and *Shakespeare and the Rival Traditions* (New York: Macmillan, 1952), which argue that Shakespeare's was a popular theater; Ann Jennalie Cook, *The Privileged Playgoers of Shakespeare's London, 1576–1642* (Princeton: Princeton University Press, 1981), which challenges Harbage's thesis; and, for a reconsideration of all existing evidence, Andrew Gurr, *Playgoing in Shakespeare's London* (Cambridge: Cambridge University Press, 1987).

4. Term used in Bradbrook, *Common Player,* 24.

5. For a reconstruction of the event see Anne Righter, *Shakespeare and the Idea of the Play* (1962; reprint, Harmondsworth: Penguin Books, 1967), 15.

6. The touring companies' failures have been recounted by, among others, Glynne Wickham, *Early English Stages 1300–1660* (New York: Columbia University Press, 1963), 2:1:104–6. But recently theater historians have challenged the traditional account. Alan Somerset's investigation of the records shows that players were welcomed about 94 percent of the time when they arrived in a town, as they are welcomed in Shakespeare's *Taming of the Shrew* (1589) and *Hamlet* (1599–1601); Anthony Munday's *Sir Thomas More* (1595); Middleton's *Mad World,* (1606) and *Hengist, King of Kent; or, The Mayor of Queenborough* (1618); and Richard Brome's *Antipodes* (1638). Alan Somerset, talk presented to the Shakespeare Association of America, 1990. See his related essay, "The Lords President, Their Activities and Companies: Evidence from Stropshire," *The Elizabethan Theatre.* Papers given at the Tenth International Conference on Elizabethan Theatre held at the University of Waterloo, Ontario, July 1983 (Port Credit, Ontario: P. D. Meany, 1988), 93–111 (hereafter, *Elizabethan Theatre X*).

7. See Michael MacDonald, *Mystical Bedlam: Madness, Anxiety, and Healing in*

Seventeenth-Century England (Cambridge: Cambridge University Press, 1981), 108, and A. L. **Beier**, *Masterless Men: The Vagrancy Problem in England 1560–1640* (London: Methuen, 1985), chap. 1. Even servants in merchants' households—like Dromio, servant to Antipholus of Syracuse in *The Comedy of Errors*—scorned "a beggar [and] her brat" (*Err.* 4.4.35–36).

8. Wickham, *Early English Stages,* 2:2:150, cited in Alvin B. **Kernan**, "Shakespearean Comedy and Its Courtly Audience," in *Comedy from Shakespeare to Sheridan: Change and Continuity in the English and European Dramatic Tradition, Essays in Honor of Eugene M. Waith,* ed. A. R. **Braunmuller** and J. C. **Bulman** (Newark, Del.: University of Delaware Press, 1986), 91–101.

9. J. Leeds **Barroll**, "Drama and the Court," in Barroll, et al., *Drama in English,* 3:3–27; Salingar, *Traditions of Comedy,* 264.

10. Scott McMillan describes the debilitating effect which the establishment of the Queen's Men had on the previously thriving London companies. Scott McMillan, "The Queen's Men and the London Theatre of 1583," in *Elizabethan Theatre X,* 1–17, esp. 5–13.

11. Cook, *Privileged Playgoers,* 99–105, argues for the continued importance of patrons.

12. Bradbrook, *Common Player,* 40.

13. E. K. **Chambers**, *The Elizabethan Stage* (Oxford: Clarendon Press, 1967), 1:350, 2:305, 2:333; Bradbrook, *Common Player,* 64.

14. "The Elizabethan common player was a 'servant' in the eyes of the nobleman to whose company he belonged and of everyone else." J. Dover **Wilson**, "The Puritan Attack on the Stage," in *The Cambridge History of Literature,* ed. A. W. **Ward** and A. R. **Waller**, vol. 6, pt. 2 (Cambridge: Cambridge University Press, 1910), 450. Many have elaborated on and reaffirmed Wilson's assessment.

15. Bradbrook, *Common Player,* 51.

16. Theseus's generosity here sounds oddly like Titania's when she orders her servants to "Tie up my lover's tongue, bring him silently" (*MND* 3.1.194).

17. Kernan discusses the inadequacies of real and staged audiences, private and public, in "Shakespearean Comedy," 91–101, and in Alvin **Kernan**, "Shakespeare's and Jonson's View of Public Theatre Audiences," in *Jonson and Shakespeare,* ed. Ian **Donaldson** (Atlantic Highlands: Humanities Press, 1983), 74–88, esp. 78–83, on private performances in Shakespeare's plays.

18. John **Davies**, "To Our English Terence, Mr. Will. Shake-speare," in *The Scourge of Folly* (S.R. 1610), cited in E. K. **Chambers**, *William Shakespeare: A Study of Facts and Problems* (Oxford: Clarendon Press, 1930), 2:214.

19. Stephen **Gosson**, *School of Abuse* (London, 1579), cited in Bradbrook, *Common Player,* 71.

20. Munday is assumed, though not proven, to be the author of this passage from the *Second and Third Blast of Retrait from Plaies,* cited in Chambers, *Elizabethan Stage,* 4:210. Bradbrook cites this and a number of similar remarks, for example from Phillip Stubbes, who includes the cliché among his fulminations. Bradbrook, *Common Player,* 75.

21. Andrew **Gurr**, *The Shakespearean Stage 1574–1642* (Cambridge: Cambridge University Press, 1970), 141.

22. C. L. **Barber**, *Shakespeare's Festive Comedy: A Study of Dramatic Form and Its Relation to Social Custom* (1959; reprint, Cleveland and New York: Meridian Books, 1963); Robert **Weimann**, *Shakespeare and the Popular Tradition in the Theater: Studies in the Social Dimension of Dramatic Form and Function* (Baltimore: Johns Hopkins University Press, 1978); Michael **Bristol**, *Carnival and Theater: Plebeian Culture and the Structure of Authority in Renaissance England* (New York: Methuen, 1985). See also Louis **Montrose**, "The Purpose of Playing: Reflections on a Shakespearean Anthropology," *Helios,* n.s., 7 (1980): 51–74, and Steven **Mullaney**, *The Place of the Stage: License, Play, and Power in Renaissance England* (Chicago: University of Chicago Press, 1988).

23. Gurr, *Playgoing,* 113.

24. Bradbrook, *Common Player,* 105.

25. Gurr, *Playgoing,* 61–63; Jean **Howard**, "Crossdressing, the Theatre, and Gender Struggle in Early Modern England," *Shakespeare Quarterly* 39 (1988): 418–40.

26. Thomas **Dekker**, *The Guls Horn-Booke* (1609) in *The Non-Dramatic Works of Thomas Dekker,* ed. Alexander B. Grosart (London: Hazell, Watson and Viney, 1885), 2:263.

27. Thomas **Nashe** names Tarlton, Alleyn, Knell, and Bentley in *Pierce Pennilesse his Supplication to the Divell,* in *The Works of Thomas Nashe,* ed. Ronald B. McKerrow (Oxford: Basil Blackwell, 1966), 1:215; Thomas **Heywood** names Knell, Bentley, Miles, Wilson, Crosse, and Lanam in *An Apology for Actors,* in *"An Apology for Actors" (1612) by Thomas Heywood and "A Refutation of the Apology for Actors" (1615), by I. G.,* ed. Richard H. **Perkinson** (New York: Scholars' Facsimiles and Reprints, 1941), E₂v; Dekker elsewhere places Bentley "among the poets in Elysium."

28. Not everyone was so sensitive to the actor's skill. When John Marston draws on this passage in *Antonio's Revenge* (1.5) he falls back into the more standard commentary on the player's hypocrisy, ignoring his acting ability.

29. Chambers, *Elizabethan Stage,* 4:239.

30. Heywood, *Apology for Actors,* G₁r.

31. Bentley, *Profession of Player,* 116.

32. Thomas **Platter**, *Thomas Platter's Travels in England 1599,* trans. Clare Williams (London: Jonathan Cape, 1937), 170.

33. Ben Jonson, *The Devil Is an Ass* (1616), (2.8.63–92), cited in Bentley, *Profession of Player,* 115–16.

34. *A Mad World, My Masters* (5.2.30–32).

35. Lording **Barry**, *Ram Alley; or, Merry Tricks* (1607–8 [1608]) *A Select Collection of Old English Plays,* 4th ed., ed. W. Carew **Hazlitt** (London: Reeves and Turner, 1875), 10:369.

36. Earle, *Micro-Cosmography,* 39–40. Compare R. M.'s claim that the player's "chiefe Admirers are commonly young wanton Chamber-maids, who are so taken with his posture and gay clothes they never come to be their own women after." **R. M.**, *Micrologia: Characters, or Essayes, of Persons, Trades, and Places* (London: T. C., 1629), B₃v.

37. Also in *Bartholomew Fair,* Whit the bawd promises, "dou shalt live like a

lady, . . . shee de players, be in love vit 'em" (4.5.30, 33–34). In *Cynthia's Revels,* Cupid describes a "nymph of a most wandering and giddy disposion . . . she'll run from gallant to gallant . . . she loves a player well, and a lawyer infinitely" (2.3.145–46, 157), and Moria says, "I would tell you which madam lov'd a monsieur, which a player, which a page" (4.1.132–33).

38. *The Actors Remonstrance or Complaint for the silencing of their profession and banishment from their severall Play-Houses,* in *The English Drama and Stage under the Tudor and Stuart Princes 1543–1664,* ed. W. C. **Hazlitt,** (London: Wittingham and Wilkins, 1869), 263.

39. Earle, *Micro-Cosmography,* 39.

40. One problem in interpreting the attacks on players is that many of them come from within. The attacks in the 1570s and 1580s were nearly all written by men who were connected with the theater themselves. We can only speculate about how Thomas Field's early sermons against players might have affected his son, Nathan Field, who later became one of the period's most famous actors and defenders of the theater; perhaps the father's public speaking ability—like that of Laurence Olivier's minister father—had something to do with the son's leaning. Elsewhere the contradiction is more overt. John Lowin, himself one of the "Principall Actors" in the first Folio edition of Shakespeare's plays, wrote a little piece called *Conclusions Upon Dances* (1607) under the pseudonym of I. L. Roscio ("J. L. the Player"), in which "he reveals himself as part of the [antitheatrical] Puritan middle class. . . . Dance retains for him the Puritan stigma attached to any physical activity that is overtly demonstrative, consciously alluring, and nonproductive." Rick **Bowers,** "John Lowin's *Conclusions Upon Dances:* Puritan Conclusions of a Godly Player," *Renaissance and Reformation,* n.s., 11 (1987): 163–73, esp. 171. Gosson, whose *School of Abuse* (1579) effectively initiated the debate, and whose *Playes Confuted in Five Actions* (1582) popularized it, had written plays himself before the debate, and William Rankins (*A Mirrour of Monsters,* 1587) went on to write plays after his attack on players. Even a prolific playwright like Anthony Munday (*Second and Third Blast,* 1580), who was praised by Francis Meres as "our best plotter" (1598)—and who may also have been an actor before he wrote the pamphlet—contributed to the early debate. Munday may have undertaken the attack on the stage as hack work, paid for by the London Corporation; but even so he showed remarkable agility in drawing on the arguments of his supposed opponents.

41. Wilson, "Puritan Attack," 421–61. The first dozen or so of Chambers's selections from "attacks on the stage" are taken from texts composed before the establishment of permanent theaters had posed any pragmatic threat. William Alley in 1565 complained about the theatrical riffraff who drew the ignorant crowds: "iuglers, scoffers, iesters, plaiers, which may say and do what they lust, be it never so fleshly and filthy? and yet suffred and heard with laughing and clapping of handes." Chambers, *Elizabethan Stage,* 4:192.

42. We make the same assumption today when we insist on rating movies to protect impressionable audiences and criticize television for depicting too much violence, or even too much consumption of junk food.

43. The contagion of emotion between stage and gallery was precisely what the

antitheatricalists feared, and their criticism likened players and audience (both are common, both constitute a rabble, etc.). The excited—and therefore contempt-ible—spectators are described in the same terms as the clown, the most contempt-ible actor, in Fennor's 1616 description of the multitude at the Fortune who "screwed their scurvy jaws and look'd awry," like Tarlton making faces on the stage or Kempe with his "scurvey faces." *Fennors Descriptions* (1616) B₂r–₃r, quoted in Gurr, *Playgoing*, 45, 230; Kempe's faces are mentioned in *The Pilgrimage to Parnas-sus* in *The Three Parnassus Plays (1598–1601)*, ed. J. B. **Leishman** (London: Ivor Nicholson and Watson, 1949), 93–132, 129, line 667.

44. Barish, *Antitheatrical Prejudice*, 159–67; Michael **O'Connell**, "The Idola-trous Eye: Iconoclasm, Antitheatricalism, and the Image of the Elizabethan The-ater," *English Literary History* 52 (1985): 279–310; David Scott **Kastan**, "Making Majesty Subject: Shakespeare and the Spectacle of Rule," *Shakespeare Quarterly* 37 (1986): 461, citing Philip Stubbes, *Anatomy of Abuses* (1583).

45. "Player is a great spender," see T. G[ainsford?], *The Rich Cabinet Furnished with Varietie of Descriptions*, in Hazlitt, *English Drama and Stage*, 230. "He is one seldome takes care for old Age; because ill Diet and Disorder, together with a Con-sumption or some worse disease have only chalked out his Catastrophe but to a Colon." R. M., *Micrologia*, B₄r. "they . . . spend all they get," Donald Lupton, *London and the Countrey carbonadoed* (London, 1632), cited in J. Dover **Wilson**, *Shake-speare's Life in England* (1911; reprint, Baltimore: Penguin, 1968), 207. Concerning usury, see Jonson, *Poetaster* 3.1; and 270; and Henry **Crosse**, *Vertues Common-wealth; or, The High-way to Honour*, in Chambers, 4:247.

46. In Barry, *Ram Alley* [1608] the Drawer who waits on the players explains that "it stands with policy / That one should be a notorious cuckold, / If it be but for the better keeping / The rest of his company together." In Hazlitt, *Old English Plays*, 10:346 (4.1). See also "Kempe's" jokes about an actor-cuckold in *The Travels of Three English Brothers* (1607). The (to us) overheated objections are familiar in any discussion of stage history: plays were "fleshly and filthy" (1565), full of "wicked wordes, and blasphemye, impudent jestures, doubtful slaunders, unchaste songes" (1574)—and all this even before Gosson initiated the real flow of abuse. Cited in Chambers, *Elizabethan Stage*, 4.

47. Anthony **Munday**, *A Second and Third Blast of Retrait from Plaies* (1580), in Hazlitt, *English Drama and Stage*, 148.

48. Stubbes, *Anatomy of Abuse* (1583), one of the examples cited in nearly every discussion of gender and the boy-actors; Samuel Harsnett, *A Declaration of Egre-gious Popish Impostures to with-draw the harts of her Majesties subjects* (London: James Roberts, 1603), 149. Gosson merely said that it was a "lie" for men (and presumably boys) to wear women's clothes, a weak objection which both Gager and Heywood could answer easily by claiming that female impersonation was no lie because the players never pretended to tell the truth. But others expressed sexual outrage and anxiety more explicitly. Prynne became most hysterical when describ-ing the effect boys had on their audiences, transforming them to Priests of Venus, clothing them in women's attire, and sending them home to self-abuse.

49. Chambers, *Elizabethan Stage*, 4:256–57.

50. Chambers, *Elizabethan Stage*, 4:216.

51. Russell **Fraser**, *The War against Poetry* (Princeton: Princeton University Press, 1970), argues for the importance of more pragmatic objections.

52. Crosse, *Vertues Common-wealth*, cited in Chambers, *Elizabethan Stage*, 247.

53. Thomas **Beard**, *The Theatre of Gods Judgments* (London: Adam Fflip, 1612), 206–7.

54. Chambers, *Elizabethan Stage*, 4:184.

55. Barish, *Antitheatrical Prejudice*, 85, citing David **Leverenz**, "Why Did Puritans Hate Stage Plays?" in *The Language of Puritan Feeling: An Exploration in Literature, Psychology, and Social History* (New Brunswick: Rutgers University Press, 1980).

56. See my discussion of similar projections in today's theater in chapter 1.

57. Answer of the Corporation of London to the Queen's Players' petition (1584), reprinted in Chambers, 4:300; Jonson, *Poetaster* 1.2.11.

58. Chambers, *Elizabethan Stage*, 1:381 n. 1.

59. Munday may be scorning only the willingness to act for money—any amount—rather than any actual success in collecting large amounts of money. Munday, *Second and Third Blast*, 152. By 1600, however, Chamberlain's and Admiral's companies had virtually monopolized the London theaters and ensured reasonable financial stability for at least some of their players.

60. Bentley, *Profession of Player*, 31–32.

61. Bentley, *Profession of Player*, 51, notes two such contracted limitations.

62. William **Ingram**, "The Cost of Touring," unpublished talk presented to the Shakespeare Association of America, 1990.

63. Chambers, *Elizabethan Stage*, 4:256.

64. The phrase is taken from an epigram on Heywood in the anonymous *Musarum Deliciae* (1640; cited in Nungezer, see n. 86 below, 191). When the epigram's speaker advises Heywood to stop "groveling on the stage," he is more likely referring to Heywood's activities as a writer than to his career as a player, which had ended twenty years earlier. But the metaphor is taken from an actor's experience on the stage and, whatever the tenor, conveys quite explicitly the speaker's contempt for an acting career and what it entails.

65. From *Theses Martinianae* (1589), cited in Chambers, *Elizabethan Stage*, 4:230. Of course Martin was mudslinging, but the caricature wouldn't have been effective without some basis in reality. Dekker, in *The Ravens Almanacke* (1609), describes players "glad to play three houres for two pence." Dekker, *Non-Dramatic Works*, 4:194.

66. Quoted by the anti-Martinist congratulating the Queen's men for undoing Martin. London, 1589, cited in G. M. **Pinciss**, "The Queen's Men, 1583–1592," *Theatre Survey* 51–52 (1970): 50–65, esp. 57.

67. Crosse, cited in Chambers, *Elizabethan Stage*, 4:247.

68. Nashe, from the epistle prefixed to Robert Greene's *Menaphon*, cited in Chambers, *Elizabethan Stage*, 4:234. It is possible that Nashe is referring to playwrights here, but he seems to distinguish those as a separate form of lowlife (the tragedian's "ideot Art-masters") later in the passage. Chambers, *Elizabethan Stage*, 4:235.

69. Gosson, cited in Chambers, *Elizabethan Stage*, 4:204. An anonymous soldier sent a letter to Sir Francis Walsingham in 1587 complaining about a related offense:

"Yt is a wofull sight to see two hundred proude players jett in their silkes, / wheare five hundred pore people sterve in the streets." Chambers, *Elizabethan Stage,* 4:304. Soldiers, however, being highly visible, well-costumed figures often drummed into town on display for the public, had more in common with players than the soldiers liked to admit. See chapter 4.

70. Chrisoganus tells them to "take heed ye stumble not with stalking hie," and a mere steward observes that "the Players now are growne so proud, ten pound a play, or no point comedy." *Histriomastix,* in John **Marston,** *The Plays of John Marston,* ed. H. Harvey Wood (Edinburgh and London: Oliver and Boyd, 1939), 3:273–74, 276 (3.1).

71. John **Davies,** *Microcosmos* (1603), in *The Complete Works of John Davies of Hereford,* ed. Alexander B. Grosart (Edinburgh University Press, 1878), 1:82.

72. Robert Greene, *Francescos Fortunes* (1590), cited in Chambers, *Elizabethan Stage,* 4:236, and *Quip for an Upstart Courtier* (1592), cited in Chambers, *Elizabethan Stage,* 4:240. As Iago said of the charming Cassio, "He hath a daily beauty in his life / That makes me ugly" (*Oth.* 5.2.19–20).

73. Attributed by Chettle to the ghost of Tarlton in *Henrie Chettle, "Kind-Hartes Dreame" (1592); William Kempe, "Nine Daies Wonder" (1600),* ed. G. B. Hamson, Bodley Head Quartos 4 (London: John Lane, 1923), 44.

74. S. P. **Cerasano,** "Anthony Jeffes, Player and Brewer," *Notes and Queries* 229, n.s., 31.2 (1984): 221–25.

75. William **Ingram,** "The Elizabethan Stage Player: In His Habit As He Lived," talk presented to the Shakespeare Association of America, 1985, MS 2. See also William **Ingram,** *Business of Playing: The Beginnings of the Adult Professional Theater in Elizabethan London* (Ithaca: Cornell University Press, 1992).

76. Bentley, *Profession of Player,* 95.

77. The author of *Histriomastix* implies that workmen turn player when "trades serve no turnes," *Plays of John Marston,* 250 (1.1). Equally untrustworthy, Gosson described the players' origins, with typical no-win logic, by sneering that they are either brought up to the profession—bad—or—also bad—that they leave other perfectly good professions to join it. Stephen Gosson, *Playes Confuted in Five Actions, Proving That they are not to be suffered in a Christian common weale,* n.d. S.R. 6 April 1582, cited in Chambers, *Elizabethan Stage,* 4:218.

78. Greene's famous slur in *Groatsworth of Wit* (1592), thought to be aimed at Shakespeare, contains the phrase "Iohannes fac totum." Chambers, 4:241. His palmer refers to a player's merely "mechanical labor" in *Francescos Fortunes.* Chambers, 4:236.

79. Berry suggests that perhaps only the most successful troupes bought apprentices; in the other cases—a more risky business which the richer companies could avoid—the father or guardian paid the actors for taking boys on, as they did in other professions. Herbert **Berry,** "The Player's Apprentice," *Essays in Theatre* 1 (1983), 73–80.

80. Goldman, *Actor's Freedom,* 58.

81. Thomas Dekker, *The Wonderfull Yeare* (1603), in *Non-Dramatic Works,* 1:100, cited in R. A. **Foakes,** "The Player's Passion: Some Notes on Elizabethan Psychology and Acting," *Essays and Studies* 7 (1954): 73.

82. S. P. **Cerasano**, "The 'Business' of Shareholding, the Fortune Playhouses, and Francis Grace's Will," *Medieval and Renaissance Drama in England: An Annual Gathering of Research, Criticism, and Reviews II*, ed. J. Leeds **Barroll** (New York: AMS Press, 1985), 237.

83. Cerasano, "'Business' of Shareholding," 233.

84. Fleay's *A Chronicle History of the London Stage* (1890), 157; J. P. Collier, *History of Dramatic Poetry* (1879), 1:292–94. Cited in Wilson, "Puritan Attack," 434.

85. Bentley, *Profession of Player*, 110, 112.

86. Edwin **Nungezer**, *A Dictionary of Actors and of Other Persons Associated with the Public Presentation of Plays in England before 1642* (Ithaca: Cornell University Press, 1929), 206.

87. S. **Schoenbaum**, *William Shakespeare: A Compact Documentary Life*, rev. ed. (Oxford: Oxford University Press, 1987), 29.

88. For the debate about the boy players, see, e.g., Lisa **Jardine**, *Still Harping on Daughters: Women and Drama in the Age of Shakespeare* (Sussex: Harvester Press; Barnes and Noble, 1983), 9–36; Catherine **Belsey**, "Disrupting Sexual Difference: Meaning and Gender in the Comedies," in *Alternative Shakespeares*, ed. John **Drakakis** (London: Methuen, 1985), 166–90; and Phyllis **Rackin**, "Androgyny, Mimesis, and the Marriage of the Boy Heroine on the English Renaissance Stage," *PMLA* 102 (1987): 29–41. For arguments that boy actors did not create special gender uncertainties, see, e.g., Kathleen **McLuskie**, "The Act, the Role, and the Actor-Boy Actresses on the Elizabethan Stage," *New Theatre Quarterly* 3 (1987): 120–30; Stephen **Greenblatt**, "Fiction and Friction," in *Shakespearean Negotiations* (Berkeley: University of California Press, 1988), 660–93, esp. 688.

89. When the boy actors come out she asks her husband, "Sirrah, didst thou ever see a prettier child? how it behaves itself, I warrant ye, and speaks, and looks, and pearts up the head!" **Beaumont**, *The Knight of the Burning Pestle* (1607; ll. 93–95). Real women remained similarly oblivious to the boy actor's sexual possibilities. Lady Mary Wroth refers twice to boy actresses in *The Countess of Montgomery's Urania* (1621). In each case she clearly distinguishes the erotically benign "play boy" from the woman he plays, and from the ardor she might attract were she real. Michael **Shapiro**, "Lady Mary Wroth Describes a 'Boy Actress,'" *Medieval and Renaissance Drama in England* 4 (1989): 187–94.

90. Chambers, *Elizabethan Stage*, 2:50. Cited in Jackson **Cope**, "Marlowe's Dido and the Titillating Children," *English Literary Renaissance* 4 (1974), 318; Cope also argues that Jupiter's dalliance with Ganymede in the Induction to Marlowe's *Dido* is a metadramatic reference to the master who might "toy" and "play" with the "wanton female boy[s]" in his charge.

91. Jonson is often explicit. The father in *Poetaster* who learns that his son wants to go on stage cries, "My son an actor's ingle?" And the children in *Cynthia's Revels* call themselves "ingles." Apart from the transvestism central to *Epicoene*, where the whole story turns on marrying a boy-bride, Jonson in *The Devil Is an Ass* describes a boy actor who dressed up offstage and passed for a ladyfriend of one of the actors. Littlewit in *Bartholomew Fair* claims innocently that some men have wives as grand as the players'—that is, dressed as lavishly as and equipped similarly to the boys who played the players' wives? But Jonson is not alone. The Pedant (schoolmasters

were as suspected of boy-love as were the boys' troupe masters) in Chapman's *Gentleman Usher* explains that the Page has been chosen to play a lady in the coming masque because of his beauty and "other hidden virtues." Another connoisseur of boys, in Chapman's *May Day,* tries to buy a page, imagining how lovely he will look as a girl.

92. *Histriomastix,* 4.1 and 6.1, in *Plays of John Marston,* 3:260, 299.

93. Bradbrook, *Common Player,* 39–66.

94. Ingram, "Elizabethan Stage Player," MS, 6. Ingram also quotes Hickes's partner in the case, Peter Hunningborne, who "said of Savage that he was 'a verrie lewd fealowe and liveth by noe other trade then playinge of staige plaies and Interleuds.'" Testimony in Public Records Office, REQ 2/266/8.

95. J. O. **Halliwell,** Introduction, *Tarlton's Jests, and News Out of Purgatory,* ed. James Orchard Halliwell (London: The Shakespeare Society, 1844). See also Bradbrook, *Common Player,* 162–77, for an assessment of Tarlton's career of "squalor and greatness" (162), and Wiles, *Shakespeare's Clown,* 11–23, for a reassessment.

96. "Tarlton's City Jests" (no author identified), in Halliwell, *Tarlton's Jests,* 13, 14.

97. Th. Bastard, cited in Halliwell, *Tarlton's Jests,* xxxiii.

98. Bentley, *Profession of Player,* 112.

99. J. Cocke, "A Common Player," in John Stephens, *Satyrical Essayes Characters and Others* (1615); John Webster, "Of An Excellent Actor," in Sir Thomas Overbury, *The Wife,* 6th edition (1615); Earle, *Micro-Cosmography* (1628); R. M., *Micrologia* (1629). The first two are reprinted and the last two cited in Chambers, *Elizabethan Stage,* 4:255–58.

100. Chambers, *Elizabethan Stage,* 1:351.

101. See examples cited in Chambers, *Elizabethan Stage,* 2:554.

102. George **Chapman,** *Bussy D'Ambois* (ca. 1604), ed. Robert J. Lordi (Lincoln: University of Nebraska Press, 1964). Though not printed until the 1641 Q_2, the epilogue may well have been written during Chapman's 1610/11 revision of the play for a production at Whitefriars.

103. Desiderius **Erasmus,** *The Praise of Folly,* trans. Clarence H. Miller (New Haven and London: Yale University Press, 1979), 44.

104. Klein cites this passage, from Johannes Rhenanus's preface to a German adaptation (1613) of Thomas Tomkis's *Lingua* (1604), as evidence that "the system of author-direction prevailed" on the sixteenth- and seventeenth-century English stage. David **Klein,** "Did Shakespeare Produce His Own Plays?" *Modern Language Review* 57 (1962), 556–58. But the play which Rhenanus's comments introduce was a university play; the rest of Klein's direct evidence also comes from either university drama or boys' plays so its import for adult professionals is not clear.

105. Heywood, *Apology for Actors,* E_3r.

106. Klein cites Shakespeare's *Midsummer Night's Dream* (1596), Anthony Munday's *Death and Downfall of Robert, Earl of Huntington* (1598), Middleton and Rowley's *Spanish Gypsy* (1623), and Brome's *Antipodes* (1638). Klein, "Did Shakespeare Produce," 558.

107. Anthony **Munday,** *John a Kent and John a Cumber* (1587–90 [1589]), ed.

Mariel St. Clare **Byrne**, Malone Society Reprints (Oxford: Oxford University Press, 1923), 33, line 1079.

108. Wickham takes this as evidence that the former carpenter Burbage was similarly in charge of Shakespearean productions. Wickham, *Early English Stages,* 2:2:187.

109. S. P. **Cerasano**, "Edward Alleyn's Early Years: His Life and Family," *Notes and Queries,* 232, n.s., 34.2 (1987), 237–43, esp. 242.

110. "Father and son relationships tended to be particularly emotive for Jonson. . . . Even in his comedies, he was rarely able to touch on paternal relations without his writing beginning to vibrate." Anne **Barton**, *Ben Jonson, Dramatist* (Cambridge: Cambridge University Press, 1984), 20.

111. Cited in Chambers, *Elizabethan Stage,* 4:193.

112. Heywood, *Apology for Actors,* B₄r.

113. Critics like Munday feared that actors were "such kind of men in their conversation as in their profession." Even in a moment of sympathy, Hippolyta in Shakespeare's *Dream* blurs character and actor, when she responds to Bottom's prolonged suicide in "Pyramus and Thisbe": "Beshrew my heart, but I pity the man" (*MND* 5.1.295). But is "the man" dying Pyramus or Bottom, whose bad acting has made the men tease him?

114. The boy who plays Sly's wife in the Induction to *Taming of the Shrew* is also instructed to use an onion (*Shr.* Ind.124).

115. David **Bevington**, *Action and Eloquence* (Cambridge, Massachusetts and London, England: Harvard University Press, 1984), 98. See his entire chapter on "The Language of Gesture and Expression," 67–98.

116. See, e.g., John **Gielgud**, *Stage Directions* (New York: Random House, 1963), 26.

117. Chambers, *Elizabethan Stage,* 4:370; Flecknoe's often-cited observation was made in 1664, years after Burbage had died, and may of course have been influenced by Betterton or other actors then on stage. Compare Mann, *Elizabethan Player,* 201–2, on John Rainold's claim that the actors' repetition of parts might "engrave the things in their mind," *Th' Overthrow of Stage Playes* (1599).

118. See chapter 4. For a recent review of differences between Elizabethan-Jacobean attitudes towards role-playing and ours, see Joan Lord **Hall**, *The Dynamics of Role-Playing in Jacobean Comedy* (New York: St. Martin's Press, 1991), and Edward **Burns**, *Character and Being on the Pre-modern Stage* (London: Macmillan, 1990).

119. For a discussion of the relation between rhetorical theory and seventeenth-century psychologies and medical tracts, see Joseph R. **Roach**, "Changeling Proteus: Rhetoric and Passions in the Seventeenth Century," in *The Player's Passion: Studies in the Science of Acting* (Newark: University of Delaware Press, 1985), 23–57. Roach cites Gayton's anecdote about an actor who "so lively and corporally personated a Changeling, that he could never compose his Face to the figure it had, before he undertook that part." Edmund **Gayton**, *Pleasant Notes upon Don Quixot* (London: W. Hunt, 1654), 144–45, cited in Roach, *Player's Passion,* 48–49. See also Jane **Donaworth**, *Shakespeare and the Sixteenth-Century Study of Language* (Urbana: University of Illinois Press, 1984), 85–86.

120. Prologue to *If It Be Not Good the Devil Is in It* (1610–12), cited in George F. Reynolds, "Aims of a Popular Elizabethan Dramatist," in *Elizabethan Studies in Honor of Hardin Craig,* ed. Maxwell **Baldwin**, W. D. **Briggs**, Francis R. **Johnson**, and E. N. S. **Thompson** (Stanford: Stanford University Press, 1941), 148–52, esp. 149–50.

121. See chapter 3 and the suggestions that Richard's supposed role-playing allows him to manifest himself after all, though admittedly an aspect of himself which he doesn't like to acknowledge.

122. Baldwin argues for his theory in T. W. **Baldwin**, *The Organization and Personnel of the Shakespearean Company* (Princeton: Princeton University Press, 1927). For an account of the ensuing debate about typecasting, see Skiles **Howard**, "A Re-examination of Baldwin's Theory of Acting Lines," *Theatre Survey* 26 (1985), 1–20. Howard's reexamination of the actor lists leads him to question the existence of acting lines and to argue instead for the versatility of Shakespearean actors. Whether or not Baldwin's extreme version of the theory holds true, it is generally accepted that there were acting lines in some cases: for the comic actors, for the boys, and briefly for certain others like John Shank who played the "hungry knave." Bentley, *Profession of Player,* 206–33, esp. 225. There was also a line for the physically distinctive thin actor, John Sincler (or Sincklo), the only actor except the clowns who is specified by name in the speech-prefixes of Shakespeare's plays. Allison **Gaw**, "Actors' Names in Basic Shakespearean Texts, with Special Reference to *Romeo and Juliet* and *Much Ado,*" *PMLA* 40 (1925), 530–50.

123. Munday, *Second and Third Blast,* 148.

124. Heywood, *Apology for Actors,* E₃r.

125. Marcus Quintilian begins book 6 of his *Institutio Oratoria,* a discussion of techniques for generating emotion in perorations, with a personal anecdote telling how he had embraced his dying son and had breathed in the "fleeting spirit" from the boy's lips. Citing Quintilian's passage, Roach suggests that, "the dying son has figuratively as well as literally inspired, breathed spirit into, the father and rhetor, who in turn has offered up his *pathos* to inspirit the 'dreams' and 'visions' of orators by engaging their imaginative sympathies with his bereavement." Roach, *Player's Passion,* 25.

126. See Robert A. **Fotherfill**, "The Perfect Image of Life: Counterfeit Death in the Plays of Shakespeare and His Contemporaries," *University of Toronto Quarterly* 52 (1982–83): 155–78; Reavley **Gair**, "Takeover at Blackfriars: Queen's Revels to King's Men," in *Elizabethan Theatre X,* 49.

127. Cited in Chambers, *Elizabethan Stage,* 4:238–39. Nashe is presumably, though not certainly, referring to Shakespeare's *Henry VI.* Perhaps Cassius's famous self-glorification in Shakespeare's *Caesar* implies a similar claim for the power of drama to resurrect: having just killed Caesar, Cassius thinks forward prophetically to the way in which this moment will be replayed in the future: "How many ages hence / Shall this our lofty scene be acted over, / In states unborn, and accents yet unknown!" (*JC* 3.1.111–13).

128. John Jones, Dedication to *Adrasta; or, The Woman's Spleen and Love's Conquest* (1635), cited in **Bentley**, *Profession of Dramatist in Shakespeare's Time 1590–1642* (Princeton: Princeton University Press, 1971), 79–80.

129. Cited in Nungezer, *Dictionary of Actors*, 78. See also the use of the term "lively," typical praise for good acting, to describe Hermione's statue, which really does come to life in Shakespeare's *Winter's Tale*.

130. Jonas Barish cites the statement from Northrop **Frye**, *The Anatomy of Criticism* (Princeton: Princeton University Press, 1957), 58, about the "theme of cynosure or centripetal gaze" in Renaissance literature in his discussion of the Puritan "distrust of outward splendor." Barish's point is that, even though "exhibitionism has tended, generally, to provoke less indignation than [consciously deceptive] mimicry," a "frank delight in [splendor] characterizes much of Renaissance culture" with its "pervasive pleasure . . . in the twin roles of actor and spectator." Barish argues that "a doctrine of ostentation, like Castiglione's, can verge on and ultimately become a doctrine of dissimulation" or, as Stephen Greenblatt calls it, of "self-fashioning." "Puritanism, Popery, and Parade," in Barish, *Antitheatrical Prejudice*, 167–68, 158, 183.

131. Cited in Chambers, *Elizabethan Stage*, 4:257–58.

132. Chettle, *Kind-Hartes Dreame*, 44; Earle, *Micro-Cosmography*, 39.

133. Davies, *Microcosmos*, 1:82; Redfield, *Letters*, 122.

134. Foakes, "Player's Passion," 73.

135. *The Belman of London* (1608), in Dekker, *Non-Dramatic Works*, 3:81. Cited in Foakes, "Player's Passion," 74.

136. Chambers, *Elizabethan Stage*, 4:256.

137. Drayton, *Idea*, Sonnet 47, *Works*, ed. Hebel, 2.334. Cited in Gurr, *Playgoing*, 215–16.

138. See chapter 8 where the influence of these two forms of display on Shakespeare is discussed in detail.

139. William Kempe, *Kemps nine daies wonder* (1600), B_1r, cited in Gurr, *Playgoing*, 215. Sir John Davies' epigram 3 (1593?) about Rufus the courtier at the theater (also cited in Gurr, *Playgoing*, 68) may refer to the presence of gallants on the amphitheater stage (as they were later to sit on the private stage).

140. See chapters 5 and 8. However sympathetic Shakespeare may have been to the populace as individuals, his crowd scenes are all more or less derogatory, and he seems to disapprove as much of the crowd's fickleness (a theater audience's failing) as of its tendency toward chaotic violence; see Annabel **Patterson**, *Shakespeare and the Popular Voice* (Cambridge and Oxford: Basil Blackwell, 1989) for a recent reassessment of Shakespeare's treatment of commoners. Shakespeare may have been known for crowd scenes in his own time—it was a crowd scene he contributed (was asked to contribute?) to the collaborative *Sir Thomas More* (1593–1601 [1595]).

141. In his dedicatory verse (not in the Second Folio) to John Fletcher's *The Faithful Shepherdess* (1608–9 [1608]), in *The Works of Francis Beaumont and John Fletcher*, ed. Arnold **Glover** and A. R. **Waller** (Cambridge: Cambridge University Press, 1906), 2:519, lines 33–34.

142. That the missiles did not entirely stop is suggested by John Tatham's 1640 reference to the audience's "wonted custome, banding *Tyle*, or Peare, / Against our *curtaines*, to allure us forth," cited in Gurr, *Playgoing*, 249.

143. See also, e.g., the narcissistic amateur actor Poggio in Chapman's *Gentleman Usher* (2.1.313).

144. Jonathan **Haynes**, "The Elizabethan Audience on Stage," in *The Theatrical Space: Themes in Drama,* ed. James **Redmond** (Cambridge: Cambridge University Press, 1987), 59–67, esp. 59. See also note 139.

145. Or even, like the author of the following, carrying on a kind of parallel play: "Love's Labour Lost I once did see a Play, / Ycleped so, so called to my paine, / Which I to hear to my small ioy did stay, / Giving attendance to my forward dame." Robert Tofte, *Alba the monthes minde of a melancholy lover* (1598).

146. Gerard **Murphy**, unpublished talk presented to the Shakespeare Association of America, 1987.

147. Tony **Church**, interview in *The Chronicle of Higher Education,* 25 April 1990, A6. Compare the Epilogue's description of the teeming audience he sees at the end of *Eastward Hoe* (Chapman, Jonson, and Marston; 1605): "Stay Sir, I perceive the multitude are gatherd together to veiw our comming out at the *Counter.* See, if the streets and the Fronts of the Houses, be not stucke with People, and the Windowes fild with Ladies, as on the solemne day of the *Pageant!*" *Plays of John Marston,* 3:171.

148. Olivier, *Confessions of an Actor,* 48.

149. Cited in David **Klein**, *Elizabethan Dramatists as Critics* (New York: Philosophical Library, 1963), 217. Thomas May, *The Heir* (1620), in Hazlitt, *Old English Plays,* 11:514 (1.1).

150. On Jonson's mistrust of visual spectacle and all theatricality, see "Jonson and the Loathèd Stage," in Barish, *Antitheatrical Prejudice,* 132–54, esp. 132–43. Gurr discusses Jonson in Andrew **Gurr**, "Hearers and Beholders in Shakespearean Drama," *Essays in Theatre* 3 (1984): 30–45.

151. Gosson, *Schoole of Abuse,* B₇r, cited in Worthen, *Idea of the Actor,* 22.

152. Cited in Chambers, *Elizabethan Stage,* 4:223, 254.

153. Michael Shapiro cites this epilogue, with its implied insult to the audience in the unmentioned but rhymingly possible last word, "fools," as an example of the boy actors' characteristically playful abuse of their audience. Michael **Shapiro**, *Children of the Revels: The Boy Companies of Shakespeare's Time and Their Plays* (New York: Columbia University Press, 1977), 45.

154. Bradbrook cites examples: Prodigality, in the Paul's play *Liberality and Prodigality* (1601), showers the audience with "buttercups—perhaps sweetmeats in this form"; Ceres casts comfits to the audience in Robert Wilson's *Cobbler's Prophecy* (1589–93 [1590]); at the Theatre (1584) "a huge rose opened to shower fireworks, white bread, pears and apples on the spectators, who scrambled for the prizes." Bradbrook, *Common Player,* 297 n. 1.

155. *Wily Beguiled* (1596–1606 [1602; Pro.1–4), in Hazlitt, *Old English Plays,* 9:221.

156. *Works of Thomas Nashe,* 3:236.

157. Ben **Jonson**, *Cynthia's Revels,* in *The Complete Plays of Ben Jonson,* ed. G. A. Wilkes (Oxford: Clarendon, 1981), 36. Klein's valuable collection of passages about actors, taken from sixteenth- and seventeenth-century plays, contains many references to similar phenomena, e.g., in the Thomas Tomkis's university play *Lin-*

gua (1607), where Communis Sensus tells the audience: "Leave jesting; you'lle put the Fresh Actor / out of countenance" (3.6). Klein, *Dramatists as Critics*, 229. See also, e.g., Sarpego in Chapman's *Gentleman Usher* [1602], who is so ashamed when he forgets his lines that he hides his face (*Usher* 2.1.203).

158. Any player, says Greene, being out of his part at his first entrance, is "faine to have the booke to speake what he should performe." Robert **Greene**, *Greens Groatsworth of Wit*, in *The Life and Complete Works in Prose and Verse of Robert Greene*, ed. Alexander B. **Grosart**, The Huth Library (London: Hazell, Watson, and Viney, 1881–83), 12:116–17.

159. T. G., *Rich Cabinet*, in Hazlitt, *English Drama and Stage*, 230.

160. Antony **Hammond**, ed., Introduction, *Richard III*, Arden Shakespeare (New York and London: Methuen, 1981), 113.

161. See Michail M. **Bakhtin**, *Rabelais and His World*, trans. Helene Iswolsky (Cambridge: M.I.T. Press, 1968), and Bristol, *Carnival and Theater*, for the "carnivalesque," and Willard **Farnham**, *The Shakespearean Grotesque: Its Genesis and Transformation* (Oxford: Clarendon Press, 1971), and Neil **Rhodes**, *Elizabethan Grotesque* (London and Boston: Routledge and Kegan Paul, 1980), for the "grotesque."

162. Kempe was said to be "Vice-gerent generall" to Tarlton, and one of Tarlton's jests tells of his adopting Armin (Nungezer, *Dictionary of Actors*, 216, 15–16). These anecdotes have been taken by some to indicate that Tarlton actually trained or officially named Kempe and Armin as successors, and this may be so. But the story about Armin in particular fits a generic pattern described by Ernst Kris, a "myth of origin" in which a young artist is rescued from oblivion by an artist who adopts him. Ernst **Kris**, "The Image of the Artist," in *Psychoanalytic Explorations in Art* (New York: International Universities Press, 1952), 64–86. Such myths serve more to indicate that a figure was unusually charismatic than that the incident really happened. Thomas Fuller's story about Tarlton himself being discovered in a field "keeping his father's swine" and brought to court because of his "*happy unhappy* answers" is probably closer to the story of Superman's birth than to the truth about Tarlton (Halliwell, *Tarlton's Jests*, ix). Among the early clowns, Robert Wilson, Tarlton, and Armin were writers, and Tarlton and Kempe were independent performers; the authors of *The Stage Players Complaint* (1641) were the clown actors Andrew Keyne and Timothy Reed. On the clown actor William Rowley's collaborations, see Bentley, *Profession of Dramatist*, 215–20; for the speculation that Robert Armin, rather than writing the entire *Two Maids of More-clacke* (1607–8 [1608]), which is attributed to him, merely added the clown's part, see J. A. B. **Somerset**, "Shakespeare's Great Stage of Fools, 1599–1607," in *Mirror up to Shakespeare: Essays in Honor of G. R. Hibbard*, ed. J. C. **Gray** (Toronto: University of Toronto Press, 1984), 74–76. Of the four players whose representative careers Bradbrook examines in her *Rise of the Common Player*, two and possibly a third are clowns; the clown is a major focus of studies—like Barber's and Weimann's—of the importance of popular theater in the Renaissance.

163. Wilhelm **Creizenach**, *The English Drama in the Age of Shakespeare* (New York: Haskell House, 1964), 184; Charles Read **Baskerville**, *The Elizabethan Jig and Related Song Drama* (1929; reprint, New York: Dover, 1965), 95.

164. Launce reenacts a tearful scene for us in Shakespeare's *Two Gentlemen of*

Verona (1590–98 [1593]); Creizenach also cites scenes in *Sir Thomas More* (1593–1601 [1595]) and *The Birth of Merlin* (1597–1621 [1608]). Creizenach, *Age of Shakespeare*, 299–300.

165. See also the Earl of Salisbury's letter referring to Tarlton's calling someone "a plaine clowne." Cited in Halliwell, *Tarlton's Jests*, xxxii.

166. Adams, however, was the man whom Tarlton's mother accused of duping her out of seven hundred pounds in Tarlton's will, a claim seemingly substantiated by Tarlton's letter asking Walsingham to protect her from Adams. (Nungezer, *Dictionary of Actors*, 352.) Jonson may have been joking ironically about Adam's off-stage attack on Tarlton rather than about his stage routines.

167. Gosson, *The Confutation of Playes* (1582), cited in Chambers, *Elizabethan Stage* 4:214; Tarlton is "quoted" in *Metamorphosis of Ajax*, cited in Halliwell, *Tarlton's Jests*, xxxi.

168. The title page attributes the play to "R.W.," assumed to be Robert Wilson. Cf. also J. Payne Collier, introduction to Hazlitt, *Old English Plays*, 6:12–13.

169. Hazlitt, *Old English Plays*, 6:327, 328.

170. Though the jests in Tarlton's own posthumously published jest book have been taken to indicate his style—e.g., by Wiles, *Shakespeare's Clown*, 12, 14—their aggressive humor resembles that in all jest book stories. They may therefore be as indicative of the genre as of his actual life. But they do suggest the myth that people associated with him as well as with the role he took on.

171. Cited in Halliwell, *Tarlton's Jests*, xxxi.

172. Halliwell, *Tarlton's Jests*, 13, 14. See also the excellent account of the aggression in the exchange in Wiles, *Shakespeare's Clown*, 14.

173. Robert Wilson's hungry clown Strumbo is similarly insulting. "What," he says to the audience he had last seen several scenes earlier, "Have you all escaped hanging?" (*Locrine*, 4.2.21–22). There are fewer anecdotes about Kempe, but one of the Shakespearean roles which we know he played, Dogberry in *Much Ado*, is based on Derick's clown scenes in the *Famous Victories of Henry V*, which starred Tarlton as Derick. I have not seen the connection between Tarlton's role and Kempe's mentioned, but a comparison of the lines in the two plays reveals the similarity of Dogberry's role—including his asshood—to Derick's:

> *Derick:* First, thou sayst true; I am an honest fellow—and a proper handsome
>   fellow too! Now, Gadshill, knowest thou me?
> *Cutter:* I know thee for an ass.
> *Derick:* And I know thee for a taking fellow upon Gad's Hill in Kent.

The Famous Victories of Henry the Fifth Containing the Honourable Battle of Agincourt in *The Oldcastle Controversy: "Sir John Oldcastle," Part 1 and "The Famous Victories of Henry V,"* ed. Peter **Cobin** and Douglas **Sedge** (Manchester: Manchester University Press, 1991), 154 (2.2.45–61). It is also possible, of course, that our text of *Famous Victories* was affected by *Much Ado*.

174. Cited in Joel **Schecter**, *Durov's Pig, Clowns, Politics, and Theatre* (New York: Theatre Communications Group, 1985), 15.

175. For Weimann the clown amicably unified the protester with those in command: the clowns' popular routines travestied the authorities, while establishing a

utopian equality with the appreciative audience, eradicating all manner of "difference"; Weimann, *Popular Tradition*, 186–88. But Bristol's Bakhtinian analysis argues that the clowns articulated greater rejection of traditional hierarchy; Bristol, *Carnival and Theater*, 140–50. Annabel Patterson has recently suggested that Shakespeare uses his clowns to represent a sophisticated, self-aware, populist movement; Patterson, *Popular Voice*, 32–51. But Wiles sees Shakespeare turning away from populism when he and Kempe split and Shakespeare started writing his clown plots for the more elitist Armin.

176. See Weimann, *Popular Tradition*, on the public theater, Shapiro, *Children of the Revels*, on how the "playful" flattery and abuse in coterie theaters established a tie between performer and audience, and chapter 6.

177. In Leishmann, *Parnassus Plays*, 135–36 (Pro.1–4, 14–16). Other prologues provide occasion for similar observations. Marston's urbane Prologue to *The Fawn* (Queen's Revels, ca. 1604), for example, parodies the genre and its "base soothings":

> For we do know that this most fair filled room
> Is loaden with most Attic judgments, ablest spirits,
> Then whom there are none more exact, full, strong,
> Yet none more soft, benign in censoring.
> I know there's not one ass in all this presence,
> Not one calumnious rascal, or base villain
> Of emptiest merit, that would tax and slander
> If innocency herself should write, not one we know't.
>   O you are all the very breath of Phoebus.

Cited as an example of ironic praise in Shapiro, *Children of the Revels*, 44.

178. William **Rankins**, *Mirrour of Monsters*, ed. Arthur Freeman (New York and London: Garland, 1973), E_1. "Vitriolic" is the editor's term.

179. Middleton, *Mad World* (5.1.55–57). See also *Histriomastix* (1.1) and the excerpts from T. G., *Rich Cabinet*, in Hazlitt, *English Drama and Stage*.

180. The Epilogue's status was of course ambiguous; speaking lines set down for him, he could not have been as spontaneously sincere as he pretended to be. But he clearly spoke more for the author (in some cases) or for himself than any other character in the play, and he distinguished himself from the play world even if he remained partially in character. Staines comes forward at the end of John Cooke's *Greene's Tu Quoque; or, The City Gallant* (1611), for example, to distinguish between what he has done to the other characters and what he has thereby done to the audience: "That I have cheated through the play, 'tis true: / But yet I hope I have not cheated you"; Hazlitt, *Old English Plays*, 11:289. Other Epilogues made it clear that at some point they stopped speaking for their author and began speaking in their own right. The epilogue to Barry's *Ram Alley* begins by saying that the author here submits his play for the audience's judgment, and then goes on: "And for ourselves [the players] we do desire, / You'll breathe on us that glowing fire, / By which in time we may obtain / Like favors which some others gain"; Hazlitt, *Old English Plays*, 10:380.

181. Of course Prospero may merely be asking the audience to pray for him, as

well as to applaud, and when he reminds them that they too "would pardon'd be" from crimes, he can hardly be addressing divinity. But it does sound as if he were praying to them, and that they were the original divine source of indulgence.

Chapter Three

1. Antony Holden, *Laurence Olivier,* 294. Cf. "[in the early history plays] portraiture balances or even tends to outweigh event, and what remains with one over the years is more likely to be an impression of personalities rather than of what happens to them"; Marco **Mincoff,** *Shakespeare: The First Steps* (Sofia: Bulgarian Academy of Sciences, 1976), 67.

2. Anne Righter, *Idea of the Play,* 88. Richard's resemblance to an actor is a critical commonplace. See, e.g., A. P. **Rossiter,** *Angel with Horns and Other Lectures on Shakespeare,* ed. Graham Storey (London: Longman's, 1961), 16–19; Peter Ure, "Character and Role from *Richard III* to *Hamlet,*" in *Elizabethan and Jacobean Drama,* ed. J. C. **Maxwell** (Liverpool: Liverpool University Press, 1974), 22–43; and Thomas F. **Van Laan,** *Role-Playing in Shakespeare* (Toronto: University of Toronto Press, 1978).

3. Muriel Bradbrook notes that Burbage's arms featured a thrice repeated boar, and while the animal may have been chosen as a pun on his name, Burbage may also have been influenced by the fact that "the badge of Richard III, who supplied Burbage's first famous part, was a boar." Bradbrook, *Common Player,* xi.

4. See Nicholas **Brooke,** "Marlowe as Provocative Agent in Shakespeare's Early Plays," *Shakespeare Survey* 14 (1961): 34–44.

5. He even dismisses the pallbearer with the scornful epithet "beggar!" (*R3* 1.2.42) as if to make a distinction between himself and such creatures.

6. Harold F. **Brooks,** "*Richard III,* Unhistorical Amplifications: The Women's Scenes and Seneca," *Modern Language Review* 75 (1980): 721–37, esp. 728–29.

7. Wolfgang **Clemen,** *A Commentary on Shakespeare's "Richard III,"* trans. Jean Bonheim (London: Methuen, 1957), 19. Clemen quotes J. Dover Wilson, who was quoting C. H. Herford.

8. Richard of course merely exaggerates the traditional attack rhetoric of courtship. See Armado's triumphant letter to Jaquenetta, likening himself to Caesar: "I came, I saw, I overcame" (*LLL* 4.1.71), discussed in chapter 4.

9. Barber and Wheeler, *Whole Journey,* 111–12.

10. Barber and Wheeler, *Whole Journey,* 111.

11. Barber and Wheeler, *Whole Journey,* 86. They compare the equally villainous Barabas, who has no past; Barber and Wheeler, 91. See also Wheeler's earlier essay arguing for the importance of Richard's birth and infancy in shaping the adult traits described in the play; Richard P. **Wheeler,** "History, Character and Conscience in *Richard III,*" *Comparative Drama* 4 (1971–72): 301–21.

12. Michael Neill argues that the Duchess rejected Richard and failed to mirror back to him an acceptable image of himself. She thus left him, Neill suggests, with only a shattered sense of himself and an estrangement from himself that made it natural for him both to act and to shape his life like a play. Michael **Neill,** "Shake-

speare's Halle of Mirrors: Play, Politics, and Psychology in *Richard III*," *Shakespeare Studies* 8 (1975): 99–129.

13. So exaggerated is York's rhetoric that, as David Riggs points out, when he goes off like a Hotspur, Clifford's response is one of puzzled amazement: "To Bedlam with him! Is the man grown mad?" (*2H6* 5.1.131). David **Riggs,** *Shakespeare's Heroical Histories* (Cambridge: Harvard University Press, 1971), 177.

14. See chapter 8 for an analysis of this scene.

15. Barber and Wheeler, *Whole Journey,* 112, calls her "the original mirror of earliest infancy."

16. Harold F. Brooks notes that Shakespeare would have learned from Hall's and Holinshed's Chronicles that the Duchess outlived Richard, but "to include the Duchess [in *Richard III*] was by no means an inevitable or even a very obvious idea." Brooks, "Women's Scenes," 723.

17. Richard also sees himself as witched: "Edward's wife, that monstrous witch, / Consorted with that harlot, strumpet Shore, / That by their witchcraft thus have marked me" (*R3* 3.4.70–72).

18. Cf. the brew in the Three Sisters' cauldron in *Macbeth,* with its "finger of birth-strangled babe" (*Mac.* 4.1.30).

19. Janet Adelman has suggested the degree to which Richard's deformity is generated by his—and Shakespeare's—sense of being tainted by his origin in a feared and hated maternal body; Janet **Adelman,** *Suffocating Mothers* (New York: Routledge, 1992). But in Shakespeare's legend about Richard's birth, we can perhaps also glimpse an opposing identification with the female's fear of men, revealed in a mother's recoil from her son, or from his masculinity. Though not the only factor in the creation of the legend about Richard, such recoil may nonetheless find expression in it. (Barber and Wheeler note the Duchess's related tendency to stifle Richard and thwart his self-expression by asking him to be someone he clearly is not—someone meek and gentle; Barber and Wheeler, *Whole Journey,* 112.)

20. Barber and Wheeler, *Whole Journey,* 116. Richard's own declaration of villainous ambition at the end of *Henry VI, Part Three* follows after he watched—again hidden—when Edward, with his queen, kissed his infant son and promised him the crown (*3H6* 5.7.19). Richard, looking on as an outsider, sounds jealous of the baby rival, as well as of his adult brother: "I'll blast his harvest; and your head were laid" (*3H6* 5.7.21). Here Shakespeare juxtaposes "the cherishing of an infant to Richard's alienation" (Barber and Wheeler, *Whole Journey,* 113). It is precisely such a moment that drives Macbeth over the edge, when Duncan elevates Malcolm as crown prince.

21. "The scene might almost be a preliminary study for the Richard-Anne scene; here too we have a widow who first rebuffs (indeed, fails to grasp) the king's demands. Here, too, there is stichomythia, with matching words and phrasing, interrupted by dialogue in different rhythms, by longer speeches of several lines, by terse and direct statements"; Clemen, *Shakespeare's "Richard III,"* 42, 11.

22. As he watches their billing and cooing, he imagines a "wanton multiplication of claimants to the throne" which seems "as much an affront to Richard's sexual capacity as it is to his ambition"; Neill, "Halle of Mirrors," 104. See also Barber and Wheeler, *Whole Journey,* 95–96.

23. The two younger women Richard courts are also in mourning, and, as we have seen, Anne's sorrow at the funeral makes his conquest of her emotions especially satisfying to him. Many of the women are mourning people Richard has killed. Shakespeare at this time seemed interested in the courtship of a mourning woman by a somewhat unsavory young man. In *Two Gentlemen of Verona*, written perhaps a year or so after *Richard III*, the Machiavellian Proteus courts Silvia with echoes of the protean Richard courting Lady Anne (*TGV* 4.2.82–136). Proteus has not actually killed Silvia's fiancé (and Proteus's best friend), Valentine, but he did have Valentine banished, and he does—in one of the play's oddest moments—go on to *claim* that "Valentine is dead" (*TGV* 4.3.109) as a way of excusing his courtship. "This excuse," Clifford Leech comments with some distaste, "is so feeble that it reflects from the incompetence of Proteus to that of the dramatist"; Clifford **Leech**, *The Two Gentlemen of Verona*, Arden Shakespeare (London: Methuen, 1969), 90 n. 109. Silvia is even more adamantly repulsed by Proteus than Anne was by Richard. She even takes up Anne's rhythms: her "Return, return, and make thy love amends" (*TGV* 4.2.96) reworks Anne's "Set down, set down your honorable load" (*R3* 1.2.1). She finally relents and agrees to give him her picture, just as Anne took Richard's ring. Like Richard (and Shakespeare?), Proteus finds that Silvia's hatred only makes him love her the more: "Spaniel-like, the more she spurns my love, / The more it grows and fawneth on her still" (*TGV* 4.2.15–16).

24. Brooks, "Women's Scenes," 724. On Hecuba see also Harry **Levin**, *The Question of Hamlet* (New York: Viking, 1961), 141–54; Lizette I. **Westney**, "Hecuba in Sixteenth-Century Literature," *CLA Journal* 27 (1984): 436–59.

25. Wheeler, "History, Character and Conscience," 314.

26. Wheeler, "History, Character and Conscience," 313. Richard had boasted that he could "cry 'Content!' to that that grieves my heart" but already in the next line sees himself crying "artificial tears" instead of the real ones he's repressed (*3H6* 3.2.182–83). His griefs betray themselves, and his need for love remains. Richard's final "despair" arises not only from conscience but from the realization that "there is no creature loves me" (*R3* 5.3.201).

27. Again political expediency seems to mask or at least to coincide with more personal needs.

28. Some have read this pronouncement as a merely opportunistic rationale. See, e.g., Carolyn **Heilbrun**'s review of the Shakespeare in the Park *Richard III* with Denzel Washington (*New York Times*, 12 August 1990, sec. 2), which suggests that Richard uses his deformity as an excuse, and is really driven by a (motiveless?) male lust for power. But Richard's lust for the crown also makes sense as an example of what we would now call the displacement of desire.

29. Janet **Adelman**, "Fantasies of Maternal Power in *Macbeth*," in *Cannibals, Witches and Divorce: Estranging the Renaissance*, Papers from the English Institute, n.s. 11 (Baltimore: Johns Hopkins University Press, 1987), 90. Revised and incorporated in chapters 1 and 6 of Adelman, *Suffocating Mothers*.

30. Adelman, "Fantasies of Maternal Power," 90, rewritten in *Suffocating Mothers*, 2. Later Edward will evoke another thorny manifestation of the female power that stifles ambition, when he calls Queen Margaret a "thorny wood / Which . . . /

Must by the roots be hewn up" (*3H6* 5.4.67–69). Cf. Birnham Wood in *Macbeth*, which closes in on Macbeth just as the witches said it would.

31. Ralph **Berry**, "Metamorphoses of the Stage," in *Shakespeare and the Awareness of the Audience* (London: Macmillan, 1985), 1–15.

32. Berry, *Awareness of the Audience*, 7.

33. In light of the way Richard's aggressive theatrics can prove dangerous to himself, it is curious that the very words Richard uses cynically to describe the actor's ability to deceive others are the words used by Theseus in *A Midsummer Night's Dream* to describe the amateur actor's painful attack of stage fright. Richard, plotting with Buckingham, coaches him in deception:

> Come, cousin, canst thou quake and change thy colour,
> Murder thy breath in middle of a word,
> And then again begin, and stop again,
> As if thou were distraught and mad with terror?

(R3 3.5.1–4)

Compare Theseus's benevolently patronizing remarks on the learned scholars too frightened to greet him with their prepared speeches:

> Where I have come, great clerks have purposed
> To greet me with premeditated welcomes;
> Where I have seen them shiver and look pale,
> Make periods in the midst of sentences,
> Throttle their practis'd accents in their fears,
> And, in conclusion, dumbly, have broke off.

(MND 5.1.93–98)

What Richard takes to be signs of Machiavellian hypocrisy, Theseus sees as signs of pure terror.

34. Richard Wheeler's phrase for reading life and text against one another; personal communication.

35. *John Aubrey's Brief Lives*, ed. Oliver Lawson **Dick** (London: Secker and Warburg, 1949), 275.

36. If this is indeed what Nashe is alluding to in his preface to Greene's *Menaphon; Works of Thomas Nashe*, 3:311.

37. Schoenbaum, *Documentary Life*, 74; Peter **Dwyer**, "William Shakespeare's First Performance: An Entertainment for Spectators," *Stratford Papers on Shakespeare 1961*, ed. B. W. **Jackson** (Toronto: W. J. Gage, 1962), 58–77; Douglas **Hamer**, review of S. Schoenbaum's *Shakespeare's Lives, Review of English Studies* 22 (1971): 484. Otherwise we do not know much about the show except that it was considered acceptable entertainment for a five-year-old child—which might explain Hamlet's scornful reference to killing "so capital a calf" in order to insult that second-time child, Polonius (*Ham.* 3.2.104). Considering Shakespeare's later sympathy for slaughtered animals in the plays, this would be a particularly significant form of violence; see Dwyer, "First Performance."

38. This specific variety of clowning—turning aggression to laughter—would have been natural to Richard.

39. Cf. C. L. Barber, *Festive Comedy*, 5. Many have found Christopher Sly in *The Taming of the Shrew* as good as anything Shakespeare created, Cade's scenes in *Henry VI, Part Two* stand out, and Launce's is the most polished part of *The Two Gentlemen of Verona*.

40. Emrys Jones, *Scenic Form in Shakespeare* (Oxford: Clarendon, 1971), 12.

41. Alexander Leggatt, "Shakespeare and the Actor's Body," *Renaissance and Reformation*, n.s., 10 (1986): 100.

42. If the Poet says to the young man, "My glass shall not persuade me I am old / So long as youth and thou are of one date" (Son. 22), Richard says to Anne, in effect, my glass shall not persuade me I am ugly, so long as you love me.

43. J. A. B. Somerset argues that Armin's stage appearances as fool suggest variety rather than a particular acting "line" of the wise fool, and that the fools about whom Armin wrote before he worked with Shakespeare were not like Shakespeare's. The wise fools were created by Shakespeare, he concludes, not Armin. "Shakespeare was to transcend, not imitate the recorded tradition"; Somerset, "Stage of Fools," 68–81, 77.

44. David Wiles has collected evidence from Armin's known roles of his ability to juggle multiple personalities. Based on allusions in the same play texts, Wiles argues that Armin was physically, though not mentally, a natural fool himself, with a "deformed body," and that he "had a physical affinity with dogs in particular"; Wiles, *Shakespeare's Clown*, 139, 147–48. Wiles is concerned to point out Armin's contributions to the roles Shakespeare created for him. Armin's resemblance to the Vice-like Richard whom Shakespeare had already imagined, however, as well as other continuities between the early plays and the wise fools, suggests that, on the contrary, Shakespeare contributed a good deal indeed to the collaboration. Cf. Somerset, "Stage of Fools," n. 43.

45. The fascination with deformity was more culturally conditioned in a society that kept dwarves and fools for amusement. Armin himself—though known for playing wise fools—was more interested in such "naturals" as Blue John (whom he is said to have created), who were made the butt of other people's wit, than in sophisticated performers like Touchstone or Feste who wittily exposed everyone else. Armin's *Nest of Ninnies* is devoted almost entirely to the ill-fated adventures of naturals.

46. Such creatures serve entire cultures as well as individual psyches, as in the "hunchback dance" of clowns among the Great Basin peoples in America. Catherine S. Fowler, "The Hunchback Dance of the Northern Paiute and Other Clown Performances of the Great Basin," in *Anthropology of the Desert West: Essays in Honor of Jesse D. Jennings*, edited by Carol J. Condie and Don D. Fowler, *Anthropological Papers* 110 (Salt Lake City: University of Utah Press, 1986), 217–28.

47. Natalie Davis, "On the Lame," *American Historical Review* 93 (1988): 572–601, esp. 574; Davis is talking about recreating the lives of real historical figures.

48. The following sketch is based on standard accounts in Chambers, *Shakespeare: A Study*. Edgar I. Fripp, *Shakespeare: Man and Artist* (Oxford: Oxford University Press; London: Humphrey Milford, 1938); Mark Eccles, *Shakespeare in Warwickshire* (Madison: University of Wisconsin Press, 1963); and Schoenbaum, *Documentary Life*.

49. Schoenbaum, *Documentary Life*, 38.

50. By the end of 1578 he had entered into a complicated legal arrangement concerning his wife's inheritance, a house, and land in Wilmcote. The property was mortgaged to his brother-in-law for two years and simultaneously leased to another man for twenty-one years, an arrangement that seems to have been intended to pay off two debts at once. Other sales of family property for unusually small sums followed. John was apparently hoping for an improvement in his circumstances, but when the Wilmcote mortgage came due in 1580, he did not—in all likelihood could not—redeem the property; nineteen years later he was still struggling over it in the courts. Eric **Poole**, "John and Mary Shakespeare and the Aston Cantlow Mortgage," *Cahiers élisabéthains* 17 (1980): 21–41.

51. Indeed "everyone of any substance in Tudor and Stuart England was in debt . . . it was not unusual for people to be creditors and debtors simultaneously"; MacDonald, *Mystical Bedlam*, 67.

52. MacDonald, *Mystical Bedlam*, 67.

53. *Errors* is dated 1590–94 [1592]. In 1591 and 1592 John Shakespeare's name was included on a list of persons absenting themselves from church and assumed to do so "for fear of process for debt," cited in Shoenbaum, *Documentary Life*, 42.

54. The phrase comes from Barber and Wheeler, who make a detailed and convincing argument for the links between the play and its biographical context; Barber and Wheeler, *Whole Journey*, 79–84. See their point about the debtor's concern for what his wife will think of his public humiliation.

55. Padel called attention to the possible importance of John's problems for Shakespeare's work; Joseph **Padel**, "That the Thought of Hearts Can Mend," *TLS*, 19 December 1975, 1519–21. Padel's thesis has been elaborated and refined by several critics, most notably C. L. Barber and Richard P. Wheeler.

56. What devastation can be wreaked on a sensitive child by the sudden collapse of a beloved father—and the attendant collapse of the family's status—we know from the story of Charles Dickens, whose view of the world was permanently shaped by his father's disgrace. The real facts do not necessarily matter. Even relatively mild disillusionment can generate—as it did for Dickens—an exaggerated picture of misfortune that leaves lasting scars, as well as generating a series of fictional Micawber-ish failures at fatherhood. In Dickens this loss seems to have fostered a particularly theatrical creativity. He was something of an infant prodigy, shown off by his proud father. Like many of the actors cited earlier, Dickens apparently inherited or adopted his mother's "astonishing" power of imitation; *Lippincott's Magazine* (1874), cited by Michael **Allen**, *The Childhood of Dickens* (London: St. Martin's Press, 1988), 58. Though Dickens was primarily a novelist and journalist, his work drew on Victorian popular theater and he himself could have been a gifted actor—perhaps one of the most gifted of his period. Even after he was established as a successful writer, Dickens remained passionately committed to giving the dramatic readings which eventually proved too strenuous and all but literally killed him. They allowed him to realize parts of himself that had to be suppressed in ordinary life, and they provided a direct and intimate contact with his supportive audience which even serial writing could not supply. It should not be surprising that the violent conjunction of two different lives—the relatively idyl-

lic early childhood and the adolescent poverty and disgrace—would not only have disrupted a sense of himself but would also have nurtured the ability to step aside from any subsequent self to create another onstage. For Dickens and acting, see Carol Hanbery **MacKay**, ed., *Dramatic Dickens* (New York: St. Martin's Press, 1989), especially Jean Ferguson **Carr**, "Dicken's Theatre of Self-Knowledge."

57. Steven R. **Smith**, "The London Apprentices as Seventeenth-Century Adolescents," *Past and Present* 61 (1973): 149–61. Smith cites Davis's claim, above. See also Paul S. Seaver's account of "what we would probably define as late adolescent identity crises," which were "reasonably commonplace" in the late sixteenth and early seventeenth centuries. Seaver's account of the crises recorded in the diaries of Nehemiah Wallington (1598–1658), London Puritan artisan, is in Paul S. **Seaver**, *Wallington's World: A Puritan Artisan in Seventeenth-Century London* (Stanford: Stanford University Press, 1985), 15ff.

58. Both the "battlefields of France" and the "nine worthies" would also provide raw material for Shakespeare's early heroical plays about "manly virtues." See chapter 4.

59. Avi Ehrlich suggests that there are an unusual number of such failures; Avi **Ehrlich**, *Hamlet's Absent Father* (Princeton: Princeton University Press, 1977).

60. Kohut, *Analysis of the Self*, cited in Barber and Wheeler, *Whole Journey*, 51, refers to an "intense object hunger."

61. Ehrlich, *Hamlet's Absent Father.*

62. Sundelson described Shakespeare's response to absence in David **Sundelson**, *Shakespeare's Restorations of the Father* (New Brunswick: Rutgers University Press, 1983). See also Barber and Wheeler, *Whole Journey*, and Coppélia **Kahn**, *Man's Estate: Masculine Identity in Shakespeare* (Berkeley: University of California Press, 1981).

63. Barber and Wheeler, *Whole Journey*, 48, 53. The importance of this configuration may also help illuminate Shakespeare's interest in the anonymous play *Arden of Faversham* [1591]. *Arden* dramatizes a true story in which a nouveau riche milquetoastian landlord is murdered by his highborn wife Alice Arden and her lover; Shakespeare draws on it for her portraits of Lady Macbeth, of Rosalind dressed as a boy in the forest of Arden, and of the shrewish Aemelia in *The Comedy of Errors*. Whether or not his mother Mary Arden resembled them, these daughters of Alice Arden were stronger than their men, or tried to be.

64. Lawrence **Stone**, *The Family, Sex and Marriage in England 1500–1800* (New York: Harper and Row, 1977), 115.

65. David Balk cites the case of one boy whose "major aim" after his sister died "was to get away from his home and begin life on his own"; David **Balk**, "Adolescents' Grief Reactions and Self-Concept Following Sibling Death: A Study of Thirty-Three Teenagers," *Journal of Youth and Adolescence* 12 [1983]: 137–61, 157. See also Albert C. **Cain**, Irene **Foot**, and Mary **Erickson**, "Children's Disturbed Reactions to the Death of a Sibling," *American Journal of Orthopsychiatry* 34 (1964): 741–52; and George H. **Pollack**, "On Siblings, Sibling Loss and Creativity," *The Annual of Psychoanalysis* 6 (1978): 443–81.

66. It is interesting that Laurence Olivier chose to open his autobiography with an anecdote about the painful "loss" of an older brother (though only to service in

India, not to death), immediately followed by his father's giving Laurence permission to become an actor; Olivier, *Confessions of an Actor,* 19.

67. Assuming that Shakespeare felt the significance of birthdays as did his Cassius in *Julius Caesar.*

68. Fripp, *Man and Artist,* 146. Ophelia's *brother* Laertes is her most ostentatious mourner.

69. Stone, *Family, Sex and Marriage,* 99, 105–15, 208–15.

70. E.g., MacDonald, *Mystical Bedlam,* Ralph A. **Houlbrouke,** *The English Family 1450–1700* (London and New York: Longman, 1984); Linda A. **Pollock,** *Forgotten Children: Parent-Child Relations from 1500 to 1900* (Cambridge: Cambridge University Press, 1984).

71. MacDonald, *Mystical Bedlam,* 82.

72. "The choice of godparents was used to strengthen friendship, reinforce kinship"; Houlbrouke, *English Family,* 131.

73. Albert C. **Cain** and Barbara S. **Cain,** "On Replacing a Child," *Journey of the Academy of Child Psychiatry* 3 (1964): 443–56; Cecily **Legg** and Ivan **Sherick,** "The Replacement Child—A Developmental Tragedy: Some Preliminary Comments," *Child Psychiatry and Human Development* 7 (1976): 113–26.

74. MacDonald's phrase, *Mystical Bedlam,* 76.

75. Phyllis **Greenacre,** "The Childhood of the Artist: Libidinal Phase Development and Giftedness," *The Psychoanalytic Study of the Child* 12 (1957), 47–72.

76. Cf. Donald **Silver,** "The Dark Lady: Sibling Loss and Mourning in the Shakespearean Sonnets," *Psychoanalytic Inquiry* 3 (1983): 513–27.

77. The replacement child's dilemma is complicated by guilt; replacement children are even less inclined than firstborns to overt competition with rivals: how can you fight someone who might die as the others had?

78. Schoenbaum, *Documentary Life,* 27.

79. Joan and Margaret are the two women who haunt the heroes of *The Henriad.*

80. Napier notes, for example, that one mother who had lost a four-year-old "took no comfort from the child she was nursing," MacDonald, *Mystical Bedlam,* 82.

81. Harris argues that mothers' attitudes towards firstborn sons differed from fathers' attitudes; Barbara J. **Harris,** "Property, Power, and Personal Relations: Elite Mothers and Sons in Yorkist and Early Tudor England," *Signs* 15 (1990): 606–32.

82. Patricia **Crawford,** "'The Suckling Child': Adult Attitude to Child Care in the First Year of Life in Seventeenth-Century England," *Continuity and Change* 1 (1986): 28–29. This is not to deny that other aspects of pregnancy were painful or frightening. See, e.g., Linda A. **Pollock,** "Embarking on a Rough Passage: The Experience of Pregnancy in Early Modern England" in *Women as Mothers in Pre-Industrial England: Essays in Memory of Dorothy McLaren,* ed. Valerie **Fildes** (London and New York: Routledge, 1990), 39–67.

83. See Robert **Harmon,** Anita **Glicken,** and Roberta **Siegel,** "Neonatal Loss in the Intensive Care Nursery: Effects of Maternal Grieving and a Program for Intervention," *Journal of the American Academy of Child Psychiatry* 23 (1984): 68–71, for discussion and bibliography.

84. MacDonald, *Mystical Bedlam,* 41 n. 91, 266, 82. Houlbrouke argues that the deaths of babies, painful though they often are, are easier to come to terms with

than those of older children. He cites Ralph Josselin's ability to overcome grief at the death of a ten-day-old son because the boy was "the youngest, and our affections not so wonted unto it"; Houlbrouke, *English Family,* 136. Even such "reasoning," however, could not apply when the lost child was the first or only one, especially if others had died before.

85. Legg and Sherick, "Replacement Child," 115.

86. See chapter 5 for possible traces of Shakespeare's replacement status in his *Merry Wives of Windsor.*

87. See Louis Adrian **Montrose**, "'The Place of a Brother' in *As You Like It*: Social Process and Comic Form," *Shakespeare Quarterly* 32 (1981): 28–54; the Girardian analysis in Joel **Fineman**, "Fratricide and Cuckoldry: Shakespeare's Doubles," in *Representing Shakespeare: New Psychoanalytic Essays,* ed. Murray M. **Schwartz** and Coppélia **Kahn** (Baltimore: Johns Hopkins University Press, 1980), 70–109; Marjorie **Garber**, *Coming of Age in Shakespeare* (New York: Methuen, 1981); all cited in Marianne **Novy**, "Shakespeare and the Bonds of Brotherhood," in Holland, Homan, and Paris, *Shakespeare's Personality,* 103–115.

88. Novy, "Bonds of Brotherhood," 106.

89. Marianne **Novy**, *Love's Argument: Gender Relations in Shakespeare* (Chapel Hill: University of North Carolina Press, 1984), 188. Perhaps influenced by Shakespeare's daughter's pregnancy and the birth of his first grandchild?

90. He compensates for his distance from her by telling her a story in her ear, displacing bodily contact with verbal exchange, as a future writer might learn to do when displaced by a sibling on his mother's lap.

91. Barber and Wheeler, *Whole Journey,* 44.

92. Sigmund Freud, "A Childhood Recollection from *Dichtung und Wahrheit*" (1917), cited in Hilda S. **Rollman-Branch**, "The First Born Child, Male: Vicissitudes in Pre-oedipal Problems," *International Journal of Psychoanalysis* 47 (1966): 404–15. Rollman-Branch studies the lives of gifted artists who were ousted from the privileged position of firstborn. She suggests that in gifted individuals, the ouster constitutes an exaggerated narcissistic injury and arouses intense rage and envy. In defense, the child identifies with "the life-giving and life-saving mother." The child is driven to exploit his own intellectual and creative resources, so that he too, like his mother, can produce. The association between biological and creative pregnancy, labor, and giving birth is also common among adults, of course. Rollman-Branch, "First Born Child, Male," 409.

93. Although Juliet has no living rival to take part in this upheaval, the play does insist—oddly—on the deaths not only of Juliet's siblings ("Earth hath swallowed all my hopes but she," says Capulet; *Rom.* 1.2.14), but also of her rival-twin, the Nurse's daughter Susan, who was "of an age" with Juliet (*Rom.* 1.3.19). The Nurse mentions Susan only once, just at the moment that she mentions weaning Juliet. In both sibling competitions, Juliet was the only survivor.

94. The fact that the children are nearly all girls does not rule them out as media for expressing Shakespeare's own concerns—quite the contrary.

95. This is especially true for sensitive and gifted children, Rollman-Branch argues; Rollman-Branch, "First Born Child, Male," 412–13.

96. Symbol of the forces of "good" which will overcome Macbeth's guilty ambition (*Mac.* 1.7.21).

97. C. L. Barber speaks of the "cherishing role of the parents" and "maternal, cherishing attitudes"; C. L. **Barber**, "The Family in Shakespeare's Development: Tragedy and Sacredness," in Schwartz and Kahn, *Representing Shakespeare,* 188–202, 190.

98. But see E. A. J. Honigman on a less idolatrous image of his character; E. A. J. **Honigman**, *Shakespeare: The Lost Years* (Manchester, N.H.: Manchester University Press, 1985).

99. Norman Holland describes Conrad van Emde Boas's theory about Shakespeare's denial of hostility toward his brother and his identification with his rival instead. "Van Emde Boas applies this model to the Sonnets. Barber and Wheeler and Marianne Novy suggest that it also accounts for Shakespeare's negative capability, his astonishing power to understand the 'other' and imagine stage characters at once like and unlike his real self"; Norman N. Holland, Introduction to Holland, Homan, and Paris, *Shakespeare's Personality,* 1–16, 9–10.

100. Barber and Wheeler, *Whole Journey,* 63. Throughout their study of Shakespeare's life and work, Barber and Wheeler return to the central question of what Shakespeare did with his aggression and to their suggestive exploration of "theatrical aggression." See also David B. **Barron**, "*Coriolanus*: Portrait of the Artist as Infant," *American Imago* 19 (1962): 171–93; and Holland, Introduction, Sherman **Hawkins**, "Aggression and the Project of the Histories," and Kirby **Farrell**, "Love, Death, and Patriarchy in *Romeo and Juliet*" in Holland, Homan, and Paris, *Shakespeare's Personality.*

101. See chapters 4–6 on the former and chapter 7 on the latter.

102. See chapter 2.

103. Anne seems to have conceived William's child within a year of her father's death. He was buried November 1581; Susanna was born May 1583, thus conceived August 1582. One year is the period of mourning specified in *Love's Labour's Lost* when an overeager young Navarre seeks to impose marriage on a mourning princess.

104. Barber and Wheeler note that Richard's wooing of Anne "mimes Petrarchan hyperbole in a sadomasochistic way"; Barber and Wheeler, *Whole Journey,* 102.

105. Andrew Gurr's speculation that the sonnet was written for Anne is based on the couplet's labored diction, which might be explained as a pun on "Hath-away"; Andrew **Gurr**, "Shakespeare's First Poem: Sonnet 145," *Essays in Criticism* 21 (1971): 221–26, cited in Schoenbaum, *Documentary Life,* 91. Schoenbaum, agreeing, adds that in Elizabethan pronunciation, "And saved my life" would have sounded just like "Anne saved my life."

106. Thirty-one percent of pregnancies recorded between 1550 and 1599 in sixteen English parishes in one study were prenuptial pregnancies; Peter **Laslett**, Karla **Oosterveen**, and Richard M. **Smith**, eds., *Bastardy and Its Comparative History* (Cambridge: Harvard University Press, 1980), 23.

107. See, e.g., Stone, *Family, Sex and Marriage,* 104; Keith **Wrightson**, *English Society, 1580–1680* (London: Hutchinson, 1982), 69; and Alan **MacFarlane**, *Mar-*

riage and Love in England, 1300–1840 (Oxford: B. Blackwell, 1986), 91–102, esp. 94–95.

108. It is just possible that Anne's dowry made her welcome—perhaps even sought after—and that the young Shakespeares were paying tenants. But this does not preclude less rational motives.

109. Recent biographers and chronologies of the plays push the dates of Shakespeare's earliest work—and, by implication, of his prior acting experience—back into the 1580s.

110. Schoenbaum cites the evidence: Nicholas Rowe says that "the top of his performance was the ghost in his own *Hamlet*," Oldys and Edward Capell say he played Adam in *As You Like It,* and Shakespeare is listed first among the "principal comediens" in Jonson's *Every Man in His Humour* in 1598 and included in the cast list of *Sejanus* in 1603; Schoenbaum, *Documentary Life,* 201–3. In addition, Kenneth Muir, analyzing Shakespeare's distribution of quotations from the old *King Leir* play in his own *King Lear,* suggests that Shakespeare may have played Perillus, the Kent figure, in the old play; Kenneth **Muir,** ed., Introduction, in *King Lear,* Arden Shakespeare (London: Methuen, 1964), xxix.

Chapter Four

1. Studies of theatrical self-consciousness usually include other phenomena among the "plays-within-plays." For example, they include induction plays or framed plays like *The Taming of the Shrew,* as well as plays-within-plays proper (e.g., the one in *Sir Thomas More*). Plays with prologues are sometimes included if, as in the case of Heywood's *Four Prentices of London* (1592–1600 [1600]), the prologue is extended. However, of the numerous plays included among the induction and prologue plays, about half, like *The Rare Triumphs of Love and Fortune* (1582), do not represent an actual theatrical performance; instead ghosts watch humans (as in *The Spanish Tragedy*), or humans watch ghosts (as in *The Second Part of the Seven Deadly Sins* [1585, revived 1590, 1592]) or other creatures (as in Peele's *Old Wives Tale* [1588–94 (1590)]). In addition many of the inner plays proper are really masques rather than plays (like the masque in Tourneur's *Revenger's Tragedy* [1607]), performed by the characters for one another, rather than being performed by characters specifically designated as either professional or amateur players.

In other words, what we refer to as "the play within a play" varied widely in form and function, depending on when it was performed (1516–1642), and on what sort of stage. (The ones most often cited are: Thomas Kyd, *The Spanish Tragedy* [1582–92 (1589)]; Anthony Munday, *John a Kent and John a Cumber* [1587–90 (1589)]; Munday et al., *Sir Thomas More* [1593–1601 (1595)]; Thomas Nashe, *Summer's Last Will and Testament* [1592]; Chettle and Munday, *The Downfall* [1598] and *The Death of Robert, Earl of Huntingdon* [1598]; John Marston, *Histriomastix* [1598–99 (1599) but possibly a revision of an earlier play], *Antonio's Revenge* [1599], and *The Malcontent* [1600–4 (1604)]; Cyril Tourneur, *The Revenger's Tragedy* [1606–7 (1606)]; Francis Beaumont, *The Maid's Tragedy* [1608–11 (1608)]; Ben Jonson, *Bartholomew Fair* [1614]; Thomas Middleton, *A Mad World, My Masters* [1604–7 (1606)], *Hengist, King of Kent; or, The Mayor of Queenborough* [1615–20 (1618)], and *Women Beware Women* [1620–27 (1621)]; and Philip Massinger, *The Roman Actor* [1626]).There were many fewer onstage representations of plays than it might at first seem. For discussion of the variety of melodramatic moments, see F. A. **Boas**, "The Play within the Play," in *A Series of Papers on Shakespeare and the Theatre* (The Shakespeare Association, 1925–26), 134–56; Leslie A. **Fiedler**, "The Defense of the Illusion and the Creation of Myth," *English Institute Essays,* ed. D. A. Robertson, Jr. (New York: Columbia University Press, 1949), 74–94; Thelma **Greenfield**, "The Transformation of Christopher Sly," *Philological Quarterly* 33 (1954): 34–43; R. J. **Nelson**, *Play within the Play: The Dramatist's Conception of His Art* (New Haven: Yale University Press, 1958); Arthur **Brown**, "The Play within a Play: An Elizabethan Dramatic Device," *Essays and Studies* 13 (1960): 36–48; Richard **Hosley**, "Was There a 'Dramatic Epilogue' to *The Taming of the Shrew,*" *Studies in English Literature* 1 (1961): 17–34; Robert Y. **Turner**, "The Causal Induction in Some Elizabethan Plays," *Studies in Philology* 60 (1963): 183–90; Righter, *Idea of the Play;* Dieter **Mehl**, "Forms and Functions of the Play within a Play," *Renaissance Drama* 8 (1965): 41–61.

2. "Kempe" appears as a character in *The Parnassus Plays* (1598–99/1599–1601/1602)—though not to put on a play—and in *The Travels of Three English Brothers* (1607)—where his play is cut short after two lines of prologue. Other professional players appear in Tailor's *The Hog Hath Lost His Pearl* (1613) (hired to play a private joke), Jonson's *Every Man out of His Humour* (1598) and *Poetaster* (1601), Marston's *Histriomastix,* Munday et al., *Sir Thomas More,* and Massinger's *Roman Actor.* Shakespeare has the players in *Taming of the Shrew* and in *Hamlet.* The rest of the period's inner plays are performed by amateurs like Munday's crew in *John a Kent and John a Cumber* or charlatans like Middleton's cheaters in *Hengist, King of Kent.* For the most illuminating treatment of the professional players see Mann, *Elizabethan Player.*

3. On the implications of the social discrepancy between players and audience, see Alvin B. **Kernan**, "Courtly Servants and Public Players: Shakespeare's Image of Theater in the Court at Elsinore and Whitehall," in *Poetic Traditions of the English Renaissance,* ed. Maynard **Mack** and George deForest **Lord** (New Haven: Yale University Press, 1982), 103–21; and Kernan, "Shakespearean Comedy," 91–101.

4. Michael **Williams**, *Americans and Their Forests* (Cambridge: Cambridge University Press, 1989), 21.

5. And Kate takes an old man for a woman, or says she does (*Shr.* 4.5.36–40).

6. Jack Cade in *Henry VI, Part Two* comes earlier, but he does not meet with the king himself.

7. G. K. **Hunter**, "Bourgeois Comedy: Shakespeare and Dekker" in *Shakespeare and His Contemporaries,* ed. E. A. J. **Honigmann** (Manchester: Manchester University Press, 1986), 3.

8. Riggs, *Heroical Histories,* describes the heroical ideal the plays embody and rework.

9. Both the chronicles and the Worthies also contributed to the "prentice literature" aimed at and consumed by seventeenth-century adolescents. The apprentices "conceived of themselves as possessing the manly virtues displayed on the battlefields of France and of the Holy Land . . . and with the romantic virtues of Johnson's

Nine Worthies." The latter was a prentice version of the famous heroes, celebrating nine London prentices all of whom made good. Smith, "London Apprentices," 149–61; see chapter 3, n. 57.

10. Berowne's playful conceit, at least when applied to lovers rather than actors, was hardly unique to Shakespeare. At about the same time that Berowne was on-stage, Arden in the anonymous *Arden of Faversham* (1585–92 [1589]) has a pre-monitory dream before his wife murders him:

> This night I dreamed that being in *a park,*
> A *toil* was *pitched* to overthrow *the deer,*
> And I upon a *little rising hill*
> Stood whistly watching for the herd's approach.
> Even there, methoughts, a gentle slumber took me. . . .
> But in the pleasure of this golden rest
> An ill-thewed foster had removed the toil,
> And rounded me with that beguiling home
> Which late, methought, was pitched to cast the deer.
> With that he blew an evil-sounding horn,
> And at the noise another herdsman came
> With falchion drawn, and bent it at my breast,
> Crying aloud, "Thou art the game we seek."

Arden of Faversham, ed. Martin **White** (New York: W. W. Norton, 1982), 6.6–19 (italics added).

11. Two scenes later Holofernes evokes the hunt again for us, when he reads his "extemporal epitaph on the death of the deer," which begins, "The preyful princess pierc'd and prick'd a pretty pleasing pricket," and notes how "the dogs did yell" bringing the pricket down (*LLL* 4.2.47–48, 55, 58). Hers is only a playful prey-fulness, but the bantering which accompanies it suggests a parallel between the Princess's attack on the deer and the French attack on Talbot. The phrase "in blood," found both in Holofernes' poem and in the description of Talbot's predicament, is another link between the two. See also Holofernes' unusual reference to Diana as "Dictynna" (*LLL* 4.2.35)—a name Ovid uses only when calling her "hunter of deer."

12. The incompatibility was being explored on the stage at the time. In *His-triomastix,* for example, the traditional opposition between soldier and scholar be-comes a conflict between soldier and player when the Captain comes to press the players into service: "What?" the Captain cries, "Playes in time of Warres? hold, sirra / Ther's a new plott," and remains unconvinced when one of the players ex-plains, "'Tis our Audience must fight on the field for us, / And we upon the stage for them" *Histriomastix,* in *Plays of John Marston,* 3:285–86.

13. For several years, across the channel, Navarre's namesake, Henri the "'white plume' of Navarre," (compare Armado, that "plume of feathers"; *LLL* 4.1.95) had become a folk hero to the English by challenging the Catholics on the French throne. Essex, a man with an eye for self-presentation, used Henri's wars to act out his expensive dreams of chivalric glory, with his old-fashioned knights errant "armed like the antique figures shown on old tapestries, with coats of mail and iron helmets . . . going into battle to the sound of bagpipes and trumpets"; Anthony

Esler, *The Aspiring Mind of the Elizabethan Younger Generation* (Durham: Duke University Press, 1966), 93.

14. Less derogatory was the new military genre in painting which deemed soldiers worthy subjects for artists. See J. R. **Hale**, *Artists and Warfare in the Renaissance* (New Haven: Yale University Press, 1991).

15. When King John besieges Angiers in Shakespeare's *King John*, for example, the citizens standing on the city walls are like an audience "in a theater, whence they gape and point / At [King John's] industrious scenes and acts of death" (*KJ* 2.1.375–76).

16. The rest of his scenes are dogged by shame: "let Talbot perish with this shame" (*1H6* 3.2.57), he cries when defeat seems likely; he and his son speak of "shame" three times (and infamy once) in seventeen lines when they meet; his fellow soldiers speak of his "shame" after he is gone. This obsessive sense of shame has a biblical flavor about it, and does actually echo the prophetic wrath in Jeremiah, where an angry God shames his people for their "abominations": "For the greatness of thine iniquity (are thy skirts discovered and thy heels made bare) . . . therefore will I discover thy skirts about thy face, that thy shame may appear. . . ." (Jer. 13.22) Talbot not only suffers from a sense of shame as physical exposure; he tries to inflict it on his enemies as well. He punishes the coward Fastolfe by publicly stripping off his garter in a technically accurate but nonetheless unhistorical defrocking ceremony. And his showiest victory in France is the attack on Orleans in which the French, as Alencon says, were "shamefully surprised" (*1H6* 2.1.65). There Talbot roused "the Dauphin and his trull" from "drowsy beds" (*1H6* 2.2.28, 23) so that they come running on stage "in their night clothes" (*1H6* stage directions after 2.1.38), and then, as another stage direction says, "fly, leaving their clothes behind them" (*1H6* stage direction after 2.1.7). He revenges his earlier shame by exposing his enemies.

17. His opponent throughout the play, Joan of Arc, threatens—though she fails to effect—a similarly fatal gaze: "O were mine eyeballs into bullets turned / That I might shoot them at your faces!" (*1H6* 4.7.79–80).

18. Little and Cantor, *Playmakers,* 90.

19. Fortinbras, it turns out, is marching for no more than a "fantasy" or a "trick of fame" (*Ham.* 4.4.61)—hardly better than the First Player caught up in his "fiction," or "dream of passion" (*Ham.* 2.2.246); while by contrast the player can make himself into Pyrrhus, a potent soldier.

20. See chapter 5 and Afterword.

21. Heroic drama was also the medium used by dramatists to compete with one another. George Peele, Robert Greene, and Thomas Kyd all tried to out-Tamburlaine Christopher Marlowe—and thus were exploring not only a national ideology but a much more pragmatic trade war.

22. Davies, *Microcosmos* 1:82; Philip **Massinger**, *The Roman Actor* (1626), ed. William Lee Sandidge (Princeton: Princeton University Press, 1929), 4.1.31–32.

23. *Pierce Pennilesse,* in *Works of Thomas Nashe,* 1:212.

24. Ibid.

25. Heywood, *Apology for Actors,* B$_3$v–B$_4$r.

26. Webster, *Excellent Actor,* cited in Chambers, *Elizabethan Stage* 4:258.

27. Like Faustus, the magician John a Kent (who is even more than Faustus a figure for the dramatist) can "from foorth the vaultes beneathe, / call up the ghostes of those long since deceast"; Munday, *John a Kent*, 5, lines 108–9. Shakespeare's magician-dramatist Prospero claims that "graves at my command / Have wak'd their sleepers, op'd, and let 'em forth" (*Tem.* 5.1.48–49), although we never see any such thing.

28. D. J. Palmer claims that Shakespeare also "resurrected" Henry V in that king's eponymous play; D. J. **Palmer**, "Casting Off the Old Man: History and St. Paul in *Henry IV*," *Critical Quarterly* 12 (1970): 267–83. This seems even truer in the context of the full cycle of history plays, which began with Henry V's death in *Henry VI, Part One* (1592) and ended with the live Henry's greatest triumph in *Henry V* (1599).

29. The proportion may have been even larger in an earlier draft. Editors have suggested that a scene with Armado and Moth is missing, and that the original play lacked the lengthy Muscovy fiasco which fills out the aristocratic plot. For a summary of the discussions see Richard **David**, ed., *Love's Labour's Lost*, Arden Shakespeare (London: Methuen, 1968), xxii, xxi. The degree of character development is such that scholars continue to search for the historical originals of the mechanicals as well as for those of the aristocrats.

30. Greene, *Groatsworth of Wit*, in *Complete Works*, 12:131–32.

31. A Spaniard in post-Armada England, Armado is already branded as an inferior "other."

32. Tomkis is cited in chapter 2, n. 157; "bashful player" is in T. G[ainsford], *Rich Cabinet*, 230.

33. Thomas **Greene**, "*Love's Labour's Lost:* The Grace of Society," *Shakespeare Quarterly* 22 (1971): 323.

34. Daniell argues that the *Henriad* contributed its imagery of civil war to *Shrew*'s love story; David **Daniell**, "The Good Marriage of Katherine and Petruchio," *Shakespeare Survey* 37 (1984): 23–31, esp. 25–26. Indeed the main extant predecessor for Petruchio's triumph over Katherine is Henry V's appropriation of Katherine in *The Famous Victories*, a likely source for the *Henry VI* plays.

35. Stephen **Brown**, "Shakespeare's King and Beggar," *Yale Review* 64 (1975): 370–95.

36. Or possibly "dug." Cf. M. R. **Ridley**, *Antony and Cleopatra*, Arden Shakespeare (London: Methuen, 1954), 194 n. 7.

37. See note on *LLL* 4.1.66, in David, Arden *Love's Labour's Lost*, n. 63.

38. James, Richard Jones's boy, played both a waiting maid and a beggar in the Admiral's production of *Troilus and Cressida*, 1599. Nungezer, *Dictionary of Actors*.

39. Lucio slanders the Duke in *Measure for Measure* by claiming that he would "mouth with a beggar though she smelt . . . garlic" (*MM* 3.2.177–78) and Armado unwittingly slanders himself by invoking the ballad.

40. Brian Morris argues that the only reference to "Sly" in the stage directions is a prompter's addition. Brian **Morris**, ed., *The Taming of the Shrew*, Arden Shakespeare (London: Methuen, 1981), 6.

41. Salingar, *Traditions of Comedy*, 271.

42. Grumio, the clown's role in the main plot, may have been played by one of the nonclown actors, John Sincklo or Alexander Cooke. This would have left the

company clown (Kempe?) free to play Sly. See Morris for Jeanne Roberts's theory about Sincklo and Dover Wilson's about Cooke; Morris, Arden *Shrew,* 49–50.

43. Geoffrey **Bullough,** *Narrative and Dramatic Sources of Shakespeare's Plays* (London: Routledge and Kegan Paul, 1957), 1:58–61.

44. Ola Elizabeth Winslow suggests Hance as a possible influence on Sly. Ola Elizabeth **Winslow,** *Low Comedy as a Structural Element in English Drama* (Chicago: University of Chicago Libraries, 1926), 55.

45. Baskerville, *Elizabethan Jig,* 313. This is a seventeenth-century Dutch singspiel which Baskerville, who retells it, believes to have been based on an earlier English jig. See Morris, Arden *Shrew,* 77.

46. Baskerville reprints a jig of "A merry discourse 'twixt him and his *Ioane*" in which she rejects him because of his drinking, he promises to reform, and she takes him back—a kind of "Taming of the Drunkard" story; Baskerville, *Elizabethan Jig,* 423–27.

47. Sly aspires to the status of the kings Shakespeare had been reading about in the chronicles, though his confusion of William the Conqueror with Richard Coeur de Lion makes his claim more like that of Falconbridge, the commoner in Shakespeare's *King John* who merely claims he is the bastard son of Richard.

48. Bullough, *Dramatic Sources,* 1:59, 372.

49. Like the Duke in *As You Like It,* who finds "sermons in stones" (*AYL* 2.1.17), he finds them in random drunks.

50. Bullough, *Dramatic Sources,* 1:109–10.

51. With his own (otherwise superfluous) hunting dog, Troilus (*Shr.* 4.1.137).

52. In light of the lord's invocation of death in the induction, it is worth noting that Shakespeare's most original contribution to the lore of shrew taming in the main plot was precisely Petruchio's plan to "kill [his] wife with *kindness*" (*Shr.* 4.1.195; italics added) (or to "kill [her] in her own humour," as the servants put it; *Shr.* 4.1.167), rather than beating her into submission like other shrew tamers. The figure of speech—it is no more than that—reverberated in Shakespeare's mind, however, for in the very passage describing his method, Petruchio elaborates on one of Shakespeare's most characteristic image clusters, the cluster *kite, sheets, bed, death,* which Armstrong first identified; Edward A. **Armstrong,** *Shakespeare's Imagination,* rev. ed. (Lincoln: University of Nebraska Press, 1963). Petruchio likens Kate to a kite, or bird of prey, "sharp" and "empty," who must not be "full-gorged" until he tames her (*Shr.* 4.1.177–78). Shakespeare's women are elsewhere associated implicitly with birds of prey, especially at moments when they seem threatening—when Hortensio fears Bianca's loyalty, for example, or when Othello fears Desdemona's; but only Kate is called a kite. A second pun on her name further consolidates the reference: "Kate" is also a common name for prostitutes (see the song in *The Tempest,* 2.2.50–55). In Katherine, Shakespeare evoked and Petruchio exorcised the qualities feared in women. Perhaps the lord's death-consciousness is not so inappropriate after all.

53. A suggestion even more likely for Shakespeare's later patron directors like Prospero in *The Tempest* and the Duke in *Measure for Measure.*

54. Karl P. **Wentersdorf,** "The Original Ending of *The Taming of the Shrew:* A Reconsideration," *Studies in English Literature* 18 (1978): 201–15, esp. 209–13.

55. Daniell, "Good Marriage," 30.

56. Morris, Arden *Shrew*, 76.

57. Morris, Arden *Shrew*, 62–63.

58. David **Bevington**, *From Mankind to Marlowe: Growth of Structure in the Popular Drama of Tudor England* (Cambridge: Harvard University Press, 1962), 15.

59. See the summary of the evidence in the notes to *Shr.* Ind.1.81–86; Morris, Arden *Shrew*, 158–59. There are problems in determining the dates of the two plays. The extant *Women Pleased* is late, and the induction exchange may have been added to Shakespeare's *Shrew* only later, in response to the spate of shrew and antishrew plays in the early 1600s. But reference to Sincklo (who died before the extant *Women Pleased*) in the Folio *Shrew* speech-prefix suggests that this exchange might have been part of the original *Shrew* after all, where it would have referred to an earlier version of *Women Pleased*.

60. Even the name of Petruchio's hunting dog, "Troilus," playfully—and again misleadingly—suggests that the woman, and not the man, will be pleased in this story.

61. Or not quite the opposite. Several critics have convincingly described the mutuality of the love between Kate and Petruchio. The line announcing this mutuality, however, may continue a pointed reference to *Women Pleased:* "If she and I be pleas'd," says Petruchio to the other couples, "what's that to you?" (*Shr.* 2.1.296).

62. Morris, Arden *Shrew*, 85.

63. Sherman **Hawkins**, "Falstaff as Mom," unpublished talk given at the section on "Marriage and the Family," annual meeting of the Modern Language Association of America, 1979.

64. On the two sets of mother-child relationships in the play, see Weston A. **Gui**, "Bottom's Dream," *American Imago* (1952): 251–305, esp. 284.

65. We may understand her silence about her own approaching wedding, but it is harder to justify her apparent indifference to Hermia's similar plight. She may disapprove silently of Hermia's enforced wedding, but she does nothing to prevent it; Theseus by contrast not only mitigates the threatened punishment, but perhaps tries also to patch things up when he goes off to speak privately with Egeus.

66. Gui, "Bottom's Dream," 268–69, 284, *passim*.

67. "Wither" is a word Shakespeare associates with "that harlot, strumpet Shore" who "wither'd" Richard III's arm (*R3* 3.4.71, 69), and with the Countess who calls Talbot a "weak and writhled shrimp" (*1H6* 2.3.22).

68. Whichever of the two antithetical meanings for "enforced chastity" we choose—"imposed" or "forced to yield"—her sympathy remains constant.

69. Callisto: Ovid, Metamorphoses II: 400ff. See Walter F. **Staton**, "Ovidian Elements in *A Midsummer Night's Dream*," *Huntington Library Quarterly* 26 (1963): 165–78, esp. 170–71.

70. "In his great Ovidian comedy, *A Midsummer Night's Dream*, Shakespeare juxtaposes all the profound associations of the Actaeon myth with the comic tradition concerning men who become, first spiritually and then physically, jackasses." Leonard **Barkan**, "Diana and Actaeon: The Myth as Synthesis," *English Literary Renaissance* 10 (1980): 317–59, esp. 352ff. See chapter 5 for a discussion of Shakespeare's use of the myth elsewhere.

71. See Barber, *Festive Comedy*, 137, and Jan Lawson **Hinely**, "Expounding the Dream: Shaping Fantasies in *A Midsummer Night's Dream*," in *Psychoanalytic Ap-*

proaches to Literature and Film, ed. Maurice **Charney** and Joseph **Reppen** (Rutherford: Farleigh Dickinson, 1987), 120–38. Hinely's is the best commentary I know on Bottom's dream and its psychological implications for the lovers.

72. Titania's first words on wakening allude to a famous example of parental devotion. "What angel wakes me from my flowery bed?" (*MND* 3.1.124) transforms Hieronimo's anguished cry in *The Spanish Tragedy* when noise of his son's murder breaks his sleep: "What outcries pluck me from my naked bed?" (*Spanish Tragedy* 2.5.1).

73. Cf. chapter 3 on the possibility that Shakespeare was a replacement child.

74. Staton, "Ovidian Elements," 175–76.

75. Bottom's experience translates many of Adonis's experiences into benign equivalents. Shakespeare's Venus had wrestled Adonis onto a primrose bed and tangled him like a bird in a net; Titania has Bottom carried to her floral bower, entangling him like an elm in ivy. Adonis was encompassed by his huge goddess, but Shakespeare emphasizes the tininess of Bottom's fairies and the largeness of his ears. Adonis had no beard; Bottom, who had an excess of beards at rehearsal, is, an ass, counterphobically hairy.

76. Hinely, "Expounding the Dream," 136.

77. When Puck at the end of the play takes up a similar protective stance around the beds of all the mortal newlyweds, he chases away the screech owl of mortality: "The screech owl, screeching loud / Puts the wretch that lies in woe / In remembrance of a shroud" (*MND* 5.1.362–64). This reminds Harold F. Brooks of the similar owl in "The Phoenix and the Turtle": "Shrieking harbinger, / Foul precursor of the fiend, / Augur of the fever's end" (*PhT* 5–7). Harold F. **Brooks**, ed., *A Midsummer Night's Dream*, Arden Shakespeare (London: Methuen, 1979).

78. Lysander evokes this blissful loss of boundaries when he is trying to convince Hermia to sleep next to him in the woods: "One turf shall serve as pillow for us both; / 'One heart, one bed, two bosoms, one troth'" (*MND* 2.2.40–41). (Or as the "Phoenix" poet put it, "Hearts remote, yet not asunder; / Distance and no space was seen"; *PhT* 29–35.) That such union terrifies Hermia does not diminish its power for us.

79. Obviously a chronological narrative of character development has no place in *Dream*—Bottom wants to play Thisbe *before* he ever sees the Fairy Queen. But it is important that Bottom's two major experiences in the play encompass *both* being treated like a beloved baby, and being an unflappable actor in a play. Titania's ministrations in Bottom's "dream" allow him to survive Pyramus's nightmare loss of Thisbe.

80. Given the ambiguity of Bottom's visionary syntax perhaps "make *it* the more gracious" (*MND* 4.1.216–17) refers to the entire play as well.

81. Cf. Aaron's description of the "solemn hunting" that is part of Lavinia's wedding celebration in *Titus Andronicus* (*Tit.* 2.1.112). Even more than the "solemnities" of marriage in *Dream*, Titus's hunt fails to contain the violence beneath its "solemn" rituals.

82. Cf. Louis Adrian **Montrose**, "'Shaping Fantasies': Figurations of Gender and Power in Elizabethan Culture," *Representations* 2 (1983): 61–94.

83. Bottom fears that Lion has "deflower'd" his Thisbe when he attacked her (*MND* 5.1.281). Mihoko **Suzuki**, "The Dismemberment of Hyppolytus: Humanist

Imitation, Shakespearean Translation," *Classical and Modern Literature* 10 (1990): 103–12. Caught between his stepmother's desire, his father's curses, and his own horse's passion, Hippolytus will be torn apart by another monster. Theseus, Phaedra, and Hippolytus constitute a far more dangerously incestuous triangle than the one constituted by Oberon, Titania, and the little Indian boy, but they are similar. The two triangles frame Bottom's triangle—one in the past, one in the future—like stages of development in a boy's life.

84. Barber, *Festive Comedy*, 151.

85. Peter **Leinwand**, "'I Believe We Must Leave the Killing Out': Deference and Accommodation in *A Midsummer Night's Dream*," *Renaissance Papers* (1986): 11–30.

86. Staton, "Ovidian Elements," 177.

87. Barber, *Festive Comedy*, 149.

88. Dorothy **Bethurum**, "Shakespeare's Comment on Medieval Romance in *Midsummer Night's Dream*," *Modern Language Notes* 160 (1945): 85–94.

Chapter Five

1. But see Richard L. **McGuire**, "The Play-within-the-Play in *1 Henry IV*," *Shakespeare Quarterly* 18 (1967): 47–52.

2. Falstaff also encounters a "real" Fairy Queen in *The Merry Wives of Windsor*; see below.

3. W. H. **Auden**, "The Prince's Dog," in *The Dyer's Hand and Other Essays* (New York: Random House, 1962), 182–208.

4. A. R. **Humphreys**, Introduction, in *Henry IV, Part Two*, Arden Shakespeare (London: Methuen, 1966), lvi.

5. There are also some odd verbal echoes: Falstaff twice identifies himself with weavers (*1H4* 2.4.130, *Wiv.* 5.1.22–23), unlike any male in the canon besides Bottom. And while Bottom concerned himself with moonshine, Falstaff calls himself a "minion[] o' the moon," one of Diana's "foresters . . . under whose countenance we steal" (*1H4* 1.2.26, 25–29). But the resemblance is more essential and touches on their histrionic core.

6. Cited in Weimann, *Popular Tradition*, 191; for a recent expansion of the argument, see Wiles, *Shakespeare's Clown*, 116–35; J. A. **Bryant**, "Shakespeare's Falstaff and the Mantle of Dick Tarlton," *Studies in Philology* 51 (1954): 149–62. See also Weimann, *Popular Tradition*, 189.

7. Another trick they share for dealing with adversity is to make ballads— Bottom in all earnestness to encompass his unspeakable vision, and Falstaff more facetiously, to get back at the prince (*1H4* 2.2.43, *2H4* 4.3.45).

8. Auden, "Prince's Dog," 185–86.

9. E.g., when drafting "dead" men (*1H4* 4.2.31–38), playing dead (*1H4* 5.3.30–33), or tricking Shallow (*2H4* 3.2.310–40).

10. Hal's intimate relation to Falstaff, whether seen as filial or as erotic, has been the focus for much of the commentary on the play. See, e.g., Auden, "Prince's Dog"; Hawkins, "Falstaff as Mom"; Theodor **Reik**, "Rosenkavalier Waltzes," in *The Haunting Melody: Psychoanalytic Experiences in Life and Music* (New York: Farrar, Straus

and Young, 1953), 121–45; William **Empson**, *Some Versions of the Pastoral* (London: Chatto and Windus, 1935), chaps. 2, 3; Ernst **Kris**, "Prince Hal's Conflict," *Psychoanalytic Quarterly* 17 (1948): 487–506; Barber and Wheeler, *Whole Journey*, 198–217; Sundelson, *Restorations of the Father;* Peter **Erickson**, *Patriarchal Structures in Shakespeare's Drama* (Berkeley: University of California Press, 1985); and Coppélia Kahn, *Man's Estate.*

11. Sherman Hawkins suggests that Hal, in his own oedipal progress, abandons Falstaff after seeing him "betray" Hal by flirting with the aged bawd Doll; indeed, he never sees Falstaff again after that encounter; Hawkins, "Falstaff as Mom." But for Falstaff himself the relation to Doll is less important.

12. "This type is afraid of the intensity of his own aggressive and hostile drives and therefore regressed to an earlier phase in which there were no serious and dangerous conflicts with the external world. The energy, otherwise used in the pursuit of aggressive, hostile and sadistic strivings, becomes redirected to protect the self that is afraid of the consequences of its repressed aggressiveness. The mechanism is thus a defense against the threatening retribution and at the same time a regression to the phase of an infantile pleasure-ego, an early organization of the individual in which the world is 'tasted,' orally tested as to whether it tastes good or bad. That defense would manifest itself not only in a lack of aggressiveness and cruelty that could endanger the self in the form of retribution, but also generally in avoidance of dangers, risks and bold adventures, and in the last consequences in physical caution and even cowardice." Reik, "Rosenkavalier Waltzes," 132.

13. *MND* 3.1.172–94, *2H4* 3.2.95–182. Bottom and Falstaff each call the members of the group individually and make a comic remark on his name.

14. Cf. Harry **Berger**, "Sneak's Noise or Rumor and Decontextualization in *2 Henry V*," *Kenyon Review* 6.4 (1984), 58–78, esp. 74–76.

15. With Hal's help, though, Falstaff can still triumph over an unsympathetic audience like John, who greets the knight's account of his service with the same skeptical words Hippolyta had used on hearing about the midsummer night's dream in Athens: "This is the strangest tale that ever I heard" (*1H4* 5.4.153).

16. In the same vein Falstaff tells Shallow, "You hunt counter" (*2H4* 2.2.88–89). See James M. **Saslow**, *Ganymede in the Renaissance: Homosexuality in Art and Society* (New Haven: Yale University Press, 1986), 73.

17. Henry Crosse (1603). See chapter 2.

18. Thersites is even more self-consciously an actor himself, and his "Pageant of Ajax" (*Tro.* 3.3.271) helps establish the theatrical context for this scene.

19. He sees them in typically oral terms: "Tut, tut, good enough to toss, *food* for powder, *food* for powder, they'll fill a pit as well as a better; tush, man, mortal men, mortal men" (*1H4* 4.2.65–67; italics added).

20. Empson, *Versions of Pastoral,* 102–15. See also Barber and Wheeler, *Whole Journey,* 198–208.

21. See Sigurd Burckhardt's brilliant speculations about the parallel in Sigurd **Burckhardt**, "'Swoll'n with Some Other Grief': Shakespeare's Prince Hal Trilogy," in *Shakespearean Meanings* (Princeton: Princeton University Press, 1968), 144–205. More recently James Calderwood has argued for a parallel between Henry's achievement of kingship and the play's achievement of unity and suggested that the

playwright's sacrifice of himself to the dramatic office is like Henry's "sacrifice of self to the political office"; James **Calderwood**, *Metadrama in Shakespeare's Henriad* (Berkeley: University of California Press, 1979), 113–64, 178.

22. It was in general a dramatically self-conscious period for Shakespeare: following the *Henry* plays he created the most metadramatic of the Roman plays in *Julius Caesar*, *As You Like It*'s superbly histrionic Rosalind, the Duke's overt speculation in the same play that "All the world's a stage," and finally, of course, *Hamlet*. It was also the period when Shakespeare inserted more prologues and epilogues than at any other time, no doubt in part because it was then the fashion, given impetus by the war of the theaters. But the *Henry* plays seem to generate the need for such an apparatus or at least to take naturally to it.

23. Burckhardt, *Shakespearean Meanings*, 183–89; Calderwood, *Metadrama*, 132.

24. Humphreys suggests that the Epilogue's first paragraph "is spoken by its author, presumably Shakespeare" (Humphreys, Arden 2 *Henry IV*, 186, headnote to epilogue), but to me he sounds more like an actor apologizing for speaking a speech "of mine own making," rather than one scripted by the author (*2H4* Epi.5).

25. Could this be a reference to a precensorship performance of *Henry IV, Part One*?

26. The Folio paragraph ends after "infinitely" and moves the prayer to the end of the Epilogue; Humphreys, Arden 2 *Henry IV*, 187, 188, textual notes.

27. See chapter 8 for Antonio.

28. Humphreys cites Wilson's editorial commentary to *Henry IV, Part Two* in his note to *2H4* Epi.16–17; Humphreys, Arden *Henry IV, Part Two*.

29. For details of the ways in which the Chorus's speeches mislead as well as for a variety of theories explaining the discrepancies, see Warren D. **Smith**, "The *Henry V* Chorus in the First Folio," *Journal of English and Germanic Philology* 53 (1954): 38–57, esp. 46–51; Anthony S. **Brennan**, "That Within Which Passes Show: The Function of the Chorus in *Henry V*," *Philological Quarterly* 58 (1979): 40–52; Sharon **Tyler**, "Minding True Things: The Chorus, the Audience, and *Henry V*," in Redmond, *Theatrical Space*; Anthony **Hammond**, "'It Must Be Your Imagination Then': The Prologue and the Plural Text in *Henry V* and Elsewhere," in *"Fanned and Winnowed Opinions": Shakespearean Essays Presented to Harold Jenkins*, ed. John W. **Mahon** and Thomas A. **Pendleton** (London and New York: Methuen, 1987), 133–50.

30. See Michael Goldman's argument that, "Once it is recognized that the Chorus sounds very much like the King, much of the play's method becomes clear." Both convey the "atmosphere . . . of strenuous activity" which defines both the actors' jobs in the play and the history (or fiction) it presents, giving a sense of "the size and energy of the subject . . . barely restrained or contained." Goldman, *Energies of Drama*, 58–59.

31. See chapter 4.

32. A. R. **Humphreys**, Introduction, in *Henry IV, Part One*, Arden Shakespeare (New York: Vintage Books, 1967), xiv. Stanley **Wells** and Gary **Taylor**, with John Jowett and William Montgomery, "The Canon and Chronology of Shakespeare's Plays," in *William Shakespeare: A Textual Companion* (Oxford: Clarendon, 1987), 119.

33. *Henry IV, Part Two* seems to have been partially completed before the

Brookes objected to Oldcastle's name, which appears in the speech-prefixes early in the Quarto. It may have been performed sometime late in 1596 or early 1597 (Humphreys), but was probably later, perhaps as late as 1598 (Wells and Taylor).

34. Cited in Wilson, "Puritan Attack," 434.

35. Schoenbaum, *Documentary Life*, 227–30.

36. Harry Berger, like Burckhardt asking about that unidentified "hidden grief," attributes it to Northumberland's secret guilt about helping cause his son's death. In the chronicles, Berger notes, Northumberland was guiltless; his responsibility is Shakespeare's invention; Berger, "Sneak's Noise." The prominence of a guilty, mourning father at the beginning of *Henry IV, Part Two* accords well with the possibility that Hamnet's recent death had affected the play. It is interesting that in *The Merchant of Venice*, probably written just after Hamnet died, Shakespeare included a similarly mistaken report about a son's death. There, in the central clown's scene, Launcelot Gobbo taunts his blind father by announcing his own death (*MV* 2.2). Only later does he identify himself and save the old man from despair. The entire play is clouded by a vague sense of mourning, beginning with Antonio's opening line, spoken not long before he discovers he is losing Bassanio: "In sooth I know not why I am so sad" (*MV* 1.1.1).

37. It has been suggested that both plays may have been performed at the same household—one with enough resident choir boys to play the fairies in *Dream* and the children dressed as fairies in *Wives*; Brooks, Introduction, in Arden *Dream*, lvii.

38. He is the Bottom-like "cavalerio" in this play; there are other curious echoes of *Dream* in *Wives*. Cf. H. J. Oliver, ed., Introduction, in *Merry Wives of Windsor*, Arden Shakespeare (London: Methuen, 1971), lxxv, 20, note to 1.1.2.

39. Like the heroines of clown jigs cited in chapter 4.

40. Bullough attributes the repetition between *Dream* and *Wives* to lack of imagination; Bullough, *Dramatic Sources*, 2:17. Leonard Barkan suggestively expands the connections in Barkan, "Diana and Actaeon," 351–53.

41. Barbara **Freedman**, "Falstaff's Punishment: Buffoonery as Defensive Posture in *The Merry Wives of Windsor*," *Shakespeare Studies* 14 (1981): 163–74.

42. Doll also calls him a "rascal," and Falstaff uses the epithet for Pistol (*2H4* 2.4.39, 212).

43. See note to *1H4* 5.4.108, in Humphreys, Arden *1 Henry IV*, 160.

44. The hunt's function as a social marker, its aristocratic trappings, and the elitism signaled by expensive costumes, traditional rituals, and special language, were more obvious to commentators in the nineteenth and early twentieth century, when the same person was likely both to take part in a hunt and to write criticism of Shakespeare. To Americans, for whom hunting has become a working-class sport, the regal aura is absent.

45. *As You Like It* is the only Shakespearean "hunting" play that is not part of the theatricality discussed here. But it is of course associated with its own sort of theatricality, centered on Rosalind's double disguise, and figured in the culminating "Masque of Hymen."

46. See the reference to the deer's theological significance in D. C. **Allen**, "Marvell's 'Nymph,'" *English Literary History* 23 (1956): 93–111, which cites traditional sources for this common symbolism.

47. "The thematic imagery of hunting held far more immediate meaning for

Shakespeare and his contemporaries than it does for us. Today few theatregoers would have followed the hounds after a deer in one of the three chases surviving in England. Even so, they would have seen a different finale because they now kill the stag at bay with a shotgun blast instead of cutting his throat with a sword. Antony's spectacular crimsoned hunters have been lost in time." A. Stuart Daily, "To Moralize a Spectacle: *As You Like It,* Act 2, Scene 1," *Philological Quarterly* 65 (1986): 149.

48. Richard Leighton Greene cites reports of "stag" hunts in "Hamlet's Skimmington"; Richard Leighton Greene, *Evidence in Literary Scholarship: Essays in Memory of James Marshall Osborn,* ed. René Welleck and Alvaro Ribeiro (Oxford: Clarendon Press, 1979), 1–11. Though primarily concerned with Hamlet's dumb show and spoken play as a skimmington, he notes that Falstaff's "curious and elaborate punishment at the end of [*The Merry Wives of Windsor*] has more than a touch of the skimmington about it . . . [and] suggests the harrying of the simulated stag which constitutes the orthodox skimmington"; Greene, "Hamlet's Skimmington," 4–5. As Greene notes, Natalie Zemon Davis first suggested the connection to *Hamlet.* See also David Underdown, *Revel, Riot, and Rebellion: Popular Politics and Culture in England 1586–1660* (Berkeley: University of California Press, 1985), 102–3, 106, 110–11; Leah Marcus, "Levelling Shakespeare: Local Customs and Local Texts," *Shakespeare Quarterly* 42 (1991): 168–78.

49. John M. Steadman, "Falstaff as Actaeon: A Dramatic Emblem," *Shakespeare Quarterly* 3 (1963): 236–37; Jeanne Addison Roberts, *Shakespeare's English Comedy: "The Merry Wives of Windsor" in Context* (Lincoln and London: University of Nebraska Press, 1979), 127–29.

50. Barkan claims that since Petrarch "Actaeon's story becomes throughout the Renaissance a means of investigating the complicated psychology of love"; Barkan, "Diana and Actaeon," 335. See also Nancy J. Vickers, "Diana Described: Scattered Woman and Scattered Rhyme," *Critical Inquiry* 8.2 (1981): 265–79.

51. Orsino evokes Actaeon in the opening lines of *Twelfth Night* to figure his lovelorn bachelor condition (*TN* 1.1.21–23). His "Diana" is the veiled and cloistered Olivia, who will not let him see her.

52. Actaeon's story resembles Hippolytus's story in that both are tales of reluctant male sexuality awakened by a mature woman—the young man's mother, in Hippolytus's story. Hippolytus, most unfairly from his point of view, was then punished for his experience when Theseus called up a monster to goad the youth's own horses into tearing him apart. But Actaeon's story, as Nancy Vickers notes, primarily belongs where Ovid puts it, with the story of Pentheus, who discovers female sexuality forbidden for its own mysterious reasons (not just because of his father's taboo) and is then torn apart by his mother. This story embodies the antagonisms and identifications between lover and beloved (Pentheus imagines, recoils, spies, and imitates) and their terrible issue in violence. Ovid, Vickers points out, juxtaposes Actaeon's story with that of Orpheus, whose forbidden glance at his own wife leads ultimately to his being torn apart; Vickers, "Diana Described," 269–70).

53. Robert Marienstras, "The Forest, Hunting and Sacrifice in *Titus Andronicus,*" in *New Perspectives on the Shakespearean World,* trans. Janet Lloyd (Cambridge: Cambridge University Press, 1985), 40–47.

54. See Vickers's argument that Petrarch uses the myth as figure for the lyric poet's relation to the object he describes; Vickers, "Diana Described," 273–75.

55. See chapter 1 for application of Canetti's term to contemporary actors.

56. See Katherine Eisaman **Maus**, "Horns of Dilemma: Jealousy, Gender, and Spectatorship in English Renaissance Drama," *English Literary History* 54 (1987): 561–83, on the cuckold's fate. He is exposed as a "fixed figure, for the time of scorn / To point his slow unmoving finger at" (*Oth.* 4.2.54–55), as Othello feared; he hears the whole world whispering, "Sicilia is a so-forth" (*WT* 1.2.218), as Leontes does. See also Coppélia Kahn, "'The Savage Yoke': Cuckoldry and Marriage," in *Man's Estate,* 119–50.

57. As in *Endimion,* often cited as a possible source for the *Wives'* fairies; John Lyly, *The Complete Works of John Lyly,* ed. R. Warwick Bond (1902; reprint, Oxford: Clarendon, 1973), 3:59–60:

> *Omnes:*   Pinch him, pinch him, blacke and blue,
>   Sawcie mortalls must not view
>   What the Queene of Stars is doing,
>   Nor pry into our Fairy woing.
> *1 Fairy:*   Pinch him blue.
> *2 Fairy:*   And pinch him blacke.
> *3 Fairy:*   Let him not lacke.
>   Sharpe nailes to pinch him blue and red,
>   Till sleepe has rock'd his addle head.
> *4 Fairy:*   For the trespasse hee hath done,
>   Spots ore all his flesh shall runne.
>   Kiss *Endimion,* kisse his eyes,
>   Then to our Midnight Heidegyes
>
>   (*Endimion* 4.3.29–41)

58. Webster, *Excellent Actor,* cited in Chambers, *Elizabethan Stage,* 4:257–58.

59. Armstrong, *Shakespeare's Imagination,* 42–49.

60. W. H. D. **Rouse**, ed., *Shakespeare's Ovid Being Arthur Golding's Translation of the "Metamorphoses"* (Carbondale: Southern Illinois University Press, 1961), 68 (bk. 3, lines 280–91). See also *A Disputation between a Hee Conny-Catcher and a Shee Conny-Catcher* (1592): "he saw more than he lookt for [i.e., wife's adultery with best friend], and so much as pincht him at the very heart"; Greene, *Complete Works,* 10:259.

61. The treatment which begins in *Errors* ends only in *The Tempest,* where Caliban is hunted like a deer and "pinch'd" for his lust (*Tem.* 1.2.331). See chapter 8 for a similar connection between "pinching" and bearbaiting in the plays.

62. And Armado in *Love's Labour's Lost.*

63. A replay also of Hal's trick on Falstaff when he hides to hear Falstaff betray him in the tavern. Appropriately enough, Parolles appears in the play which explicitly identifies the player as a "beggar" in the epilogue (*AWW* Epi.1), and which constitutes Shakespeare's most extended study of masochism outside of the sonnets. Helen, the lowborn orphan whom Bertram has been made to marry against his will, loves the arrogant snob and goes to extraordinary lengths of self-denial in order to win him. Parolles's relation to Bertram condenses all that is ugliest in Helen's love (or a player's profession)—or the poet's love for the young man of the sonnets.

64. Actaeon's story contributes fleetingly to the hunting and theatrical ambiance

elsewhere in the plays. In *As You Like It* the hunt's implications for marriage are visually explicit when cuckold's horns are paraded ostentatiously across the stage as soon as Orlando thinks about marrying Rosalind. But Orlando also plays a kind of bachelor Actaeon to Rosalind's Diana, when he courts her and she turns on him (albeit wittily) to describe the shrew she'll be: "I will weep for nothing, like Diana in the fountain, and I will do that when you are disposed to be merry" (*AYL* 4.1.145–47). In *Twelfth Night*, Orsino wishes to penetrate Olivia's self-imposed cloistered chastity (and her "veil"; *TN* 1.5.167, 1.1.28). He himself evokes Actaeon in the first lines of the play.

65. Actaeon's story is linked even more closely to the rejection of women in Marlowe's *Edward II*, where Edward's lover Gaveston plans to seduce the king by calling for "Italian masks by night" (*Edward II* 1.1.55):

> Sometime a lovely boy in Dian's shape,
> With hair that gilds the water as it glides,
> Crownets of pearl about his naked arms,
> And in his sportful hands an olive-tree,
> To hide those parts which men delight to see,
> Shall bathe him in a spring; and there, hard by,
> One like Actaeon peeping through the grove,
> Shall by the angry goddess be transform'd,
> And running in the likeness of an hart
> By yelping hounds pull'd down, and seem to die;—
> Such things as these best please his majesty.
>
> (*Edward II* 1.1.61–71)

66. Folio and Quarto editions differ; the Quarto omitted the Windsor Castle and Garter speeches completely (e.g., vol. 5, 56–74). See Oliver, Introduction, in Arden *Wives*, xxxii, xiv.

67. Barbara Everett links these two performers as epitomes of the embodied actor, physically and almost palpably present to an audience; Barbara Everett, "The Fatness of Falstaff," *London Review of Books*, 16 August 1990, 18–22, esp. 19. Maggie Smith tells about an actress aunt of hers who played both parts in repertory, moving from one to the other merely by shifting the hump from shoulder to belly. Given this context of gender reversal for each in this histrionic feat (a female actor playing both Richard and Falstaff), it is interesting to note that hunchbacks and pregnant women are interchangeable in the hunchback dances cited in connection with Richard in chapter 3.

68. In one of Shakespeare's sources the Falstaff figure was in fact "Anne's" suitor. Cf. Bullough, *Dramatic Sources*, 2:9.

69. Cf. Richard:

> And will she yet debase her eyes on me . . .
> On me, that halts and am misshapen thus?
> Upon my life, she finds—although I cannot—
> Myself to be a marvelous proper man.
> I'll be at charges for a looking-glass,

And entertain a score or two of tailors . . .
Since I am crept in favor with myself,
I will maintain it with some little cost.

(*R3* 1.2.251–64)

70. See chapter 3 and Richard's description of the thorny wood that keeps him from the open air and rends his flesh as he seeks to be impaled by the crown.

71. In one final shared physical fate, both Falstaff and Richard are notoriously unhorsed. See Harry **Levin**, "Falstaff Uncolted," *Modern Language Notes* 61 (1946): 305–10.

72. Shakespeare's first "pinching" play, *The Comedy of Errors*, ends with the "rebirth" of the thirty-three-year-old twins, Antipholus of Syracuse and Ephesus, when their long-lost mother emerges from the abbey to claim that she has but been in travail for thirty-three years and only now given birth.

73. See Patricia Parker's suggestion about his function in a self-conscious reference to rhetorical strategies and ideals; Patricia **Parker**, *Literary Fat Ladies: Rhetoric, Gender, Property* (London: Methuen, 1987), 29–31.

74. See chapter 3.

75. Like the heroes of the early histories—or the would-be warriors in *Love's Labour's Lost*—Hamlet is called to play an impossibly heroic role: as "worthy," bequeathed to him by his mythic father; as the morality-play scourge of God (Howard **Felperin**, *Shakespeare as Representation: Mimesis and Modernity in Elizabethan Tragedy* [Princeton: Princeton University Press, 1977], 44–67); as the revenge play revenger (Mark **Rose**, "*Hamlet* and the Shape of Revenge," *English Literary Renaissance* 1 [1971]: 132–43); or any number of other roles including, simply, "hypocrite." But unlike Navarre, Hamlet puts those roles in perspective. He is not so much an actor as an actor-manqué, overwhelmed by his sense of the futility of action in the larger theater of the world.

76. In the Quarto they almost literally save him from suicide, arriving as they do after his "to be or not to be" soliloquy. In the Folio, Hamlet does not think about self-slaughter until after his first encounter with the players, but such thoughts disappear when he briefs the players for their court performance. On the timing of the players' arrival see Leo **Salingar**, "The Players in *Hamlet*," *The Aligarh Journal of English Studies* 6 (1981): 168–83, esp. 170–71.

77. Francis **Fergusson**, *The Idea of a Theatre* (Garden City: Doubleday, 1953), 135; Barber and Wheeler, *Whole Journey,* 264.

78. Mann, *Elizabethan Player,* 51.

79. See chapter 3.

80. Before the play when Hamlet explained his plan to Horatio, he had already likened Claudius to his prey: "Observe my uncle. If his occulted guilt / Do not itself unkennel in one speech / It is a damned ghost that we have seen" (*Ham.* 3.2.85–87). Just after the play he suspects that Claudius has sent his agents Rosencrantz and Guildenstern to hunt Hamlet: "Why do you go about to recover the wind of me, as if you would drive me into a toil [net as used in deer hunting]?" (*Ham.* 3.2.37–38).

81. Greene, "Hamlet's Skimmington," 8.

82. Fergusson, *Idea of a Theatre*, 142.

83. Throughout this section I am indebted to Richard P. Wheeler, who points out the Duke's tendency to live vicariously through the people he manipulates. Richard P. **Wheeler**, *Shakespeare's Development and the Problem Comedies: Turn and Counter-Turn* (Berkeley: University of California Press, 1981), 121–39, esp. 121, 132.

84. Then he goes on in a litany of denial like Hamlet's self-accusations ("What should such fellows as I do crawling between heaven and earth?"; *Ham.* 3.1.128–29): "Thou art not noble; . . . Thou'rt by no means valiant; . . . Thou art not thyself; . . . Happy thou art not; . . . Thou art not certain; . . . Friend hast thou none; . . . Thou hast nor youth, nor age" (*MM* 3.1.13–32).

85. Leah S. Marcus notes the topical implications of Shakespeare's having set *Measure* in the moral badlands of Gonzago's Vienna. Leah S. **Marcus**, *Puzzling Shakespeare: Local Reading and Its Discontents* (Berkeley: University of California Press, 1988), 162.

86. J. W. **Lever**, Introduction, in *Measure for Measure*, Arden Shakespeare (London: Methuen, 1965), xcvii.

87. Mary Ellen **Lamb**, "Shakespeare's 'Theatrics': Ambivalence toward Theater in *Measure for Measure*," *Shakespeare Studies* 20 (1988): 129–46. I quote page 129, but the whole essay establishes nuances of the play's implications as commentary on offstage theatrics. See also Judd **Herbert**, "The Theatrical Presence of Staging and Acting in *Measure for Measure*," *New Literary History* 18 (1987): 583–96.

88. Like Berowne sitting "like a demi-god . . . in the sky, / and wretched fools' secrets over-eye" (*LLL* 4.3.76)—but then implicated in those very crimes.

89. Wheeler, *Problem Comedies*, 130–31.

90. Cf. Lever, note to *MM* 4.1.62, in Arden *Measure for Measure*, n. 99.

91. Prospero, the last of Shakespeare's directors, follows a trajectory similar to Hamlet's and Duke Vincentio's when he proceeds from thinking about death and sex to directing plays. Prospero's chosen actors are Ariel and his troop of obedient spirits, but Caliban's fellows are like actors when they dress up in frippery to play king. Like the lord in *Shrew*, Prospero had invited Caliban into his house, taught him lines, and tried to transform the lowly creature until Caliban tried to rape Prospero's daughter. Angelo had taken Isabel, Falstaff Mistress Ford, Bottom Titania, and Sly the lord's page-"wife"; and Caliban tried to take Miranda. For this crime Prospero had Caliban's troop literally hunted down with dogs.

92. Cf. Kernan on the centrality of the posture; Alvin **Kernan**, "'A Wilderness of Tigers': *Titus Andronicus*" in Barroll et al., *Drama in English*, 3:354–60. Barber and Wheeler suggest that the scene's importance grew as Shakespeare wrote: the sacrifice seems to have been merely summarized by Marcus in an earlier version, before it was expanded into the focus of the opening scene in the current text; Barber and Wheeler, *Whole Journey*, 130.

93. One spectator, perhaps Henry Peacham, was so struck by the scene that he used it to illustrate the whole play; it is the only such illustration we have for any Shakespearean play. Peacham (if it was he) need not have made the drawing at an actual performance. But whoever drew the picture knew the play well enough to

choose the moment which constitutes what Francis Fergusson might call the "idea" of the play: Tamora on her knees pleads to an unresponsive Titus, while Aaron stands by, personifying Titus's inhuman pitilessness. The text conflates this moment with another when Aaron recites his most villainous lines. See J. Dover Wilson, "'Titus Andronicus' on the Stage in 1595," *Shakespeare Survey* 1 (1948): 17–22; Gustav Ungarer, "An Unrecorded Elizabethan Performance of *Titus Andronicus,*" *Shakespeare Survey* 14 (1961): 102–9.

94. As Prince Clarence says, pleading for his life in *Richard III* when Richard's hit men come to murder him: "A begging prince, what beggar pities not?" (*R3* 1.4.257), but the plea goes unheard. Anne Pasternak Slater notes that "the misplaced kneelings of [a disordered state's] citizens" is "somewhat over-used in . . . the early plays"; Anne Pasternak **Slater**, *Shakespeare the Director* (Totowa, N.J.: Barnes and Noble, 1982), 66. Actually many of the other varieties of kneeling which she distinguishes are overused. The relationship which kneeling expresses— whether overtly political or personal—was at the heart of Shakespeare's dramatic explorations in the early plays.

95. In Maynard **Mack**, *King Lear in Our Time* (Berkeley: University of California Press, 1965), 49.

96. The original *Leir* is a pious story about an old man who has none of Lear's majesty—or egotism—and who is truly more sinned against than sinning. His daughters Ragan and Gonorill outdo Shakespeare's evil sisters by arranging to have Leir murdered (and warning the murderer not to be dissuaded by their father's moving speech), but the heavens thunder at the crime, the murderer repents, and both Leir and Cordella survive. Shakespeare's *Lear* follows the old play's narrative, with certain obvious omissions—no attempted murder, no happy ending—and many additions. But the history of Shakespeare's *Leir* borrowings suggests that at first Shakespeare ignored the larger design of the *Leir* play and focused instead on two specific "begging" fragments, which mark exchanges between loved ones, ruptures or healings of intimacy. The first is a moment of betrayal, when Leir begs the would-be murderer for mercy ("'Sblood, how the old slave claws me by the elbow!" says the murderer. "He thinks, belike, to escape by scaping [scraping?] thus." 2.1516–17). Leir tries to bribe the murderer by promising to use his influence with his daughter the Queen; but the murderer tells him that it was the Queen herself who sent him. Then Leir and his loyal follower (the original Kent), each rather comically offers himself to the murderer and begs him to save the other. This scene may have contributed to the kneelings that dominate *Titus Andronicus,* as victim after victim is newly surprised by his captor's cruel indifference. It certainly was a primary source for the murder of Clarence, the "begging prince," in *Richard III* (there was no such scene in the chronicles), and it must have contributed to "The Scene of the Beggar and the King" in *Richard II,* when the Duke and Duchess of York try to outdo one another kneeling to Bolingbroke, one begging for and one against forgiveness for their son. Shakespeare would use the scene again in *King John* and *Cymbeline.* (Other lines from the scene appear in *Richard III* 4.4.369–89 and perhaps in *The Tempest.*) The second begging scene Shakespeare took from the old *King Leir* is an exchange of kneelings and blessings between Leir and Cordella

so exaggerated that it seems all but impossible to stage seriously. Shakespeare pares the exchange into one of the unbearably poignant moments of his own *Lear*, but Jacqueline Pearson suggests that it also contributed to the comic begging in *Richard II*; Pearson, "The Influence of *King Leir* on Shakespeare's *Richard II*," *Notes and Queries* 29 (1982): 113–15. It later reappears transformed in *Coriolanus*, where father and daughter are replaced by son and mother when Coriolanus kneels to his mother because he cannot bear to see his mother kneeling to him.

97. Stanley Cavell, "The Avoidance of Love: A Rereading of *King Lear*" (1969), in *Disowning Knowledge in Six Plays of Shakespeare* (Cambridge: Cambridge University Press, 1987), 72.

98. There are other resemblances: the story of "good" versus "bad" sister affects both *Shrew* and *Lear*, for example, and Grumio in *Shrew* mutters to his rival, "Your father were a fool / To give thee all" (*Shr.* 2.1.393–94).

99. Lear's restoration is not overseen by a great lord but is facilitated by the devotion of men who, unlike his daughters, stay with him when he is down. Only Kent is willing to give him that uncritical adoration which actors demand; only Kent recognizes Lear as king when he is no longer willing to act like one: "You have that in your countenance which I would fain call master. . . . Authority" (*Lr.* 1.4.27–30).

100. Why did this scene disappear from the Folio?

101. In act 1, scene 4 Lear enters to the sound of hunting horns; in act 2, scene 3 Edgar announces his Poor Tom disguise also to the sound of the hunt: "I hear myself proclaim'd; / And by the happy hollow of a tree / Escap'd the hunt" (*Lr.* 2.3.1–3).

102. See William R. Elton, *King Lear and the Gods* (1966; reprint, Lexington: University Press of Kentucky, 1988), 84–93; William C. Carroll, "'The Base Shall Top th' Legitimate': The Bedlam Beggar and the Role of Edgar in *King Lear*," *Shakespeare Quarterly* 38 (1987): 426–41.

103. See Cavell, "Avoidance of Love," and Janet Adelman, Introduction, in *Twentieth Century Interpretations of "King Lear"* (Englewood Cliffs: Prentice Hall, 1978), 1–21, esp. 1–5.

104. Michael Goldman's vivid description of Edgar and the Poor Toms he imitates (to which he adds, "the kind who sticks his stump in your face"), in "The Worst of *King Lear*"; Goldman, *Energies of Drama*, 37, 98.

105. Apropos of audience identification and the confusions between actor and witness, passion and sympathy, it is interesting to consider the response of three patients in Broadmoor, Britain's hospital for the criminally insane, to a 1992 performance of *King Lear*. All three were greatly moved by the reunion scene where Cordelia forgives Lear and he blesses her by asking her to hide away with him: "Come, let's away to prison; / We two alone will sing like birds i' th' cage" (*Lr.* 5.3.8–9). Consulting psychiatrist Dr. Margaret Orr later reported that upon seeing this scene, all three patients "said the same thing. It was that they wished they could have been reunited with their parents in the way Cordelia was. And these were people who had all killed parents" (*London Observer*, Sunday, 16 February 1992, 49–50). Were they identifying with Cordelia, who had done no real harm—certainly not murdered Lear—and didn't need forgiveness? Or were they identifying with Lear who nearly did murder Cordelia? Or were they identifying with the whole situation of forgiveness which subordinates individual roles to a dynamic of love and hate, and

can foreground the child in Lear, the mother in Cordelia, as well as the literal father in Lear and daughter in Cordelia? Literal correspondence hardly matters in these complex identifications. Few spectators in a "normal" audience will have killed a parent, but all will have wished to do so, and most will have deeply wounded both their parents and children. Because theatrical identifications move in such mysterious ways, all can respond emotionally to the play though it flouts their moral beliefs.

106. Annabel **Patterson**, *Censorship and Interpretation: The Condition of Reading and Writing in Early Modern England* (Madison: University of Wisconsin Press, 1984), 59. The attention to beggars, unique though it seems in "all the tragedies" as class analysis, is not entirely new. Shakespeare's tragic vision had already incorporated a similar moment of social concern, when Hamlet had distanced himself from the "natural shocks," listed early in his famous soliloquy, which describe wrongs he himself has suffered at the hands of fortune, Claudius, and Ophelia:

> The whips and scorns of time,
> Th'oppressor's wrong, the proud man's contumely,
> The pangs of dispriz'd love, the law's delay,
> The insolence of office, and the spurns
> That patient merit of th'unworthy takes.
>
> (*Ham.* 3.1.70–74)

From these he moves to identify—at least figuratively—with those, who like Lear's poor beggars, "fardels bear, / To grunt and sweat under a weary life" (*Ham.* 3.1.76–77).

107. In Jonathan Dollimore's radical rereading of the tragedy; Jonathan **Dollimore**, *Radical Tragedy: Religion, Ideology, and Power in the Drama of Shakespeare and His Contemporaries* (Chicago: University of Chicago Press, 1984), 197; italics added.

108. While Westerners now see radical politics implied by the family struggles in the play, Czechoslovakia's Vaclav Havel, on the contrary, was "much taken by the current relevance of Shakespeare's king" because *Lear* showed how much of the political was personal: "After my year as President, [said Havel] I realize again and again what I didn't know before, that personal relations, sympathies, jealousies and rivalries play such an important role among nations. It's a bit frightening when you realize this. In *King Lear* this is demonstrated in a very drastic way, how in history people will kill and nations fight, all because of personal rivalries" (*New York Times*, 11 August 1991, H7).

109. We know that *Lear* was written at least partly in response to other contemporary historical pressures as well, including particularly James's controversial effort to heal the division of the kingdoms by uniting England and Scotland. Patterson suggests that James's family metaphors in discussing the union in a recent speech had prompted Shakespeare's use of the family to treat the politically difficult issue; and many believe that the republication of the old *King Leir* (1588–94 [1590]; reprint, 1605), Shakespeare's source, had already been prompted by these debates; Shakespeare's use of it would thus reflect its larger political context. The horrors of internal strife and civil war are surely important for the play, and it would be hard to imagine that Shakespeare or his audience would not think of England preying upon itself "like monsters of the deep" when they saw the private aristocratic quar-

rels rending the country's map before their eyes (*Lr.* 4.2.50). But whatever *Leir's* import for Shakespeare in 1605, that play's treatment of intimate relations between loved ones, rather than its treatment of social parameters, had shaped Shakespeare's first response to it as well as shaping the outline of his own *Lear* play.

Chapter Six

1. See the list of mirror titles in Herbert **Grabes**, *The Mutable Glass: Mirror-Imagery in Titles and Texts of the Middle Ages and Renaissance,* trans. Gordon Collier (Cambridge: Cambridge University Press, 1982), 235–329. In England, Grabes notes, "the mirror occurs with especially marked frequency . . . between 1550 and 1650" and is explored so extensively that he calls the period "The Age of the Mirror"; Grabes, *Mutable Glass,* 12, 14.

2. Or more like what Lacan posits in the "mirror stage" than anything we ordinarily mean by "mirror." Lacan's Subject evolves only by passing through the mirror stage, during which he sees not what he *is*—a mass of disconnected impressions—but a much tidier, more neatly organized visual entity, what he *ought* to be. Later experience repeats the mirroring figuratively, as the Subject is continually shaped by the strictures of external authorities, the "ones who are supposed to know." So too with Hamlet, whose mirror shows the audience what they ought to be; the difference is that while Lacan rails against such externally imposed ideals, Hamlet dies trying to find one.

3. There was a group of perceptually accurate "mirror" books, which served in some cases as compendia of information, in others as textbooks about specific professions (e.g., *The Mirror for Mariners*), but as time went on these were greatly outnumbered by specifically moral mirrors; Grabes, *Mutable Glass,* 37, 52. In any case, they too in some sense showed "virtue her own image" by showing what the *best* mariners were like.

4. Peter Ure notes that there were literal flattering glasses—Queen Elizabeth spoke of one—as well as figurative ones like Sylvius in *As You Like It.* Peter **Ure,** "The Looking Glass of Richard V," *Philological Quarterly* 34 (1955): 220.

5. "What, has *this thing* appear'd again tonight?" (*Ham.* 1.1.24; italics added). "The play's *the thing* / wherein I'll catch the conscience of the King" (*Ham.* 2.2.600–1; italics added).

6. Perhaps Marlowe in turn expected to make *Tamburlaine* a mirror of his own "honor"—a triumph over other dramatists (the "jygging vaines of riming mother wits, / And such conceits as clownage keepes in pay")—when he introduced Tamburlaine at the beginning of the play, and concluded confidently, "View but his picture in this tragic glass, / And then applaud his fortunes [i.e. my skill in putting them before you] as you please" (*Tamburlaine* Pro.1–2, 7–8).

7. Chapter 1, n. 42.

8. Of the period's approximately thirty-five plays-within-plays, some twenty are revenge masques rather than true inner plays like Armado's or Bottom's or the players' at Elsinore. In fact, in one of the three Middleton comedies which include a "professional" play-within-a-play (*Hengist King of Kent; or, The Mayor of Queenborough*), the troupe of "players" turns out to be ordinary characters in disguise.

They are cheaters pretending to be players in order to gain entrance to a great house, and in two of the plays they themselves live in the house. For discussions (and various listings) of the play-within-a-play in all forms, see chapter 4, n. 1.

9. See chapter 5 regarding *Wives*.

10. See Thomas **Kyd**, *The Spanish Tragedy* (1.5.22), in *The Works of Thomas Kyd*, ed. Frederick Boas (Oxford: Clarendon Press, 1901), 19.

11. See chapter 7 on Titus's (*Tit.* 5.3) and Timon's (*Tim.* 3.6) peculiar alternatives to the revenge play.

12. There are almost twice as many induction plays as plays-within-a-play (about sixty and thirty-five respectively). In most cases the inner action or main plot of an induction play is not literally a theatrical production. Instead most generate theatrical self-consciousness without the theater by juxtaposing actions from two different periods, two different places, or two different levels of reality ("natural" and "supernatural") in the two separate plots. Gods or ghosts watch the events on earth as if watching a play (*The Rare Triumphs of Love and Fortune* [1582]; Kyd, *The Spanish Tragedy* [1582–92 (1587)]; Greene and Lodge, *A Looking Glass for London* [1587–91 (1590)]); or people watch ghosts (Tarlton, *Seven Deadly Sins* [1590–91 (1590)]); or they watch make-believe creatures materialize before them (Peele, *The Old Wives Tale* [1588–94 (1590)]). Among the induction plays identified self-consciously as theater, the hostility is often subdued, particularly in the earlier examples. Nashe's *Summers Last Will and Testament* (1592), privately performed, includes a running commentary by its presenter, Will Summers, who merely feels superior to the actors; in Greene's *James IV* (1590–91 [1590]), Bohun orders his unidentified helpers, joined later by his two sons, to act out a play justifying his cynicism; Heywood's *The Four Prentices of London* (1592–1600 [1600]) is introduced by quarreling Prologues; and Chettle and Munday's *The Death* and *The Downfall of Robert, Earl of Huntington* (both are 1598) are presented as relatively friendly rehearsals. At the very least, the framing device, largely associated with didactic plays, often marks off a dire experience for the unwitting players; if it isn't a literal revenge it may simply be a nasty lesson.

The same is often true of devices which frame briefer unhappy moments *within* the main action as separate, though not literally as play. Here as well, violence often lurks in the separation effected by the frame, as magicians watch distant events in a perspective glass as if watching a play; or characters hide "above" to watch, unbeknownst to those below, planning to do them in.

13. Though not always. Sly does no harm to the players in *Shrew*, for example.

14. In plays like Jonson's *Poetaster* (1601), Marston's and Middleton's plays, Beaumont's *The Knight of the Burning Pestle* (1607), and Day's *The Isle of Gulls* (1606), witty antagonism between players and audience was common. Plays like the *Parnassus* plays, written for university audiences, tended to elaborate even more baroquely in the self-conscious induction and to make comic coin of the playhouse antagonisms.

15. As C. L. Barber and Richard Wheeler point out, Hamlet's advice ignores any personal "purpose" of playing, though in his own production such motives were foremost. Barber and Wheeler, *Whole Journey*, 263.

16. Gloucester tells Lear that he knows how this world goes, although he is

blind, because he now can "see it feelingly" (*Lr.* 4.6.147). Gloucester speaks of ordinary life and not of theater, but it may not be accidental that Lear's mad ravings, which frame Gloucester's reply, take him from "how this world goes" to "this great stage of fools" in less than forty lines (*Lr.* 4.6.148–49, 181). What Lear says we do in this version of the *theatrum mundi* is, not surprisingly, to "cry" (*Lr.* 4.6.180).

17. Levin, *Question of Hamlet,* 141–64, esp. 159.

18. As in René Girard's description of the triangulation of desire, or Lacan's of the intrasubjective creation of subjectivity.

19. The first sign of Hal's withdrawal from Falstaff is Hal's battlefield rebuke, "What, is it a time to jest. . . ?" (*1H4* 5.4.55).

20. Notice that he does not discover a cue for action—he does not grab his sword—but for passion.

21. Emrys Jones notes the resemblance between the two speeches in Jones, *Scenic Form,* 104–5. Hamlet's relative immobility may be as monstrous as the player's ability to "force his soul," but players were frequently seen as monstrous (see the following section of this chapter) and Hamlet's term would probably be heard first as a description of the player.

22. See Chapter 3.

23. For recent discussion of the encounter in similar terms see, e.g., Linda **Charnes,** "So Unsecret to Ourselves: Notorious Identity and the Material Subject in Shakespeare's *Troilus and Cressida,*" *Shakespeare Quarterly* 40 (1989): 413–40, and Edward **Burns,** *Character: Acting and Being on the Pre-Modern Stage* (London: Macmillan, 1990), 99ff.

24. If Hamlet associated playing and hunting, Ulysses too had spoken in terms of the hunt when he first tried to goad Achilles into action: "There's no tarrying here; the hart Achilles / Keeps thicket" (*Tro.* 2.3.258–59).

25. As Shakespeare put it in sonnet 25:

> The painful warrior famousèd for [fight],
> After a thousand victories once foiled,
> Is from the book of honor razèd quite,
> And all the rest forgot for which he toiled.
>
> (Son. 25, 9–12)

26. "A gate of steel" that renders the sun's heat is one of Shakespeare's more formidable images for an audience, matched perhaps by the "gleaming rows of teeth" the modern actor saw when looking out to the balconies (see chapter 1). Cf. also Falstaff's impression of Page's wife looking at him: "the appetite of her eye did seem to scorch me up like a burning-glass!" (*Wives* 1.3.67). The flatterer's "glass" that melts is also related (see chapter 7).

27. Ulysses teaches Achilles the lesson which the Princess in *Love's Labour's Lost* taught the would-be warrior Berowne. Achilles learns that he does need his audience's "looks," and Berowne learns that he needs to take account of his audience when he is condemned to jest a twelvemonth in a hospital for the speechless sick, where his task shall be

> With all the fierce endeavour of your wit
> To enforce the pained impotent to smile.
> . . . that's the way to choke a gibing spirit,

Whose influence is begot of that loose grace
Which shallow laughing hearers give to fools.
                              (*LLL* 5.2.845–46, 850–52)

28. Roach, *Player's Passion,* 41.

29. Greene, "Groatsworth of Wit," in *Complete Works* 2:145.

30. The ridiculously vain Ajax is a monster because he is also a "landfish" and "languageless" (*Tro.* 3.3.262–63) like Caliban.

31. The degradation in display, *even one intended as triumph,* makes Coriolanus rather give up his battle reward than hear his "nothings monster'd" (*Cor.* 2.2.77) before his people. He is of course quick enough to call the crowd itself a "monster" (*Cor.* 3.1.92, 94).

32. Is there a similarity between Benedick's fate and the tradition behind Falstaff's imprisonment in a "bottle" or basket of laundry? Steadman, "Falstaff as Actaeon," 237–38.

33. Perhaps as an unwitting symptom of the monster jealousy, the jealous Master Ford keeps a "monster" as household pet in *Merry Wives* (3.2.74), and shows him off to his friends for sport before setting out to humiliate Falstaff.

34. The taint of exposure lingers perhaps when she is on display again as a statue. Though admired and praised, it is a statue fashioned by Julio Romano, the famous painter also known for his lewd drawings illustrating the various postures of love (*WT* 5.2.96).

35. The Player-King in *Hamlet* acknowledged a similarly love-bound monstrosity in that play's inner play or pageant: "Our thoughts are ours, their ends none of our own" (*Ham.* 3.2.208). In both cases the vision of monstrosity follows a vision of hopeless love: the Player-King predicts his own posthumous betrayal by the Queen, and Troilus just as rightly predicts Cressida's betrayal of him.

36. Of the characters most often taken to be histrionic to the core, only two of the most important—Rosalind and Cleopatra—are women; the men include Richard III, Richard II, Hamlet, Iago, and Falstaff. Many of Shakespeare's best-known disguisers, however, are women who dress as men to follow their lovers: Julia, Portia, Rosalind, Viola, Imogen. Such women could be associated with the male players who were already feminized in the eyes of their critics: irrational, undisciplined, and dangerously attractive. Cf. Novy, "Female Characters," 256–70, esp. 264–68; Laura **Levine**, "Men in Women's Clothing: Anti-theatricality and Effeminization from 1579 to 1642," *Criticism* 28 (1986): 121–43; Howard, "Crossdressing," 418–40.

37. Launce does have a human mistress, but—not surprisingly—she herself is described as "spaniel-like" (*TGV* 4.2.14). Launce seems to be taking the feminine position even more overtly than does the typical male Petrarchan lover before his mistress. Harold F. Brooks and Clifford Leech each find a parallel between Launce's despair about Crab's behavior and Julia's about Proteus's. We might note the similar parallel between Launce and the sonnet poet. Harold F. **Brooks**, "Two Clowns in a Comedy (to say nothing of the Dog): Speed, Launce (and Crab) in 'The Two Gentlemen of Verona,'" *Essays and Studies,* n.s., 16 (1963): 99; Leech, Introduction, in Arden *Two Gentlemen,* lxvi.

38. There are signs that Shakespeare added Launce to the original draft of the

play (though probably not long after writing that draft) for some independent purpose. His presence contributes to several cruxes because he introduces questions about who received the letter he delivered (Julia or Lucetta?), about which dog he was later told to bring to Silvia (an appropriate lap dog or his own outsize Crab?), and about whose servant he is (Proteus's, but there are signs that originally Valentine and Proteus shared one servant, Speed, some of whose lines were later transferred to Launce). See Leech, Arden *Two Gentlemen*, xxvi–xxx.

39. States, "Dog on the Stage," 373–88.

40. Barish, *Antitheatrical Prejudice*, 3.

41. Launce's reincarnation, the citified Launcelot Gobbo in *The Merchant of Venice*, repeats the error when he says of Shylock, "my master's a very Jew" (*MV* 2.2.100). But here of course the jolt is not so thorough. Shylock is indeed a symbolic "Jew" or tightwad, as well as a real Jew or member of a particular faith. But the *actor*, one can venture with near certainty, was not a Jew in the same way that the actor of Crab was a dog.

42. Weimann, *Popular Tradition*, 257.

43. Leech assumes that Kempe would have played the part; Leech, Introduction, in Arden *Two Gentlemen*, xxvi; see also Wiles, *Shakespeare's Clown*, 73–77.

44. Weimann, *Popular Tradition*, 259, 260.

45. In tragedy, as States notes, the equivalent of the clown mediating between actors and audience is a villain like Iago. Iago, revealed as an "inhuman dog" himself (*Oth.* 5.1.62), may seem more in control of his intimacy with Othello than Launce was with Crab; Iago lets us in on his secret and even mocks his own servant persona: "Were I the Moor, I would not be Iago. / In following him, I follow but myself. . . . / I am not what I am." (*Oth.* 1.1.57–58, 65). But Iago's duplicity has its price as well; nor is he completely free of Launce's confusion. Insofar as he is obsessed with and perversely attached to the Moor, he *is* what he is after all. He is Othello's servant ("I am your own forever"; *Oth.* 3.3.486), no matter how much he denies the identity (like Viola disguised as Orsino's page and subordinating her will—her identity?—to his: "I am not what I am"; *TN* 3.1.143).

46. Sigmund **Freud**, *Jokes and Their Relation to the Unconscious*, in *Standard Edition*, 8:228–30.

47. Weimann, *Popular Tradition*, 257.

48. Typically, Shakespeare lets his clown in on the joke—in contrast to the corresponding figure in Kyd's *Spanish Tragedy*, who thinks he is to be saved at the last minute, but waits in vain (*Spanish Tragedy* 3.6.41–110).

49. Feste, we may remember, enters jesting about having to "fear no colors" (i.e., fear no collars or hanging) (*TN* 1.5.6).

50. Stephen **Booth**, *Shakespeare's Sonnets* (New Haven: Yale University Press, 1977), 454.

51. Everett, "Fatness of Falstaff," 18.

52. See, for example, Ralph M. Tutt's argument that it is possible "to detect in Launce's monologues [about "false friendship and love"] a comic foreshadowing of the anger and cynicism with which the dog image is employed in *Lear* and *Timon*." Launce's situation, Tutt says, brings to mind "the Fool's remark in *Lear* that 'Truth's a dog must to kennel; he must be *whipped* out, when Lady the Brach may stand by the fire and *stink*'" (*Lr.* 1.4.124–26; italics added). Ralph M. **Tutt**, "Dog Imagery in

The Two Gentlemen of Verona, King Lear, and *Timon of Athens,*" *The Serif* 1–2 (1964–65): 15–22, esp. 18.

53. "One that I saved from drowning, when three or four of his blind brothers and sisters went to it" (*TGV* 4.1.3–4).

54. Antonio had made a similar complaint earlier:

> This youth that you see here
> I snatch'd one half out of the jaws of death,
> Reliev'd him with such sanctity of love,
> And to his image, which methought did promise
> Most venerable worth, did I devotion.
> . . . But O, how vild an idol proves this god!
> (*TN* 3.4.359–63, 365)

55. On the "goose" cluster image, see Armstrong, *Shakespeare's Imagination,* 57–65, esp. 59.

56. Hamlet, like *Histrio-Mastix or, the Player whipt* (Marston's version, 1599) written after the statute condemning rogue players to be whipped, may be alluding specifically to the player's fate.

Chapter Seven

1. See chapter 6 for the complicated dynamics created by theater's mirroring relationships, which merged and at the same time opposed audience and player.

2. Walter **Whiter**, *A Specimen of a Commentary on Shakespeare* (1765); Caroline Spurgeon, *Shakespeare's Imagery,* 194–95.

3. C. H. **Hobday**, "Why the Sweets Melted: A Study in Shakespeare's Imagery," *Shakespeare Quarterly* 16 (1965): 3.

4. The association between Actaeon and flattery is made explicit in Sandys's moralized Ovid, where Actaeon's dogs are flatterers, sycophants first eating up his substance and then turning to please a more powerful being; Barkan, "Diana and Actaeon," 328. See chapter 5.

5. Cited in Chambers, *Elizabethan Stage,* 4:222.

6. See chapter 4 for a discussion of aggression in the exchange between actor and audience.

7. "And *Shakespeare* thou, whose hony-flowing Vaine, / (Pleasing the World) thy Praises doth obtaine"; Richard **Barnfield**, "Poems in Divers humors" (London: 1598), E$_2$r. See also: "Honie-tong'd *Shakespeare,* when I saw thine issue, / I swore Apollo got them and none other"; John **Weever**, Epigram 22 (1.1–2), in *Epigrammes,* 2d ed. (London: Thomas Bushell, 1599) E$_6$. Both cited in C. M. **Ingleby**, ed., *Shakspere Allusion-Books, Part I: A.D. 1592–8* (London: Trübner and Co., 1874, for the New Shakspere Society), 182, 186.

8. Sigmund **Freud**, "A Child Is Being Beaten" (1919), in *Standard Edition,* 17:175–204.

9. England's cycle of civil wars ends only when "the bloody dog [Richard] is dead" (*R3* 5.5.2).

10. Both flattery and jealousy derive from flaws in an intense relationship where the Other is an adoring object whose function is to serve and mirror one's desires.

Flattery signals the Other's false devotion, while jealousy signals the Other's betrayal of devotion, but both begin in the same kind of totalizing intimacy. While the jealousy plays tend to be about heterosexual relationships, the flattery plays portray homoerotic attachments.

11. *Gorboduc* and *King Leir*, both flattery plays, were revived at the time, presumably in an attempt to warn James about his behavior.

12. Chapter 5. The intimate relation between flattery and slander is suggested by the etymology of our word "sycophant," which derives from the Greek *sukophantema*, "slanderer."

13. Spurgeon, *Shakespeare's Imagery*, 197.

14. Spurgeon, *Shakespeare's Imagery*, 195.

15. Morris Palmer **Tilley**, *A Dictionary of the Proverbs in England in the 16th and 17th Centuries* (Ann Arbor: University of Michigan Press, 1950), 622, S704; James L. **Jackson**, "Shakespeare's Dog-and-Sugar Imagery and the Friendship Tradition," *Shakespeare Quarterly* 1 (1950): 260–63.

16. Frank **Whigham**, *Ambition and Privilege: The Social Tropes of Elizabethan Courtesy Theory* (Berkeley: University of California Press, 1984), 132. See also Wallace T. **MacCaffrey**, "Place and Patronage in Elizabethan Politics," in *Elizabethan Government and Society: Essays Presented to Sir John Neale*, ed. S. T. **Bindorf**, J. **Hurstfield**, and C. H. **Williams** (London : University of London Athlone Press, 1961), 95–126; Esler, *Aspiring Mind*; Javitch, *Poetry and Courtliness*.

17. Whigham, *Ambition and Privilege*, 116.

18. Cf. Norman **Sanders**, Introduction, in Robert **Greene**, *The Scottish History of James the Fourth* (London: Methuen, 1970), xxvii.

19. Richard Burton, *Anatomy of Melancholy* (1621); cited in Barish, *Antitheatrical Predjudice*, 106; *Euphues* in Lyly, *Complete Works*, 1:249; cited in Jackson, "Dog-and-Sugar Imagery," 63. Erasmus, *Praise of Folly*, 70: "Is there any animal more fawning than a dog? But then again is there any more faithful?"

20. William **Empson**, *The Structure of Complex Words* (London and Colchester: Spottiswoode, Ballantyne and Co., n.d.), chaps. 7 and 8, 158–84. Empson cites Erasmus (n. 19, above), noting that the first English translation has "spaniels" rather than dogs; Empson, *Structure of Complex Words*, 177.

21. See chapter 2. William **Vaughan**, *The Spirit of Detraction, Conjured and Convicted in Seven Circles* (London: W. Stansby for George Norton, 1611), P_3v; Wiles, *Shakespeare's Clown*, 148.

22. George Whetstone, "Description of Coseners," cited in Jackson, "Dog-and-Sugar Imagery," 262; Philip Sidney, in his list (in *The Defence of Poesie* [1595]) of the educational benefits to be gained from poetry.

23. E. P. **Vandiver**, "The Elizabethan Dramatic Parasite," *Studies in Philology* 32 (July 1935): 412.

24. *A Knack to Know a Knave*, in Hazlitt, *Old English Plays*, 6:510.

25. They did include some fun-loving and relatively harmless apolitical schemers like Merygreke in *Ralph Roister Doister* (1533, printed 1567), but the malignant type prevailed.

26. *The Three Ladies of London*, in Hazlitt, *Old English Plays*, 6:308–9.

27. It is interesting that Edward rejects his wife's "fawning" ("Fawn not on me, French strumpet"; *Edward II* 1.4.145) while accepting Gaveston's.

28. Vandiver, "Dramatic Parasite," 426.

29. In Thomas **Norton** and Thomas **Sackville**, *Gorboduc, or Ferrex and Porrex,* ed. Irby B. Cauthen (Lincoln: University of Nebraska Press, 1970); cited in Vandiver, "Dramatic Parasite," 416.

30. Once again Richard III casts his shadow on an experience associated with playing. Though the poet does not have in mind one specific "monster" or "thing indigest," these are the terms Shakespeare frequently associates with Richard. Richard, who knows "love foreswore me," seeks the crown instead.

31. Rankins, *Mirrour of Monsters,* 12, 13.

32. Tilley, *Dictionary of the Proverbs,* 721, W327.

33. The complete passage (from Rainoldes's *Th' Overthrow of Stage-Playes* [1599]) is cited by Lisa Jardine as evidence that cross-dressing was erotically suggestive; Jardine, *Still Harping on Daughters,* 15. "Dog" also referred to a sexually ambiguous male ("gelded like a spaniel" [*Per.* 4.6.124–25]; "Achilles' brach" for Patroclus [*Tro.* 2.1.116]). "Male prostitute" is not listed among the meanings for "dog" in the *O.E.D.,* although Frankie Rubinstein finds the sense in other uses of "dog." See also Buckingham's letters to James I referring to himself as "your humble slave and doge," and to the two of them as "Master and his Doge," cited in Jonathan **Goldberg,** *James I and the Politics of Literature: Jonson, Shakespeare, Donne and Their Contemporaries* (Baltimore: Johns Hopkins University Press, 1983), 144, 145.

34. Could the satire in the lost and censored *The Isle of Doggs* (1597)—so scandalous it sent both authors and actors to prison—perhaps have included sexual as well as political attacks?

35. Rankins, *Mirrour of Monsters,* 11; Tilley, *Dictionary of the Proverbs,* 622, S704.

36. Hobday, "Sweets Melted," 5; italics added.

37. An intimation borne out by sonnet 114's acknowledgement that "my mind, being crown'd with you / Drink[s] up the monarch's plague, this flattery" (Son. 114, 1–2).

38. In *Two Gentlemen* both the true lover, Valentine, and the false lover, Proteus, are fawners. Valentine, in love with a woman socially above his station, is scorned by her father and told to "bestow thy smiles on equal mates" (*TGV* 3.1.158).

39. Adults who might not blanch at being accused of Machiavellian flattery do not want to be associated with the indignities of the infantile. In the lines quoted above, Hamlet seems aware of the various and subtle implications of flattery when he assures Horatio that his favor is no flattery (Hamlet recoiled from flattery as from acting and pretense) and draws on Spurgeon's cluster to do so.

40. Or as Greene wrote, "lick[ing] the pan" (*James IV* 1.2.79).

41. John **Hunt,** "A Thing of Nothing: The Catastrophic Body in *Hamlet,*" *Shakespeare Quarterly* 39 (1988): 27–44.

42. Harold **Jenkins,** ed., *Hamlet,* Arden Shakespeare (London: Methuen, 1982), 405.

43. The Parasite in Plautus's *Menaechmi* introduces the play with a monologue about these things. Shakespeare, perhaps with such belly ties as well as emotional ties in mind, changed Plautus's play to incorporate the central symbols of the rope and the golden chain which bind the characters together in his *Comedy of Errors.*

44. Hobday, "Sweets Melted," 7. See V. Österberg, "The 'Countess Scenes' of Edward III," *Shakespeare Jahrbuch* 65 (1929): 49–91; Kenneth **Muir,** "A Reconsid-

eration of Edward III," *Shakespeare Survey* 6 (1953): 39–47, and *Shakespeare Collaborator* (New York: Barnes and Noble, 1960); Frank **O'Connor**, *The Road to Stratford* (London: Methuen, 1948), and *Shakespeare's Progress* (Cleveland: World Publication Company, 1960); Irving **Ribner**, *The English History Play in the Age of Shakespeare* (Princeton: Princeton University Press, 1957), 146–47; Inna **Koskenniemi**, "Themes and Imagery in *Edward III*," *Neuphilologische Mitteilungen* 65 (1964): 446–80; Eliot **Slater**, *The Problem of "The Reign of King Edward III": A Statistical Approach* (Cambridge: Cambridge University Press, 1988). In their recent reexamination of the canon, Taylor and Wells conclude that *Edward III* has the "strongest claims to inclusion" in the canon of any of the apocryphal plays; Gary **Taylor** and Stanley **Wells**, with John Jowett and William Montgomery, *William Shakespeare: A Textual Companion* (Clarendon: Oxford University Press, 1987), 136. Critics place the play between the *Henry VI* plays and *Love's Labour's Lost,* "Venus and Adonis," "Lucrece," and *Richard III* (1590–95).

45. "Arise, true English Ladie, whom our Ile / May better boast of, then ever Romaine might / Of *her, whose ransackt treasurie* hath taskt / the vaine indevor of so many pens" (*E3* 2.2.195–98; italics added). Shakespeare later returns to the outrageous courtship in *Measure for Measure,* where Isabella first kneels to Angelo to beg her brother's life, and he then demands the same kind of bribe that Edward IV used with Lady Jane. It is of course possible that some other playwright was so impressed by a large number of early Shakespearean works (including *Love's Labour's Lost,* which would most likely have been unavailable) that he used them all to create *Edward III.* But if so, Shakespeare in turn was equally impressed by the mysterious playwright, for he drew almost as heavily on *Edward III* as the author of that play drew on early Shakespeare. As Østerberg says, "why should Shakespeare . . . have kept up a constant, even doting fondness for this little production, of all others, and felt prompted to go on drawing upon it through the greater part of his career?"; Østerberg, "Countess Scenes," 89. The text is so enmeshed in reciprocal relations to Shakespeare's other works that it seems rather to issue from the same mind than to have come from outside and impressed Shakespeare so totally.

46. Østerberg notes the resemblance of the image to images in *Venus and Adonis* and in *Lucrece*; Østerberg, "Countess Scenes," 57. The lines are also a precursor of Ulysses' advice to Achilles, that no man can know his parts,

> Till he behold them form'd in the applause
> Where th'are extended; who
> . . . like a gate of steel
> Fronting the sun, receives and renders back
> His figure and his heat.
>
> (*Tro.* 3.3.119–123)

Such mirroring, needless to say, is more destructive than constructive. Cf. Falstaff's fantasized come-on from Mistress Page, who turns the "burning-glass" of her eye on him, or so he thinks (*Wiv.* 1.3.63).

47. Cf. chapter 3 for Richard, Proteus, and the oddity of the dead rival in these scenes.

48. Also, Lear's expectations about Cordelia's "kind nursery" (*Lr.* 1.1.123), cru-

elly disappointed not only by Cordelia but also by Goneril's locked doors and Regan's empty house.

49. Hobday, "Sweets Melted," 8.

50. Richard's peculiar image of death may even be related to the skewering death suffered by Marlowe's Edward II. Death strikes by boring a hole in the king's body:

> Within the hollow crown
> That rounds the mortal temples of a king
> Keeps Death his court, and there the antic sits . . .
> Allowing him a breath, a little scene,
> To monarchize, be fear'd, and kill with looks;
> Infusing him with self and vain conceit,
> As if this flesh . . .
> Were brass impregnable; and, humour'd thus,
> Comes at the last, and *with a little pin*
> *Bores through* his castle wall, and farewell king!
> (*R2* 3.2.160–62, 164–70; italics added)

Further resemblance to the erotics of Marlowe's play is suggested by the fact that Bushy, Bagot, and Green, the flatterers who stop Richard's "open ear" with praises and "lascivious metres" (*R2* 2.1.19–20), not only destroy his kingdom but, like Gaveston, with their "sinful hours" they have "made a divorce betwixt his queen and him, / Broke the possession of a royal bed, / And stain'd the beauty of a fair queen's cheeks / With tears, drawn from her eyes by your foul wrongs" (*R2* 3.1.12–15).

51. As Murray Schwartz and Richard Wheeler have suggested. Murray M. **Schwartz**, "Anger, Wounds, and the Forms of Theater in *King Richard II*: Notes for a Psychoanalytic Interpretation" in *Assays: Critical Approaches to Medieval and Renaissance Texts* 2 (1982), ed. Peggy A. **Knapp** (Pittsburgh: University of Pittsburgh Press, 1983), 123. Wheeler, *Problem Comedies,* 158–59. For a different opinion, see Harry **Berger**, *Imaginary Audition: Shakespeare on Stage and Page* (Berkeley: University of California Press, 1989), 66.

52. It is a bond so close that mother and child may change roles, Schwartz suggests, first Richard playing mother to the earth, then being mothered and fed by it (Schwartz, "Anger, Wounds," 123): "Dear earth, I do salute thee with my hand . . . / As a long parted mother with her child . . . / Feed not thy sovereign's foe, my gentle earth, / Nor with thy sweets comfort his ravenous sense" (*R2* 3.2.6–13, *passim*).

53. "Newts and blindworms" come not near (*MND* 2.2.11); they are to reserve their poison for his enemy. (Cf. also "The gilded newt and eyeless venom'd worm"; *Tim.* 4.3.184.) Apropos of mothers in the play we may note that Richard is a glorious sun because he is a glorious son. Later, even in decline, Richard will choose to model himself on the famous sons Phaeton and Christ.

54. A few scenes earlier, his Queen Isabel had rejected the flattering "perspective glass" offered by Bushy and had called all hope a flatterer (*R3* 2.2.14–32, 69). Only in his fall does he see to reject flattery.

55. Georges A. **Bonnard**, "The Actor in Richard II," *Shakespeare Jahrbuch* 88 (1952): 96. Hardin **Craig**, *An Interpretation of Shakespeare* (New York: Dryden, 1948), 128; cited in Peter **Ure**, Introduction in *King Richard II*, Arden Shakespeare

(London: Methuen, 1966), lxxviii. See also Righter, *Idea of the Play*, 110–14, and Leonard **Dean**, "*Richard II:* The State and the Image of the Theater," in *Shakespeare: Modern Essays in Criticism*, ed. L. Dean (New York: Oxford University Press, 1961), 159–68, for discussions of Richard as actor.

56. Appropriately enough, the next time the flattery cluster appears is in Hotspur's contempt for this very "king of smiles" (*1H4* 1.3.243): "Why, what a candy deal of courtesy / This fawning greyhound then did proffer me! / . . . 'gentle Harry Percy,' and 'kind cousin': / O, the devil take such cozeners!" (*1H4* 1.3.247–51).

57. Though Harry Berger argues that Richard knows what he is doing from the first; Berger, *Imaginary Audition, passim*.

58. See Lois **Potter**, "The Antic Disposition of Richard II," *Shakespeare Studies* 27 (1974): 33–41. Could it be that Richard is defensively taking up the humiliation of uncrowning himself which Falstaff will later feel when he is forcibly dis-horned by the citizens of Windsor?

59. Perhaps a tendril of the flattery cluster reaches out to affect Hamlet's words (considering his defeat by a Bolingbrokian Claudius) in his famous wish: "O that this too, too sullied flesh would *melt,* / Thaw and resolve itself into a dew" (*Ham.* 1.2.130–31).

60. Shakespeare's identification of Richard's position with a woman's is suggested by the way in which Richard's description of himself—the face that ruled a thousand men—echoes Faustus's description of Helen, the symbol of Desired Woman. It is also possible that Richard's self-consciously melodramatic response to Bolingbroke echoes Cordella, in the old *Leir* play, after she has been thrown out by her father, and offers to be a "Palmer's" wife:

> Ile hold Palmers staffe within my hand,
> And thinke it is the Scepter of a Queene.
> Sometime Ile set thy Bonnet on my head,
> And thinke I weare a rich imperiall Crowne,
> Sometime Ile helpe thee in thy holy prayers,
> And thinke I am with thee in Paradise.
>
> (*King Leir* 698–703)

So Richard:

> I'll give my jewels for a set of beads; . . .
> My sceptre for a palmer's walking staff,
> My subjects for a pair of carved saints.
>
> (*R2* 3.3.147, 151–52)

61. See chapter 4.

62. The speech goes on: "Because we thought ourself thy lawful king; / And if we be, how dare thy joints forget / To pay their awful duty to our presence?" (*R2* 3.3.74–76).

63. James **Black**, "The Interlude of the Beggar and the King," in *Pageantry in the Shakespearean Theatre*, ed. David M. **Bergeron** (Athens: University of Georgia Press, 1985), 104–13.

64. Shakespeare's two Richards, while both actors, differ greatly of course, as do the contexts in which they are defined. But Richard II's histrionic bent, while not originating like Gloucester's in deformity and maternal rejection, is nonetheless

linked to an announcement of a deformed birth like Gloucester's. The image appears in *Richard II* to herald Richard II's fall. When Isabel hears that Richard's followers have fled to Bolingbroke—a sign that Richard is defeated—she tells the messenger,

> thou art the midwife to my woe,
> And Bolingbroke my sorrow's dismal heir;
> Now hath my soul brought forth her prodigy,
> And I, a gasping, new-deliver'd mother,
> Have woe to woe, sorrow to sorrow join'd.
>
> (*R2* 2.2.62–66)

Since Bolingbroke is in a real sense Richard's heir, she speaks as if the prodigy she has given birth to and recoiled from is Richard himself—just as the Duchess of York had given birth to and recoiled from Gloucester.

65. Shakespeare stresses, as Plutarch does not, Caesar's vulnerability to flattery as an important part of the conspirators' plans.

66. I thought the phrase came from Michael **Platt**, *Rome and Romans According to Shakespeare* (Salzburg: Institut für Englische Sprache und Literatur, 1967), Jacobean Drama Studies 51, but I cannot locate it.

67. The source in Lucan mentions immortality but no actors or theater; Emrys **Jones**, *The Origins of Shakespeare* (Oxford: Clarendon Press, 1977), 275 (app. B).

68. The pervasive influence of playing in *Julius Caesar* has often been discussed. See Ralph Berry's survey of these discussions in *Awareness of the Audience*, 79.

69. Little and Cantor, *Playmakers*, 165.

70. Plutarch's Caesar did this in private—he made no such gesture when Antony offered the crown (cf. Bullough, *Dramatic Sources*, 5:81). The offer of his throat is a warrior's traditional battlefield submission, but Richard had already appropriated it for the erotic realm. Richard's offer to Lady Anne repeats Phaedra's abject offer to Hippolytus in Seneca's play. Perhaps Caesar is in some sense playing the maid's part here too.

71. J. L. **Simmons**, "*Julius Caesar*: 'Our Roman Actors,'" in *Shakespeare's Pagan World: The Roman Tragedies* (Charlottesville: University Press of Virginia, 1973), 87–90.

72. Spurgeon, *Shakespeare's Imagery*, 194–96.

73. In the past when Caesar denied vulnerability by projecting it outward in this way, he also unwittingly confessed it. So he had betrayed his fear of Cassius by denying it: "I fear him not: / Yet if my name were liable to fear, / I do not know the man I should avoid / So soon as that spare Cassius" (*JC* 1.2.195–98).

74. Within a year or so, Orsino opened Shakespeare's *Twelfth Night* (1600–2 [1600]) by claiming melodramatically that "my desires, like fell and cruel hounds . . . pursue me" (*TN* 1.1.22–23).

75. The reversal from sweetness to attack is repeated the next time the flattery cluster appears in the play, when Cassius contrasts Antony's *honeyed* words to his underlying aggression, and Antony retorts:

> Your vile daggers
> Hack'd one another in the sides of Caesar.
> You show'd your teeth like apes and *fawn'd* like *hounds*,
> And bow'd like bondmen, kissing Caesar's feet;

> Whilst damned Casca, like a *cur*, behind
> Struck Caesar on the neck. O you *flatterers!*
>
> (*JC* 5.1.39–45; italics added)

76. The association with Falstaff's sexual humiliation is appropriate insofar as Caesar has—ritually but nonetheless suggestively—"cuckolded" himself at the beginning of the play, when he asked the naked Antony to strike Caesar's barren wife to make her fertile (*JC* 1.2.6–8).

77. For a humanist perspective on this paradox, see Erasmus's description of hunting as a form of madness or folly: "What exquisite pleasure they [these hunters] feel when the quarry is to be butchered! Lowly peasants may butcher bulls and rams, but only a nobleman may cut up wild animals. Baring his head and kneeling down, he takes a special blade set aside for that purpose (for it would hardly do to use just any knife) and exercises the most devout precision in cutting up just these parts, with just these movements, in just this order. Meanwhile, the surrounding crowd stands in silent wonder, as if they were seeing some new religious ceremony, although they have beheld the same spectacle a thousand times before. Then, whoever gets a chance to taste some of the beast is quite convinced that he has gained no small share of added nobility. Thus, though these men have accomplished nothing more by constantly chasing and eating wild animals than to lower themselves almost to the level of the animals they hunt, still in the meantime they think they are living like kings." Erasmus, *Praise of Folly*, 60–61.

78. So the dying Hamlet laments his "wounded name," and asks Horatio to live to "tell my story" so that his name can be cleared (*Ham.* 5.2.355, 360).

79. Gail Kern **Paster**, "'In the Spirit of Men There Is No Blood': Blood as Trope of Gender in *Julius Caesar*," *Shakespeare Quarterly* 40 (1988): 18, citing Caroline Walker Bynum.

80. Henry **Ebel**, "Caesar's Wounds: A Study of William Shakespeare," *Psychoanalytic Review* 62 (1975): 121. Antony does this out of love, but the result is strangely like Corvino's jealous fantasy in *Volpone*, when he imagines his wife a whore and threatens to "make thee an anatomy, / Dissect thee mine own self, and read a lecture / Upon thee to the city and in public" (*Volpone* 2.5.70–72). The "lecture" Antony reads to the public upon Caesar's anatomy effectively prostitutes Caesar.

81. T. S. **Dorsch**, *Julius Caesar*, Arden Shakespeare (London: Methuen, 1965), 85.

82. Caesar might also be seen as a feminized sacrificial body, object of both Brutus's idolatry and his violence—like Desdemona's body when Othello comes to do justice on her: "Thou . . . mak'st me call what I intend to do / A murder, which I thought a sacrifice" (*Oth.* 5.2.64–66).

83. Ebel, "Caesar's Wounds," 124.

84. The latter of whom as we saw, was betrayed by a flattering "Sinon" just as Caesar was betrayed by flatterers.

85. "Her dazzling sight makes the wound seem three" (*Ven.* 1064). To Venus, the boar was nuzzling and kissing Adonis when the tusk wounded him (*Ven.* 1114–15).

86. Caesar had begun as a colossus—huge, upright, marble, Olympian. The colossus was replaced by mere statues (decorated by the people and then "disrobed"

by the tribunes), and then by the violated statue of Calpurnia's dream, before finally melting or thawing into flesh itself, open and wounded.

87. Like an embarrassed actor, those wounded "does," as they are called, Lavinia (*Tit.* 2.1.93, 117; 2.2.26) and Lucrece (*Luc.* 581, 1149) are as mortified by the exposure of their wounds as by the wounds themselves. When Lavinia's wounds are discovered, she blushes and runs away, while Marcus is left—like Antony—to interpret her wounds. When Lucrece's wounds are discovered, she kills herself.

88. Richard **Wilson**, "'Is This a Holiday?' Shakespeare's Roman Holiday," *English Literary History* 54 (1987): 31–44, argues that this exchange defines the anti-populist stance of the tribunes, and thus of the play.

89. Kenneth **Burke**, "Antony in Behalf of the Play," in *The Philosophy of Literary Form* (Baton Rouge: Louisiana State University Press, 1941), 331.

90. He does this in part by *flattering* us: "I awaken in you the satisfactions of authorship, as you hear me say one thing and know that I mean another"; Burke, "Antony," 338.

91. Burke, "Antony," 334.

92. By contrast, Brutus cannot "work" his audience. See Booth, "Actor as Kamikaze Pilot," 564–65.

93. As the second half of the play unfolds, Brutus, having killed Caesar, now takes on the spirit of Caesar himself. This scene contains many echoes of the assassination scene.

94. G. Wilson **Knight**, "The Eroticism of Julius Caesar," in *The Imperial Theme* (London: Methuen, 1951), 63–95.

95. As, e.g., Simmons, *Pagan World,* 102–5, says it is.

96. For the importance of debt to male bonds in *Comedy of Errors* and its relation to Shakespeare's own experience, see chapter 3.

97. All of which, as Janet Adelman says, he treats as flattery. For this observation and for the general understanding of the psychodynamics of the play—on which my own analysis is based—see Adelman's brilliant chapter on *Coriolanus* in *Suffocating Mothers*. See also Barron, "Artist As Infant," 171–93.

98. See Hobday, "Sweets Melted," 14.

99. Adelman, *Suffocating Mothers,* 155.

100. John **Holloway**, *The Story of the Night: Studies in Shakespeare's Major Tragedies* (Lincoln: University of Nebraska Press, 1961), 122, 123. Holloway argues that the pattern is "peculiarly, though not uniquely, Shakespearean" (136).

101. Goldman, *Energies of Drama,* 109–14.

102. Brian **Parker**, paper given at the Sixteenth International Conference on Elizabethan Theatre, Waterloo, Ontario, 1989.

103. Holden, *Laurence Olivier,* 340.

104. Gary **Wills**, "*Coriolanus*: A 20th-Century Power Play," *New York Times,* Sunday, 20 November 1988, H5, H25.

105. Volumnia's manipulativeness is not in Plutarch; Shakespeare invented it, and as a result his Volumnia fits the psychoanalytic textbook description of an actor's mother. It is not mothers who fail to mirror their infants who produce flawed selves, but rather mothers who mirror selectively, bending the working of their child's heart to an image of their own (see chapter 1).

Insofar as Tamora in *Titus Andronicus* was a first sketch of Volumnia (as *Titus* was Shakespeare's first version of the Coriolanus story), it is interesting that Tamora's efforts at manipulating Titus take the form of a *literal* play in which she hopes to make him play a fatal role. She comes to him disguised as Revenge, with her two sons disguised as Rape and Murder, and asks him to come down from his viewer's gallery to join the three characters.

106. "You might have been enough the man you are, / With striving less to be so" (*Cor.* 3.2.19–20).

107. In *Love's Labour's Lost,* Shakespeare's earlier play about show-off warriors, the Princess makes clear her disdain for anyone who shows off "for praise, for an outward part," and "bend[s] to that the working of the heart" (*LLL* 4.1.32–33). *Love's Labour's Lost's* histrionic concern with shame as the other side of fame is also suggested by Coriolanus, whose supposed lack of concern for fame is dogged by the possibility of "shame." He never admits shame. But he reveals a concern for it when he makes a wish for his son (projecting onto him as his own mother had projected her wishes onto him) "that thou ma'st prove / To shame unvulnerable, and stick i'th'wars / Like a great sea-mark standing every flaw / And saving those that eye thee!" (*Cor.* 5.3.72–75). Forgetting for a moment the phallic aspiration of this monumental dream, note how it reverses the potential vulnerability usually implied in situations when one is a lone target, eyed by many others. The watchers here cannot overpower the hero because the hero is saving them. They are the ones who need help, not him.

108. The equivalent realization for Richard II comes during his last scene, when he sees himself as Bolingbroke's "Jack-of-the-clock," or mechanical figure, striking the hours (*R2* 5.5.60).

109. She even suggests ad-lib lines (*Cor.* 3.2.72–86).

110. Elvis Presley's mother came to all his performances so that she'd be there when he asked her for a kiss just before he went on stage ("Mother, give me a sugar"). Holt, Quinn, and Russell, *Star Mothers,* 259.

111. The intricate connection between the two directions of flattery, being flattered and offering flattery, is indicated at the beginning of the play, in the passage quoted earlier, where Coriolanus refuses to listen to Cominius's praise and silences the cheering soldiers. His objection is couched in such tortured syntax, Brockbank says, that it constitutes "the play's most disputed passage":

> May these same instruments, which you profane,
> Never sound more! When drums and trumpets shall
> I'th'field prove flatterers, let courts and cities be
> Made all of false-fac'd soothing! When steel grows
> Soft as the parasite's silk, let him be made
> An ovator for th' wars! No more, I say!

> (*Cor.* 1.9.41–46)

(Philip **Brockbank**, ed., *Coriolanus,* Arden Shakespeare [London: Methuen, 1976], 144.) It is impossible to tell who is the flattering parasite and who the soldier being flattered. Coriolanus, presumably, is telling the soldiers not to flatter him—like Caesar at the Capitol saying he cannot respond to flattering prayers. But, unlike Caesar, Coriolanus does not even mention himself in the passage. Instead he seems to be saying, you should flatter a soldier (make "him" an ovator for the wars) only when *he* is a flatterer (when his "steel grows soft as the parasite's silk")—as if there were a connection between being flattered and being soft and compliant like a parasite. The confusion is telling, because it reveals Coriolanus's own confusion between giving and receiving flattery, praise, or ultimately any nurturance and concern.

112. Dekker, *Guls Horn-booke,* in *Non-Dramatic Works,* 2:246.

113. Redgrave, *Ways and Means,* 34. In this anecdotal mood I contribute Gerard Murphy's comment when asked about how he became an actor. Murphy recalled being rejected by his childhood sweetheart and then discovering his vocation when he was chosen to play Coriolanus (unpublished discussion before The Shakespeare Association of America, 1987). Rock star is not among Shakespeare's options, but if we entertain the possibility of essential experiences beneath historic evolutions, even singers like Orpheus fit the pattern—and his fate was on Shakespeare's mind at the end of his early portrayal of actors in *Midsummer Night's Dream* (*MND* 5.1.48–49).

114. Many editors find an allusion here to Hephaestos caught in Venus's embrace. Hephaestos, a mighty god caught indulging an effeminate or affective side, was thus made an object of scorn and mockery. The potential shame both in Hephaestos's adult sexual vulnerability and in Coriolanus's "boy"-ish vulnerability to his mother are related.

115. Cited in H. J. Oliver's survey of arguments for *Timon's* unfinished status. H. J. **Oliver**, ed., Introduction, in *Timon of Athens,* Arden Shakespeare (London: Methuen, 1959), xxv.

116. Una **Ellis-Fermor**, "*Timon of Athens:* An Unfinished Play," in *Shakespeare the Dramatist and Other Papers,* ed. Kenneth **Muir** (New York: Barnes and Noble, 1961), 170.

117. Bullough, *Dramatic Sources,* 250.

118. Cf. the illuminating discussions of Timon in terms of maternal dependence and ambivalence about it: Susan **Handelman**, "*Timon of Athens:* The Rage of Disillusion," *American Imago* 36 (1979): 53; Coppélia **Kahn**, "'Magic of Bounty': *Timon of Athens,* Jacobean Patronage, and Maternal Power," *Shakespeare Quarterly* 38.1, (1987): 37; Adelman, *Suffocating Mothers,* 167–68; Barber and Wheeler, *Whole Journey,* 305.

119. Barber and Wheeler, *Whole Journey,* 305–6; Kahn, "Magic of Bounty," 167–68; Handelman, "Rage of Disillusion," 53.

120. As had the fairies describing "the cradle of the Fairy Queen" Titania (*MND* 3.1.74) where Bottom found himself; cf. *MND* 2.2.11–12.

121. Cf. **Burke**, "*Timon of Athens* and Misanthropic Gold," in *Language as Symbolic Action* (Berkeley: University of California Press, 1966), 122.

122. Cf. Chaucer's "Pardoner's Tale" and its equation between buried gold and death.

123. G. Wilson **Knight**, "The Pilgrimage of Hate: An Essay on *Timon of Athens,*" in *The Wheel of Fire: Interpretations of Shakespearean Tragedy* (London: Methuen, 1961), 210–11.

124. Empson, *Complex Words,* 182.

125. E. C. **Pettet**, "*Timon of Athens:* The Disruption of Feudal Morality," *Review of English Studies* 23 (1947), suggested that the play is a "tract for the times," and

that, despite Ellis-Fermor's claim that Timon's story is not firmly related to Athenian politics, it is a critique of the Elizabethan shift from feudal to capitalist society (321). Timon represents the noble world of feudal patronage, and his friends reflect the new world which was destroying it—a world of commercialism and early capitalism, "calculating and profit-seeking" (329). When *Timon* was written there were many tracts for the times, constituting an extensive literature on the theme of "the prodigal and the miser" and deploying creatures like Usury and Hospitality. Indeed, with so much commentary, it's a wonder that Shakespeare's play was not more of a tract. The problem with seeing the play as a "tract for the times" is first that Shakespeare is as wary of Timon's "feudalism" as he is of capitalism and the cash nexus; even more, Shakespeare is wary of Timon's perverse and unique misuse of feudalism to support fantasies which are finally independent of economic or political structures. Timon used a public exchange system (with relatively rational goals) for private—and often irrational—ends. He tried to make an exchange of goods into an exchange of emotion. Here, as in the case of *King Lear,* the play's impact depends on the fusion of timely and timeless concerns and of the catalytic interaction of personal motives and political structures. Not only does Timon's affliction reach forward to Marx—Marx quoted Timon's arguments against gold—but it goes backward to feudal hatred of Avarice conceived in moral terms. "Calculating and profit-seeking" are both older than capitalism, though only in capitalist societies are they openly accepted as admirable goals. The point about Timon is that he is as calculating and profit-seeking as the overt capitalists, but he doesn't even know it.

126. Lear wants to "unburthen'd crawl toward [his] death" (*Lr.* 1.1.40); Timon welcomes the relief of crawling unburdened towards his *debt.*

127. See chapter 8 and discussion of the passion play as model for scenes in several of the flattery plays.

128. Other elements in the cluster follow: "Will the cold brook, / *Candied* with ice, caudle thy morning taste / To cure thy o'er-night's surfeit? Call the creatures . . . / Bid them *flatter* thee" (*Tim.* 4.3.227–29, 233; italics added).

129. The confusion between the flatterer and the one who is flattered, between player and audience, which we have seen in Coriolanus's refusal of flattery, appears here too. We cannot tell whether Timon is offering the play for his guests' delight, or whether the masquers are offering it to Timon for his. Because of the ambiguous grammar there has been much editorial speculation about who offers what to whom. The passage thus matches the passage about flattering drums and the parasite's silk in *Coriolanus,* where the great man is being flattered but sounds instead as if he is therefore flattering his flatterers (*Cor.* 1.9.42–46).

130. Munday's "Will gratulate your *feast* with some rare merriment or pleasing jest" (*John a Kent,* 18; italics added).

131. Apemantus rejects the illusory nurturance with appropriately oral imagery:

> What a sweep of vanity comes this way.
> They dance? They are madwomen, . . .
> We . . . spend our flatteries *to drink those men*
> Upon whose age we void it up again

With poisonous spite and envy. . . .
I should fear those that dance before me now
Would one day stamp on me. 'Tas been done.
(*Tim.* 1.2.128–40; italics added)

132. Maurice **Charney**, Introduction, in *Timon of Athens,* Signet Classic Shakespeare (New York: New American Library, 1965), xxvi.

133. John W. Mahon notes that "Elizabethan audiences would recognize a reference to Revelation 3:16: 'Therefore, because thou art luke warme, and nether cold nor hote, it will come to passe, that I shall spewe thee out of my mouth' (Geneva)"; John W. **Mahon**, "'For Now We Sit to Chat as Well as Eat': Conviviality and Conflict in Shakespeare's Meals," in Mahon and Pendleton, *Shakespearean Essays,* 231–48, esp. 240.

134. Apemantus had predicted that we "spend our flatteries to drink those men / Upon whose age we void it up again / With poisonous spite and envy" (*Tim.* 1.2.133–35).

135. Ellis-Fermor, "Unfinished Play," 169.

136. Ellis-Fermor has tried to connect the trial to the main action by suggesting that Alcibiades' friend is Timon himself. But, as others have argued, the literal connection is not warranted by the play itself. The connection lies instead in analogy: the friend expresses Timon's anger at a betrayal. The friend, significantly, committed the murder while he was drunk, i.e., orally sated. As Timon tells Apemantus, betrayal is much worse if you are accustomed to such satisfactions, to having "the world as my confectionary . . . The mouths, the tongues . . . / At duty" (*Tim.* 4.3.162–64). In this "unfinished" play, the "poetic" suggestion that Timon and the friend are one is so strong that readers have been picking up on it and taking it literally.

137. Thersites has a similar epilogue at the end of Shakespeare's *Troilus and Cressida.* He addresses his fellow "traders in the flesh," says he will return to make his will in two months, "and at that time bequeath you my diseases" (*Tro.* 5.10.46, 57). Speaking as a not quite dead man rather than a "corse," Thersites, like Timon, wishes a plague of sorts on those who are left in the audience. Shakespeare's own epitaph, which he is said to have composed for himself (Schoenbaum, *Documentary Life,* 306–7), is more conventionally addressed to future sextons who might dig up his grave—as Hamlet's gravediggers do—to make room for someone else:

Good frend for Jesus sake forbeare,
To digg the dust enclosed heare:
Bleste be yᵉ man yᵗ spares thes stones,
And curst be he yᵗ moves my bones.

Timon's epitaph, by contrast, defends him against the mere presence of cursing spectators. But see E. Honigman's speculations about Shakespeare's misanthropic tendencies during his last days, when he drew up his will; E. **Honigman**, "The Second-Best Bed," *New York Review of Books,* 7 November 1991, 27–28. The seeming contradiction between "Seek not my name" and "Here lie, I, Timon"

(*Tim.* 5.4.71–72) is partially explained by Shakespeare's double source: cf. note to *Tim.* 5.4.71, Oliver, Arden *Timon,* 140. But it turns out to be an appropriate contradiction in that it speaks the inevitable opposition between the actor and his role.

Chapter Eight

1. "A key feature of the scaffold, the stocks, the whipping-post, and the pillory was that they depended for their efficacy on the active participation of the public"; J. M. **Beattie,** "Violence and Society in Early Modern England," in *Perspectives in Criminal Law,* ed. A. **Doob** and E. **Greenspan** (Aurora, Ontario: Canada Law Book, 1984). Cited in David **Garland,** *Punishment and Modern Society: A Study in Social Theory* (Chicago: University of Chicago Press, 1990), 231.

2. It is customary to assume that Shakespeare's contemporaries saw in plays and baitings the same kind of sport. See, e.g., John Briley, "Of Stake and Stage," *Shakespeare Survey* 8 (1955): 106–9; Bradbrook, *Common Player,* 197–200; Wiles, *Shakespeare's Clown,* 164–81; Robert F. **Willson,** Jr., "Gloucester and Harry Hunks," *The Upstart Crow* 9 (1989): 107–11; Stephen **Dickey,** "Shakespeare's Mastiff Comedy," *Shakespeare Quarterly* 42 (1991): 255–75.

3. E. K. Chambers deals with "the whole rather troublesome question of the Bankside Bear Gardens" in his discussion of the Hope Theater, citing and quoting the relevant contemporary documents describing the sport, its history, and its location; Chambers, *Elizabethan Stage,* 2:448–71. See also Sir Sidney **Lee,** "Bearbaiting, Bullbaiting, and Cockfighting," in *Shakespeare's England* (Clarendon: Oxford University Press, 1916), 2:408–27, esp. the bibliography; and the more recent articles cited above.

4. Chambers, *Elizabethan Stage,* 2:454; Dekker, *Worke for Armourers,* cited in Chambers, *Elizabethan Stage,* 2:457 n. 6.

5. Sir Andrew Aguecheek in Shakespeare's *Twelfth Night* is another fatuous devotee (*TN* 1.3.92).

6. Wiles, *Shakespeare's Clown,* 169.

7. Chambers, *Elizabethan Stage,* 2:452.

8. Lee, "Bearbaiting," 431–32.

9. Among the live appearances may have been one by a white bear in Shakespeare's *Winter's Tale.* Wiles, *Shakespeare's Clown,* 170.

10. Dekker, "Warres," in *Worke for Armourers; or, The Peace is Broken* (1609), in *Non-Dramatic Works,* 96.

11. Baskerville, *Elizabeth Jig,* 98–99.

12. Cf. Wiles, *Shakespeare's Clown,* 162–71.

13. A wager is mentioned in Edward Alleyn's papers, cited in Chambers, *Elizabethan Stage,* 2:297; Poggio, in Chapman's *Gentleman Usher* (1602–4 [1602]) "gives it out in wagers he'll excel" in his role in a play (1.2.27); and the Citizen's Wife in Francis **Beaumont,** *The Knight of the Burning Pestle* (1607), ed. John Doebler, Regents Renaissance Drama Series (Lincoln: University of Nebraska Press, 1967), 11, is certain that her Rafe would win any such competition when the citizen suggests that "he should have play'd Jeronimo with a shoemaker for a wager" (Ind.85–86). See Chambers, *Elizabethan Stage,* 2:554.

14. Willson, "Harry Hunks," 108, notes that Carolyn Spurgeon claims not to have "found a single bearbaiting image [in the drama] except in Shakespeare." Spurgeon, *Shakespeare's Imagery,* 110.

15. The *Oxford English Dictionary* includes the definition "to find fault with, blame, reproach, reprove" (*pinch,* def. 9b).

16. As in the case of Falstaff, the scene of public attack and humiliation in *Errors* is enriched by allusions to a medley of texts and events. One of the most interesting allusions in this case is to the death of Edward II in Marlowe's eponymous play. Edward was both skewered and suffocated, invaded and stifled, in addition to being forced to stand in puddled mire while his tormentors interrogated him, singed his beard, and otherwise nipped at him. Antipholus echoes Edward's cry at being attacked, though later he changes places and imitates Edward's tormentors when he gets back at Pinch. Edward was being punished in part for his homosexual attachment to Gaveston. Perhaps Antipholus's same-sex experiences of intimacy (as a twin) evoked Edward's same-sex attachment. Antipholus was also literally bound to his male servant Dromio, once as an infant when they were lashed to a mast together, and then again when Pinch tied them so tightly he had to gnaw his way out of the cords. For both Edward and Antipholus, what is involved is an identification with another person—like an actor's, or like an infant's with its mother—so close that it can seem stifling as well as exhilarating.

17. Ralph **Berry**, "*Twelfth Night:* The Experience of the Audience," *Shakespeare Survey* 34 (1981): 111–20. See Dickey's elaboration of the full extent of the bearbaiting figure in *Twelfth Night;* Dickey, "Mastiff Comedy," 264–75.

18. Cf. Ford's similar plight—and similar complaint—in *Wives:* "There's a knot, a ging, a *pack,* a conspiracy against me" (*Wiv.* 4.2.108–9; italics added).

19. Berry, "*Twelfth Night,*" 118, 119. The audience's betrayal would be even more obvious if Malvolio had taken them into his confidence when he discovered "Olivia's" letter, as Donald Sinden's Malvolio did in John Barton's 1969 production of *Twelfth Night.* As Sinden describes his performance, upon reading "'I may command where I adore,' Malvolio tells *the audience,* 'I serve her; she is my Lady.'" Then, when he comes to "some have greatness thrust upon them," "He flashes a plea to the audience. Do they understand the importance of that? His speech now becomes faster and faster, growing in excitement." Still more involved, Malvolio reads on: "'Go to, thou art *made* if thou desir'st to be so. If *not,* let me see thee a . . .' (does it? Yes it does! Joy can know no bounds!)—to the gallery, 'STEWARD still?' They obviously don't believe him, so he shows them the *very* word and mouths it a second time." Donald **Sinden**, "Malvolio in *Twelfth Night,*" in *Players of Shakespeare 1* (Cambridge: Cambridge University Press, 1985), 41–66, 57–58; italics added.

20. Shakespeare was not completely alone in his sympathy for the bear. Although Puritans were opposed to baiting for other reasons, they "also felt for the animals," and others also began "to turn against these 'filthy sports,' as Sir John Davies called them in the 1590s." Keith **Thomas**, *Man and the Natural World: A History of the Modern Sensibility* (New York: Pantheon Books, 1983), 157, 159.

21. Dickey, "Mastiff Comedy," 265.

22. Cf. Benedick's boast in *Much Ado About Nothing* that if ever he loses any blood in love, his friends can "pick out mine eyes with a ballad-maker's pen,

and hang me up at the door of a brothel-house for the sign of blind Cupid" (*Ado* 1.1.233–35).

23. Willson says this line "seems to be intended to evoke the baiting motif, especially in the use of 'sport,'" Willson, "Harry Hunks," 108.

24. Exorcism was on Shakespeare's mind in the blinding scene. Gloucester's torture echoes details from Samuel Harsnett's account of a mock exorcism, in which the supposedly possessed woman was tied down while priests invaded her body to extract the demon, pouring noxious liquids into her throat and "a more homely place"; Harsnett, *Declaration of Egregious Popish Impostures*, 59, 62. Cf. Bullough, *Dramatic Sources*, 7:414–20 (excludes the actual exorcism); Muir, Arden *King Lear*, 239–42 (app. 7).

25. Note in Humphreys, Arden *2 Henry VI*, 145. Or "a rampant bear chained to a staff"; Herschel Baker's note to *2H6* 5.1.144, in *The Riverside Shakespeare*, ed. G. Blakemore Evans (Boston: Houghton Mifflin, 1974), 663.

26. Jones argues that the mystery plays, which Shakespeare could have seen as a child, gave Shakespeare a model for his earliest sense of dramatic structure in the histories, particularly in *Henry VI, Part Two*, where the fall and the death of Humphrey, Duke of Gloucester form "a tragedy in little." Emrys Jones, "Shakespeare and the Mystery Cycles," in *Origins of Shakespeare*, 31–84, esp. 35.

27. Jones, *Origins of Shakespeare*, 48.

28. Jones, *Origins of Shakespeare*, 35–46.

29. Jones, *Origins of Shakespeare*, 42.

30. Jones, *Origins of Shakespeare*, 57–59.

31. Jones, *Origins of Shakespeare*, 59–63.

32. Religious celebration confronted Elizabethan passion play audiences with the complex phenomenon of the Incarnation incarnated in a merely human player whose function was to remind them of Christ's example.

33. "He that played Christs part hanging upon the Crosse, was wounded to death by him that should have thrust his sword into a bladder full of bloud tyed to his side"; Beard, *Theatre of Gods Judgements*, 206. Beard of course is concerned to demonstrate the falseness and impropriety of the play, while Arcand sees the actor's death as an ironically accurate repetition of Christ's death. But both are provoked by the strangeness of the actor's position.

34. Daniel's "resurrection" will occur through donated organs, as we discover later when the film flashes through a sequence of hospital scenes showing people awaking from surgery with their new hearts, eyes, etc.

35. Nicolas-Marc Des Fontaines, *L'Illustre Comédien, ou le martyre de S. Genest* (1646); Lopa de Vega, *Lo Fingido Verdadero, Villan de Xetafe* (1622); and Jean Rotrou, *Le Véritable Saint Genest* (1645). The title of Sartre's biography of Jean Genet (*Saint Genet: Actor and Martyr*) alludes to Rotrou's play about a professional actor.

36. Shylock's description of Antony as a "*fawning* publican" (*MV* 1.3.36; italics added) makes sense in this context as well as in the biblical context. Apropos of names we should note also that Antonio in Renaissance drama is a name often reserved for foolish though harmless characters, from Erasmus's true fool, to the old uncle Antonio in *Much Ado*, to the charlatan Tony in *The Changeling*; R. P. Corballis, "The Name 'Antonio' in Renaissance Drama," *Cahiers élisabéthains* 25 (1984):

61–72. In *Twelfth Night* and *The Merchant of Venice* the name is given to a man so devoted to a boy that his devotion verges on foolishness. In Marston's *Antonio and Mellida* (1599–1600 [1599]) Antonio is "an hermaphrodite"; John Marston, *Antonio and Mellida* (Ind.68), ed. G. K. Hunter, Regents Renaissance Drama Series (Lincoln: University of Nebraska Press, 1985), 7.

37. Antonio's speech about Portia immediately follows his description of Lady Fortune's treatment of him. In both cases his words say "I accept this woman's action" but his manner conveys the opposite. Fortune and Portia are even for a moment confused, when Antonio moves directly from saying how glad he is that Fortune "cut me off" from misery to commending himself to Bassanio's unnamed wife, both referred to by the general pronoun: "Of such misery doth *she* [Fortune] cut me off. / Commend me to your honorable wife, / Tell *her* the process of Antonio's end" (*MV* 4.1.268–70; italics added). Portia and Fortune are elsewhere conflated in the play, just as Timon conflates Fortune with the maternal earth who can either sustain him or reject him.

38. J. R. **Brown**, "Love's Wealth and the Judgement of *The Merchant of Venice*," in *Shakespeare and his Comedies* (London: Methuen, 1968), 45–81.

39. See the discussion of gold and emotional debts in *Julius Caesar*, chapter 7.

40. Or, as the sonnet poet put it:

> Thee have I not locked up in any chest,
> Save where thou art not, though I feel thou art,
> Within the gentle closure of my breast,
> From whence at pleasure thou mayst come and part.
>
> (Son. 48, 9–12)

Cited in M. M. **Mahood**, "Love's Confined Doom," *Shakespeare Survey* 15 (1962): 50–61, esp. 54.

41. Unless the "sever'd lips" (*MV* 3.2.118) in her counterfeit portrait be a displacement upwards of what was seen as a severing or a wound elsewhere. See Kahn, *Man's Estate*, 132, on a similar displacement in *Lucrece*.

42. Blau, *Take Up the Bodies*, 25. The entire passage is worth quoting because it likens all theater to the ceremony of the trial—and thus implies that trial scenes in plays can be interesting metadramatic reflections on their own medium. "If," Blau says, "as Vico remarked, jurisprudence with its rites of punishment was 'an entire poetic,' so theater—particularly dramaturgy with its rites of punishment—is an entire jurisprudence. There is still (as old actors used to tell me) nothing more dramatic than a trial, although trials can reflect thought . . . or a set of procedures, more or less brainless, having nothing to do with justice. The same is true of theater. There is a sense in which every performance is a trial, offering up evidence."

43. In that same play, King Henry VI himself prepares for death with a theatrical model in mind. "What scene of death hath Roscius now to act?" he asks, when his enemies surround him (*1H6* 5.6.10).

44. Nungezer, *Dictionary of Actors*, 74.

45. Muriel C. **Bradbrook**, "The Triple Bond: Audience, Actors, Author in the Elizabethan Playhouse," in *The Triple Bond: Plays, Mainly Shakespearean, in Performance* (University Park: Pennsylvania State University Press, 1975), 59.

46. R. A. **Foakes**, ed., Introduction, in *The Comedy of Errors*, Arden Shakespeare (London: Methuen, 1962), xlix.

47. Egeon is a father, as Gloucester and York were, and as most Shakespearean Christ figures are.

48. Cf. Jardine, *Still Harping on Daughters*, 19. Sebastian was a beautiful youth beloved of Diocletian. But when he converted to Christianity, Diocletian ordered him shot through with arrows ("like a porcupine," John Foxe says in his book of martyrs, *Actes and Monuments* [1563], a fate not entirely unlike Edward II's skewering). Oscar Wilde took "Sebastian" as his pseudonym after he was released from prison, and seems to have been as much compelled by the posture of sacrifice as by the physical posture implied by his being pierced. "For a man who condemned sacrifice," Richard Ellman writes in his biography of Wilde, "he wrote plays that were full of it"; Richard **Ellman**, *Oscar Wilde* (New York: Alfred A. Knopf, 1987), 436.

49. Empson, *Versions of the Pastoral*, 114–15; Marianne Novy, *Love's Argument*, 68–69.

50. Booth, *Shakespeare's Sonnets*, 176.

51. Booth, *Shakespeare's Sonnets*, 177.

52. Notice also the stage implications of two nearby sonnets, 23 and 25. The first of these (which will be discussed next) begins with a reference to stage fright; the second contains a Ulysses-like statement about the brevity of fame. Then comes sonnet 26 with its interest in "showing."

53. W. G. **Ingram** and Theodore **Redpath**, *Shakespeare's Sonnets* (London: University of London Press, 1964), 56–58.

54. Ingram and Redpath, *Shakespeare's Sonnets*, 56.

55. Further denigration of the actor may be implied by other, more general senses of "unperfect." An "unperfect actor" can be a bad actor, one who is *always* fearful and *always* forgets his lines, or the phrase, at least momentarily before the reader goes on to the next line, can even allude to a person who is a perfectly acceptable actor but is therefore "unperfect" as a person, just because he is an actor. See Booth, *Shakespeare's Sonnets*, 171.

56. Booth, *Shakespeare's Sonnets*, 171.

57. Like Antony who wants to "put a tongue / in every wound of Caesar" (*JC* 3.2.230–31), the poet wants to put a tongue in his poems or even in his breast.

58. Cf. C. L. Barber's essay on the sonnets citing those which explicitly liken the youth to the poet's glass, a child to his mother's glass, etc. C. L. **Barber**, "Full to Overflowing" (review of *Sonnets*, ed. Stephen Booth), *New York Review of Books* 25, 6 April 1978, 34.

59. Cited in *A New Variorum Edition of Shakespeare: The Sonnets*, ed. Hyder Edward **Rollins** (Philadelphia and London: J. B. Lippincott, 1944), 1:275. From Lamb, *On the Tragedies of Shakespeare* (1811).

60. Anne Goble suggests that "he is talking at least as much about playwriting as acting" in such phrases as "gored mine own *thoughts*," "sold cheap what is most dear," and "looked on *truth* / Askance and strangely" (Goble, personal communication, 1991; Son. 110, lines 3, 5, 6; italics added).

61. Booth, *Shakespeare's Sonnets*, 354.

62. Cited in Chambers, *Elizabethan Stage*, 4:230.

63. Ingram and Redpath, *Shakespeare's Sonnets*, 254.

64. Booth, *Shakespeare's Sonnets*, 355.

65. Booth, *Shakespeare's Sonnets*, 355.

66. "Gore" as a noun, of course, also brings to mind the matter coming out of the wound, as in Venus's imagined "picture of an angry chafing boar, / Under whose fangs on his back doth lie / An image like [Adonis], all stain'd with gore" (Ven. 2.662–64).

67. Booth, *Shakespeare's Sonnets*, 355.

68. See chapter 6.

69. The "goddess" who presides over the poet's fate here is the same classical Fortuna on whose bosom Timon climbed, though now all she provides to drink is bitter "eisel."

70. Because it replaces his arrows in sonnets 153 and 154, perhaps even "Cupid's brand," though literally a torch, suggests sexual implications of being branded.

71. Cf. the thorns Richard had associated with the crown (*3H6* 3.2.172–75); see chapter 3. But see "graven" instead of "branded," textual note in Hammond, Arden *Richard III*, 282.

72. Herschel Baker glosses "stigmatic" as "a branded person, hence one marked with deformity (i.e., branded by God)"; Baker, *Riverside Shakespeare*, 664. Cairncross glosses it as "branded deformity. Applied to a criminal branded or 'stigmatized' with a hot iron"; Andrew J. **Cairncross**, ed., *Henry IV, Part Two*, Arden Shakespeare (London: Methuen, 1969), 148.

73. Booth, *Shakespeare's Sonnets*, 363.

74. Shortly, "the monarch's plague, this flattery" will become the primary subject (Son. 114, 2). There the poet will claim that he knowingly drinks the poisoned cup, the flattering illusion being that the fair young man is as perfect as he seems and loves the poet as he seems to. The draught convinces the poet that he is not one of the "monsters and things indigest" (Son. 114, 5; like Richard III, the unlicked bear-whelp, still lurking behind the self-loathing in these poems), but is instead "crowned with you" (Son. 114, 1).

75. Booth, *Shakespeare's Sonnets*, 369.

Afterword

1. Paul's, a private theater, was also circular ("This round . . . this ring," *Antonio's Revenge*, Ind.13, 23), as was the Cockpit in Whitehall, perhaps the original referent for the Chorus's "wooden O" in *Henry V*; Smith, "*Henry V* Chorus," 38–57, esp. 46–51. But the configuration was associated most consistently with the public amphitheaters.

2. Cited in Chambers, *Elizabethan Stage*, 4:258.

3. Thomas **Middleton**, *Father Hubbard's Tales; or, The Ant and the Nightingale*, in *The Works of Thomas Middleton*, ed. A. H. Bullen (London: John Nimmo, 1886), 8:64. Cited in Gurr, *Playgoing*, 91.

4. Michael Drayton, *Idea*, Sonnet 47, *Works*, ed. Hebel, 2.334, cited in Gurr, *Playgoing*, 216.

5. Originally pointed out by M. W. Sampson, *Modern Language Notes* (1915); cited in Harbage, *Shakespeare's Audience*, 114. Citing Harbage, Ralph Berry quotes the passage to introduce Berry, *Awareness of the Audience*, 1.

6. Canetti, *Crowds and Power*, 27.

7. Charlotte **Spivack**, "Elizabethan Theatre: Circle and Center," *The Centennial Review* 13 (1969): 424–43.

8. Heywood, cited in Spivack, "Circle and Center," 433. Heywood goes on: "Built with starre galleries of hye ascent, / In which Jehove doth as spectator sit. . . . / He that denyes then theaters should be, / He may as well deny a world to me."

9. Georges **Poulet**, *The Metamorphoses of the Circle* (Baltimore: Johns Hopkins University Press, 1966), esp. "The Renaissance," 1–14.

10. See Richard Wheeler and C. L. Barber's elaboration of the maternal subtext in the histories (Wheeler and Barber, *Whole Journey*, 92–114) and Janet Adelman's brief but compelling discussion of mothers in the early histories, where she cites the scene between Margaret and Suffolk (Adelman, *Suffocating Mothers*, 8). Cf. Marston's association of the playhouse "round" with a similar embrace:

> If any spirit breathes within this round
> Uncapable of weighty passion
> (As from his birth being huggèd in the arms
> And nuzzlèd 'twixt the breasts of happiness)
> . . . let such
> Hurry amain from our black-visaged shows.
> (*Antonio's Revenge* Ind.13–16, 19–20)

11. These are related to the womblike tombs in the early tragedies *Romeo and Juliet* and *Titus Andronicus,* which become pits of charnel (and carnal) horror, figured by a finger through a ring.

12. Cf. Vindice's reference to the "luxurious circle" where his revenge masque will be performed for two adulterous couples (*The Revenger's Tragedy* 3.5.22).

13. The attack is later seen as rape, when Henry tells Harfleur's governor to give up or Harfleur's "pure maidens [will] fall into the hand / Of hot and forcing violation" (*H5* 3.3.20–21).

14. No one is suffocated in Richard's overrun garden, but the last time Richard's Queen Isabel had appeared before she came to the garden to hear all this about its transformation, she had just learned about Richard's imminent fall and called herself a "gasping new-deliver'd mother" (*R2* 2.2.65). (In Kyd's *Spanish Tragedy,* another Isabell comes to destroy the garden where her son had been found hanged, if not strictly suffocated.) Hamlet's Denmark is not only an "unweeded garden" (*Ham.* 1.2.135), but one where the enemy pours poison in a king's ear and kills him.

15. Cf. the jealous wife Adriana in *Comedy of Errors,* who fears that her philandering husband like "an unruly deer breaks the pale" (*Err.* 2.1.100).

16. Talbot is the only one to call himself and his men deer (*1H6* 4.2.46, 48, 54). Elsewhere he is described in similarly circular terms: he is "girdled with a waist of iron, / And hemmed about with grim destruction" and is "ringed with bold adversity" (*1H6* 4.3.20–21; 4.4.14). A deer is perhaps latent also in *Troilus and Cressida,*

when Achilles tells his Myrmidons to "empale him [Hector] with your weapons" for the final inglorious kill (*Tro.* 5.7.5).

17. See chapter 5.

18. He rallies for a moment by asking rhetorically, "Is not the king's name twenty thousand names?" to rescue himself from despair over the news (*R2* 3.2.85).

19. Foakes notes of these lines that "a quibbling allusion to stage-rails may be intended." R. A. **Foakes,** ed., *King Henry VIII,* Arden Shakespeare (London: Methuen, 1957), note to *H8* 5.3.86–89.

20. J. W. **Saunders,** "Vaulting the Rails," *Shakespeare Survey* 7 (1954); 69–81, esp. 70. See also Foakes's addition to Saunders's claim; Foakes, Arden *Henry VIII,* note to *H8* 5.3.86–89.

21. Like the scenes alluding to bearbaiting or the passion play baiting of Christ, this one contains an allusion to "baiting of bombards" (harassing drunkards?) (*H8* 5.3.80).

22. The Chorus's commentary may have been written specifically for a performance at the Cockpit, a stage even smaller than other stages, in which the normal constraints would be made more severe; see n. 1.

23. The iambic pentameter line is not spacious enough to contain the Chorus's material either; his sentences are repeatedly interrupted just after the verb and thus also convey his breathless sense of confinement. Michael Goldman argues convincingly that "once it is recognized that the Chorus sounds very much like the king, much of the play's method becomes clear. . . . Henry's theme is physical limitation overcome by supreme effort," and, similarly, the Chorus's reference to the limits of the stage gives us a "sense of the size and energy of the subject . . . barely contained or restrained"; Goldman, *Energies of Drama,* 59. Goldman's discussion of the Chorus's metadramatic impact is continued by Brennan, "That Within," 40–52; Tyler, "Minding True Things"; and Hammond, "Plural Text," 133–50.

24. Like the paradox of Henry's own achievement, with so much accomplished in so short a time: "Small time, but in that small most greatly liv'd / This star of England" (*H5* Epi.6).

25. Poulet, *Metamorphoses of the Circle,* xviii–xxvii.

26. Like Sir Alexander Wengrave in *The Roaring Girl,* the Chorus also turns the stage into a ship at sea on an amphitheater full of waves:

> O, do but think [he tells the audience]
> You stand upon the rivage and behold
> A city on th' inconstant billows dancing;
> For so appears this fleet majestical,
> Holding due course for Harfleur.
>
> (*H5* 3.0.13–17)

In the prologue to act 2, the theater had already become a ship to carry the audience to France:

> There is the playhouse now, there must you sit;
> And thence to France shall we convey you safe,
> And bring you back, charming the narrow seas

To give you gentle pass; for if we may,
We'll not offend one stomach with our play.

(*H5* 2.0.36–40)

27. Goldman calls attention to this odd figure ("divide one man") as one of the means by which Shakespeare creates this play's pervasive impression of energy exploding outward—here, of the actor himself exploding outward. Goldman, *Energies of Drama*, 60.

Index

CAPITALS AND SMALL CAPITALS denote authors or actors; **boldface** page numbers denote major discussions or full bibliographic details. Where both text and a note are referenced, only the text page number is given; e.g., **57n163** takes the reader to page 57 of the text and thence to note 163.